Champlain

The Life of Fortitude

MORRIS BISHOP

Champlain

The Life of Fortitude

New York: Alfred A. Knopf

1 9 4 8

THIS IS A BORZOI BOOK,
PUBLISHED BY ALFRED A. KNOPF, INC.

FIRST EDITION

CONTENTS

Contents

ILLUSTRATIONS AND MAPS

Champlain

The Life of Fortitude

CHAPTER I

Youth

MAN'S URGE has always been westward, face into the winds that ring the globe. The currents of his migration are marked on maps like the currents of the sea and air. The history of modern America is the record of this westward urge. It still exists, in attenuated form, in the hearts of ardent youths and aging burghers, dreaming over road maps in their tidy garages.

Nowhere and at no time was the westward urge more strong than in the seaport town of Brouage in the latter part of the sixteenth century.

You will find Brouage only on a large-scale map, a Carte Michelin. It lies close to France's west coast, twenty miles south of La Rochelle, seventy miles north of Bordeaux. This is a sad region, a flat plain inclined ever so slightly toward the sea, sand blending imperceptibly with salt marsh, and salt marsh with salt water. The town has the melancholy charm of all great things decayed. It was a stronghold once; its walls, bastions, and bartizans remain, decorated with wallflower and ivy. The works have no purpose now. There is nothing to protect; and anyway, wide breaches have been made to permit a highway to enter and quickly depart.

Brouage is nothing now: a handful of houses, built of the stone from greater houses. Its few inhabitants tend the dazzling salt beds, grapple for mussels in the mudbanks, put to sea for fish by way of a drainage canal, and nurse their little vineyards, which feed, one would think, more on sunshine than on soil. Brouage, to its shame, is less than a commune, being attached, for administrative ends, to a neighboring village. But once it was an important city, "the second harbor in France," said writers of its heyday, "the most sure and convenient port of Europe." That was when the sea, now some three miles distant, lapped its walls, and when ships from all countries came to it for salt.

The abundant life has made us forget the importance of salt to the Old World. As beasts cluster at their salt licks, the traders of the past gathered at the great deposits of salt: the oases of the Sahara, the salt pans of Ostia, the *marais salants* of France. Salt was a dietetic necessity in the vegetable diet of the poor, and also a necessity for the preservation of meat and fish. The young of our age, the age of refrigeration, have never tasted salt cod or salt pork, even a half century ago the inevitable foods of sailor, farmer, and cit. No corruption wins against salt. The Spanish and Portuguese found that dry salt cod alone was proof against equatorial heat, and salt fish was the thirsty staple of the crews and passengers who crossed the Line.

Catholic Europe demanded fish as Lenten and Friday fare, and the Atlantic fishermen supplied its salted ration. They ranged far out on the ocean; even in the fifteenth century a great fleet annually visited Iceland waters. Christopher Columbus himself made the Iceland journey, no doubt to find out the fishermen's secrets. There are suggestions, though no actual proof, that the Basque and Breton fishers discovered Labrador and the Newfoundland Banks well before 1492 and jealously kept their secret hidden.

In the sixteenth century, Brouage was one of the principal sources of salt for the fishing fleet. Here came the tough little ships from La Rochelle, Brittany, and Normandy to load a precious ballast of salt in hogsheads, then to head west for the Grand Banks or northwest for the milky seas below the Pole.

It was in this town, conscious of the ocean, of the great west, that Samuel Champlain was born.

The year of his birth is not attested by any contemporary

4

document. A *Biographie Saintongeoise*, published in 1852, gives us the date of 1567 with an air of assurance but without any allegation of authority. The date is at least a reasonable one and fits with the circumstances of his life. He could not have been born more than a year or two earlier or a year or two later.[1]

His birthplace is still pointed out to the rare tourist. It is no more than a crumbling heap of stone, for some forty years ago its decorated stone doorway was sold to an artistic Englishman, and the remainder of the house naturally fell down. (A stone arch from the rear is in the Château de Ramezay in Montreal.) If this was actually Champlain's home, his family was one of substance, living in bourgeois comfort. But the attribution is too vague to build on, the inference unclear.

His father was Antoine Champlain, his mother, Marguerite Le Roy. The *Biographie Saintongeoise* of 1852 says summarily that the parents' families were fishermen, but gives no authority for the statement. It is probable enough. In our Champlain's marriage contract, dated in 1610, his father is described as the late Antoine de Champlain, in his lifetime a sea captain. (Notice the *de*, the *particule*, which gives a hint of elevation, of lost landed proprietorship.) There is no discrepancy here. In those days, when the French marine was expanding rapidly, it was not hard for an energetic and intelligent fisherman to become a ship's captain. The great Jean Bart, a fisherman's son, rose to be admiral of Louis XIV's navy. Our Champlain's own uncle, whether on his father's or his mother's side, entered the service of Spain and attained a respectable rank in the Spanish navy. This uncle was known as *"le capitaine Provençal"*; his nickname became a surname, according to the easygoing fashion of the times. The name indicates that one branch of the family came from Provence, the French southland.

In fact we know little of Champlain's origins. We do not even know the religion in which he was baptized. His Christian name, Samuel, hints strongly of Protestantism, for French Protestants commonly gave their children Old Testament names, while the Catholics chose the names of saints, thus affording their off-spring a personal advocate in heaven. Also, Brouage was in the heart of the Huguenot country. But these are mere indications,

[1] See Appendix A: "Date of Champlain's Birth."

not proofs. We know only that Champlain was at thirty a nominal Catholic, and that in his later years he was ardent and devout in the faith.

What did he look like?

There is a portrait of Champlain showing a plump, middle-aged face with prideful, espaliered mustaches, and an overfed, sedentary body. The portrait has been much reproduced, usually with reference to an original by Moncornet, who flourished in the mid-seventeenth century. This face ornaments most editions of Champlain's works; it is the original document for every statue of the explorer, gazing ecstatically heavenward, surrounded by ramping Indians, in the public parks of Canadian cities; it appears in the most blameless historical manuals, such as the recent *Album of American History*; it has figured in countless local histories and pious advertising booklets. But it is not the face of Champlain. It was demonstrated as long ago as 1904 [2] that the portrait was not by Moncornet, but by L. C. J. Ducornet, who died in 1856, and who is chiefly memorable in art history for the fact that he was born without arms, and with only one foot, and with only four toes on that foot. He was also born without a conscience. With brush in teeth and palette in his toes, he produced a considerable body of work in the fields of historical painting and lithography. His portrait of Champlain, the ancestor of all the modern reproductions, appeared in 1854.

Ducornet credits Moncornet with the original portrait from which he made his own. But no such original portrait of Champlain has been discovered. In 1920 Mr. H. P. Biggar showed that there exists a portrait by Moncornet which so closely resembles the Ducornet Champlain in composition, feature, and costume that beyond question it served as a model for Ducornet.[3] But the Moncornet portrait is not of Champlain, but of Michel Particelli, *Contrôleur-général des Finances* under Louis XIV. And thus the school children who dream of the Champlain pictured in their texts, and the tourist gaping at the puffing statues of the valiant explorer, are still giving a shadowy life to the features of Michel Particelli, *Contrôleur-général des Finances de*

[2] Victor Hugo Paltsits, in *Acadiensis*, IV, 306–11.
[3] *Canadian Historical Review*, I, 379–80.

France and a sharp, unscrupulous rogue, according to his contemporaries.[4]

Champlain was, in fact, a lean, ascetic type, dry and dark, probably rather under than over normal size. Only the lean ascetic could have endured the trials of his life uncomplaining, or could have, when nearly fifty, kept pace with Indian braves on a war expedition of near a thousand miles. His southern origin is indication enough of dark hair and dark eyes. He was of mean stature, most likely; for in 1615 he was wounded in a battle in central New York, and Indians carried him on their backs in a flight of sixty miles through the forest. The Indians would not have carried a great fat man, even if they could.

Of formal education Champlain certainly had little. He wrote good serviceable French, with none of the graces of scholastic rhetoric. He never ornamented his pages with Latin tags and classical allusions, in an age when the sorriest author cited his school texts for decorum's sake. He learned something of mathematics, enough to write in his later years a practical treatise on navigation. He was handy with the pencil and brush; he became an excellent cartographer, and he could make sketches, crude but vivid, of curious objects and scenes. But these abilities do not prove attendance at a school. He could have learned them from his father in the leisure of calm days at sea.

The best of his education was had on shipboard. "From my childhood," he writes to Queen Marie de Médicis, "the art of navigation has won my love, and has impelled me to expose myself nearly all my life to the impetuous waves of the ocean." What were these childhood adventures? As a cabin boy, did he accompany his father on some fishing trip across the Atlantic? It would be idle to speculate on the unknowable. We know only that he became a competent ship's captain and an authority on the art of navigation.

There was also education to be had on shore. For a boy trained early to observe the lines of ships and their canvas and rigging, there was endless delight in visiting the ships moored

[4] With one exception, all the imaginative portrayals of Champlain I have seen show him plowing through the wilderness freshly shaven and with his anachronistic imperial and mustache (which came in only with Richelieu) neatly trimmed. The exception is the fine mural by C. W. Jeffreys, who knows history as well as art, in the Château Laurier, Ottawa.

to the city walls. With his sea-conscious comrades, he would discuss learnedly the merits and defects of Portuguese carracks, of Flemish flyboats and clinker-built cogs, and of the big round-bowed English hookers constructed expressly for the salt trade. The salt business itself had its interest, especially when there was a threat of rain and the red-eyed salt workers whipped to a gallop their horses carrying great cones from the evaporating pools to ship or shed. And surely the boy watched the sailors, ritually drunk before affronting the dangers of the Atlantic. He heard strange foreign songs bawled in the streets. He saw the national battles that came tumbling out of taverns. He learned the lingua franca of the sailors, and he listened open-mouthed to the reminiscences of Brouageais who had made the journey to Canada and Brazil.

There was excitement enough within the city. The ever-lasting wars of religion flowed and ebbed against the walls of nearby La Rochelle, the holy city of the Huguenots, and the important seaport of Brouage was often submerged in the tide of conflict. In 1570 Brouage was held by the Huguenots, and was captured by the Catholics, with a loss of 1,200 Protestant dead, there and thereabout. In the following years it was occasionally raided by corsairs from La Rochelle, whose citizens united commercial with religious hate. By 1576 it was Protestant again, and was visited by Henry of Navarre, the Huguenot leader, later to be Catholic King Henry IV of France. He was magnificently received with the spectacle of a naval battle between a vessel manned by horrid Moors and four light craft that attacked it and most artfully set it on fire. This was Champlain's first sight of the gallant white-plumed Henry, whom he was ere long to know and serve well. Then in 1577 Protestant Brouage was besieged by the royal army. Battered and hungry, it capitulated. In 1585 the city, now stanchly Catholic, underwent a cruel but unsuccessful siege by Condé, the Protestant duke. In the following year the Protestants attempted an all-out attack on the stronghold. Jealous La Rochelle gladly contributed a fleet of fifteen ships and a swarm of small boats. The commander of Brouage, d'Epinay Saint-Luc, assembled his own fleet. The two navies bombarded each other for a month without doing any serious harm. Then the Protestants succeeded in penetrating the harbor and sank there twenty vessels loaded with sand and stone. D'Epinay Saint-Luc did his best to raise the craft, but in vain; there they lay in the soft sand, and there they still lie. La Rochelle had gained its end, the crippling of the trade of Brouage. From this blow the little city never recovered.

It is possible that Champlain served in the defending fleet. He was soon to be a staff officer under d'Epinay Saint-Luc; it would be natural that he should have first commended himself to his chief in the naval action off his native city.

It is at least clear that Champlain in his boyhood and youth knew war, terror, hunger, and the sight of death. Such an education is toughening.

Now he disappears for some years. The chances are that he was learning the sailor's trade, observing the ways of the sea and the ways of men. We find him again about 1593. He says of himself: "Having been employed in Henry the Fourth's army in Brittany as *maréchal des logis* under the Marshal d'Aumont, Marshal d'Epinay Saint-Luc, and Marshal Brissac, for some years, until 1598. . . ."

Henry of Navarre was now King Henry of France, and a Catholic. The war was no longer a war of Catholic against Protestant; it was a war of the Catholic monarch, aided by many Protestants who found his lukewarm faith tolerable, against the die-hard ultra-Catholic League, which had made an ally of Spain. The bitter end of the war was fought in Brittany. The Spanish sent an army to aid the League, but with secret instructions not to aid it too much. Spain did not wish the League's triumph; it wished only the weakening of France. For ten years the armies of the King and of the Leaguers and of Spain crossed and crisscrossed Brittany, seldom coming to grips, but always leaving behind them a trail of death, famine, and tears.

Marshal d'Aumont, the first of Champlain's chiefs, was appointed commander of the King's forces in Brittany in 1592, but he did not get into action until a year later. It is fairly safe, then, to assume that Champlain did not go to war before 1593, when he was twenty-six. He was *maréchal des logis*, billeting officer (not the *maréchal des logis* of the modern French army, who is a kind of sergeant-major).

In the first days of August 1594, Marshal d'Aumont's army set out from Rennes and marched westward. (In the first days of August, exactly 350 years later, the American Sixth Armored Division set out from Rennes, moving westward, but at what a different pace!) D'Aumont's army, wonderfully enough, was well disciplined. One morning he hanged twenty-eight soldiers for insubordination and looting. This was an impressive example for a young *maréchal des logis*. D'Aumont forced about four hundred retreating Spaniards onto the rocky point of Crozon, which guards the southern entrance to the harbor of Brest. The marshal pursued them there, being in turn pursued by the main body of the Spaniards. On the dreary, lichened rocks of Crozon, under the unceasing rain, the Spaniards fortified themselves, and in a heroic defense they refused all composition and died one by one before the French, who were now joined by the allied English. When their fort was finally taken by assault, only eleven out of 401 Spaniards remained alive, and of the eleven, nine were wounded. The scene of their death is still known as the *Pointe des Espagnols*. The French and English lost nearly three thousand men.

Champlain was at Crozon and fought bravely, says a careful modern historian, though, regrettably, he does not give his authority.[5] Champlain must have learned there some military lessons that would later serve him in the American wilderness. He learned too how brave men can die, hopeless, for fidelity.

One of those who died at Crozon was Sir Martin Frobisher, the explorer of the Canadian Arctic. Champlain later knew and praised his work; but he was probably unaware that he had heard the shot that killed England's naval hero.

The war dragged on. In the summer of 1595 Marshal d'Aumont was wounded in attempting to capture the Château of Comper to oblige a charming countess with whom he was in love. He died; he was seventy-three, old for wounds, and old for love.

D'Epinay Saint-Luc, former governor of Brouage, Champlain's immediate superior, took d'Aumont's place as com-

[5] E. Pocquet: *Histoire de Bretagne*, V, 260.

mander in chief. Probably he showed favor to his fellow townsman. All we know is that Champlain's war service was sufficiently eminent to bring him, later, a pension from King Henry
and the royal friendship.

In 1596 d'Epinay Saint-Luc was transferred away from the
Breton sector. He was succeeded by his brother-in-law, the
Marshal de Cossé-Brissac.

The endless war in Brittany had laid that thriving province
waste. Brigands terrorized the countryside after the regular
armies had passed by. When soldiers of any sort appeared in a
village, the inhabitants fled to the woods, having less fear of
the wild than of the military. Yet in the forest the wolves, accustomed to the taste of human flesh, learned to hunt men, and
especially women. They invaded the city of Quimper and
brought men down in the city streets. A chronicler says: "They
had gained the cunning to seize men always by the throat to
prevent their victims from crying out; they knew how to mangle
men without injuring their clothes, which one would find intact
beside the bones of the eaten dead."

In the degeneration of the army through a long war, one may
imagine the trials of a humane man in the post of billeting officer. The action of the soldiers was always the same, says a
modern historian,[6] and is to be summarized by five phrases: to
loot the possessions, to carry off the cattle, to burn the houses,
to kill the men, to rape the women.

The war ended with the complete triumph of the royal armies.
In May 1598 King Henry came to Rennes, ceremonially reviewed his victorious troops, heard a *Te Deum* in the cathedral,
and touched for the King's evil. Five days of festivities followed.
Then the troops were demobilized, given their separation pay,
and told to shift for themselves. It occurred to no one that a
grateful country should have any further obligation toward
veterans or interest in their doings.

Samuel Champlain, ex-officer with five years' service, was
now thirty-one years old. His body and his spirit had been
toughened by the privations of life on board a deep-sea fishing
smack, and later by the hardships of a long, cruel war. He had
learned how to take care of himself in conflicts with the ele-

[6] E. Pocquet: *Histoire de Bretagne*, V, 320.

ments, in conflicts with angry men, ready with fists and knives. He knew the devices of the old soldier for keeping himself comfortable in adverse circumstances, for sleeping in rain and snow, for finding food when there was no food to be had. He had learned something of the art of war: a war of small marauding bands in a lonely forest land, a war of cunning and surprise. He was on easy terms with death; no doubt he had killed with his own hand. He had served his apprenticeship to fortitude, and, unknowing, an apprenticeship for life and war among the savages of a savage and distant continent.

Now he was in no mood to settle down to some dull, virtuous trade. "Seeing myself," he writes, "without any charge or employment, I resolved, not to remain idle, to find some means of making a voyage to Spain, and being there, to make and cultivate acquaintances, so that by their influence and intercession I might ship in one of the vessels that the King of Spain sends every year to the West Indies, and thus inform myself of those facts which have not been ascertained by any Frenchmen, because they have no free access there; and so on my return I would make a truthful report of them to His Majesty." The words are contained in the introduction to a report he later made to His Majesty. Certainly in 1598 his purpose was not so much to make a truthful report to his sovereign as to appease his own curiosity, his postwar restlessness, his still unweakened desire for adventure. In this moment of self-counsel, with no duties and no demands claiming him, it was the westward urge that stirred in his heart.

To gain his purpose he had a stout string to pull. He made his way to Blavet, now Port-Louis, opposite Lorient on the south coast of Brittany. Here were quartered the Spanish troops awaiting repatriation according to the terms of the peace treaty. And here he found his uncle, Captain Provençal, "considered to be one of the good mariners of France, and who, in that status, had been employed by the King of Spain as pilot-general in his navy." [7] Captain Provençal received his nephew cordially and evidently spoke well of the Spanish service. He found a place

---

[7] He was not the *piloto general*, the august chief of all the Spanish pilots. He was probably a ship's master. I have searched in vain for his name in the many published Spanish documents of these years.

for Champlain on the *Saint Julien*, a five-hundred-ton vessel
that had been in the Newfoundland fishing trade. On the ninth
of September 1598 Champlain set sail for Spain.[8]

[8] G. de Carné: *Correspondance du duc de Mercoeur* (Arch. de Bretagne, 11, 12),
II, 159. Champlain says August.

CHAPTER II

The First Voyage

THE SPANISH TROOPSHIPS headed southwest across the Bay of
Biscay to Cape Finisterre, halted a week in Vigo Bay to repair
storm damage, coasted south around Cape Saint Vincent, and
came to anchor in Cadiz. Here the soldiers were disembarked,
and all the chartered French transports except the *Saint Julien*
returned to France. The Spanish admiral liked the *Saint Julien*,
her size, speed, and seaworthiness; he held her for the Spanish
service. Thus circumstances favored Champlain's purpose. He
spent a month in Cadiz, and three in Sanlúcar de Barrameda, at
the mouth of the Guadalquivir, Seville's river. He visited
Seville and made plans, not very good plans, of that city and
of the seacoast towns he saw. Certainly he carried out his announced purpose, "to make and cultivate acquaintances" who
would be useful to him.

The admiral of the convoy for New Spain, Don Francisco
Coloma, inspected the *Saint Julien* and chartered her at the rate
of one crown per month. (The crown, the écu, was worth three
livres. The livre, the standard base of reckoning, became the
franc at the Revolution.) As Captain Provençal was summoned
to other duties, uncle and nephew proposed to the admiral that
Champlain should accompany the ship for the transatlantic
voyage. "The Admiral freely granted me this, with every evi-

dence of satisfaction, promising me his favor and assistance, which he has not denied me when occasion arose."

Champlain was neither master nor pilot of the *Saint Julien*; he could not have fulfilled the strict requirements for these posts. He evidently made the journey as a kind of supercargo, the representative of the ship's owners.

The fleet set sail from Sanlúcar de Barrameda on February 3, 1599.[1] It followed the classic route to the Canary Islands, then southwest to the sixteenth parallel, and directly west with the trade winds astern until the fleet ran inevitably into America.

Of the crossing Champlain tells us nothing. The incidents seemed to him not worthy of remark. It was normal for the food to shorten day by day, for the water to turn foul and rank, for weevils to appear in the biscuit, for giant cockroaches to take their ease like first-class passengers. Was he not struck by the shipboard gaieties, the cockfights, the mimic bullfights, the illuminations, ceremonies, amateur theatricals? Thomas Gage, sulky English Dominican, made the journey in 1625; he tells how thirty Jesuits celebrated Saint Ignatius's day, trimming their ship with fine linen, "her flags and topgallants representing some the Jesuits' arms, others the Picture of Ignatius himself, shooting off that night at least fifty shot of Ordnance, besides four or five hundred Squibs, and all her Masts and Tacklings hung with Paper lanthorns having burning lights within them; the Waits ceased not from sounding, nor the Spaniards from singing all night." On St. Dominic's Day the Dominicans on their vessel strove to outdo the Jesuits with decorations, music, and explosions. After dinner "they had prepared a Comedy out of the famous Lope de Vega, to be Acted by some Souldiers, Passengers and some of the younger sort of Friers, which I confess was stately acted and set forth both in shows and good Apparel, in that narrow compass of our Ship, as might have been upon the best Stage in the Court of Madrid."

Two months and six days after leaving Sanlúcar the fleet raised Deseada, a small uninhabited island east of Guadeloupe. The ships were on their course; to hit Deseada squarely was a pilot's triumph! The convoy touched at Guadeloupe to take

[1] Champlain says "at the beginning of January." For the chronology of the trip see Appendix B.

1 5

on water, to pick fruits, and to shoot small game. Here Champlain saw his first savages, a band of three hundred. The Spaniards immediately gave them chase, and they fled away into the mountains. Champlain noted that here white man and brown were hunter and quarry.

Thence the fleet passed among the high, barren, uninhabited Virgin Islands. Champlain's mariner's eye picked out a number of good harbors from the quarterdeck.

And now he says a very curious thing. "From these islands we went to Margarita Island, where pearls are fished for. In this island is a good-sized city called by the same name, Margarita. The island is very fertile in grain and fruits. From this port more than three hundred canoes leave every day, going a league offshore to fish for pearls in ten or twelve fathoms. The fishing is done by negro slaves of the king of Spain, who take a little basket under their arm, and with it plunge to the bottom of the sea, and fill it with oysters, and climb back into their boats, with which they return to the said port to unload at the proper place, where the officers of the said king receive them. From the said island we went to Puerto Rico. . . ."

This is a fair enough description of the pearl fisheries, and Champlain supplements it with a sketch of the Negro fishermen and a chart of the island. But Margarita lies off the Venezuelan coast, five hundred miles almost due south from the Virgin Islands, which adjoin Puerto Rico, According to Champlain's narrative, the fleet made a side trip of a thousand miles to visit the pearl fisheries and then returned almost to its point of departure! But this is insane, this defies all common sense, and naturally, this contravenes all the Spanish records. The convoys followed a fixed route, almost a timetable. The Margarita ship left the main convoy, usually at Deseada, and rejoined it at Havana for the return voyage.

In describing the trip to Margarita, Champlain lied, or he was confused.

Perhaps he lied. The purpose of his report to King Henry IV was to demonstrate the wealth of the Spanish colonies and to gain favor for himself. Nothing would so stir his gallant master's cupidity as the mention of a sea carpeted with pearls. It would be a pity to leave them out. He put them in, with a picture and a chart.

Yes, but why did he lie so clumsily? Any attentive reader, one would think, would exclaim at the fantastic itinerary. (Though to be sure, no editor or biographer of Champlain seems to have been at all disturbed by it.) Champlain's chart of Margarita only vaguely resembles the actual island. He even shows Panama and the Pacific Ocean a dozen miles away. A liar, one would think, would be more careful.

Perhaps he was confused. This, I think, is the better explanation of the discrepancies and perplexities of his journal. He brought home a sketch of pearl fishers, whom he had seen somewhere in the West Indies. As he could not remember just where, he concluded that they must have been off Margarita, *ergo* he must have visited that island; so he put a few notorious facts concerning it into his record. I will grant you that such confusion is hardly worthy of a great navigator.

From the Virgin Islands, then, Coloma's fleet proceeded west to Puerto Rico and cast anchor in the noble harbor of San Juan. The city itself was found to be desolate and deserted. "Most of the houses were burnt, and there were not four persons to be found, except a few negroes, who told us that the merchants of the said place had been carried off prisoners by the English, and the others who had been able to flee had escaped into the mountains, whence they had not yet dared to emerge for fear that the said English would return." The English, Champlain tells us, had left the city only fifteen days before his arrival.

Now this is curious too. The Duke of Cumberland had, in fact, captured San Juan in June 1598. According to Spanish sources, no great injury was done. The English carried off some legitimate prizes, cargoes of hides, sugar, and ginger, but committed no wanton destruction in the city. The only looting recorded is of a stained-glass window. Worsted at length by dysentery and yellow fever, the English abandoned the city finally on November 23, 1598.[2] The news of its freedom reached

[2] Iñigo Abad y Lasierra: *Historia de Puerto Rico*, 159; L. Cabrera de Córdoba: *Relaciones*, 2; Julian S. Corbett: *The Successors of Drake*, 250.

Spain by January 4, 1599, before the departure of Champlain.
He arrived in San Juan probably in mid-April. It is strange that
the timorous merchants should still be hiding in the mountains.
It is perhaps less strange that Champlain should have misunderstood a Negro's excited Spanish concerning the time of the
Englishmen's abandonment of the island. Champlain's Spanish
was evidently not good. (He transcribes San Juan de Ulúa as
St. Jean de Luz, Portobelo as Portouella, Vera Cruz now as
Lauelle Croix, now as Vereaciux. Anyone who, after three
years among the Spanish, so garbles a recurring word like Vera
Cruz has no sense of language. Poor Champlain was no linguist;
in thirty years' association with the Algonquins he did not learn
to speak their language.)

In Puerto Rico he remained a month. He tasted and sketched
the tropic fruits, and noted the island's products, its abundant
parakeets, its luxuriant forests. He made a drawing of a tree
called the sombrade, whose branches take root and grow like
those of the banyan. "I have seen one of these trees of such extent that it covered more than a square league." [3]

The admiral had so far kept his fleet united, no doubt for
security against European pirates. In San Juan he divided the
convoy, taking four large vessels with him to the Main, or
north coast of South America, sending three to Portobelo with
the shipments of Panama and Peru, and consigning three galleons to Mexico. Champlain's ship was one of these last three.

The Mexican detachment, accompanied by four *pataches* (dis-
patch boats, or gunboats), coasted along the northern shore of
Santo Domingo. Off Tortuga Island, the pirates' home, they
had an encounter with thirteen French, English, and Dutch
ships, which alternated contraband trade with piracy. The
Spanish galleons, which heavily outgunned the enemy, bottled
him in the bay by Saint Nicolas. But the corsairs dared a
desperate trick. At dawn they drove out of the harbor, bearing
down directly on the anchored Spaniards. "This resolution,"
says Champlain admiringly, "brought down the Spaniards'

---

[3] This is identified, in the various editions of Champlain's works, as *ficus
americana maxima*, or *ficus sp.* Dr. J. I. Otero, Director of the Instituto de Agri-
cultura Tropical in Mayaguez, rejects this identification, and proposes the man-
grove (*rhizophora mangle L*).

courage and softened their rhodomontades. We had to up anchor
with such speed that in the vice-admiral's ship they cut the
cable at the hawse-hole." The pirates got to windward and
escaped. "But it is very certain that if the vice-admiral had
wished, he could have taken them, having better ships and more
men and munitions; and the foreign ships were saved only
through the Spaniards' lack of courage." Here speaks the old
scorn of the sailor for sailors of other nations. Champlain's
sympathy was all with his enemy, some of whom were French,
all of whom were bold and dexterous with their little ships.

This was the only exciting event that Champlain records.

The squadron went through the Windward Passage and
coasted westward along the south side of Cuba. It paused at the
Caymans and, according to Champlain, departed thence toward
evening and, "with a very fair wind," arrived at the Yucatan
Bank at three the following afternoon. It was a very fair wind
indeed; it was a miraculous wind that could move square,
bluff-bowed cargo ships four hundred miles in twenty hours.

(I am a little sorry to mock at Champlain's ingenuous errors,
which I can correct at my ease with an atlas. But patience; I
have a case to prove.)

The ships came safely to San Juan de Ulúa, the present Vera
Cruz. Two weeks later Champlain had leave from his commander to visit the City of Mexico. In the capital he spent a
month. His description of Mexico is the most ample and interesting portion of his report.

He was amazed by the beauty of the country and the mag-
nificence of the city, "which I hadn't thought to be so superbly
built of fine temples, palaces, and houses, and the streets so well
laid out, with fine big shops, full of all sorts of very rich merchandise." He describes the resources of Mexico, its fertility,
its wealth in cattle. Three subjects particularly interested him:
the natural products, especially the trees, the wild life, and the
lot of the Indians.

He sketched and described the trees and novel plants, with
some allegations that still bemuse the botanist. He made his
first acquaintance with Indian corn, which later he was to know
only too well. He describes the method of serving chocolate,
and the cacao tree, which somehow he gets inextricably en-

tangled with the maguey. He tells in some detail of the cochineal plant, and of the methods of gathering, drying, and beating the seeds. Today scientists seem to be agreed that the cochineal is an insect.

He saw, and illustrated, rattlesnakes, llamas, fireflies, and the curious quetzal bird, which has no feet and which never descends to earth until it falls dead. "It is said that the female lays a single egg on the back of the male, and when the little bird leaves its shell, it stays in the air." He pictures also a dragon with a head like an eagle, wings like a bat, and a body like a lizard. It is as big as a sheep. "They are not dangerous and do no harm to anyone, though to see them one would say the contrary."

He feels pity for the oppressed Indians, "poor people, deprived of reason." He tells how the Inquisition had tortured them, so that they fled to the mountains and ate whatever Spaniards they could capture. Now, he says, the Spanish rule is milder, and there is an effort to bring them to the knowledge of God and the belief of the Church. To that end each village priest calls the roll before Mass, and any absentees are sought out and given thirty or forty blows with a stick. Champlain is already impressed by the importance of converting the Indians, and by the unwisdom of doing so by compulsion. Religion imposed by fear is no religion.

After his month in Mexico, Champlain returned to Vera Cruz. As there was no sign of activity in the fleet, he made another side trip, in a *patache*, to Portobelo on the Isthmus of Panama. He describes vividly that unhealthy port and notes that there is a good landing near by for an enemy of the King of Spain, who would thus control the trade route from the west coast. He made a plan of the city of Panama; evidently he crossed the Isthmus and saw the great South Sea, beyond which lay China. All the rest of his life he dreamed of seeing that sea once more.

Still, he makes a curious error for a cartographer who spent a month in the country. He twice says that the Chagres River, one of the two channels of trans-Isthmian trade, flows into the Caribbean at Portobelo. In fact the mouth of the Chagres is at Fort San Lorenzo, 130 miles west.

"One may suggest," he says, "that if the four leagues of land between Panama and this river should be cut through, one would come from the South Sea to the hither sea, and thus one would shorten the [sea] journey by more than 1,500 leagues, and from Panama to the Straits of Magellan would be an island, and from Panama to the Newfound-lands another island, so that all America would be two islands."

Here is a clear proposal for a Panama Canal. Champlain deserves every credit for his shrewd and logical suggestion. He does not, however, deserve the credit awarded him by his biographers of being the first to make the suggestion. It was an old idea, which had occurred to many travelers. Emperor Charles V appointed a commission to study the already familiar project in 1534. The commission reported that the obstacles were insurmountable. A Portuguese, Antonio Galvão, published a book in 1550 to demonstrate the feasibility of a canal.

From Portobelo, Champlain returned to Vera Cruz, where the Mexican fleet was assembled. It sailed for Havana, the rendezvous for the ships from the whole Caribbean. Clearly a long delay was foreseen, for Champlain made another side trip to Cartagena in present Colombia. Returning after two and a half months' absence, he found the fleet still serenely waiting in Havana harbor. The admiral "gave me a very good reception, for having seen at his order the places where I had been." One may conclude that Champlain had been dispatched on an official errand to the ships of the Main, and that he had gained the confidence and esteem of his superior.

After four months in Havana harbor the fleet set sail, following the classic route homeward: northeast through the Florida Strait and the Bahama Channel, on the warm, tugging current of the Gulf Stream, within sight of the future Miami and Palm Beach. When past the Bahamas it headed northeast, keeping to northward of Bermuda, and thence to 38 degrees, the latitude of the Azores, and so comfortably homeward to Seville without misadventure and without the loss of a single ship. Champlain's journey ended, according to his own reckoning, in March 1601. I believe that in fact he landed on August 11, 1600.[4] At any

⁴ See Appendix B.

rate, he was in Cadiz on July 2, 1601, for on that date a French friend, Guillaume Hellaine of Marseille, made over to him some property before a Cadiz notary.[5]

At some time before the summer of 1603 he wrote his account of the journey, his *Brief Discours des choses plus remarquables que Samuel Champlain de Brouage a reconneues aux Indes Occidentales.* His manuscript is preserved in the great John Carter Brown Library in Providence. (The text was not printed until 1859.) It is a beautiful little book. Evidently Champlain began by ornamenting his pages with sixty-two water-color maps and illustrations, depicting remarkable trees, plants, birds, and animals. He included also some dramatic scenes: the burning of Indians, silver mining, the beating of absentees from Mass. The water colors are graceful and charming, done in pure colors: viridian, cobalt blue, raw sienna.

When his illustrations were done (or at least blocked out), he had the text filled in by a second hand, clerkly, professional. The text does not always fit the space allotted to it.

As a record of travel, his book has its interest. As a guide to the mariner, it is loose and faulty. It contains nothing not already available to the French and English. Compare it, for instance, with the two excellent "ruttiers," or pilot guides to the Caribbean, published by Hakluyt in 1598. Its errors, amazing on the part of a skilled navigator, make one wonder if he made the trip at all. He says, for instance: "From the said Bahama Channel one sees to the southeast the Island of Santo Domingo." Santo Domingo is in fact five hundred miles distant.

But no, he must have made the journey, for he could have copied his errors nowhere.

His style is heavy and dull. He has no sense of vivid detail, of the striking phrase. Only when he drew in sight of Mexico City was he at all stirred. This visitor, who came out of curiosity to these entrancing lands, seems to have been unable to note any but the most obvious facts, and the most fantastic tales of tongue-in-cheek natives. For instance, after six weeks in Cartagena, arrogant and lovely pearl, he remembers only that the harbor is good, that the King keeps two galleys there, and that the country round about is fertile.

[5] A.-L. Leymarie, in *Nova Francia* I, 80 (October 1925).

Yet Champlain was no dullard. We shall see that, when he writes about the savages and the wilds of Canada, he can be racy as well as accurate. Why then is his first effort in writing so false and flat?

I suspect that he did not write his *Discours* immediately on his return, when his impressions were fresh in mind. I suspect that he wrote it early in 1603, when the opportunity presented itself of making a journey to the St. Lawrence, and when it suddenly seemed a good idea to prove his experience to his new commander and to his King. During the trip to the Indies he had kept his sketchbook handy, and had brought back with him the charts and the drawings of fruits and animals from which he made the illustrations for his text. With these in hand he reconstructed his journey with no aid but memory, a memory from which all but a few oft-told tales had faded. He may have learned from his experience to take notes, to keep a log of his journeys from day to day.

His voyage to the Indies was at any rate of the utmost importance to him. He saw a great American empire under the rule of Spain, supporting Spain's might in the Old World. He saw a colonial system, fully organized, operating on the whole smoothly, with the native populations working docilely to supply their masters with wealth and goods. He saw a capital city in Mexico as noble and as well built as any in Europe, with, as he estimated, twelve to fifteen thousand Spaniards, six times as many Christian Indians, and a great number of Negro slaves. He saw such a city as might, in his mind's eye, rise above the St. Lawrence and in the endless, dark, dripping forests beside Lake Huron.

In Mexico he saw a colonial organization that his righteous spirit could only condemn. He saw the conquerors at ease, resting upon the labors of the conquered. His own procedure was to be one of honest trade and honest co-operation with the natives. The Spanish colonial system implied the exploitation of the natives; the English system in North America was to imply their expulsion or extermination; the French system, as Champlain established it, implied their alliance, on an equal footing, for a common end.

In Mexico he saw also the unsubstantial structure of the city of the soul. "At the beginning of the King of Spain's conquests," he says, "he had established the Inquisition among the Indians, and enslaved them, or caused them to die in such great numbers that the mere story of it rouses one's pity. This bad treatment was the reason that the poor Indians would flee to the mountains like desperate men. : : . If the Spanish still wanted to chastise them according to the rigor of the said Inquisition, they would cause them all to die by fire." This lesson he laid up in his heart. We shall see that in New France there were no forced conversions. Nowhere else in the New World were the savage peoples treated with such kindness and with such regard for their human dignity as possessors of immortal souls that must be won, little by little, to God.

CHAPTER III

Canada before Champlain

Long before Champlain's time, white men had visited the Canadian coast. The Northmen were there in the eleventh century. If their decision to abandon their North American colony in favor of Greenland seem peculiar to us, we must recall that the European white man has bested the aboriginal red man only when he held a musket or an arquebus in his hand. The Northmen fought the Indian with equal weapons, and the Northmen were driven back bloodily to their boats. For five hundred years these shores were left in peace, though no doubt the Greenlanders made occasional trips hither for ship timber. The trees of Iceland and Greenland grow no higher than the knee.

In the summer of 1497 John Cabot, probably born Giovanni Caboto in Genoa, naturalized citizen of Venice, and domiciled in Bristol, England, discovered the continent of North America. He landed, apparently, in Newfoundland and Cape Breton, possibly in Labrador. He assumed that he had reached the territories of Marco Polo's Grand Khan. He set up a cross and an English flag, thus legally establishing England's claim to a North American empire. Beside the English flag he planted the banner of Venice. The claim of Venice to our soil has not yet been invoked.

When Cabot returned to England, King Henry VII rewarded him with a gift of ten pounds from his privy purse, and on the same date granted twelve pounds to "the damsel that danceth" (a lesson for explorers). Cabot made a new expedition in the following year with two ships and three hundred men, and coasted south from Labrador, perhaps as far as Virginia. He returned empty-handed, shamed. For many years England took little interest in this wild land of cold and poverty.

In 1501 and 1502, two Portuguese, Gaspar and Miguel Cortereal, visited these shores from Labrador to the Bay of Fundy. They were probably trying to learn if any new-found lands lay within the area assigned to Portugal by Pope Alexander VI in 1494, and in fact a good Portuguese claim was established. We have evidence of four expeditions from Bristol, probably fishing trips, between 1501 and 1505. There is reason to believe that Sebastian Cabot, son of John, penetrated Hudson Strait to Hudson Bay in 1509. The Portuguese Fagundes explored the Gulf of St. Lawrence, without finding the river, in 1520. In 1524 Esteban Gómez, a Portuguese in Spanish service, ranged the coasts from Cape Breton to Florida. In the same year Verrazano, a Florentine commissioned by the French King Francis I, came as far north as Cape Breton, or farther. There was an English attempt in 1527 to find a northwest passage. The explorers landed briefly in Newfoundland. The skipper wrote from the harbor of St. Johns that he counted there "eleven saile of Normans, and one Brittaine, and two Portugall Barkes, and all a-fishing."

For, almost unobserved by history, the gallant fishermen of western Europe had made themselves at home on the shores of Newfoundland and Nova Scotia. It has even been earnestly alleged that the Bretons and Basques were familiar with the great fishing grounds of the Grand Banks and with the near-by coasts long before the sacred date of 1492, and that they kept the knowledge a secret of their guild. It is possible; but in the nature of things the fishermen wrote no records with their tarry fingers, and we cannot now interpret the hints they dropped in sailors' taverns. What is secure is that John Cabot's report of the abundance of codfish was bruited over Europe. For, said

Cabot, he had only to lower a basket overside with a stone in
it to draw up a basketful of noble fish. In the early years of the
sixteenth century various documents began to appear which
show that fishermen, especially French and Portuguese, were
building an important trade in Newfoundland cod. In 1517 there
were reckoned to be over a hundred ships in the business.

These brave fishermen knew the coasts well, for they must
needs go ashore to dry the cod, and as well to obtain wood and
water, bait and fresh meat. They made friends with the shy
Indians, and soon learned to supplement their fishing revenue
by buying furs for bits of ribbon, for knives, for cooking kettles.
The great American fur trade began.

One of these Breton fishermen was Jacques Cartier of St.
Malo, bold and enduring, as every adventurer in tiny ships must
be, and also a man whose observations fructified in ideas, and
also one who could impose his ideas on others and convert them
into achievement. In fact Cartier was one of that little group
of the elect who, from the given data of knowledge, make
history.

Cartier was probably a shipmate of Verrazano in 1524. From
observation, or from fishermen's tales, he had the hint of a great
gulf lying to the west of Newfoundland, and he surmised that
this might be a channel leading to the Pacific Ocean and to the
riches of Cathay. He gained an interview with his monarch,
Francis I, and proposed a journey of exploration. The King
immediately recognized the gamble to be a good one. Cartier
set sail from St. Malo in April 1534 with two ships and sixty
men. He made Newfoundland in three weeks, a fortunate passage. Here he salted down ten casks of great auks—news to
make the ornithologist shudder. He entered the Gulf of St.
Lawrence by the Straits of Belle Isle, the ten-mile gap between
Newfoundland and Labrador. He went west for about a hundred
miles along the southern coast of Labrador, which looked to
him like the land God gave to Cain. He found in a harbor,
without surprise, a great ship from La Rochelle. The French
fishermen had discovered the Gulf but kept quiet about it for
business reasons. Cartier then turned south and west to the
Gaspé Peninsula. Here he raised a cross thirty feet high, with

the royal lilied shield and an inscription: *Vive le Roy de France*. Thus simply does one gain title to half a continent. He then made most of the circuit of Anticosti Island and, in fear of autumn storms, headed home.

His report to the King was on the whole encouraging. He had found a beautiful and fertile country, peopled by friendly natives, two of whom he carried to France as curiosities and also for training as interpreters. More important, he had found a wide gap to the westward, salt and tidal. This might well be the Northwest Passage, the existence of which was firmly fixed in men's minds by the mere process of speculation on its possibility. The King was convinced, reasonably, that the exploration should be pursued.

Cartier left on his second expedition in May 1535 with three ships. He entered the Gulf at the Straits of Belle Isle and followed the Labrador coast west past Anticosti Island. He beat his way up the vast estuary, whose banks may be only dimly discerned, one from the other. Day by day the two shores neared, the tide dwindled, the water grew sweeter. It became evident that this was no sea channel, but a great river. Cartier came to a lovely spot where the waterway narrows to a half mile in breadth, a gap between abrupt hills. He had penetrated eight hundred miles from the sea and had reached the site of Quebec.

On the shore stood the Huron-Iroquois village of Stadacona. The chief, Donnaconna, received the explorers with a long, incomprehensible speech, and the women danced and sang without ceasing, up to their knees in water. Visitors in canoes came to board the ship; they were given ship biscuit and red wine, in the great French tradition of the *vin d'honneur*. A century later this reception was still remembered among the Indians, with the report that the French ate wood and drank blood.

(Too little recognized is Cartier's achievement in navigation in bringing his three ships safely up the treacherous, unknown channel of the St. Lawrence. Even a hundred years later the ocean-going ships were regularly berthed at Tadoussac, and the traffic to Quebec carried on with pinnaces of ten or fifteen tons.)

Cartier's dream of an open passage to the Orient was dashed.

Whether he hoped, as modern writers suppose, that the St.
Lawrence might flow from the interior of Asia, or whether he
hoped only to find gold and other wealth, is not now clear. At
any rate, he pushed on up the river in his smallest ship. A little
above Lac St. Pierre his men took to the ship's boats and so
came to Hochelaga, the present Montreal. A fortified Huron
village stood on, or adjacent to, the campus of McGill University, asleep in destiny's womb.

There is good reason to believe that Cartier received from
the Indian chief of Hochelaga a dozen bars of gold.[1] This evidence persuaded the King to equip two more expeditions to
Canada.

Cartier and his men climbed Mount Royal and looked, like
Moses from Mount Nebo, westward to the promised land they
were not to tread upon. He could go no farther. The Lachine
Rapids, flooding downward at a speed of thirty miles an hour
and more, barred any passage by the ship's boats. The season
was late (it was the second of October); it was high time that
the explorers should rejoin their main party at Stadacona.

During the absence of their chief the Frenchmen at Stadacona
had built a fort at the junction of the little St. Charles River
with its tiny tributary the Lairet. Present-day antiquarians lo-
cate this first dwelling of white men in Canada on the dank
flats just to the north of the Dorchester Bridge.

It was a dreadful winter. The snows came down to a depth
of four feet, making mountainous drifts against the fort. The
ships, anchored in the St. Charles to be out of the angry current
of the great river, were bound fast in ice. Wine froze in its
casks. Food ran short; the French appealed to the Indians, but
it was the Indian way rather to starve in winter than to lay up
a surplus. The natives gave, grudgingly, a few smoked eels but
demanded a high price in knives and hatchets. Scurvy attacked
the French horribly; twenty-five of the seventy-four men died,
and only three or four remained sound. In the nick of time they
learned the native remedy, the amedda, apparently a decoction
of new green shoots.[2] Meanwhile they conceived a great fear of

---

[1] Gustave Lanctot: *Jacques Cartier devant l'histoire* (Montreal, 1947) 46.

[2] Much labor has been spent in the effort to identify the amedda, or anedda,
which was the cure for scurvy employed by the St. Lawrence Indians. It is vari-

the natives' intentions, and Cartier made the sick in the ship's hold beat with sticks and stones on her sides to give a sound of activity. He would emerge from the palisade of his fort with two or three of those able to walk, and he would make a great pretense of rage, "crying and throwing sticks after them, sending them aboard, showing by signs to the said savages that he made all his folk work in the ships, some to calk, others to make bread and do other work, and that it was not good that they should come to idle outside."

It would be interesting to know if the Indians could make any sense out of this elaborate mimicry. But they too were afflicted with scurvy and were probably in no mood for attacking their visitors.

Early in May, as soon as the great river was clear of ice, Cartier set sail for St. Malo, first kidnapping Chief Donnaconna and some ten of his braves.

His report to his King dwelt little upon the trials and tragedies of the expedition, and much upon the potential richness of the land and the wonders rumored to lie beyond. The King, fondling his gold bars, was not discouraged. He appointed Cartier captain-general and master pilot, and authorized another and greater venture.

Kings are, however, subject to mysterious influences. He delayed the new expedition from year to year. Early in 1541 he appointed as viceroy of New France, outranking Cartier, Jean François de la Roque, sieur de Roberval. He instructed Roberval to found colonies, to grant fiefs and lordships, in brief, to establish a New France that should rival the New Spain to the south.

Unfortunately there was a complete lack of colonists. The survivors of Cartier's expedition gave the worst possible report of the country. The king fell back on the only available source of manpower—the jails. Prisoners condemned to death were

---

ously supposed to be the white pine or white spruce. Certainly the Indians made such a "fir-water." (Wm. Inglis Morse, *Acadiensia Nova*, I, 49.) W. F. Ganong gives references to show its use recently in Labrador and by Soviet soldiers. (*Ste-Croix Island*, St. John, 1945, 123.) However, Dean David Thomson of McGill University points out that the Indians, who suffered with Cartier from scurvy, had to wait for spring to obtain their cure. The amedda must, then, have been a deciduous tree, unless the spring sap gives the spruce its healing virtue.

offered Canada as a commutation of sentence. Those who accepted were marched, chained together in gangs, to St. Malo.

Cartier set sail in May 1541 without waiting for Roberval. In Stadacona (which we might as well begin calling Quebec) he was well received by the Indians, who saw in the French the bringers of miraculous knives, hatchets, and kettles. They looked about for their companions whom Cartier had carried off to France five years before. Cartier replied that they had become great lords in France and had married happily. (In fact they were all dead of civilization's maladies.) The Indians, especially the new chief, were delighted with the news.

Cartier chose for his winter quarters a pleasant site at Cap Rouge, on the north shore of the St. Lawrence, eight miles above Quebec. High overhead rises today the splendid Quebec Bridge.

We have no information of the winter, save that the garrison was largely busied in collecting samples of gold, silver, and diamonds. In the spring Cartier decided to return to France. He was resentful of Roberval's failure to appear; he wanted to dazzle the court with his gold and diamonds. He arrived in June at St. Johns, Newfoundland, and found there Roberval with three ships, a year late. After high words on both sides Cartier sailed for France by night, without a farewell.

Roberval resumed his journey to the St. Lawrence. He re-occupied, apparently, Cartier's fort at Cap Rouge. He dispatched two of his ships to France, with plenty of diamonds, to report to the King and to bear witness against Cartier.

The winter of 1542–3 was a cruel one. Food was short; scurvy killed fifty colonists, a third of the party. There were no survivors of Cartier's winter to point out the salutary tree amedda. Roberval ruled sternly over his convict band. "He punished every man according to his offense. One was hanged for theft. . . . Others also were put in irons, and divers were whipped, as well men as women, by which means they lived in quiet."

In the early summer of 1543 Roberval made an effort to ascend the St. Lawrence. How far he went we do not know, as the record comes mysteriously to a sudden end. We know only that he succeeded in returning to France.

The gold and diamonds, when inspected by French jewelers, were a disappointment.

Now silence settles down on the great river for nearly sixty years, for a man's lifetime. Yet perhaps the silence is not absolute; perhaps there were white men's voices, too faint to reach our ears. There are three vague indications that traders may have made their way to Hochelaga, our Montreal.[3] In reading history one must always be impressed by the fact that our knowledge is only a collection of scraps and fragments that we put together into a pleasing design, and often the discovery of one new fragment would cause us to alter utterly the whole design. Few men write of their deeds, and few write down the talk of others; and fires, wars, damp, and mildew destroy the written words. And in the old days pastrycooks bought letters and sheets of books to wrap their dainties in; and many a manuscript has gone to light fires; and of the great, universal annihilator of paper I am too prudish to speak.

The fishermen made their annual journeys to the Grand Banks in constantly increasing numbers. Catholic Europe must have fish; it kept its fast days with great rigor, to the confusion of lax Reformists. In 1579 Sir Humphrey Gilbert found 36 ships in the harbor of St. Johns, Newfoundland. The French had at least 150 vessels in the business; the English, probably as many; the Spanish, over 100; the Portuguese, about 50. Some 20 or 30 Basque ships were engaged in whaling, penetrating the Gulf of St. Lawrence for its famous white whale.[4]

And the fishermen, following the immemorial habit of sailors, bartered with the natives for their possessions, to be taken home as souvenirs or for profit. The only possessions of these dark northern men worth having were their furs, most of all their beaver skins.

The beaver is an unlucky beast. He was plentiful throughout Europe during the Middle Ages; Dante mentions him in the *Inferno*. His soft, warm fur made bare-skinned man jealous, and man rendered him practically extinct by the mid years of the sixteenth century. At this moment the fishermen began bringing home skins of the American beaver, richer even than the rare

[3] H. P. Biggar: *The Early Trading Companies of New France*, 47n.
[4] Harold A. Innis: *The Cod Fisheries*, 30–51.

and prized pelts of Europe. His fur is full of tiny barbs, water-shedding, admirable for felting. The skins most prized by felters and connoisseurs were those which had been worn by an Indian, preserving his oily sweat. Fashion proclaimed that every gentle-man must have a hat of beaver felt, and of no inferior fur. A gentleman's hat was a great magnificent burden, the unique creation of an artist, as women's hats are today. When a man died he bequeathed his hat specifically in his will. Its high crown was commonly decorated on the left side with feathers, nose-gays, or furbelows, while the right side was left bare to permit swordplay. Hence all men's hats now have a discreet bowknot, a vestigial falbala, on the left.

It was men's fashions, male vanity, that sent traders across the sea, and Indians to the beaver ponds to capture the creatures under the ice with their bare hands. It was the fashion set by the courts that tempted the hardy Dutch and the hardier French *coureurs de bois* into the interior of America. And it was this courtly vanity which set Indian tribe against tribe, which caused endless war for the domination of the trade routes and sources of supply, which exterminated the whole great race of Hurons, which caused, eventually, the wars of white man against white man in deep forests by nameless rivers.

And the beaver—the humble, virtuous beaver, fashion's quarry—only precariously survived. He is the sole animal save man that builds houses and landscapes his home. He is the engineer of the animals, the artisan, the worker. He works for himself and not for man, so man destroyed him and wore his skin for a hat.

The beginning of the American fur trade cannot be dated. Certainly when in 1534 Cartier first reached the New Bruns-wick coast, the behavior of the Indians showed that they knew what white men are and what they want. The Indians held up furs on their paddles and signaled the Frenchmen ashore. After some hesitation the French accepted the invitation and traded until the Indians were left stark naked. There are other indica-tions of a developing trade through the course of the century.

The impulse of the trade was felt in the interior. River dwell-ers and lake dwellers heard of the wonderful steel hatchets, knives, awls, and fishhooks, and learned that they could be had for the skins of beasts. They brought or sent their furs to market.

The channels of trade already existed. Before the white man appeared, the Indians had built up a remarkable system of commerce. Some tribes specialized in manufacture, others in transport. Copper from Lake Superior found its way to Texas, Virginia, and New England. Pipestone, flint, obsidian, crossed half the continent. Walrus tusks from Eskimo land were used by the New York State Iroquois as scrapers.

Indian entrepreneurs organized the old commercial channels for the purposes of the fur trade and developed new ones. Obscure battles were fought for the control of the outlets.

By the end of the sixteenth century, Tadoussac, at the mouth of the Saguenay, was the established rendezvous for the French traders and the natives. Here came the Montagnais and others of Algonquin stock,[5] who in turn traded with the wild primitive hunting tribes to the north as far as Hudson Bay and to the west as far as the Ottawa.

The volume of furs steadily increased, and the demand in France increased with the supply. The profits were enormous. In 1602, one had a beaver for two biscuits or two knives.

The English began to raid the returning vessels and to take them into English ports, war or no war. The French realized that to guarantee their trade they must protect their source of supply and their lines of communication. In short, they must plant colonies.

The failure of Cartier and Roberval, and of French colonizers in Florida and Brazil, had made the government suspicious of such enterprises. Men who argue from experience found only precedents of calamity in the French record. Sully, the great minister of Henry IV, opined that the planting of distant colonies was contrary to "the nature and mind of the French, whom I recognize, to my great regret, to have neither the perseverance nor the foresight requisite for such matters, and who ordinarily devote their vigor, intelligence, and courage only to the conser-

---

[5] Indianists make great play with the distinctions between Algonquins, Algonquians, Algonkins, and Algonkians. This seems really too much trouble. I think it will be clear whether I am referring to a particular tribe, to the far-flung "stock," or to the language.

vation of what touches them close and is constantly present before their eyes, as the experience of the past has made only too plainly visible, so that things which are separated from our substance by foreign lands and seas will never be anything but a useless burden to us." Fortunately there were others in council to oppose prudence with dreams. Michel Hurault, *conseiller d'Etat*, published two discourses in 1588 and 1592, pointing out the aid that the Spanish colonies gave the homeland in its effort to dominate Europe. He made clear that the strength of a European power must in the future depend upon its overseas possessions. King Henry, adventurous by instinct, inclined to accept the bold and confident advice rather than the prognostications of timid good sense.

The first of the new series of colonial enterprises has no important place in history, but it is an extraordinary tale of courage and folly. There was in Brittany a turbulent, wrong-headed gentleman, Troïlus du Mesgouez, marquis de la Roche-Helgomarc'h. He obtained from Henry III the right to occupy Newfoundland. Setting sail in 1584 with a hundred colonists, he went first to Brouage for salt, and there his ship was wrecked. Samuel Champlain of Brouage was then about seventeen. Did he inspect the wreck and learn from the survivors their purposes, their wild hopes and imaginations? Was this the beginning of Champlain's own hopes? Here are questions we dare not answer, except to say "possibly," or even "very likely."

After a period in war and prison, the Marquis de la Roche resumed his colonizing efforts. He attempted to settle a band of beggarmen on Sable Island, a fog-bound, sandy grave of good ships off the Nova Scotia coast. As the story of his enterprise and of his unfortunate victims has nothing to do with Champlain, I have interred it in Appendix C. It is really well worth reading, if you are not too pressed for time.

Pierre Chauvin, a Huguenot of Honfleur, had four vessels in the fish and fur business during the last years of the century. His chief associate was François du Pont-Gravé, or briefly Pontgravé, a hearty, full-blooded adventurer, of whom we shall hear more. Pontgravé had ascended the St. Lawrence as far as Trois Rivières, half way between present Quebec and Montreal. Chauvin obtained from the king a monopoly of fur trading on the river, on condition that he settle fifty colonists a year in the area. In 1600 he went out with Pontgravé and the Sieur de Monts, of whom also we are to hear much. He arrived at Tadoussac, the usual meeting place with the Indians. Here he established his colony, against the advice of Pontgravé and de Monts, who recommended a location farther upstream. At Tadoussac, comments Champlain, "the cold is so great that if there is an ounce of cold forty leagues up the river, there will be a pound of it here." But Chauvin was more concerned with commercial advantages than with his colonists' comfort. When he sailed away in the autumn, their number had unaccountably dwindled to sixteen and to fewer still by spring. It was the court of King Petaud, where every man is master, says Champlain. "Idleness and sloth, with the diseases that attacked them, reduced them to hard straits and forced them to have recourse to the savages, who charitably took them in when they abandoned their quarters. Some died miserably; the others, suffering much, awaited the return of the ships." Chauvin rescued the survivors in 1601. Apparently he made no further effort to colonize.

The merchants of the French seaports bitterly assailed Chauvin and his monopoly of the fur trade. They petitioned the King for relief, pointing out incidentally that they had already left one of their own agents to winter with the Indians. After much hesitation the King annulled, in effect, Chauvin's monopoly in 1602 but proposed to study the matter further. He commissioned his loyal subject Aymar de Chastes, governor of Dieppe, to meet with representatives of the cities interested, and, with Chauvin, to draw up regulations for the fur trade and for the colonization of New France. De Chastes carried on the negotiations with vigor. As Chauvin opportunely died, de Chastes took his place as organizer of a fact-finding expedition in 1603. The master of the ship was Pontgravé; and de Chastes sent along as observer and cartographer his good friend Captain Samuel Champlain.

CHAPTER IV

The Second Voyage

SAMUEL CHAMPLAIN arrived in France from his Spanish and Mexican adventures probably in the autumn of 1601. He was in his mid thirties, toughened by privation, ripened by experience. He was a good soldier, a good navigator; he was handy with pencil and brush and had some experience in cartography. He was looking for a job, by preference an interesting and exciting job.

There are two years to account for. The *Biographie Saintongeoise* of 1852 says, without giving a reference, that he was an *armateur*, a ship's outfitter, in Dieppe. It is quite possible. The governor of Dieppe, Aymar de Chastes, was an old wartime friend of his, and Champlain might naturally have sought his powerful aid.

And naturally he sought the fountainhead of all aid, King Henry himself. King Henry remembered, perhaps after a little jogging of the memory, his old companion in arms. The royal favor went by preference to those who had fought by his side up and down the fields of France. His Majesty was pleased to grant Champlain a pension, and to command him to attend upon the King's person.[1]

---

[1] Champlain speaks of *"sadite Majesté, à laquelle i'estois obligé tant de naissance, que d'vne pension. . . . "* (III, 315.) Why *"de naissance"*? I cannot find that Brouage

To reinforce his claim for a pension, or to justify it, Champlain wrote and illustrated his record of his journey to New Spain. Evidently King Henry turned it over to de Chastes, for from de Chastes's estate it fell into the hands of a Dieppe convent, and in the nineteenth century it was sold to the John Carter Brown Library in Providence.

Champlain and de Chastes were thoroughly congenial: de Chastes was vice-admiral of the French Navy, and had captained a military expedition to the Azores in 1583. Though he now had "as many gray hairs as years," he proposed to lead in person a band of colonists to the New World when proper reconnoissance had been made. He offered a place in his exploring party to Champlain, who replied that he would like nothing better but that he must have the King's permission. This was soon obtained by de Chastes. Armed with a letter from the royal secretary, Champlain presented himself to his new captain, Pontgravé, in the little seaport town of Honfleur.

To his captain Champlain took an immediate liking, and the friendship was lifelong. "I was his friend, and his years would make me respect him as my father," he said later. Pontgravé was now close to fifty, a loud, hearty, back-slapping fellow, always with a ready jest, especially when starvation was at hand, when death rode the Atlantic gales. Meeting fishing vessels at sea, he would greet them with a famous bellow: *"Malouins!"* (men of St. Malo!), and would shout some Breton song. Despite his gout and the doctor's orders he yielded too readily to the temptation of calvados, which he drank without water. Everybody loved Pontgravé, or nearly everybody; some blamed his sharp practice in business deals. He was an old hand in the fur trade; he had already ascended the St. Lawrence as far as Trois Rivières.

The 1603 expedition consisted of three ships: Pontgravé's *Bonne Renommée*, 120 tons, out of Honfleur; a ship equipped by the Rouen merchants, under Captain Prévert; and one from St. Malo. The risks of such an enterprise may be judged from the fact that the marine insurance rates were thirty-five per cent.

---

had any special dependence on Henry of Navarre in 1567. Was there some family loyalty of the Champlains to Protestant Henry? If so, some color is given to the supposition that Champlain was baptized a Protestant.

Pontgravé carried two interesting passengers: Montagnais Indians he had picked up at Tadoussac on a previous voyage and had brought to France to train as interpreters and ambassadors of good will—commercial good will, to be sure. They had been royally entertained, in the strict sense of the word; they had gone to court and had been exhibited to the King of France himself.

The *Bonne Renommée* sailed from Honfleur on March 15 and sighted Newfoundland on May 7. Beating her way among icebergs and floes, some of them twenty miles long, she entered the Gulf and came on May 20 to Anticosti Island.

Of the first crossing to Canada, Champlain tells us such facts as would concern a mariner: the course, the latitudes, the ice. He does not record the incidents of travel that impressed landsmen at sea; the bad food, the increasing stench of the barreled water, the profane valor of sailormen in storms. Nor the welcome first sight of birds, a hundred leagues from Newfoundland, by which navigators knew their longitude. Such travelers as the candid Brother Gabriel Sagard, who came over in 1623, were more impressed by marvels. He describes with wonder the aerial maneuvers of the clouds of birds in the Gulf, and the islands where the birds huddle so thick that one cannot walk without treading on eggs, where the sailors smite down birds with a club until overcome by the frightful guano smell. He tells how the sailors take birds by trailing a baited fishhook overside or by holding up a herring as bait and seizing the bird by the leg when he swoops. He describes the strange and beautiful fish, the brilliant, chameleonlike dorad and the salmon, six feet long. And that great clumsy creature, the manatee, which sailors averred they could mount and ride like a horse. The waters of the Gulf teemed with life: porpoises, walrus, and whale, which were so abundant off Gaspé as to disturb one's sleep with their hoarse spouting. With luck one might see a swordfish attack a whale, leaping into the air and plunging its harpoon into the whale's back.

Sagard tells us too of the burlesque baptism‾that the sailors performed on reaching Gaspé, despite the shocked protests of clerical passengers. "One of the mariners counterfeits the priest and feigns to confess the novices, muttering between his teeth, then baptizes them by pouring on their heads a great panful of cold water, and preaches and exhorts and mishandles them so much that to escape they ransom themselves with a bottle of wine or brandy. And anyone who hangs back makes his case the worse, for five or six sailors seize the gallant and plunge him head first into a great tub full of water."

Amid such sights and diversions the *Bonne Renommée* made her way up the St. Lawrence, past the Shickshock Mountains of Gaspé. The Gulf became gradually river. The pilot picked his way timidly in morning fogs, boldly when bright day gave him a view of familiar reefs and mountain formations. A cloud of gulls convoyed the vessel. Close above the water skimmed parties of ducks and geese in formation, rapid, full of purpose. From time to time a beluga, or white whale, rose and stared, incredulous.

The pilot, watchful to the north, picked up the mountainous mouth of the Saguenay. He turned in to Tadoussac, at the junction of the two rivers, the rendezvous of French and Indian fur traders. He cast anchor off a little sandy beach, above which today rises the imposing bulk of a sumptuous hotel. It was a grim country, as it is still, with its beetling mountains, its twisted granite descending into the water, its hardy evergreens exploiting every crevice full of soil.

It was on May 27, 1603, that Champlain first set foot on the land that was to be his home, the land whose history he was to shape.

There were signs of great activity on shore, many fires, and many birch-bark canoes drawn up along the beach. Pontgravé took Champlain and his two Indians in a ship's boat to shore, making signs of amity.

Champlain had his first impression of the Canadian natives. Their bodies, naked save for breechclouts, were the color of French beggars half roasted by the sun. Their faces, immobile under plastered paint, were both terrifying and comic. Some were bright red with blue noses and black eyebrows. Some were striped with red, black, and blue from ears to mouth; some bore a single wide black stripe from ear to ear, around the eyes, with three stripes on each cheek. The thought of devils occurred to every pious mind.

"As soon as we had landed we went to the lodge of their great Sagamore, named Anadabijou, where we found him and some eighty of his companions, making *Tabagie* (that is to say, a feast.) He received us very well, after the fashion of the country, and made us sit down beside him, while all the savages ranged themselves one next to the other on both sides of the lodge. One of the savages whom we had brought began to make his oration, of the good reception that the King had given them, and of the good entertainment they had received in France, and that they might feel assured His Majesty wished them well, and desired to people their country, and to make peace with their enemies (who are the Iroquois) or send forces to vanquish them. He also told of the fine castles, palaces, houses, and peoples they had seen, and of our manner of living. He was heard with the greatest possible silence." [2]

How curious would be a transcript of their report! A little later, a missionary who knew the language overheard a traveled savage describing French carriages as "moving cabins drawn by moose." This traveler was chiefly impressed in France by the Swiss Guards and the mighty rumble of their drums, and by the multitude of cookshops. But to return:

"Now when he had ended his oration, the said Grand Sagamore Anadabijou, who had listened to him attentively, began to smoke tobacco, and to pass on his pipe to Monsieur du Pont-Gravé of Saint Malo, and to me, and to certain other Sagamores who were near him. After smoking some time, he began to address the whole gathering, speaking with gravity, pausing sometimes a little, and then resuming his speech, saying to them that in truth they ought to be very glad to have His Majesty for their great friend. They answered all with one voice: 'Ho, ho, ho!' which is to say 'Yes, Yes!' Continuing his speech, he said that he was well content that His said Majesty should people their country and make war on their enemies, and that there was no nation in the world to which they wished more good than to the French. Finally, he gave them all to

---

[2] I reproduce, and shall continue to reproduce without further acknowledgment, the translation by H. H. Langton in the Champlain Society edition of the *Works of Champlain* (Toronto, 1922–1936.) The translation is a model of fidelity and felicity, save only that it improves Champlain's often slipshod style.

understand the advantage and profit they might receive from His said Majesty.

"When he had ended his speech, we went out of his lodge, and they began to hold their *tabagie* or feast, which they make with the flesh of moose, which is like beef, with that of bear, seal, and beaver, which are their most ordinary meats, and with great quantities of wild fowl. They had eight or ten kettles full of meats in the midst of the said lodge, and these were set some six paces apart, and each on its own fire. The men sat on both sides (as I said before), each with his porringer made of the bark of a tree; and when the meat is cooked, one of them apportions to every man his part into these dishes, out of which they feed very filthily, for when their hands are greasy they rub them on their hair, or else on the hair of their dogs, of which they have many for hunting. Before their meat was cooked, one of them rose up and took a dog and went leaping about the said kettles from one end of the lodge to the other. When he came in front of the said Sagamore, he threw his dog violently on the ground, and then all with one voice cried: 'Ho, ho, ho!'; having done this, he went and sat down in his place. Immediately another rose and did the like, and so they continued until the feast was cooked. Then when they had ended their feast, they began to dance, taking in their hands as a mark of rejoicing the scalps of their enemies, which hung behind them. There were one or two who sang, keeping time by the beat of their hands, which they strike upon their knees; then they stop sometimes, and cry: 'Ho, ho, ho!' and again begin to dance, panting like a man out of breath.

"They were celebrating this triumph for a victory they had won over the Iroquois, of whom they had slain about a hundred, whose scalps they cut off, and had with them for the ceremony. Three nations had taken part in the war, the Etchemins, Algonquins, and Montagnais, to the number of a thousand; and these went on the warpath against the Iroquois, whom they encountered at the mouth of the River of the Iroquois [the Richelieu, which flows north from Lake Champlain into the St. Lawrence] and slew a hundred of them. The mode of warfare which they practise is altogether by surprises; for otherwise they would be afraid, and too much in dread of the said Iroquois, who are in greater number than the said Montagnais, Etchemins, and Algonquins."

This passage is of more than casual interest. Champlain listened bemused to the Algonquin speech, most musical of Indian tongues, with its rich vowels and soft, whispered syllables. He understood, of course, nothing. The substance of the discourses was reconstructed by the interpreters after the fact, though no doubt with care. According to instructions, they reported to the Indians that King Henry IV wished to people the country, in other words, to establish permanent French colonies on the St. Lawrence. The Indians, unwitting the future, were politely pleased. They were unfeignedly delighted at the other statement of French policy, that the King would support, in peace or war, the alliance of the Montagnais (Algonquins of the lower St. Lawrence), Etchemins (Penobscot Algonquins of Maine), and Algonquins proper, whose headquarters was the Ottawa River. The alliance was formed against one enemy only, the Iroquois confederacy of upper New York State. Already this aggressive, well-organized group was raiding the St. Lawrence country, taking plunder and captives and gaining honor according to the savage code.

It was an old war. In 1535 King Donnaconna of the Quebec Hurons complained bitterly to Cartier of the Toudamans (Tsonondowanen, or Senecas), who harassed his people with continual war. Two years before, this Iroquois enemy had surprised an encampment of his people and had killed all but five out of two hundred. By 1603 the Hurons had disappeared from the Quebec and Montreal region, having been expelled, very likely, by the Iroquois. And the Algonquins, from the Penobscot to the Ottawa, were allied against the Iroquois.

The history of the Iroquois, most advanced of Eastern Indians, is much disputed by anthropologists. There are two chief theories of their origins. One is that they migrated from the Southwest and on reaching the Great Lakes split into two groups. One group, the Hurons, made their way north of the lakes and down the St. Lawrence. The southern group, the Five Nations, with some offshoots, settled in central New York and there established a mainly agricultural civilization.

According to the other theory, the Iroquois originated in the northeast. By 1000 A.D. they occupied the north shore of the St. Lawrence. Their territory was invaded by the Algonquins; by 1200 A.D. they were conquered by the Adirondacks. Two branches emigrated, the Iroquois to northern New York, the Hurons to the shores of Georgian Bay. A third branch, the natives whom Cartier found in Stadacona and Hochelaga, lingered on. The Iroquois dreamed forever of revenge; the Hurons forgot it and joined the Algonquins against their terrible kinsmen.[3]

Other bold theories have been advanced. According to one, the Iroquois invaded the Atlantic seaboard from the Caribbean, whither they had come from South America.[4] Certainly there are striking resemblances between their customs and those of the Guaranís of the southern continent. According to another theory, the Huron-Iroquois, markedly dolichocephalic, are Aryan, and they came to America from Europe, by way of Iceland and Greenland, in very far-off times. Their language is said to bear resemblances, at least curious, at most significant, with Indo-European. Few philologists, unfortunately, are equipped to judge this fascinating theory.

Why did the war rage between Iroquois and Algonquin? Parkman sets it down to the "insensate fury," the "homicidal frenzy" of the Iroquois. Against this judgment of racial character may be alleged the fact that in the sixteenth century the Iroquois prophet Dekanawidah dreamed of universal peace and devised a code of laws for the United Indian Nations. His minister was Hiawatha. Modern students, vowed to the economic interpretation of history, see in the war a long effort to control the fur trade, first with the French on the St. Lawrence, then with the Dutch in New Amsterdam. My own conclusion is that the war was a traditional relic of the struggle for an Iroquois homeland, that by the sixteenth century it had degenerated into a noble sport, and that by the end of the century it was being converted into a commercial war, under the sanction of old ideologies. The curious are referred to the comfortable quarters of Appendix D.

Here it will be enough to accept that Champlain on his first

[3] A. Beaugrand-Champagne, in *Cahiers des Dix* (Montreal, 1936), I, 171.
[4] W. D. Lighthall, in *Trans. Roy. Soc. Can.* 3d Ser. Vol. XXV (1931), II, 71.

landing in Canada found the Iroquois already the dreaded enemy, and throughout his life they became more terrible and more dreaded.

The two Indians with the French reported to their kinsmen that King Henry had promised to support the Algonquin alliance against the Iroquois. One can hardly suppose that the King would have made such a statement of policy without giving some instructions to his own representatives. The policy was evidently authorized in Paris. Champlain, setting it down in his report for publication, implicitly approves it. And since he was still ignorant of Indian affairs, he must have favored the alliance on the advice of Pontgravé.

As it turned out, their support of the alliance was of far-reaching and long-lasting importance. Champlain—and France—had a choice of two courses. The first was a policy of strict neutrality, of aloofness from Indian wars. Such a policy has been approved, in retrospect, by historians. It would have strengthened the position of France with regard to the Iroquois, whose power was on the rise, and was destined to continue rising for a century and a half. It would have enabled the French to establish a dominating military force in America, to judge and arbitrate native quarrels, to impose peace, as the British imposed peace in India. It would have given the French access to the Iroquois country, and hence control of the whole American hinterland.

The trouble is that such a course was practically impossible. French colonial policy was still unformed; not for a half century were the royal ministries to send more than a handful of armed men to Canada. Never during Champlain's lifetime were there a hundred French residents in all of Canada. In the circumstances, any effort on the part of the French to impose peace by force would have been simply grotesque.

What the French wanted of America was furs and fish. Pontgravé and Champlain took the only course possible, if they wished to continue their explorations and obtain furs. If they had said to the Algonquin allies, who, according to their own statement, had mustered a war party of a thousand men, that they proposed a lofty neutrality, they would have been received with distrust and would have found their progress barred. Since the favor of the Algonquins, who commanded the river, was necessary to them, they offered alliance, though recognizing, from the Grand Sagamore's own words, that they were allying themselves with the weaker party.

The alliance thus made determined the character of the French penetration of America. Eight years later Champlain's agent, Etienne Brûlé, wintered with the Indians beside Lake Huron. Before Champlain's death Frenchmen were west of Lake Michigan and on the shores of Lake Superior. Before the century was over they had descended the Mississippi to the Gulf of Mexico. Meanwhile the English in their colonies, advancing step by step, consolidating their positions, had barely reached the Alleghenies.

The alliance made at Tadoussac by Champlain and Pontgravé lasted for a century and a half, as long as New France lasted. The sides were already chosen for a hundred-and-fifty-years war, of French, Algonquins, and Hurons against Iroquois, Dutch, and English. The die was cast on this May 27, 1603.

Champlain's first impressions of the natives are otherwise interesting. He made acquaintance with their astounding filthiness. The gorge of the Frenchmen rose at their first savage banquet, though the Europeans of his time were none too squeamish. (Indeed, Macaulay tells us of the London tripe shop where the guests, including the young Dr. Samuel Johnson, wiped their greasy hands on a Newfoundland dog, quite in the Montagnais manner.) To be sure, the Indians had no textiles for napkins and no soap. Dry and rotten wood was used for cleaning, in great emergencies.

At this *tabagie* (one of the few Indian words that have become familiar French, though in Quebec, to the horror of Parisians, it means a tobacco shop), Champlain watched for the first time one of the native dances that were later to bore him to the limit of endurance. He heard the Indian songs, grave, heavy, monotonous, as befits a liturgy. And the drums, for the Montagnais were great drummers. Their drum was like a tambourine, with rattling pebbles between skin surfaces. "They do not strike it, as do our Europeans, but they turn and shake it, to make the stones rattle inside," says sprightly Father Le Jeune in the *Jesuit Relations*. "They strike it upon the ground, sometimes its edge and sometimes its face, while the sorcerer plays a thousand apish tricks with this instrument. Often the spectators have sticks in their hands, and all strike at once upon pieces of wood, or upon hatchet handles they have before them, or upon their bark plates turned upside down. To this din they add their songs and cries, I might indeed say their howls, so much do they exert themselves at times; I leave you to imagine this beautiful music."

After the *tabagie*, the French and the Indians spent a fortnight in polite conversations, and certainly in fur trading. Champlain inspected the bark lodges of the Indians and noted the routine of their lives. He was much impressed by the birch-bark canoes, which a man could carry easily and which could transport half a ton. He admired the physical perfection of the natives; "all these peoples are well proportioned in body, without any deformity; they are agile, and the women are well shapen, filled out and plump, of a swarthy color on account of the profusion of a certain pigment with which they rub themselves, and which gives them an olive hue." He noted their cheerfulness and laughter, the deliberation of their speech in council, their vengefulness and mendacity, their amazing endurance, and especially their intelligence. "I think that if anyone should show them how to live, and teach them to till the ground, and other matters, they would learn very well; for I assure you that plenty of them have good judgment, and answer very properly any question put to them." He inquired at length into their religion, and was grieved at its diabolical falsity, and gave them a summary of Christian theology. "I think they would speedily be brought to be good Christians if their country were colonized, which most of them would like."

He attended a victory ball, which impressed him, as it could hardly fail to do. The Indians, their faces painted like French maskers in carnival time, performed a solemn cotillion. "They arranged all their women and girls side by side, and themselves stood behind, singing all in unison. Suddenly all the women and girls proceeded to cast off their mantles of skins, and stripped themselves naked, showing their privities, but retaining their ornaments of matachias, which are beads and braided cords made of porcupine quills, dyed of various colors. After they had made

4 7

an end of their songs, they cried all with one voice: 'Ho, ho, ho!' At the same instant all the women and girls covered themselves with their mantles, which were at their feet, and they had a short rest; then all at once beginning again to sing, they let fall their mantles as before. They do not stir from one spot when they dance, but make certain gestures and motions of the body, first lifting up one foot and then the other, and stamping upon the ground.

"While they were performing this dance, the Sagamore of the Algonquins, whose name was Besouat [probably the same as Tessouat, whom we shall meet again in 1613], was seated before the said women and girls, between two poles, on which hung the scalps of their enemies. Sometimes he arose and moved away to address the Montagnais and Etchemins, saying to them: 'See how we rejoice for the victory which we have obtained over our enemies; ye must do the like, that we may be satisfied.' Then all cried together: 'Ho, ho, ho!' As soon as he had returned to his place, the Grand Sagamore and his companions cast off their mantles, being stark naked save for their privities, which were covered with a small piece of skin, and each of [the Montagnais and Etchemins] took what seemed proper to him, such as matachias, tomahawks, swords, kettles, pieces of fat, moose flesh, seal; in a word, everyone had a present, which they proceeded to give to the Algonquins. After all these ceremonies the dance came to an end, and the Algonquins, both men and women, carried away their presents to their lodges. They also matched two of the fittest men of each nation, whom they caused to run, and he who was swiftest in the race had a present."

This genial strip tease yielded before many years to the forces of reform. Father Le Jeune tells us in 1637 that he and Father de Quen were invited to a feast of Tadoussac Indians, but it was hinted that they should not remain long, "because, as it is a war feast, the women will serve there entirely naked." The priests argued and threatened, and invoked God's anger and justice. "In fact, neither in their feasts nor at their departure did they conserve this filthy custom."

On June 11 Champlain made a day's trip up the Saguenay.

This awesome chasm, which arouses the most romantic emotions in today's tourist, seemed to Champlain merely "a most unpleasant country; very deserts, unfit for animals or birds." He questioned the natives about the country beyond and had from them a good description of Chicoutimi, and Lac St. Jean, and the far lonely land to the north. In those frozen wastes primitive hunters already sought the beaver and marten, to trade with the Montagnais middlemen for the French goods unloaded at Tadoussac. Beyond the northern wilderness, said the Indians, they were in sight of a salt sea; Hudson Bay, of course. "I hold that, if this be so, it is some gulf of this our sea, which overflows in the north into the midst of the continent; and indeed, it can be nothing else." We must commend Champlain's cautious judgment, for he must have been tempted to take this salt sea as a branch of the western ocean, leading to the wealth of Cathay. It was only six years later that Henry Hudson discovered the bay that bears his name, and thus confirmed Champlain's opinion.

On Wednesday, June 18, Champlain began his journey up the St. Lawrence in a twelve-ton pinnace that had crossed the Atlantic on the *Bonne Renommée's* deck. Pontgravé was captain and pilot. Champlain noted the landmarks, the channel, the dangers to navigation, the character of the soil. He was charmed by the Ile d'Orléans (which Cartier had called Bacchus Island because of its abundant grapes.) He was unimpressed by the Falls of Montmorency. On Sunday the pinnace reached the Quebec narrows. It was a beautiful country, Champlain observed, a good land covered with oaks, cypresses, birch, firs, aspens, fruit trees and vines. The soil, if tilled, would be as good as that of France. There were rock-crystal diamonds in the slaty rocks.

Did Champlain dream that here was to rise his city, his lasting memorial? And that here he was to die?

From here on, the navigation became more ticklish, but the country more inviting. Champlain took careful notes on the channel to be followed, on the pleasing aspect of the land, on the fine black soil, promising great increase if cultivated, on the abundance of grapes, cherries, currants, and "swamp sugar pear" or shadbush, of hazel nuts and ground nuts or Indian potato, "tasting like truffles, which are very good roasted or boiled."

At the Three Rivers, the head of tidewater, the St. Maurice flows into the St. Lawrence from the north. Champlain records that this river provides a waterway to the far west, alternative to the St. Lawrence and the Ottawa. In fact, out of fear of the raiding Iroquois, the Indians already took this course, climbing beside high Shawinigan Falls, treading innumerable lakes, making endless weary portages, emerging at last on the upper Ottawa. Champlain, with his military eye, recognized at the Three Rivers a good emplacement for a permanent fort, which would protect the native traders. It might do more; it might impose and enforce peace. "If this river were inhabited we might make friends with the Iroquois and with the other savages, or at the very least under protection of the said settlement the said savages might come freely without fear or danger." Here is a statement of his policy for the next thirty years: peace, if attainable; if peace is unattainable, protection for France's allies.

On the St. Lawrence above Trois Rivières the country was new to Pontgravé. The explorers crossed broad Lac St. Pierre, penetrated the nest of islands at its head, and came to the mouth of the River of the Iroquois, in our time the Richelieu, which drains Lake Champlain and now carries canal traffic to New York. Here the French found a camp of their Algonquin allies, the base for their operations against the Iroquois.

Champlain went a dozen miles up the Richelieu in the longboat, until he found hard going at the rapids of St. Ours. He questioned his guides and learned that some distance farther to the south lay a long lake. It was the lake destined to be known, presumably forever, by his name. And beyond and above this lake lay another [Lake George], and at its extremity dwelt the terrible Iroquois. And beyond this, said his informants, was a river that led down to the coast of Florida [the Hudson]. And all the country of the Iroquois was somewhat hilly, but nevertheless a very good country, temperate, without much winter, nay, very little.

The French returned to the St. Lawrence and continued upstream. The country was rich and delightful, well forested with

oak, aspen, poplar, ash, maple, beech, white cedar, and few pine
or fir trees. Champlain noted the butternuts and chestnuts, the
wild cherries, hops, strawberries, raspberries, currants, and
gooseberries, and other small fruits he could not name.

On Wednesday, July 2, he came to rapids and anchored the
pinnace in the lee of a small island by the north shore. This was,
in fact, Market Gate Island, and the craft lay at the foot of St.
Joseph Street in the future city of Montreal.

The Huron town of Hochelaga, which Cartier had visited,
had disappeared. Probably the Hurons had been driven westward by their dread kinsmen the Iroquois. There were no river-
side dwellers to recall the past, to point out the vine-covered
ruins of Huron long houses.

Champlain and his companions inspected the rapids, the famous Lachine Rapids. "I assure you I never saw any torrent of
water pour over with such force as this does, although it is not
very high. It descends as it were step by step; and wherever it
falls from some small height, it boils up extraordinarily, owing
to the force and speed of the water as it passes through the said
rapid, which may be a league in length. There are many rocks
out in the stream, and about the middle are very long narrow
islands, where the current runs both beside the islands that are
toward the south, and also to the north; and it is so dangerous,
that it is beyond the power of any man to pass with any boat,
however small it may be. We went by land through the woods,
to see the end of the rapid, which is a league away, and there
we saw no more rocks or falls, but the water runs with the
utmost possible swiftness; and this current extends for three or
four leagues, so that it is vain to imagine that any boats could
be conveyed past the same rapids."

Only by canoe could Champlain proceed further, and time
was too short to permit exploration up the river. All he could
do was to question the natives as to what lay beyond. They told
him that there was a succession of rapids and reaches, and many
leagues beyond, a great lake [Ontario], at the extremity of
which the water was brackish and the winters mild. Then there
was a waterfall, somewhat high [Niagara]. Then another lake
[Erie], sixty leagues long, with water very brackish. Then a
broad strait [Detroit] leading into the interior. "They told us

that they themselves had passed no farther, and had not seen the farther extremity of a lake [Huron] which is fifteen or sixteen leagues beyond where they themselves had been, nor had they who told them of it known any man that had seen it, because it is so vast that they will not venture to put out into the same, for fear lest some storm or gale should surprise them. And the water there is very salt, like our sea."

Champlain asked them if the water in these far countries still flowed eastward into the St. Lawrence. No, they said; beyond the high fall the water was almost still, and the lake might find an outlet by other rivers. This was exciting news. "In my judgment," says Champlain, "if so many rivers fall into this lake, which has so small a discharge at the said fall, it must of necessity have an outflow by some very large river. But what makes me believe there is no river by which this lake has its outflow (considering the number of rivers which fall into it) is that the savages have not seen any river taking its course into the interior, save in the place where they were; which makes me believe that this is the South Sea, being salt as they say. Nevertheless we must not give too much credence to this view, except it be with manifest reason, even though there be some small grounds."

Champlain questioned some other Algonquins as to the western country. In general they corroborated the previous story, although giving widely varying estimates of distance. Some of them denied that the far lakes were salt or brackish. One gave a new picture of Niagara, "a fall that may be a league broad, over which an exceeding great current of water descends into the said lake." Champlain inquired about mines. They replied that the Hurons, "the good Iroquois," knew of a mine of pure copper to the north. Proudly they showed the French some copper bracelets they had obtained from these good Iroquois. On the whole their testimony was very encouraging. Four hundred leagues to the west lay a great water, whose end no one knew. "Without doubt, from their account, this can be nothing else than the South Sea, the sun setting where it does."

How facts acquiesce to our desires! How much Champlain learned, through jumbled translation, through signs, through the sketching of maps on white birch bark! And how little, despite his effort to be objective and cautious! And how clumsy is our communication! Even Champlain, writing in lucid French for Frenchmen, clouds his meaning several times by using the word *salubre* where he can only mean *salé*. "Salubrious" seemed to him a fine scientific-sounding synonym for "salty."

On July 4 the party renounced further exploration and sailed rapidly downstream to Tadoussac. They then made a brief trip to Gaspé, probably for trade. They saw Ile Percée, familiar to numberless tourists in quest of the quaint. "It is a sort of very high rock, steep on both sides, with a hole in it, through which shallops and boats can pass at high water; and at low water one can walk from the mainland to the said island, which is only some four or five hundred paces off." (Ile Percée was one of the regular points of rendezvous for the French in these lonely waters. There were certain others, like Tadoussac, like the Gut of Canso. They were chosen because they were unmistakable among the interminable bays and headlands of the bewildering coast. When you reached the Pierced Isle of Gaspé, you knew you were where you wanted to be.)

Returning to Tadoussac, the voyagers found the Algonquin warriors, whom they had last seen on the Richelieu River, preparing to invade the Iroquois country. The expedition had been a success. The allies had attacked three Iroquois canoes on their lake, the future Lake Champlain, and had returned with the scalps for a fitting celebration at Tadoussac. Now they were preparing a second raid. They donned their richest furs of mink or beaver, adorned with beads and varicolored cords. "They marched one behind the other, with their bows and arrows, clubs and round shields. And they went leaping one after the other, striking attitudes with their bodies, and executed many turns and twists like soldiers doing evolutions." Then they held their *tabagie*, and the women stripped themselves naked, "and thus naked and dancing got into their canoes, and then they put out on the water, and struck at one another with their paddles, splashing a quantity of water over one another. Yet they did not hurt, for they warded off the blows which they struck at one another. Having ended all these ceremonies, they withdrew into their lodges, and the savages went off to war against the Iroquois."

On August 16 the French set sail for home with a satisfactory cargo of furs in the hold. As passengers they carried an Iroquois woman and the son of a Montagnais sagamore off for a Parisian education.

At Ile Percée they found Captain Prévert of St. Malo, whom they had not seen since they had left France together. He had spent the summer on the coast of New Brunswick and Nova Scotia. He reported that he had found a rich copper mine in Minas Channel off the Bay of Fundy. He had given the natives wedges and chisels to extract the ore; he had promised to return and collect it the following summer. Champlain was much impressed.

He was impressed also by a strange story the Indians told of a frightful monster called the Gougou, twice as tall as a ship's mast, who devoured savages while uttering most horrible noises. Captain Prévert backed up the Indians; he had passed close to the haunt of this creature and had heard its evil hissings. Champlain was inclined to think that the evidence was good and that this devil, the Gougou, must exist.

So Champlain, we must grieve to admit, was still gullible. As in Mexico, he accepted the tall tales told him by others as gullible as himself or by jokers with marvels for greenhorns. Captain Prévert was evidently such a joker. His copper mine has never been discovered. He tried once to persuade a newcomer that he had seen an Indian playing lacrosse with a devil and that he had clearly seen the devil's lacrosse stick in the air, but as for *Monsieur le diable*, he was invisible.

On August 24 the vessels of Pontgravé and Prévert set off together. They passed Cape Race in Newfoundland on Sept. 2 and made an excellent crossing in only eighteen days. Champlain was busy in the cabin drawing up a report for His Majesty complete with maps.

It had been a most successful trip, promising well for the future. Champlain had carefully observed the soil, the natural resources, the communications. He found the country most fit for colonization. "The country and coast of Florida may have a different climate, and be more abundantly productive of fruits and other things than that which I have seen; but there cannot be lands more level nor of better quality." The fur trade, already organized in the northland, promised immediate profits. The natives were cordial and malleable. There was, to be sure, a lurking danger to the south, but with a strong military force in the interior, the French could impose peace, or failing that, could make an alliance with the native suppliers of furs and defend their trade routes.

Most of all he was convinced, by what seemed the best of testimony, that not far to the west, by none too difficult a journey, lay the South Sea and access to all the wealth of the East. Even sixteen years later this conviction was not shaken. He then represented to the King and lords of his Council that the natives had "given him such and so faithful report of the north and south seas that one cannot doubt but that this would be the means of reaching easily to the Kingdom of China and the East Indies, whence great riches could be drawn."

He had his conviction, his dream, and his purpose, to which he would devote all the labors of his life. He was a fortunate man.

CHAPTER V

The Third Voyage—Sainte Croix

WHEN THE *Bonne Renommée* arrived in Honfleur, Champlain learned to his sorrow that his chief, stout de Chastes, was dead. The whole question of the Canada trade was once more before the King and council for settlement. Champlain was annoyed to find that King Henry and Queen Marie had been regally entertained in Honfleur only a week before his return. He had missed the opportunity for a dramatic entrance.

He repaired, then, to Fontainebleau with his baggage of curiosities and mysterious minerals for the monarch, since polite as well as savage kings like to receive presents. His best curiosity was the son of the Montagnais sagamore. (We hear no more of the Iroquois woman.) The unhappy boy was baptized, dressed in a blue coat and bonnet, and lodged in the palace of Saint-Germain, to the delight of the three-year-old Dauphin Louis. The prince, charmed with his "Canada," would send him from his own nursery table the soups and jellies he refused to eat. Unhappy "Canada" sickened of civilization through the winter and died in June 1604. I see him in his last months, looking palely across the trim parterres of the palace to the spires of Paris, dreaming of his snows, and love, and liberty. The savage can endure every hardship, except the hardship of the shut room.

But let us rejoin Champlain in Fontainebleau. Henry received him cordially and was pleased to learn of the fertility and promise of the St. Lawrence region. Champlain dwelt particularly on the likelihood that his river was a way to China, between the icebergs of the north and the horrid heats of the Equator. He insisted further that the fur trade should not be thrown open to all, for only by granting a monopoly could the government stipulate and enforce the planting of colonies. King Henry agreed; indeed, he had probably come to the same conclusion independently.

No doubt by Henry's order, a license was granted to Champlain to print his report. But unfortunately the King kept Champlain's first map of Canada, and then he lost it, or someone lost it; for we are still hunting it in vain.

Before the end of the year Champlain was an author, with a book in pocket to inscribe for his friends and with a budding fame in the small literary world of Paris. *Des Sauvages; ou Voyage de Samuel Champlain de Brouage* is a trim little book, pleasing to the eye. It is dedicated to Charles de Montmorency, Admiral of France, who might, of course, turn out to be helpful to explorers. It is graced by a liminary sonnet by a certain de la Franchise, who otherwise appears in literary history only as the author of a book entitled *In Defense of Ladies*. His sonnet, hardly an anthology piece, does contain the interesting statement that Champlain promises to go farther, to reduce the gentiles and find the East, in order to reach China.

Champlain had now committed himself to the further exploration of Canada. He was put in touch with a gentleman who had offered to explore and colonize the New World for France, with the monopoly of the fur trade for his fee.

This gentleman was Pierre du Gua, sieur de Monts, an old companion in arms of the King and a Huguenot of Saintonge, Champlain's own country. His hardihood had already been rewarded by the governorship of the town of Pons in Saintonge, and it is alleged that he succeeded de Chastes as governor of Dieppe.[1] (It is further alleged that he was *Très Respectable* of the

[1] Ed. Buron, in *Rev. des questions historiques*, LXII, 29 (September 1934). But Henry IV confirmed Sigogne as governor of Dieppe in September 1604. (L'Estoile: *Journaux-Mémoires*, VIII, 100.)

Grand Orient Lodge of Freemasons in 1604.[2]) To these veterans whose constancy he had tested the King turned in need, regardless of their faith. De Monts had made at least one trip to the St. Lawrence, with Chauvin in 1600 (probably), apparently merely for adventure's sake.

On October 31, 1603, the King's Council appointed de Monts vice-admiral and lieutenant-general, with authority over all North America from the fortieth to the forty-sixth degrees of latitude, or from Philadelphia to Cape Breton. For his reward he was given the exclusive right to the fur trade for ten years, with authority to seize any illicit traders. Permission was granted to honest merchants to join with de Monts, under rather severe conditions. On the positive side, de Monts was required to establish the name, power, and authority of the King of France throughout his new territory; to summon the natives to a knowledge of the Christian religion; to make peace with the said peoples and their princes; to people, cultivate, and settle the said lands; to make explorations and especially to seek out mines of precious metals.

By limiting de Monts's territory by the fortieth parallel to the south, Henry implicitly abandoned the French claims to the rest of America, from Carolina to Brazil. For all the area he claimed for France he adopted the appellation that appeared on the title page of Champlain's book: New France. (Though Champlain called it *France nouvelle*, and Henry *Nouvelle France*. There is a subtle distinction here. Champlain emphasized that the France was new; Henry, that the newness was France.)

It appears from King Henry's action that he renounced the old policy of establishing colonies under government auspices in favor of private, or company, colonies, on the Dutch plan. These colonies would serve commerce and be served by it.

It was an important decision. As a result of it New France was to be ruled for many years by merchants and their factors, and the policies of the New World were to be determined in the interests of trade. And of course, as an afterthought, religion. But always as an afterthought.

[2] Dr. Erl A. Bates of Ithaca, Indianist and student of Masonic History. Dr. Bates has reason to believe that Champlain and Lescarbot were also members of this lodge. But I can find no corroboration from profane sources.

Henry's great minister Sully—sulky Sully—opposed the whole business. "One never draws great riches from anything north of the fortieth parallel," he said. But Henry would not listen, and Henry was right.

Champlain called, then, on de Monts and gave him a full account of his recent journey. De Monts, impressed by Champlain's character as well as his knowledge, offered him the post of geographer and cartographer, without, however, any clearly defined rank. Champlain asked nothing better. He had first, however, to ask the King's permission, for he was the recipient of a royal pension, and Champlain was a prudent man. The King gave his assent to Champlain's journey, requiring him only to make a faithful report of all he should see and discover. The King formally commissioned him captain in his Navy and appointed him geographer to the new expedition.[3]

M. de Monts spent the winter of 1603–4 preparing his venture. He chartered Pontgravé's good ship, the *Bonne Renommée*, with Captain Morel to serve as master under Pontgravé. He engaged also a 150-tonner under the command of Captain Timothée of Le Havre.

After the ships, the men. A number of gentlemen, even noble gentlemen, joined up, restless with the peace of France. Chief among them was Jean de Biencourt, seigneur de Poutrincourt. This was another old soldier of King Henry's, one of the bluff, enduring, simple hearts that Henry loved. A courtly musician, he played the lute and manichord. He was nearly fifty, with grown sons, but not too old for dreams. He had a romantic purpose; to establish himself with his family in a lordship in the wilds. The opinion of Mme de Poutrincourt, if it was asked, is not recorded.

De Monts was far too intelligent to overload his ship with gentlemen, handy only with the sword. Faithful to his engagement, he recruited 120 artisans, carpenters and masons, and soldiers, apparently Swiss mercenaries. And surgeons, for the expedition's health. And for its spiritual comfort, a priest, Father Aubry. De Monts, himself a Huguenot, welcomed re-

[3] The statement is frequently made, with much drawing of inferences, that Champlain was appointed royal geographer, which gives a hint of high eminence. I have found no record of such a lofty appointment.

cruits of his own faith. There were to be loud arguments in the 'tween-decks, and high words, and hatred, and division of purpose.

Unfortunately de Monts was unable to budge any French farmers from their beloved farms. And his recruits were a turbulent lot, insubordinate, dangerous. Whether de Monts availed himself of a cause in his contract authorizing him to take by force vagabonds, vagrants, and exiles is not clear. What is clear is that he had few passengers of the true colonist stamp.

The business organization of the expedition caused many wrangles. A company was formed to control the monopoly of the fur trade and to engage in fishing, timbering, and mining. The capital of 90,000 livres was subscribed by the merchants of Rouen, St. Malo, La Rochelle, and St. Jean de Luz, the Basque town that specialized in whaling. In addition to the two colonizing vessels, two fur-trading ships and a whaler were dispatched.

De Monts's two ships sailed from Le Havre on March 7, 1604. De Monts set the rendezvous for Cape Canso, on the east coast of Nova Scotia, looking across the strait to Cape Breton Island.

The plan was to settle on the St. Lawrence, and this was certainly Champlain's recommendation, for his eager purpose was to visit the upper river, the salty seas beyond, and China. However, de Monts changed his mind during his long reflection on the high seas and decided to find a more southern location on the Atlantic coast. Champlain suggests that he feared unprofitable warfare with illicit French fur traders on the St. Lawrence. Probably he feared still more the Canadian winter, for he must have talked with survivors of Chauvin's party who had wintered at Tadoussac in 1600–1, and he must have read the calamitous record of Cartier's stay at Stadacona. But if he sought a refuge from the cold, he was indeed sadly befooled.

One thing is clear. If he turned south, away from the fur-trading centers, he was less concerned with commercial profit than with establishing a colony. He was more governor than business man. As we are to hear much of the French businessmen of the French ports, greedy, shortsighted, mean-spirited, it is a pleasure to salute de Monts, an honorable gentleman who strove to fulfill his King's orders and purposes.

The passage was long and stormy, with icebergs aplenty. (Perhaps de Monts resorted to a humorous French device for obtaining a fair wind, that of flogging a cabin boy soundly.) On May 1 the ship sighted Sable Island and was nearly lost on it, for the pilots were a hundred miles off in their reckonings. On the eighth they came to shore at Cape La Have, a little south of present Halifax.

De Monts then headed south, hunting a good site for temporary headquarters. His first discovery was a ship from Le Havre trading in furs in defiance, or ignorance, of the legal monopoly. De Monts ran out his guns and seized the ship and its captain, Rossignol, screaming with magnificent fury.

The ship proceeded with caution southwesterly along the enchanting coast, rounding a series of rocky points connected by broad semicircles of hard white sand. It passed White Point Beach and entered a wide, sheltered, lovely bay. This the French named Port Mouton, because here a sheep was drowned, recovered, and eaten. The colonists, we perceive, had provided themselves with livestock. The name still persists, though indeed the local pronunciation is "Matoon."

The ship anchored, and the passengers came ashore on a perfect beach under Bull Point, where in the transparent water kelp-furred rocks rise like the backs of buffaloes. Friendly Indians appeared, and some of them were persuaded to guide the shallop north to Cape Canso. By this means de Monts informed Pontgravé of his whereabouts and directed him to bring the *Bonne Renommée* to Port Mouton with all speed.

While awaiting Pontgravé, who seems to have had the major part of the supplies, the colonists pitched a casual camp on a spruce-shaded upland, which may still be identified. They fished and hunted hares and consumed their provisions in happy confidence of the future.

Champlain, with de Monts's secretary, Ralluau, and ten men, was sent exploring to the south in the eight-ton pinnace. They coasted among dangerous capes, shoals, and rocky islands, rounded menacing Cape Sable, turned northwest, and entered St. Mary Bay, which is separated only by a narrow peninsula from the Bay of Fundy. Champlain made careful notes and charts and observed the tides, the vegetation, and the animal life. The waterfowl were so abundant and so unsuspecting that the explorers could knock down all they wanted with a stick. Simon the miner, a sanguine fellow, found an iron mine and a silver mine. After about three weeks the reconnoissance party returned to Port Mouton.

On finding his friends again, Champlain had news that must have given him pause. The reckless colonists had already consumed most of their provisions and those from Captain Rossignol's ship. Some of them, too quick despairers, had proposed to abandon the enterprise—and Champlain—and return to France. Probably, they said, Champlain and his party were drowned or cast away. Should the whole expedition perish for their sake? At what point does enlightened self-interest outweigh fidelity to the absent, etc.? But de Monts and Poutrincourt, old soldiers, said they would rather die than be so base. In the midst of the argument the *Bonne Renommée* arrived. Pontgravé explained his delay by the fact that he had found at Canso four Basque ships trading for furs, and according to his rights he had seized the ships, confiscated the furs, and taken the captains prisoners. The vessels he evidently sent home with prize crews.

You can see how the word went up and down the coast that the new monopolists were violently interrupting an established trade legitimized by time, and that no aid should be given these interlopers, these King's toadies, taking the bread out of poor men's mouths.

The *Bonne Renommée* unloaded its supplies. De Monts promised himself, no doubt, to watch them more closely in the future. Pontgravé then departed for the St. Lawrence and the pressing business of the fur trade.

De Monts acted on Champlain's favorable report of his exploration. He reloaded his ship, bade farewell to Port Mouton, rounded Cape Sable, and came to anchor in the shallow haven of St. Mary Bay. After only two or three days in that wide valley with its tidal flats, he found no site naturally strong and fit for fortification as a permanent settlement. He decided to look farther.

Unfortunately he had lost his priest, Father Aubry. The adventure of Father Aubry is too good a story, as Lescarbot tells it, to be abridged. "There was a certain Churchman of a good family in Paris that had a desire to perform the voyage with Monsieur de Monts, and that against the liking of his friends, who sent expressly to Honfleur to divert him thereof and to bring him back to Paris. The ships lying at anchor in the said Bay of Saint Marie, he put himself in company with some that went to sport themselves in the woods. It came to pass that, having stayed to drink at a brook, he forgot there his sword, and followed on his way with his company; which when he perceived he returned back to seek it; but having found it, forgetful from what part he came and not considering whether he should go East or West or otherwise (for there was no path), he took his way quite contrary, turning his back from his company, and so long travelled that he found himself at the seashore where no ships were to be seen (for they were at the other side of a nook of land far reaching into the sea); he imagined that he was forsaken, and began to bewail his fortune upon a rock. The night being come, everyone being retired, he is found wanting: he was asked for of these that had been in the woods; they report in what manner he departed from them, and that since they had no news of him. Whereupon a Protestant was charged to have killed him, because they quarrelled sometimes for matters of religion. Finally, they sounded a trumpet through the forest; they shot off the cannon divers times, but in vain; for the roaring of the sea, stronger than all that, did expel back the sound of the said cannons and trumpets. Two, three, and four days pass; he appeareth not. In the meanwhile the time hastens to depart; so, having tarried so long that he was held for dead, they weighed anchors to go further."

A fortnight later a small party returned to St. Mary Bay to look for mines. "After some abode they going a-fishing, the said Aubry perceived them, and began with a feeble voice to call as loud as he could; and for to help his voice he advised himself to do as Ariadne did heretofore to Theseus:

> Candidaque imposui longae velamina virgae,
> Scilicet oblitos admonitura mei.[4]

[4] I bound upon a staff my finery
    To make them think, oblivious ones, of me.

For he put his handkerchief and his hat on a stave's end, which made him better to be known. For, as one of them heard the voice and asked the rest of the company if it might be the said Monsieur Aubry, they mocked and laughed at it. But, after they had spied the moving of the handkerchief and of the hat, then they began to think that it might be he. And coming near, they knew perfectly that it was himself, and took him in their barque with great joy and contentment the sixteenth day after he had lost himself. During these sixteen days he fed himself but by I know not what small fruits like unto cherries, without kernel, yet not so delicate, which are scarcely to be found in those woods." [5]

When de Monts gave up Father Aubry for lost, he left St. Mary Bay and sailed northeast along Digby Neck, on the west coast of Nova Scotia. Riding the enormous Fundy tides, he turned into the chasm of Digby Gut. The enormous, beautiful harbor of Annapolis Basin opened wide before him. The seamen exclaimed with delight. Champlain promptly reckoned that two thousand ships could ride there in safety. He proposed that it should be named Port Royal, and that name persisted as long as the French ruled this land. The ship went up the bay as far as safety permitted, to near the present Annapolis Royal.

The party was enchanted by the pleasant aspect and the security of the region. "I should like to have it for my own," said M. de Poutrincourt. "I should like to settle here with all my family." M. de Monts, exercising his new authority as lord of all this country, promptly made out to him a deed of gift, which was later to be ratified by the King himself.

Quitting the happy harbor, the ship followed northeast along the eastern shore of the Bay of Fundy. The explorers were anxious to find the copper mine reported by Captain Prévert in the previous year. They looked eagerly under the towering cliffs of Cape Chignecto and Cape d'Or, and indeed found two copper mines, which the optimistic miner pronounced very good. (Professor W. F. Ganong, Champlain's learned editor, tells us

[5] Probably partridge berries. Marc Lescarbot, *Nova Francia*, translated by P. Erondelle, 1609. (London, 1928). This reminds me of the wonderful story of Juan Ortiz, who strayed from Narváez's expedition in Florida in 1528, and was rescued eleven years later by de Soto.

that in fact native copper occurs in the trap rocks of this region,
but so far it has never been profitably worked.) However, there
was no sign of Captain Prévert's rich veins of pure copper.

It was now the twentieth of June, high time to establish the
permanent camp. De Monts decided to continue his exploration
and return later to hunt the great copper mine. Since clearly
he had reached the head of the Bay of Fundy, he turned west,
raised the New Brunswick coast, and followed it southwest.
He found a good harbor, the mouth of a broad, deep river. A
short way inland the river narrowed to form the famous "revers-
ible falls," which today's tourist dutifully inspects. As it was
June 24, St. John's Day, the captain named the place St. John.
Here was destined to rise the city of New Brunswick's pride.

De Monts was not satisfied. He continued southwest along
the island-dotted shore, past the rocky group now called the
Wolves to Passamaquoddy Bay. He turned up the broad tidal
estuary of the Sainte Croix. A half dozen miles upstream he
came upon a little island, placid and welcoming. It was a beautiful spot for a home, with a friendly look, as it still has on a
bright midsummer day, in the wide river's peace, with the
swallows skimming the calm water, with the hazy mountains
asleep to the north. It seemed comfortable and secure. This,
decided de Monts, would be his settlement.

This fateful island, Sainte Croix Island, has an area of about
five acres. Its eastern rim is a continuous bluff rising about fifty
feet above mean tide level; it slopes gently to the water on the
western side. Thus there is no protection against the fierce
northwest winds of winter. But this consideration did not occur
to the explorers in the genial end of June. Champlain noted the
good anchorage, the fine growth of firs, birches, maples, and
oaks, the supply of clay for brickmaking, the evident fertility
of the soil, and especially the island's security. "This place we
considered the best we had seen, both on account of its situation,
the fine country, and for the intercourse we were expecting with
the Indians of the coasts and of the interior, since we should be
in their midst. In course of time we hoped to pacify them, and
to put an end to the wars which they wage against one another,
in order that in the future we might derive service from them,
and convert them to the Catholic faith."

6 5

Thus the disastrous choice of the island was determined largely by fear of the natives. In fact the Indians of these parts were a mild and inoffensive race who never raised their hands against the future settlers, French and English. But Champlain is hardly to be blamed for seeking security first. The Algonquins he had seen on the St. Lawrence had talked only of war. He had seen their victory dance, their mowing before the scalps of their enemies. We cannot condemn a military man for prudence. Still, prudence is myopic and is always looked to the wrong quarter.

De Monts and his men, high-hearted, set to work. The long-boat was dispatched to St. Mary Bay to summon the men on Captain Rossignol's confiscated ship. (It was on this journey that Father Aubry was rescued.) Artisans and gentlemen together mounted their cannon and built a barricade. Security being attained, a plan was drawn, the ground cleared, and buildings erected: a storehouse fifty feet long, a house for M. de Monts, two for the gentlemen (including Champlain), three for the artisans, one for the priest, one for the Swiss soldiers. There was also a chapel, a kitchen, a forge, an oven, a hand mill for grinding grain. The men labored with a will, though tortured by black flies and mosquitoes. Some of the men's faces were so swollen that they could hardly see.

De Monts had brought out woodwork for his buildings from France. The fact has been adduced to show the ignorance of the French about the country they were to inhabit. But the woodwork (*charpenterie*) was probably doors and windows, tables and benches. The provision of such fittings shows mere good sense. These men had no sawmill; the sawing of planks from newly felled trees would have been an endless task.

Outside the enclosure was a reserved area for gardens. Every man had his own plot. Some rye was sown, which throve very well. But most of the other shoots withered in the sun. The soil was sandy, hungry, and there was no water save the occasional rains.

De Monts established a beachhead on the mainland, with a barn and cleared land for sowing and a mill on Beaver Brook. Upon its site today stands the Red Beach Plaster Mill.

So the summer passed, with the erection of a French fort on

the American shore. De Monts built well, so well that the remains of his works were visible two hundred years later. He
made all tidy and secure—but secure against the wrong enemy.

While the work was in progress Champlain made a second,
and again ineffectual, effort to discover Captain Prévert's copper
mine at the head of the Bay of Fundy. If Captain Prévert ever
heard of Champlain's persistence he probably regarded it as a
magnificent joke.

On the last day of August, Poutrincourt sailed for France
with the two large ships. The settlers were left with a pinnace
of seventeen or eighteen tons and another of seven tons.

On September 2 Champlain took the seventeen-tonner for a
reconnoissance to the southwest. Carrying a lateen sail, with
oars for auxiliary, it was well fitted for exploration along difficult coasts. Twelve sailors formed the crew; two friendly Indians
went as passengers, guides, and ambassadors. Evidently one of
the sailors was interpreter; he had been on these coasts before;
or perhaps he was merely a remarkable linguist by nature.

While Champlain picks his way in fog and storm, we may
review the history of this Maine coast before his coming.

In reading, and in writing, this history (as indeed all history)
one must be struck by the discrepancy between the record and
the truth. The record is scanty enough, but it gives us a handful
of clear and positive facts. These scattered facts are merely indications, aspects, of the truth. Most of the truth is never written
down, for there are many actors and few recorders. Of the truth
that is written, most is lost, for time has a thousand devices to
destroy men's industry. So to find the truth we must soon leap
from the fact, to hazard, to guess. And do we find the truth?
Why no; only at best, a good guess, a provisional truth.

On the record we have John Cabot, who passed this way in
1498 and may have seen, first of white men, the coast of Maine.
Or it may have been Cortereal, who was hereabouts in 1502.
More likely, though still not certain, is the visit of Verrazano
in 1524. Verrazano relates a curious story of his visit to Maine
(if indeed it was Maine. It was probably Maine, not surely
Maine.) The inhabitants, he says, were rude, barbarous, and
suspicious, unlike the gentle Indians of Narragansett Bay. "If
we wished at any time to traffic with them, they came to the

seashore and stood on the rocks, from which they lowered down by a cord to our boats beneath whatever they had to barter, continually crying out to us to come nearer; and instantly demanding from us that which was to be given in exchange, they took from us only knives, fishhooks, and sharpened steel. No regard was paid to our courtesies; when we had nothing left to exchange with them, the men at our departure made the most brutal signs of disdain and contempt possible."

From this fact we may make a cast at truth. The Indians saw the white men without surprise. They took every precaution to prevent their visitors from getting within reach of them. They knew what the white men wanted: fresh food, perhaps furs. They knew what they wanted from the white men: knives, fishhooks, steel. They did not look at steel with incredulous wonder. They knew about barter and had devised a method for bartering in security. Obviously white men had been there before. And obviously the white men had given the natives cause for fear. Perhaps they had killed some Indians for their furs, or perhaps they had carried off some squealing natives as souvenirs.

Estebán Gómez in 1525 explored Penobscot and Casco bays (and this is fairly close to certain.) Thevet (probably) visited Penobscot Bay in 1556. He tells us the surprising news that "upon its banks the French formerly erected a little fort about ten or twelve leagues from its mouth, which was surrounded by fresh water, and this place was named the Fort of Norembegue."

A fort? What Frenchmen? Is this really the Penobscot? Is Thevet merely a liar, as some investigators assert? I have no time to argue the case, nor have you to listen. Let us merely agree with Henry F. Howe [6] that the story is probably true and that we have here an indication that unknown fishermen had come ashore and established a post where they could exchange cheap knives for precious furs.

In 1580 Sir Humphrey Gilbert sent John Wallace to this Penobscot country; he returned with a good cargo of furs, which he sold for forty shillings apiece. In 1593 Richard Fisher and Richard Strong met trading boats "up and down the coast of Arembec to the west and southwest of Cape Breton" in latitude 44.

[6] *Prologue to New England*, 33.

With the seventeenth century our information becomes more exact. Bartholomew Gosnold was in Maine in 1602. Off Kennebunkport (probably) he had a very surprising adventure. He saw a Basque shallop, with mast and sail, standing toward him and naturally supposed the occupants to be Christians. But it was manned by eight savages. One of Gosnold's passengers describes the meeting: "After signs of peace, and a long speech by one of them made, they came boldly aboard us, being all naked, saving about their shoulders certain loose deer skins, and near their waists seal skins tied fast like to Irish dimmie trousers. One that seemed to be their commander wore a waist-coat of black work, a pair of breeches, cloth stockings, shoes, hat and band; one or two more had also a few things made by some Christians. These with a piece of chalk described the coast thereabouts, and could name Placentia in Newfoundland. They spoke divers Christian words, and seemed to understand more than we, for want of language, could comprehend." Another witness adds that they had an iron grapple and a copper kettle, and that they were tall men, "of broad and grim visage, of a black swart complexion, with their eyebrows painted white. They showed by signs that some Basques of Saint Jean de Luz had fished or traded in this place."

Yes, but how had they come by their shallop and their Christian clothes? Is the story we half glimpse one of shipwreck and death or one of deception and murder?

In 1603 Martin Pring made a landfall in Casco Bay and coasted south to Plymouth Bay, where he took on a valuable load of sassafras, sovereign remedy for the pox.

Such is the record of fact. From it the truth is plain enough. Up and down our coast bold, greedy fishermen, Basque and French, were invading the coves and trading for furs. They sought only gain and were careless of history; indeed they kept their knowledge secret, as fishermen still do. So all our statements of first discoveries, our celebrations of centenaries, our memorial plaques, are based on fragments, and are probably wrong.

Now we return to Champlain in his pinnace, feeling his way along the Maine coast in September 1604. There was a mull of fog, as they say in Maine today. He passed many islands, sandbanks, shoals, and rocks, and rounded point after point, where Maine dabbles her innumerable bony fingers in the sea. He noted safe and pleasant harbors. Then he raised a high, well-wooded island with a bare summit, and this he named, for all time, Mount Desert.

On some perilous reef he stove a hole in the pinnace and was nearly lost but got her ashore in time. The next day he saw smoke rising from a cove, probably Otter Creek Cove.[7] Two canoes filled with Indians appeared. Champlain put his two Indians into a canoe and sent them to make contact, but the shy natives fled. Champlain knew how to deal with Indians, how to tempt them with patience. He cast anchor and waited through the night. The next day the inquisitive wild men came alongside. They were quickly won with tobacco and biscuit; they proposed a visit to their chief, Bessabez, who lived on the Great River. And so they guided Champlain through the tiny channel that divides Mount Desert Island from the mainland, and into Blue Hill Bay, and past Deer Island into the broad waters of the Penobscot.

This noble river, says Champlain, must be the Norumbega, concerning which many fables were current, of civilized white tribes on its headwaters, possessing great riches. "But," says Champlain, "I am convinced that the majority of those who mention it never saw it, and speak of it only by hearsay from people who had no more knowledge of it than themselves." Champlain is losing some of his credulousness. We shall hear no more of Gougous and fantastic monsters.

He may have taken for a moment the wide tidal Penobscot for a northwest passage. The mountains stand far from the river banks, the solid green comes down to the water, and there leaves at low tide a wet, barren strip; the shore seems to smile with bared gums. But soon the river narrows, the rocky walls come close, sailing becomes difficult. Champlain went cautiously up with the tide till he reached Kenduskeag Stream, the heart of Bangor today. Here the rocks barred all further progress. Champlain walked up the shore to the falls, the present Salmon

[7] Edmund F. Slafter: *Voyages of Samuel de Champlain*, I, 209. But Allen Forbes and Paul F. Cadman (*New France and New England*, III, 7) prefer Hull's Cove.

Pool, where the coffee-colored water pours over with caramel foam.

He was familiar with hope and with hope confounded. "I landed to see the country; and going hunting, found the part I visited most pleasant and agreeable. One would think the oaks had been planted there designedly."

Some of the Indians went into the interior to summon their great chief, Bessabez, and a minor chief, Cabahis. Bessabez appeared shortly with half a hundred companions. "As soon as the Indians on shore saw Bessabez arrive, they all began to sing, dance, and leap, until he had landed, after which they all seated themselves on the ground in a circle, according to their custom when they wish to make a speech or hold a festival. Cabahis, the other chief, also arrived a little later, with twenty or thirty of his companions, who kept by themselves; and they were much pleased to see us, inasmuch as it was the first time they had ever beheld Christians. Some time afterwards I landed with two of my companions and two of our Indians who acted as our interpreters. I ordered the crew of the pinnace to draw near to the Indians, and to hold their weapons in readiness to do their duty in case they perceived any movement of these people against us. Bessabez, seeing us on shore, bade us sit down, and began with his companions to smoke, as they usually do before beginning their speeches. They made us a present of venison and waterfowl.

"I directed our interpreter to tell our Indians that they were to make Bessabez, Cabahis, and their companions understand that the Sieur de Monts had sent me to them to see them, and also their country; that he wished to remain friends with them, and reconcile them with their enemies, the Souriquois and Canadians; moreover, that he desired to settle in their country and show them how to cultivate it, in order that they might no longer lead so miserable an existence as they were doing; and several other remarks on the same subject."

A politic speech, and a severe test of the interpreter's capacity. "We want only to do you good," was Champlain's theme. "We offer you peace, security, prosperity." There was no mention of the other part of the bargain. But that was perfectly comprehended by these barbarians.

"This our Indians made them understand, whereat they signified that they were well satisfied, declaring that no greater benefit could come to them than to have our friendship; and that they desired us to settle in their country, and wished to live in peace with their enemies, in order that in future they might hunt the beaver more than they had ever done, and barter these beaver with us in exchange for things necessary for their usage. When he had finished his speech, I made them presents of hatchets, rosaries, caps, knives, and other little knick-knacks; then we separated. The rest of this day and the following night they did nothing but dance, sing, and make merry, awaiting the dawn, when we bartered a certain number of beaver skins. Afterwards each returned, Bessabez with his companions in their direction and we in ours, well pleased to have made acquaintance with these people."

In this episode one will observe the boldness of Champlain in penetrating sixty mies into unknown country with only a dozen sailors for protection. More, one will observe the tact of his speech, manner, and action. He accepted the protocol of savage diplomacy with, I think, a fundamental honesty. He had his commercial purpose, which he openly displayed, but in its proper place. He promised friendship, aid, and peace, with the intention of keeping his promises. He always kept his word, even to the disadvantage of his own side. His sincerity was recognizable and recognized. He was not patronizing; he treated the Indians as equals. Thus he came to be the one man whom the Indians always trusted. In fact the friendship of the Maine and Acadia Indians with the French, established by Champlain, was to continue unbroken as long as there were French and Indians.

On September 17 Champlain resumed his journey westward. He worked his way among the bewildering islands, the lovely Sporades of Penobscot Bay. He passed the river where Cabahis dwelt, either the Orland or the Belfast. In Rockland Harbor the escorting Indians left him, out of fear of their enemies along the Kennebec. Champlain rounded the headland of Port Clyde and crossed Muscongus Bay in the neighborhood of Pemaquid. Then, as the weather was bad and the provisions short, he decided to return to the settlement and make a more extended exploration in the following year. On October 2 he was back at the base of Sainte Croix.

Four days later snow fell. Winter set in early and hard. The wind blew fiercely from the north and west, wailing through the cracks between logs ill fitted and ill chinked with crumbling clay. The colonists had deforested their little island; there was no screen against the weather, and soon insufficient firewood. Snow fell to the depth of three or four feet and lay unmelting till the end of April. The thin springs of the island froze. At first the settlers felt no alarm; they counted on ferrying wood, water, and perhaps fresh meat from the mainland. But soon great cakes of ice began to appear in the water and were driven to and fro on the twenty-five-foot tides. As the ice increased, it became impossible to make the short half mile to shore.

All the beverages froze except the Spanish wine. Frozen cider was issued by the pound. (Though nowadays if you freeze cider the result seems to be applejack.) The men drank melted snow and ate cold salt meat and frozen vegetables; fuel was too short to permit much cooking. To grind their grain they labored at the hand mill, but weakly and in pain. For sickness came, the scurvy.

"There was engendered in the mouths of those who had it," says Champlain, "large pieces of superfluous fungous flesh (which caused a great putrefaction); and this increased to such a degree that they could scarcely take anything except in very liquid form. Their teeth barely held in their places, and could be drawn out with the fingers without causing pain. This superfluous flesh was often cut away, which caused them to lose much blood from the mouth. Afterwards, they were taken with great pains in the arms and legs, which became swollen and very hard and covered with spots like flea-bites; and they could not walk on account of the contraction of the nerves; consequently they had almost no strength, and suffered intolerable pains. They had also pains in the loins, stomach, and bowels, together with a very bad cough and shortness of breath. In brief, they were in such a state that the majority of the sick could neither get up nor move, nor could they even be held upright without fainting away; so that of seventy-nine of us, thirty-five died, and more than twenty were very near it. The majority of those who kept well complained of some minor pains and shortness of breath."

Concerning those who were not stricken, Father Biard, who came out in 1611, reports a story current in his time: "Of all Sieur de Monts's people who wintered first at Sainte Croix, only eleven remained well. These were a jolly company of hunters, who preferred rabbit hunting to the air of the fireside; skating on the ponds, to turning over lazily in bed; making snowballs to bring down the game, to sitting around the fire talking about Paris and its good cooks." Although his description does not fit Sainte Croix in the depth of that winter (particularly the bit about hunting with snowballs), he may have been right in substance.

Several of the dead were dissected, in an effort to find the origin of the malady. Champlain gives a horrible description of the state of the internal organs. The cause he could not determine. The only cure was the coming of spring.

Lescarbot, who came over in 1606 and saw plenty of scurvy himself, examines the evidence with his usual perspicacity. It is a winter disease; it was known to Hippocrates and to Dutch sailors. The causes appear to be salted meats and bad provisions in general, and also the vicious air of the country. "One must take heed to salt meats, smoky, musty, raw, and of an evil scent, likewise of dried fishes, as Newfoundland fish, and stinking rays; briefly, from all melancholy meats, which are of hard digesting, are easily corrupted, and breed a gross and melancholy blood." The corruption of running water may be a cause, and the air of boggy and waterish Northern lands. "But there is yet in New France another bad quality of the air, by reason of lakes that be thick there and of the great rottenness in the woods." Sailors on long voyages take the illness from rotten biscuit and meat and stinking water, whilst "they which carry sweetmeats, be it flesh or fruits, and that use good bread, good wine, and good broths, do easily avoid these sicknesses; and I durst, in some sort, be answerable unto them for their healths, unless they be very unhealthful by nature." Sedentary people are especially apt and subject to the disease. "A physician might say that a student is not fit for that country, that is to say, he shall not live there in health; nor those who groan over their work, nor vain dreamers, nor enthusiasticks, nor those that be often visited with agues." The remedy, he says, is proper food, especially the tender herbs of springtime. Some recommend frequent gargling with lemon juice. "It resteth a preservative, necessary for the accomplishment of mirth and to the end one may take pleasure in the work of his hands; it is for everyone to have the honest company of his lawful wife."

With the new season the scurvy dwindled on the pestilential island. In March, Indians began to call, trading fresh meat for trinkets. Green shoots showed amid gray snowbanks and were devoured by the sufferers. The ice in the river thinned, and the stronger settlers ranged the mainland for game. The terrible winter was over, and hope came on the warm winds.

It had been, evidently, a winter of unusual severity for the region. Had the winter been as mild as many are, the settlers would have suffered little. They would have fished and hunted, perhaps have defied the scurvy entirely. They would have made their permanent settlement in this region, if not on Sainte Croix Island itself. If the winter had been mild the center of French influence would have been Maine and not Nova Scotia. Here is a dotted line that one may prolong indefinitely into the realm of the imaginary.

As it was, the settlement of Sainte Croix was momentous in our history. It was the first white man's colony in the United States north of the Carolinas. When the boundaries of the new republic were established in the Treaty of Paris in 1783, the Ste-Croix River was chosen as the limit between Maine and New Brunswick. But which of several rivers was the Ste-Croix of de Monts and Champlain? A boundary commission was appointed. At length, in 1797, the British commissioner obtained a copy of Champlain's original map. With this in hand the commissioners examined the coast. On Dochet Island they found the ruins of de Monts's settlement, corresponding exactly to their position on Champlain's map. The question was settled, and the boundary between Canada and the United States was set and marked forever by the graves of that forlorn little band of adventurers.

Today not even a historical marker on the shore recalls this notable and tragic site. There is no way by which the land-bound traveler may visit the island, unless the genial Coast Guardsman in charge of the lighthouse chances to come ashore. He is, however, proud of his historical charge and gladly shows the outlines of de Monts's settlement as W. F. Ganong and others have determined them.

Sainte Croix Island should be a national monument, because of its historical importance and because of its nostalgic beauty. The federal government should acquire it, guard it from the devouring tides, excavate the sites, and restore the de Monts settlement, as the National Parks Bureau of Canada has nobly restored Port Royal. The federal government should not wait too long; as the lighthouse keeper points out, the southern shore is crumbling away at the rate of forty feet a year.

part of the proposed journey. Champlain's particular duty was to make charts of the coast. Also on the pinnace were some gentlemen adventurers, twenty sailors, including the pilots Champdoré and Cramolet, and an Indian named Panounias with his wife. Champlain had already discovered the usefulness of a friendly Indian, to be an ambassador, a witness to good treatment, and a decoy.

The party set sail on June 18, 1605, and followed the coast west to Pemaquid, the limit of Champlain's explorations of the previous year. They found the mouth of the Kennebec and headed into it. Here they met two canoes of natives hunting birds, which at this season are molting and are easily taken. It appeared that the explorers had passed a boundary between Indian races. New Brunswick and eastern Maine were occupied by Etchemins; from the Kennebec west the inhabitants were Almouchiquois, also of Algonquin stock, but speaking a different language. Panounias was an Etchemin, his wife Almouchiquois.

Good relations were soon established. The Indians led the pinnace up the Back River and the Hockomock to the present Wiscasset, where a formal parley was held with their chief. The French then returned down the Hockomock and through the Sassanou, past the difficult tidal fall at Upper Hell Gate, where they were obliged to tie a hawser to a tree to warp their boat through. Thus they came into the Kennebec again (opposite Bath), and then upstream to Merrymeeting Bay, that lovely sheltered haven, whose soft green islets pose self-consciously in the summer's blue and gold. Thence they returned to sea, rounded Small Point, and sailed west, past the strewn islands of Casco Bay, where the seed of Portland was to be sown, and so past Cape Elizabeth and Richmond's Island to little Ram Island, close to the mainland. Here they were greeted by eighty dancing Indians, with whom a good understanding was soon had. Richmond's Island roused their admiration, with its fine oaks and nut trees, its grapevines, the first they had seen, and its cleared land. They named it the Island of Bacchus:

Then past bold Prout's Neck and the glittering sands of Old Orchard Beach to the gray, piled rocks of Biddeford Pool, and up the placid Saco River some distance on the tide. Many Indians danced on the shore. They were a vigorous and well-

formed race, their faces painted a startling black and red. They
shaved the fore parts of their heads (what with?) and wore their
back hair very long, plaited and adorned with feathers. These
were the first agricultural Indians Champlain had seen. They
tilled the soil with wooden hoes. Champlain inspected their
planting and observed the typical hills of corn, serving as a
support for twining bush beans. He noted also squash, pumpkins, tobacco, hickory nuts, grapevines. The Indians lived in
wigwams in a palisaded village. It was an attractive region,
obviously more temperate than cruel Sainte Croix.

On July 12 the French resumed their journey, coasting southward along a sandy shore, past Cape Porpoise and Kennebunkport. They noticed the red-winged blackbirds, the multitude of
passenger pigeons, the abundance of swamp red currants. They
rounded the red-brown rocks of Cape Ann and hove to in its
lee, probably due east from Rockport. Five or six Indians
danced on the beach. "The Sieur de Monts sent me ashore to
visit them, and to give to each a knife and some biscuit, which
caused them to dance better than ever. When this was over, I
made them understand as well as I could that they should show
me how the coast trended. After I had drawn for them with a
charcoal the bay and the Island Cape, where we then were,
they pictured for me with the same charcoal another bay which
they represented as very large [Massachusetts Bay]. Here they
placed six pebbles at equal intervals, giving me thereby to
understand that each one of these marks represented that number of chiefs and tribes." Indeed, Champlain may have inter-
preted their symbols correctly, for the Massachusetts Indians
were composed of six divisions.

The cordial natives ran along the shore and lighted signal
smokes to show the sites of their villages. This coast was the
most populous Champlain had yet seen.

The pinnace picked its way into Boston Harbor and anchored
off Noddle's Island, now East Boston (though possibly it was
Nahant). The Boston Indians greeted the visitors. The usual
distribution of knives, rosaries, and biscuits was followed by
the usual rapturous dancing on the shore. These Indians had
much cleared land sown with corn. They used dugouts made
with great labor by burning and chipping out tree trunks; we

have now come too far south for the birch-bark canoe. Their language was entirely incomprehensible.

Champlain saw the mouth of a river that, he opined, led inward to the land of the Iroquois. This he named the Rivière du Gua, in compliment to Pierre du Gua, sieur de Monts. It is Boston's Charles River. Remember that the first known white men to look on the site of Boston were Champlain and his companions. The date was July 16, 1605.

The next day the travelers continued southeast along the coast, past the hook of Nantasket, and Cohasset, and Scituate. They anchored off Brant Point, just north of Plymouth. A flotilla of dugout canoes came out, some containing fifteen or sixteen persons. The chief, Honabetha, boarded the pinnace. "We received the chief very kindly and gave him good cheer. After remaining with us some time, he went back. The men we had sent to them brought us little squashes as big as your fist, which we ate as a salad like cucumbers, and they were very good. They brought us also some purslane, which grows abundantly among the Indian corn."

The pinnace entered wide, sunny Plymouth Bay. Champlain noted with interest the natives fishing from their canoes with bone hooks and lines of Indian hemp. He went on shore and carefully charted the harbor. He was kindly received by a multitude of Indians.

Had Champlain possessed any effective means of communication with these Indians, he would have learned that white men were no great novelty in Plymouth Harbor. Two years before, Martin Pring had spent seven weeks there gathering sassafras. Pring remarked, among other things, the good looks and tall stature of the natives, the fruitfulness of their soil and the prosperity of their agriculture. He noticed their treacherousness, their jealousy of their women, their fear of the expedition's great mastiffs, and especially their delight in music. "We had a youth in our company that could play upon a zither, in whose homely music they took great delight, and would give many things, as tobacco, tobacco-pipes, snakes' skins of six foot long, which they use for girdles, fawns' skins, and such like, and danced twenty in a ring, and the zither in the midst of them, using many savage gestures, singing lo, la, lo, la, la, lo; him that first brake the ring, the rest would knock and cry out upon."

From Plymouth the explorers followed the coast along the south shore of Cape Cod Bay, until they discovered that they were in a pocket. They then headed north and doubled the Cape, recognizing well the dangers of its winds and sands. They went south along the seaward side of the Cape, past the line of bluff-headed dunes, rounded a long sandspit and anchored in green, sluggish Nauset Harbor. All this region was delightfully wooded; today only a poor scrubby growth remains. The bay was bordered by wigwams, and the beach gay with welcoming dancers.

De Monts, Champlain, and nine or ten armed men inspected the settlement. They admired the corn, already five and a half feet high, and the beans, squash, tobacco, and tasty Jerusalem artichoke. Champlain noted that the Indians let their fields lie fallow and grow to weeds. They would then prepare them for planting by burning the weeds and turning the soil with wooden spades. Their wigwams were round and thatched with reeds. "We asked them if they had their permanent residence in this place, and whether there was much snow; but we could not find this out very well since we did not understand their language, although they attempted to explain by signs, taking up sand in their hands, then spreading it on the ground, and indicating that the snow was the same color as our collars, and fell to the depth of a foot. Others indicated that it was less, giving us also to understand that the harbor never froze over; but we were unable to ascertain whether the snow lasted a long time. I consider, however, that the country is temperate and the winter not severe."

De Monts's preoccupation with finding a better site than Sainte Croix is perfectly clear. The proficiency of his men in communicating by signs is also evident.

Champlain observed that these Cape Cod Indians had no furs, or very few; they wore breechclouts of grass and hemp. "I saw, among other things, a girl with her hair quite neatly done up by means of a skin dyed red, and trimmed on the upper part with little shell beads. Some of her hair hung down behind, while the rest was braided in various ways. These people paint their faces red, black, and yellow. . . . I do not know what government they have, but believe that in this they resemble their neighbors, who have none at all. They do not know what it is to worship or pray. : : : In appearance they seem to be of good disposition, and better than those to the northward; but the whole of them, to tell the truth, are not worth much. The slightest intercourse with them at once discloses their character. They are great thieves, and if they cannot lay hold of a thing with their hands, try to do so with their feet, as we have repeatedly learned by experience. . . . One must be on one's guard against these people and mistrust them, yet without allowing them to perceive it."

His last words, singularly moderate, were the product of harsh experience, of tragedy, indeed. Champlain tells the story in excellent narrative style: "Four or five sailors having gone ashore with some large kettles to fetch fresh water from among the sand-hills at a distance from our pinnace, certain Indians, being desirous to possess some of these kettles, watched for the time when our men went there, and snatched one by force out of the hands of a sailor who had filled his the first and who had no weapons. One of his companions, starting to run after the Indian, quickly returned, being unable to catch him, inasmuch as the latter was a swifter runner than himself. The other Indians, when they saw our sailors running towards our pinnace and shouting to us to discharge some musket shots at the Indians, who were in considerable numbers, took to flight. At the same time there were a few Indians on board our pinnace who threw themselves into the sea, and we were able to seize only one of them. Those on shore who had taken to flight, seeing the others swimming, turned back straight to the sailor from whom they had taken the kettle and shot several arrows at him from behind and brought him down. Perceiving his condition, they at once rushed upon him and despatched him with their knives.

"Meantime we made haste to go on shore, and fired muskets from our pinnace. Mine exploded in my hands and nearly killed me. The Indians, hearing this fusillade, again took to flight, and redoubled their speed when they saw that we had landed, being frightened on seeing us run after them. There was no likelihood of catching them, for they are as swift-footed as horses. The dead man was brought in, and some hours later was buried.

Meanwhile we kept our prisoner bound hand and foot on board our pinnace, fearing lest he should escape. The Sieur de Monts determined to let him go, feeling persuaded he was not to blame and knew nothing of what had occurred, as was the case also with those who were at the time on board and alongside our pinnace. A few hours later some Indians came toward us, making excuses by signs and outward show that it was not they who had done this evil deed, but others farther off in the interior. We were unwilling to do them harm, although it was in our power to avenge ourselves."

The extraordinary forbearance of the French when one of their number was murdered was probably due to the God-fearing virtue of de Monts. Lescarbot, who had the story at second hand, adds that the French were earnest for revenge, and that the men on the pinnace were taking aim at the natives when M. de Monts ordered them to lower their weapons, since their targets were not the murderers.

This is the first recorded death by violence of a European in New England. De Monts's magnanimity is in striking contrast to the tenfold and hundredfold punishments soon to be imposed by the whites upon the red men. De Monts's action has been ascribed to his awareness that he might yet settle in this country and need the native good will; "better one murder than a war." [1] But I think he had no time for such long views; I think his command was the instinctive act of a merciful man, a pious Huguenot, who rebelled at the thought of killing the innocent as a lesson to the guilty.

And now fogs and storms hindered a further journey to the south. Provisions began to run short. "The Sieur de Monts decided to return to Sainte Croix Island, in order to find another spot more suitable for our settlement; for we had been unable to find such a place on any of the coasts we had explored on this voyage."

Indeed? One would have said that they had found many places more suitable than their Calamity Island, Scurvy Island. All this lovely New England coast lay open to them; so far they had heard of no European rivals. There is only one reasonable explanation of de Monts's decision. He had found New England

[1] Henry F. Howe: *Prologue to New England*, 118.

swarming with Indians, and he had learned to fear their treachery. He did not dare to plant a colony of two score white men among thousands of Indians, who would kill for a kettle.

So on July 25 he turned his vessel north. On leaving Nauset Harbor she was nearly wrecked on a bar; Champlain blames the clumsy pilots, Champdoré and Cramolet. They made good speed past Cape Cod and Cape Ann to Saco, where a friendly interview was held with the chief. Then to the mouth of the Kennebec for a little fur bartering. Here the chief, Anassou, gave them some bad news. A European ship had put in near by and, under the guise of friendship, had killed five Indians. "From his description of the men on the ship we judged they were English."

English they were indeed. The ship was the *Archangel* of Dartmouth, Captain George Waymouth. It was sent out under the patronage of Henry Wriothesley, Earl of Southampton, who was also the patron of William Shakespeare. Waymouth had traded and explored in the Kennebec region, and had kidnapped, not killed, five Indians, to serve as future interpreters and guides. Thus the preparations for racial mistrust and bloodshed were laid. He had set sail for England on June 16. Three weeks later de Monts and Champlain, outward bound from Sainte Croix, had crossed his track but had had no news of him.

Now de Monts, returning from the Kennebec, sailed past Monhegan Island, which was to be a landmark for the English sailors, past Ile au Haut and Great Wass Island, and so to Sainte Croix, where he arrived happily on August 2, 1605.

CHAPTER VII

The Third Voyage—Nova Scotia and New England

WHEN THE EXPLORERS returned to Sainte Croix, an urgent necessity lay upon them to find a refuge against the coming winter. A cold August night sent their thoughts forward; this was the first chill of the new season, not a straggler from the last. What to do? Sainte Croix promised death from cold and scurvy; the New England coast, death from swarming, hostile natives. De Monts's thoughts turned back to the welcoming harbor of Port Royal, on the sheltered western coast of Nova Scotia. He immediately dispatched Champlain and Pontgravé to make a reconnoissance, to find a home.

The two sailed in their pinnace to Digby Gut, entered broad Annapolis Basin, and visited its shores. They went up the bay until it shallowed, and picked a smiling site on the north side, on a little rise, well protected from the northwest winds by a low range of hills, well fed with water, beside a good landing place. Their settlement is now the Port Royal National Historic Park, and here the Canadian Government has built a reproduction of the Port Royal of 1605. The architect has followed the illustration in Champlain's works, which erred on the side of tidiness; he has filled the gaps with imitations of the massive Norman farm architecture of the period. The roofs are handsomely shingled with hand-split pine and oak. The floors are accurately fitted by skilled German prisoners of war, working happily in their camps. The hardware is of hand-wrought elegance. The result does the scholarly, loving architect credit; its only fault is that it gives the visitor an impression of richness and comfort that would have surprised the colonists of 1605. However, this is a small cavil. The Canadian government has most worthily commemorated the first permanent and lasting settlement of white men on our continent north of Florida and New Mexico.

De Monts soon followed Champlain with two pinnaces loaded with supplies and with the precious fitted woodwork from Sainte Croix. He inspected the site and approved. All hands set to work, felled the trees, cut them into lengths for log houses, leveled the land. Buildings were erected within a rectangle enclosing a central court. The establishment was more compact than that at Sainte Croix, no doubt for security and for protection against the cold winds. It included a house for M. de Monts, "of pretty good woodwork," quarters for the workmen, storehouses, a kitchen, an oven, and a forge. At one corner was a raised platform on which were mounted four cannon. Near by were the gardens and the inevitable cemetery.

The workmen had by now some practice in building houses of logs and some knowledge of the menaces to be met. Still, there was little time for refinements. No doubt in this first year the rain dripped through a summary thatch and the wind soughed between the warping green logs of the walls. However, the settlers did not repine; they were very proud of their cozy home.

Within a month or two—in September, probably—the lodgings seemed fit to withstand the winter. A council was held. The necessities of the colony were great; obviously the only person fit to represent its needs at court was the Sieur de Monts, who held in his person all the rights of trade and settlement. He had been absent from France for a year and a half, and jealous rivals were surely at work to annul his privileges. It was high time that he should be seen at court.

As deputy governor of Port Royal, and indeed of all North America, he appointed sturdy Pontgravé. Forty to forty-five men constituted his force. These were the new arrivals who had come out in this year of 1605; the survivors of Sainte Croix, all but three, thankfully returned to France.

Three brave men who had lived through the winter at Sainte Croix volunteered to stay. These three were the Sieur de Fougeray of Vitré, the pilot Champdoré, and Champlain.

Champlain, who was in a sort of independent position as cartographer and geographer with a royal commission, elected to remain, "in the hope of making new discoveries toward Florida; and of this the Sieur de Monts highly approved."

The mind and character of Champlain are gradually becoming clear. The passion of his mind was exploration, discovery. He was possessed by the old *libido sciendi*, the lust of knowing. His lust turned to the great unknown of his time, the white void on sailors' maps. He looked, longing, to the west, the land of mystery. Thus he had embarked for the New World in the Spanish service, thus he had contrived to join the St. Lawrence expedition of 1603. Now he had had the experience of discovering and charting regions unknown and uncharted. He had not had enough; no discoverer has enough of discoveries. More than ease, more than security, more than any consolations of love and familiarity, he desired the knowledge of strange and perilous lands.

This was his passion. His character was fit for the fulfillment of his passion. The mark of his character, as it had been developed through war, adventure, and privation, was fortitude.

Fortitude is, I think, strength to endure for a purpose. Champlain possessed this strength. When others complained, he did his work; when others turned back, he persevered; when others died, he lived. His strength was physical, for only a man of extraordinary toughness could have survived his trials. His strength was also mental, for, as we shall see, his whole long life was a battle against the fainthearts, the mean-spirited, the avaricious, the sensual.

The life of fortitude is a noble thing to contemplate.

So Champlain, with the memory of cold, scurvy, and suffering fresh in his mind, elected to stay in America.

De Monts sailed away in the ship of Captain des Antons of Saint Malo. Pontgravé, an energetic commander, kept all his men hard at work. Champlain took advantage of a spell of fine weather to seek again for Captain Prévert's copper mine, which had become an obsession. He took with him a Slavonian miner, Master Jacques. He sailed to the present St. John, New Brunswick, and persuaded the Indian chief Secoudun to be his guide. They explored once more the Minas Channel, but all in vain.

On Champlain's return to the settlement he found a few men already down with scurvy.

Winter came late to Port Royal, in comparison with bitter Sainte Croix. The first snow fell on the twentieth of December. But the settlers were reasonably at ease. Their cabins were stout, their hearths supplied with limitless fuel. The hunters brought in rabbits and hares, ducks, partridge, plover, Canada geese, in plenty; the fishermen had fruitful sport.

The shy but curious Indians drew near. These were Souriquois, or Micmacs, of the great Algonquin stock. They were dressed in cloaks of patched skins, flung over one shoulder, with the arm bare; and breechclouts, leggings, and moccasins. They wore crowns of moose hair painted red, and necklaces of porcupine quills dyed red, white, and black. The French tempted them with red jackets, beads, and knives; the Indians paid in furs, in moose meat, in seal oil bottled in moose bladders. The settlers, guardedly cordial, soon concluded that these were mild and friendly folk, like the natives about Sainte Croix. The French accepted the proffered peace pipe and puffed at it with diplomatic distrust, but some, eventually, with wicked gusto.

The chief of the Indians was their sagamore, Membertou, a gay and humorous old gentleman, tall, large-limbed, with the air of a leader. Though he claimed to be over a hundred and to remember Cartier's visit, his eyesight was uncommonly keen, his chin was adorned with an honorable tuft of black hairs, and he was still capable of leading a war expedition against the Indians of Maine. He was destined to become an excellent friend of the French, the first convert to Christianity, and the representative, in their minds, of the good savage.

Some of the French with a taste for languages got some knowledge of the soft, unguttural Micmac tongue. But the wild woodland creatures seemed to learn a serviceable French more readily than the French could master their speech. They had already picked up some Basque words from unknown traders, and these they wove comically into their French jargon. Despite some difficulties with the consonants *v* and *f*, "they pronounce the rest of the French tongue better than our Gascons," says Lescarbot. Civilization has not made its children the apter linguists.

The winter wore on. It was a mild season, in comparison with that of the previous year, with beating rains between the snows. But there were troubles enough. Water seeped under the cabins, making the floors damp and chill. Many suffered from thirst, fearing to drink melted snow and the water of the brooks. Scurvy claimed twelve men out of the forty, and five recovered only with the coming of spring.

Among the confined settlers the inevitable quarrels and hatreds arose. Some of the party were Catholic, some Huguenot. Leaders of the religious disputes were a priest and a minister, whom de Monts had provided to insure spiritual health, but who brought only constant war. These two shouted at each other until, at a loss for argument, they fell to with their fists. The French and Indians too watched the bouts with delight, betting on their favorites. It would appear that the priest out-pointed the minister. But the two died simultaneously of the scurvy, and, according to a perhaps untruthful story, "the sailors who buried them put them both in a single grave, to see if they would be at peace when dead, since, living, they had never been able to agree." [1] If the story is true we may see in the common interment a disposition of rowdy Pontgravé, not of sober Champlain.

There were sullen men and grumbling days. Everyone hated the dreary duty of grinding wheat in the small portable hand mill. The Indians refused the dull task, though they were offered half the flour in pay. The French, like the Indians, much preferred to hunt the moose, even though vainly, to fish, and to pry through the ice with long wooden tweezers for oysters.

Champlain himself had enough to do. He had brought back from his exploration of the New England coast a collection of rough charts and notes. Of these he made sets of fair copies, for

---

[1] Sagard: *Histoire du Canada* (1866) I, 26. The battles of priest and minister are often assigned to 1604–5. Sulte ("*Poutrincourt en Acadie*," *Trans. Roy. Soc. Can.*, 1883, p. 32) argues convincingly for the following year.

the future use of authorized French navigators, for his report to the King his master, and for the illustration of the book he was to write. According to the best of modern students, W. F. Ganong, the charts mark a great advance in the cartography of this country. "It is well-nigh impossible for anyone who has not himself mapped the country to realize the difficulty of transferring topography to paper accurately. The impression made by a complicated topography upon the eye at its own level is so different from that given by the inspection of a modern map that the two hardly belong to the same psychological order. The historian with accurate modern maps has the advantage of the use of three dimensions over the explorer, whose wanderings, for the most part, are confined to the two dimensions of a single plane. It is surprising how deceptive an appearance the actual country can present, how limited is at times the range of human vision, how opaque the hills, how like to islands the peninsulas the connections of which are hidden, how deep may seem a bight and how shallow a bay, and how completely telescoped in a uniform line a varied coast may become when seen in the haze of distance. The physical obstacles such as wind, weather, weariness, and the exceeding speed of time also play their part. All these difficulties, which the modern charts abolish for us, Champlain had to face, and to make his maps in the teeth of them. It is therefore not in comparison with the modern charts that his maps should be judged, but rather with the blank darkness out of which they were boldly and laboriously carved." [2] They were true sea charts, Professor Ganong continues, designed to show safe entrances and good anchorages of ports, and as such they are surprisingly accurate, both in bearings, soundings, and relations to neighboring features.

Champlain had time, also, to meditate on his on purposes. As cartographer to the expedition, he did his duty by making his scrupulous maps of the coast. As geographer, he had the duty of discovery and of claiming new empires for France. He listened eagerly to the news the Indians could give him of canoe routes to the interior. Forever in his mind was the thought of discovering an easy way to the Orient. He seems to have had

[2] *Champlain's Works* (Champlain Society) I, 196–7.

no faith in the fabled strait dividing the continent in two. His hope was to find a river route to the hinterland, where other rivers, logically, should lead down to the western sea. It was his misfortune, and that of France, that he did not find the mouths of the Connecticut River and the Hudson.

He was certainly more concerned at this time with discovery than with the fur trade. De Monts also seems to have pictured himself as a colonizer rather than a merchant. De Monts was constantly trying to find a site for his colony far to the southwest, where furs were poor and scant, where he would be in no position to control the northern fur trade and punish the contraband dealers. Champlain saw eye to eye with his chief. His purpose was almost an animal desire, to push forever westward, to discover, to see, to know. For the glory of France? No doubt; but chiefly for the satisfaction of a craving he could recognize but not define.

Spring came early in this year of 1606. By March 16 Champlain and Pontgravé were ready "to proceed on a voyage of discovery along the coast of Florida." But when hardly started they were driven by a storm upon (apparently) White Head Island, southeast of Grand Manan. Champdoré, a better shipwright than pilot, repaired the pinnace. The party continued as far as the mouth of the Sainte Croix, where the snow still lay deep. Persistent fogs and head winds determined Pontgravé to return to Port Royal. On his arrival he fell ill with an affection of the heart.

On April 9, "although still indisposed, he embarked again, because of his desire to explore the coast of Florida." The pinnace lay at anchor for the night inside Digby Gut. In the early morning Champdoré attempted the passage of the Gut in a dense fog, with the wind contrary. Says Champlain: "Pontgravé and I, who were in bed, heard the sailors crying out and exclaiming: 'We are lost!', which soon brought me to my feet to see what had happened. Pontgravé was still ill, and this prevented him from getting up as quickly as he wished. I was no sooner on deck than the pinnace was thrown upon the coast." The pinnace was badly battered; she filled with water but did not break up. When the tide ebbed, the crew was able to go ashore and to unload a good part of the stores. A New Brunswick chief, Secoudun, and some companions who had wintered at Port Royal arrived in their canoes to save the men and goods. The pinnace went to pieces at the return of the tide.

On reaching the settlement, Pontgravé held a formal investigation of Champdoré's action. As prosecutor, he accused the pilot of running the pinnace ashore maliciously. As jury, he declared him guilty. As judge, he sentenced the culprit to be jailed and handcuffed and to be delivered for further trial to de Monts in France. The judgment satisfied Pontgravé's rancor, but not Champlain's desire, for there was a pinnace in the stocks that only Champdoré could complete.

Had he not been twice baffled by weather and mishap in this spring of 1606, Champlain, with plenty of time and ample supplies, would have proceeded far down the Atlantic coast. He could have chosen a site for settlement anywhere north of Florida, for there were as yet no Dutch in New York, no English in Virginia. Clumsy Champdoré was fate's instrument to make Champlain the founder of Canada, not of the area of these United States.

Time dragged on. The settlers gave up all thought of exploration and thought only of return to France. Day after day passed with no sign of de Monts and his relief. Finally Pontgravé released Champdoré after two months' imprisonment and ordered him to complete the half-built pinnace. From later evidence it appears that she was of eighteen tons, decked or half decked, with a four-foot draft.

Champlain consoled himself with his pretty garden, for every man, even the chiefs, had to work his own allotment. "I made one which I surrounded with ditches full of water wherein I placed some very fine trout; and through it flowed three brooks of very clear running water from which the greater part of our settlement was supplied. I constructed in it near the seashore a little sluiceway, to draw off the water when I desired. This spot was completely surrounded by meadows, and there I arranged a summer house with fine trees, in order that I might enjoy the fresh air. I constructed there likewise a small reservoir to hold salt-water fish as we required them. I also sowed there some seeds which throve well; and I took therein a particular pleasure, although beforehand it had entailed a great deal of labor. We often resorted there to pass the time, and it seemed as if the little birds thereabouts received pleasure from this; for they gathered in great numbers and warbled and chirped so pleasantly that I do not think I ever heard the like."

You may still see Champlain's garden and the descendants of his little birds, still warbling and chirping pleasantly, at Port Royal.

By mid-July no sail had appeared to gladden the tired eyes of the watchers. Perhaps de Monts had been unable to raise funds for a new expedition. Perhaps he lay at the bottom of the Atlantic. It was impossible to brave another winter of privation and scurvy in Port Royal without supplies and medicines. Pontgravé determined to carry his settlers in the pinnace to Cape Breton or Gaspé, where they might hope to find a fishing vessel that would bring them back to France.

Two brave men volunteered to remain in Port Royal to guard the settlement. Their names were La Taille and Miquelet; they deserve what preservation these transitory pages can give. Good Membertou promised to look after them, "and that they should be no more unhappy than if they were his own children. We had found him a good Indian all the time we were there."

On July 17 the party set off in two crowded pinnaces, one of eighteen tons, one of seven or eight. As Champdoré's construction work was done, he was formally rehandcuffed. The craft ran into storms. Amid mountainous seas off an evil coast the rudder irons of the large pinnace broke. Champdoré was unhandcuffed and succeeded in attaching the rudder. The passengers united to obtain his pardon from the still vengeful Pontgravé.

On July 24 they were off Cape Sable. And there the voyagers perceived a shallop making westward. It drew near; Ralluau, de Monts's secretary, stood in the sheets and waved and screamed. Poutrincourt was on his way to Port Royal in a ship of 120 tons, he shouted; and he himself was following along the coast in the hope of intercepting the settlers, if by chance they were already on their way home. By great good luck he had indeed found them, in this open sea off the fog-bound, islanded coast.

The three little boats headed again for Port Royal. There they found Poutrincourt's ship, the *Jonas* (a name to make a seaman shudder.)

Let us now go back several months, to the arrival of de Monts in France in the late autumn of 1605. He seems to have landed a good quantity of furs in his own ship and in those of his subordinates on the St. Lawrence. While the shareholders were pleased, the jealous Norman merchants, enemies of his monopoly, made trouble. It seemed advisable that he should remain in France, close to the ear of His Majesty and his ministers.

He immediately set about preparing his expedition for the spring of 1606. For its commander he fixed on his companion of the 1604 journey, Poutrincourt, the courtly soldier, who dreamed of establishing his line in his seigniory of Port Royal. Though Poutrincourt was involved in certain tangled lawsuits he welcomed the chance to return to the land he remembered green, pure, and gleaming under the summer sun.

The ship *Jonas*, Captain Foulques, was commissioned and ordered to load at La Rochelle. M. de Poutrincourt began to assemble his party.

Immediately he ran into great difficulty. The survivors of Sainte Croix had spent the winter in the taverns of the Norman and Breton coast. Their tales of terror, cold, and death grew more dreadful with every round of drink. They showed the marks of scurvy on their bodies; they gaped to point where their teeth had fallen from spongy gums. The savages, in their remembrance, became baleful as demons. When their stories had spread through the seaports, no volunteers could be had, save the desperate, the disappointed, and those few in whom the lust for adventure overmastered the fear of death.

Poutrincourt's first recruit was his eldest son Jean, commonly called Biencourt, a hardy youth of fifteen. The second was stalwart young Robert du Pontgravé, eager to join his father in the land of wonder. There were other good men, fascinated by the unknown. There was Louis Hébert, master of pharmacy of Paris, son of Catherine de Médicis's apothecary. (And as Catherine de Médicis once nearly died of overeating, her apothecary must have been a man of substance.) And there was Daniel Hay, a lover of danger, "a man whose pleasure it is to display his courage amid the dangers of the deep." And Jean Ralluau, of course, who went out for the summer only.

Best of all, there was Marc Lescarbot. He was a Paris lawyer, a poetaster, a piddling scholar, with some published orations and translations from the Latin to his credit. Though formally a Catholic, he had marked Huguenot sympathies. In 1606 he had just suffered some dreadful disappointment in the courts, which moved him, he says, to flee an evil world. Naïf, gay, and passionately curious, he was to write a delightful classic of the literature of discovery.

There were no priests. Lescarbot lays their absence to the timorousness of the clergy. It appears, however, that Poutrincourt contented himself with casually inquiring for clerical volunteers during Holy Week, when all were busy hearing confessions. A priest is not a free man; naturally none could give an immediate consent. By this transparent device Poutrincourt saved himself the obligation to carry an idle passenger, and put all the blame on the clergy.

One of the recruits was a Negro, the first recorded in the history of northern North America. The chances are that he was Mathieu d'Acosta or de Costa, and that he had learned the language of the Acadian Indians while serving as a crewman on a Portuguese fisherman.[3]

Many, if not most, of the colonists were a villainous lot, who had good reason for leaving France. Ordered to assemble in La Rochelle on April 1, they immediately set that prim Protestant town in an uproar, and some of them were jailed until the city should be quit of them. "The common people is a strange animal," sighs Lescarbot.

After many mishaps the ominous *Jonas* set sail on May 13. She took the Azores route, to avoid storms and to get an assured reckoning of latitude. The journey was interminable. During

---

[3] The Negro is not named by Lescarbot. But he sounds like the Mathieu d'Acosta who was the subject of a suit between de Monts and a Rouen merchant, Bauquemare, who was associated with Dutch traders. Bauquemare apparently kidnapped d'Acosta from de Monts, and de Monts went to law to get him back. His knowledge of the Indian language made him very valuable. How had he learned Micmac? I make the reasonable supposition from his Portuguese name that he had served with a fisherman on these coasts. See William Inglis Morse: *Pierre du Gua de Monts* (London, 1939), 51.

sunny calms the passengers bathed in the ocean, danced on the deck, climbed to the crosstrees, sang in harmony. They arrived finally at Port Royal on July 27. Their cannon roared, and were answered by the joyous cannon of the settlement, fired by the two lone watchmen, La Taille and Miquelet. The newcomers set foot on the heaving land and, amid greetings, embracings, and tears, visited the little fort. Old Membertou capered with delight.

Three days later the expedition's shallop with Jean Ralluau, and Pontgravé and Champlain in their pinnaces, arrived. M., de Poutrincourt ordered a tun of wine to be set on end, and gave all leave to tap it freely, "so that some of them drank until their caps turned round."

Lescarbot found this a good land, similar to that which God promised his people through his servant Moses, saying: "The Lord thy God bringeth thee into a good land, a land of brooks and water, of fountains and depths that spring out of valleys and hills; a land wherein thou shalt eat bread without scarceness, thou shalt not lack anything in it." Poutrincourt had his men sow wheat, rye, cabbage, turnips, and other vegetables, and these began to sprout promptly. Lescarbot was delighted. He had the proper view of the colonist: that wealth must come from agriculture, not from the vain search for gold. "Farming must be our goal. That is the first mine for which we must search, and is better worth than the treasures of Atahualpa; for whoso has corn, wine, cattle, linen, cloth, leather, iron, and lastly codfish, need have naught to do with treasure."

As soon as might be, Poutrincourt assembled his chief men in council. His instructions from de Monts were to push south beyond Cape Cod and to re-establish the colony on some warm southern shore. Prudence dictated that a reconnoissance should first be made in the pinnace, which "draws little water, ferrets everywhere, and finds suitable places for settlement." It was decided to make the reconnoissance immediately and to move the colony in the spring.

The colonists were divided into three groups. The first, composed of the survivors of the previous winter, was to return to France under the captaincy of Pontgravé. The second, the main body of the newcomers, remained at Port Royal. Lescarbot was one of this party. The third, Poutrincourt, with Champdoré for pilot and a crew of sailors, would explore the coast of future New England.

Champlain elected, without hesitation, to stay in America, in order to join the exploring party. This was his duty as geographer. He had survived two calamitous winters; he would risk a third. Only he and Champdoré and Fougeray remained of the men who had come out in 1604.

For Pontgravé and the party returning to France, Lescarbot wrote a long heroic poem, *Adieu aux Français*. This deserves some literary commemoration as the first recorded poem written in North America north of the Spanish country. Not much more can be said in its praise.

The *Jonas* sailed for France amid many a cannonade. The exploring party headed west and south. On September 7 they visited the tragic island of Sainte Croix, and discovered that their wheat and garden vegetables had come up fair and fine. There they found two Indian friends, Secoudun of St. John and Messamouet of La Have, on the Nova Scotia coast. Messamouet had once visited France and had been entertained by Philibert de Gramont, governor of Bayonne. The two chiefs accepted the invitation to join the tourists.

Champlain urged that the pinnace should head directly for Cape Cod, to take up the exploration where it had been dropped in the previous year, and to save a precious week or two before winter's onset. He was overruled by Poutrincourt, who chose to skirt the coast.

We shall see many similar episodes in Champlain's life. He argues his case, and he is right. Another, not always his superior, argues the opposite. And Champlain, not sufficiently self-confident, or dominating, or ruthless, is half persuaded and yields to the contrary view. Later his judgment is proved right, and he is sorry. The fact is, he thought too much to be a proper man of action, and thought has a certain sterilizing effect. He did not well persuade others, and there was a secret doubt in his air of command.

The pinnace followed the coast, then, pausing for parleys and trade. The French found the Indians "waiting upon the seashore, sitting on their rumps like apes." There was some trouble at Saco, where Messamouet gave handsome presents to the local tribes and was dissatisfied with the poor things he received in return. His dissatisfaction was one of the circumstances leading up to a war.

The pinnace rounded Cape Ann and turned into the harbor of Gloucester, whose beauty and commodiousness, whose tumbled rocks and green forest rim, delighted Champlain. He named it "Le Beau Port," and made of it a careful chart. According to a modern authority, "his harbor chart of Gloucester is so accurate that by reference to it a shoal draft boat of today could be piloted in with perfect safety and without recourse to modern aids to navigation." [4]

Here the French surgeon dressed the wound of a savage who cut his foot badly on a sharp rock. "But two hours after he came again, the most jocund in the world, having put about his head the binding cloth wherewith his heel was wrapped, for to seem the more gallant."

On the last day of September the party sailed on and came to the inner side of Cape Cod. They landed at Wellfleet, or possibly Barnstable, and named the cove Oyster Harbor. They then rounded the Cape and turned into familiar Nauset Harbor for shelter from untoward winds. Champlain and Champdoré reported that this was the limit of their previous journey, and here was the grave of a French companion. Thence they continued south, past dazzling beaches and jutting dunes, crowned with scrub pine and arthritic oaks, past low, green-topped Monomoy. They turned the southern point of Monomoy spit, headed north, and anchored in Stage Harbor, in the present village of Chatham. They came to shore about where Alton Kenney's marine railway and boathouse stand. The presumed landing place is marked by a concrete monument bearing a bronze tablet. Its builder, Professor Carol V. Wight of Johns Hopkins, reinforced his concrete with some dozens of discarded New England bean pots. "Some future archæologist," says Professor Loren Petry of Cornell, "will conclude that Champlain introduced baked beans into New England."

[4] Alfred F. Loomis: *Ranging the Maine Coast*, 24.

The voyagers set up camp on shore, among the beach plums, the bayberry, the wild roses, the flies. And the omnipresent poison ivy of today? Strangely enough, none of these early explorers mention poison ivy, which, one would think, must have tortured flesh that had developed no resistance to its poison. Possibly the heyday of poison ivy has come only with the clearing of our forests.

Here they remained a fortnight, making some necessary repairs to their craft and laying in supplies. Game was plentiful; Poutrincourt (it is alleged) killed twenty-eight plover with a single shot. An oven was erected on shore and bread baked. Champlain observed the habits of the Indians, who had a different language and a different economy from the coastal Indians farther north. I shall here report only that they swarmed astoundingly with fleas.

M. de Poutrincourt, inspecting the Indian settlements, noted that the inhabitants were taking down their wigwams, preparing to depart. He immediately suspected that they were meditating an offensive action. He gave orders that all his men should return to their craft. He seems to have had little control over his unruly crew, for five of them remained on shore by their oven, eating hot biscuits. Poutrincourt thought they were aboard; he should have known.

"The next morning, the fifteenth of October, the Indians did not fail to come and see in what state were our men, whom they found asleep, except one who was before the fire. Seeing them in this condition, the Indians, to the number of four hundred, came quietly over a little hill, and shot such a salvo of arrows at them as to give them no chance of recovery before they were struck dead. Fleeing as fast as they could toward our pinnace, and crying out: 'Help, help, they are killing us!' some of them fell dead in the water, while the rest were all pierced with arrows, of whom one died a short time afterwards. These Indians made a desperate row, with war-whoops which it was terrible to hear.

"At this noise, and that of our men, the sentinel on our vessel cried out: 'To arms! They are killing our men!' Thereupon each quickly seized his weapons, and at the same time some fifteen or sixteen of us embarked in the shallop to go ashore. But being unable to land on account of a sand-bank which lay between us and the shore, we jumped into the water and waded from this bank to the mainland, a distance of a musket-shot. As soon as we reached it, the Indians, seeing us within bowshot, fled inland. To pursue them was useless, for they are wonderfully swift. All we could do was to carry off the dead bodies and bury them near a cross which had been set up the day before, and then to look about to see whether we could catch sight of any Indians; but in this we wasted our time. Realizing this we returned. Three hours later they reappeared on the shore. We discharged several shots at them from our little brass cannon; but whenever they heard the report, they threw themselves flat on the ground to avoid the charge. In derision of us they pulled down the cross, and dug up the bodies, which displeased us greatly, and made us go after them a second time; but they fled as fast as they had done before. We again set up the cross, and reinterred the bodies, which they had scattered here and there among the heaths, where they had kindled a fire to burn them. We returned without having accomplished more than before, seeing clearly that there was hardly any chance of taking vengeance for this blow, and that we must postpone the matter until it should please God."

So writes Champlain. Lescarbot adds, among other details obtained from Poutrincourt, the fact that three of the unruly five were killed on shore, the leader being found dead, face downward, with a little dog on his back, both transfixed and transpierced with the same arrow. A fourth later died of his wounds; the fifth, Duval, was saved, only to be hung by Champlain in Quebec two years later. Lescarbot tells also how the capering Indians on the shore dug up one of the dead, and one put on the dead man's shirt. "And with all this they also turned their backs to the long-boat and made mock at us by taking sand in their two hands and casting it between their buttocks, yelping the while like wolves."

Filled with impotent anger, the French left this haven, which they named, by antiphrasis, Good Luck Harbor.

They sailed westward along the south coast of Cape Cod. They descried an island to the west, perhaps Martha's Vineyard, perhaps merely the Horseshoe Shoal. They observed a little river, probably the Mashpee, which enters Nantucket Sound just west of Cotuit. To this Champlain gave his own name; he was indeed modest.

A high west wind arose. The voyagers were forced to turn back.

This was the farthest south and west that the Frenchmen came. Had they started earlier in the season, had the winds favored them, they would certainly have found Narragansett Bay, the Connecticut shore, the harbor of New York. We can hardly question that among the cordial Cuttyhunk Indians or the Manhattans of New York they would have found sufficient security for a settlement. And all our history would have been altered. Perhaps I would be writing this story in French.

Heading eastward, the travelers brooded on their discomfiture by the natives of Good Luck Harbor. "We determined to seize a few Indians of this place, in order to take them to our settlement and make them grind wheat at a hand-mill as a punishment for the murderous assault committed upon five or six of our men. But to do this when we were armed was very difficult, since whenever we went to them prepared to fight, they ran away, and betook themselves to the woods, where we could not catch them. It was necessary, therefore, to resort to stratagem, and this is what we decided: that when they should come to make friends with us again, we should coax them, by showing them beads and other trifles, and should reassure them repeatedly; then we should take the shallop well armed, and the stoutest and strongest men we had, each with a chain of beads and a fathom of match-fuse on his arm, and should set these men on shore, where, pretending to smoke with them (each with one end of his match alight, in order not to arouse suspicion, it being customary to carry light at the end of a cord for lighting the tobacco), we were to coax them with soft words in order to draw them into the shallop; and, should they be unwilling to enter, each of our men as he approached was to choose his man, and throwing the beads about his neck should at the same moment put a cord around the man to drag him on board by force; but should they raise too great a commotion, and our men be unable to master them, then, by tightening the cord well, our men were to stab them; and if by chance any should escape, there were to be men on shore to charge against them with swords. Meanwhile on board our pinnace the small cannon were to be in readiness to fire upon their companions in case any should come to their assistance, under cover of which cannon the shallop would be able to withdraw in safety."

It was a good idea for a commando raid, but a little too fanciful, too dependent on the enemy's acting according to plan.

The French came duly to shore in Good Luck Harbor and tempted some of the Indians into the water. But the enemy did not co-operate properly. When Poutrincourt gave the signal an aimless huggermugger ensued. Five or six Indians were killed, but no slaves to work the hand mill were taken. Secoudun secured a scalp, "but by ill luck it fell into the water, whereat he was so chagrined that he wept openly and loud."

This treacherous attack by the French has been severely censured by modern writers.[5] Indeed, it is in sharp contrast with the forbearance under provocation shown by de Monts in the same region in the previous year. But stratagems of this sort were normal and unreproved in their time. Poutrincourt and Champlain had been trained in the civil wars of France, when every sort of duplicity had come to be practiced without blame, save for failure. In all history an inferior but well-armed force has always imposed its will on a superior, ill-armed mob by the punishment of innocent hostages for the offenses of the guilty. On such a principle, and with such treacherous shows of friendship, the English and Dutch settlers dominated and slew the Indians ringing their forts.

Still, it was an ugly trick, however justified by need and precedent, even Biblical.[6] Lescarbot gives Poutrincourt full credit for the plot; and to him, and not to Champlain, we may happily ascribe it.

Poutrincourt now took sober counsel with his chief men. He had lost three men out of about a score; he had four or five sick and wounded. One of these was young Pontgravé, who had

[5] H. F. Howe: *Prologue to New England*, 143; H. C. Kittredge: *Cape Cod*, 19.

[6] "And Joab said to Amasa, Art thou in health, my brother? And Joab took Amasa by the beard with the right hand to kiss him. But Amasa took no heed to the sword that was in Joab's hand: so he smote him therewith in the fifth rib and shed out his bowels to the ground, and struck him not again; and he died." II Samuel 20: 9, 10.

lost three fingers through the explosion of an overcharged musket. The smell of the men's wounds in the confined hold was frightful, and the surgeon had run out of ointment. Supplies for only eight or ten days remained. And a squall of snow came down. Poutrincourt decided to run for Port Royal.

On the first of November the pinnace was off the coast of Maine. Champlain noted ice two inches thick and sadly compared this country with the warm south.

The coastal Indians reported to Secoudun that some women of his race had been carried off by the Almouchiquois of western Maine and put to death. This was a declaration of war. Secoudun would attend to it in the spring.

On November 14, 1606, the pinnace entered the harbor of Port Royal.

CHAPTER VIII

The Third Voyage—Port Royal

WHEN THE returning voyagers cast anchor off Port Royal and stepped into their shallop to go ashore, they rubbed their eyes in wonder. A longboat pushed out from land, towing a dinghy, painted blue. In this was melodramatically camped a figure with long seaweed beard and draped in a blue cloth. In his right hand he brandished a trident. A canoe with four painted Indians followed him. Neptune (for it was no other) arose and proclaimed, in reproachable French Alexandrines:

> *Arrête, Sagamos, arrête-toi ici,*
> *Et regardes un Dieu qui a de toi souci.*
> *Si tu ne me connais, Saturne fut mon père,*
> *Je suis de Jupiter et de Pluton le frère. . . .*

Neptune, under whose disguise we may see the features of Marc Lescarbot, concluded with a swelling climax, prophesying that ten thousand French ships would one day ride these waters. A trumpet sounded. Poutrincourt, being prompted, drew his sword. The six Tritons who rowed the longboat each made a suitable declamation, one of them using the Gascon tongue. Then the four painted savages, betraying themselves by their perfect French, offered to Poutrincourt a quarter of elk, beaver skins, native adornments, and fish, with poetic allocutions in which Indian words were whimsically entangled with Cupid and Diana. Poutrincourt responded suitably, though impromptu. Then the welcoming band sang in four parts:

> *Vrai Neptune donne-nous*
> *Contre les flots assurance,*
> *Et fais que nous puissions tous*
> *Un jour nous revoir en France.*

The trumpet sounded and the cannon roared, making such echoes that one would have sworn Proserpine was giving birth to a child. As Poutrincourt stepped ashore he was greeted by a poetic scullion, welcoming him and his companions, as sturdy of tooth as of kidney, adjuring them to sneeze high and loud before drinking, thus to discharge all their chill humors and to fill their brains with the sweet vapors of wine.

This pageant, or masque, fondly called by Lescarbot, its author, "Le Théâtre de Neptune," might perhaps better be known as "The Descent of Literature upon America," indeed, the first North American drama.

Feasting done, the colonists set busily to work. Poutrincourt had a drainage ditch dug around the settlement, and constructed a water mill, which set the savages agape. Every man prepared his own garden, ready for spring planting. Champlain built a road, two thousand paces long, to his troutery.

The winter of 1606–7, for all its threats, was mild and genial. No serious snow fell until the last day of December. In mid-January Lescarbot and some friends picnicked joyously in the sunshine. There were frequent rains and thaws, hindering the hunt for the moose, who can be caught only when he flounders in deep snow.

Scurvy returned, but less violently than in previous years. Four men died, melancholic idlers.[1] One of the victims was the Negro. Others developed sore gums and swollen legs. But a varied diet and an active life saved most of the settlers scot-free.

Poutrincourt, well warned, kept his men constantly busy, without doors and within. They gathered hickory nuts and, in season, the ground nut, or Indian potato. They collected mus-

---

[1] Lescarbot. Champlain says seven, but Lescarbot is usually more accurate in details.

sels, crabs, and cockles. They fished incessantly, venturing out in the Indians' bark canoes, so cranky that a Frenchman upset one, he averred, by merely turning his head. Everyone enjoyed the hunting. Parties sought the noble moose, who weeps when he is captured. (He has a quaint cure for epilepsy; with his left hind foot he scratches himself behind the ear until the blood flows.) The Indians, wearing snowshoes, would pursue a moose for as much as three days till he sank exhausted in the snow. Says Lescarbot: "We once went to the spoil of a moose left dead upon the brink of a great brook about two leagues and a half within the lands, where we passed the night, having swept aside the snows to make our camp. We made there a very dainty feast with this venison, more tender than any other kind of flesh; and after the roast we had sodden meat, and broth abundantly, made ready at an instant by a savage, who did frame with his hatchet a tub, or trough, of the body of a tree, in which he boiled his flesh."

Occasionally an Indian would smell out a hibernating bear, and a party would spear him in his torpor. (He feeds, they say, by licking his paw, which yields a nourishing juice.)

Then there were caribou and deer, and small game: rabbits, raccoons, muskrat, otter. Best of all was the beaver, who supplied not only good food, but fur negotiable for wealth.

Lescarbot picturesquely describes the beaver, noting his powerful teeth. "With these teeth he cutteth small trees and poles in sundry pieces, wherewith he buildeth his house. That which I say is an admirable and incredible thing. This creature lodgeth himself upon the brinks of lakes, and there he first maketh his couch with straw or other things fit to lie upon, as well for him as for his female; raiseth a vault with his wood, cut and prepared, which he covereth with turf in such sort that no wind enters therein, forasmuch as all is covered and shut up except one hole which leadeth under the water, and by that way he goeth forth to walk where he listeth. And because the waters of the lake do sometimes rise, he maketh a chamber above the lower dwelling, for to retire himself in, if in case any inundation should happen; in such sort that some beaver's cabin is above eight foot high, all made with wood, pyramid-wise, and daubed with mud. Moreover, it is held that being amphibious, as we have said, he must always participate with water, and that his tail be dipped in it—which is the cause why he lodgeth himself so near a lake. But, being subtle, he contenteth not himself with that which we have said, but hath moreover an issue into another place out of the lake, without any cabin, by which way he goeth on the land and beguileth the hunter. But our savages being aware of it take order for the same, and stop this passage.

"When they will, then, take the beaver, they pierce through the ice of the frozen lake, about his cabin; then one of the savages thrusteth his arm into the hole, tarrying the coming of the said beaver, whilst that another goeth upon this ice, striking with a staff upon it for to astonish him and make him return into his lodging. Then one must be nimble for to seize on his neck, for if one catch him by any part where he may bite, he will bite very sore. The flesh thereof is very good, almost as if it were mutton."

The hunting, the outdoor life, guarded the colony's health better than all the apothecary's drugs. Champlain well recognized the necessity of keeping the men too physically tired for quarrelsome moodiness. To that end he established the Order of Good Cheer, *l'Ordre de bon temps*. A chain ceremoniously conferred on the day's best hunter encouraged rivalry; a formal dinner, with proper toasts and allocutions, roused the ready gaiety of the Frenchman at meat. Poutrincourt, an excellent musician, led the choruses.

Each man of M. de Poutrincourt's high table was appointed chief steward in his turn, says Lescarbot. "Now his care was that we should have good and worshipful fare, which was so well observed that, although the belly-gods of these parts do often reproach unto us that we had not *la rue aux Ours* [the Paris street of the cooked-meat sellers] with us, we have ordinarily had there as good cheer as we could have at the *rue aux Ours*, and at far lesser charges. For there was none but, two days before his turn came, was careful to go a-hunting or fishing, and brought some dainty thing, besides that which was of our ordinary allowance. So well that at breakfast we never wanted some modicum or other of fish or flesh; and at the repast of dinners and suppers, yet less; for that was our great banquet.

where the Governor of the feast or Steward, having made the cook to make all things ready, did march with his napkin on his shoulder and his staff of office in his hand, with the collar of the order about his neck, which was worth above four crowns, and all of them of the order following of him, bearing every one a dish. The like also was at the bringing in of the dessert, but not with so great a train. And at night, after grace was said, he resigned the collar of the order, with a cup of wine, to his successor in that charge, and they drank to one another."

Smacking his lips, Lescarbot lists the native meats, game, and fish. These were added to the rations brought from France, and to the wine, which was in plenty; they had started off with forty-five hogsheads.

"We had always twenty or thirty savages, men, women, girls, and boys, who beheld us doing our offices. Bread was given them gratis, as we do here to the poor. But as for the Sagamos Membertou and the other Sagamos, when any came to us, they sat at table eating and drinking as we did; and we took pleasure in seeing them, as contrariwise their absence was irksome unto us."

It is a pretty picture, of the good-fellowship of Frenchman and savage. Here was inaugurated a policy that Champlain and all the French rulers in Canada were to follow. The French have never taken kindly to the racism of other colonial powers. They respected the Indian's dignity and admired his hardihood; often they liked him as an individual. As we shall see, many found the Indian's way of life more agreeable than that of the underling in a harsh civilization.

M. de Poutrincourt himself, who had willingly left the privileges of the noble in France to establish his line in the wilderness, set the example for his men. He ruled the natives, as he did his colony, kindly but firmly, and all tendered him their affection and respect. The Jesuit Father Biard, who was out with him in this same country in 1611, bears witness to his liberality and magnanimity, his high Christian principle, and his due severity on occasion. Father Biard praises also the music he composed for the religious services of the Indians.

The two youths, Biencourt, son of Poutrincourt, and Robert du Pontgravé, most readily adapted themselves to Indian life and manners and best learned the Micmac speech. Their aptitude gave Champlain the idea of a policy he was soon to adopt in the St. Lawrence: to bring out mere boys, who would become apprentices to Indian life, and thus his agents and interpreters.

Champlain, Lescarbot, and others who came soon after have left us a precious description of the life of the Acadian Micmacs. They were a handsome, vigorous race, healthy and long-lived. Their bodies were well formed; among them were no misshapen monsters, no hunched backs or fat bellies. They sneered at the one-eyed, the squinters, the flat-nosed, among the French. Their color was tawny, from the sun's action, and from their habit of greasing themselves against the flies, "which are very troublesome not only where we are, but also through all that new world and even in Brazil, so that it is no wonder if Beelzebub, prince of flies, hath there a great empire." Their eyes were black, as was their hair, which grew, commonly, only on their heads. The Frenchmen's hairy faces and breasts seemed disgusting to them. The mocking French encouraged them to believe that French women too were bearded and mustachioed. Their sight, their smell, were marvelously keen. They swam like fish; they ran like horses, like greyhounds.

Their dwellings were conical wigwams. Women fetched poles from the woods and stuck them in the ground in a circle, inclining so that the tops interlaced. On the poles they tied skins, matting, and bark. The stores were put at the foot of the poles; the fire was built in the middle. The space between baggage and fire was strewn with fir needles, and on these were thrown mats and soft sealskins. As many as fifteen Indians could lie here in a wheel, their heads on the baggage, their feet toward the fire.

Their clothing in summer was a mere breechclout, so that the women resembled the pictures of St. John the Baptist (though, says Lescarbot slyly, he would not press the comparison). For hunting they wore moccasins and leggings. For festivals they had superb robes of moose skin, white, ornamented with bands of embroidery in red, violet, and blue, representing animals or done in formal designs. On great occasions they painted their faces red and violet. Their hair was elaborately adorned with colored porcupine quills.

Their tools were stone axes, bone needles, and thread made

of the root of the black spruce. Their artistic taste was marked, and they made pretty beasts, birds, and men of stone and wood. They had dishes of bark and bags of plaited rushes. Wonderful to the French were their showshoes, of beechwood corded with moose skin dressed to the state of parchment. Most wonderful of all were their canoes, framed of cedar, sheathed with birch bark sewn with bone needles and spruce-root thread, calked with fir gum chewed to a paste by the women and applied with fire. Indeed, we wonder still at these dancing craft, which a boy can carry, and which can carry the weight of five or six men.

For weapons they had lances and wooden clubs, but chiefly the bow and arrow. The bows were of maple scraped with oyster shells till they shone like glass. The arrows were of cedar tipped with bone or the tail of the horseshoe crab, and fletched, by preference, with the eagle's tail feathers.

They had no agriculture and made no bread. Their diet was mostly meat and fish, roasted or boiled. Their kettles were tree stumps, hollowed out by fire and stone axes. In these their stew was heated with red-hot stones. Their greatest delight was grease, which they would drink like water; no, they abhorred water.

Until the white man came their health was excellent. They knew nothing of fevers, nor of gout, gravel, and rheumatism. For wounds and other mischances they had recourse to herbs, whose properties they knew well. Their commonest therapeutic was the sweat bath, which was exactly like the baths of modern Finland.

In case of serious illness ("for one must die in the end," says Lescarbot), they summoned the aoutmoin, the medicine man. He bled the patient and sucked his wounds. He did his magic, danced till balls of foam emerged from his mouth, drew the sickness out with his hands, saying: "Here, it is gone! You are cured!" He would dig a pit for the devil, and summon him, and struggle with him, forcing him against his will to confer health on the patient. Lescarbot wisely comments: "If they do not always work a cure, one must remember that our doctors are often in like case."

They were a modest and well-mannered race. Though polyg-

amy was practiced, the wives were chaste, and adultery rare.
They had indeed a system of trial marriage, lasting as much as
a year, but this convention was strictly ordered. Lescarbot avers
that he never saw any immodest gesture or look among them.
Their nakedness did not increase lechery, rather the contrary.
Lescarbot ascribes their decorum to their lack of salt, hot spices,
and wine, to their keeping bare the head, where lies the fountain
of procreative desire, and to the dulling effect of tobacco smoke.

The life of the women seemed hard, even to men who knew
the cruel lot of peasant women in France. Theirs was all the
labor of the camp and the household, while their husbands played
the gentleman. They were soundly beaten, for any misdemeanor
or for none. Father Biard tells how a Frenchman reproved a
savage for mistreating his wife; the savage retorted: "Have you
got nothing to do but look into my house, to see if I am beating
my dog?"

As among all the Indians, the children were greatly loved,
never scolded, and according to all civilized standards, shame-
fully spoiled. They were given anything they asked for, even
a morsel of food out of their father's mouth. "The greatest
persons give way to the little ones." The French were fascinated
by the papoose, with its ingenious system of drainage: a little
aperture for a boy, a leaf gutter for a girl. (For excrement, a
pocket filled with powdered rotten wood.) When the child cried,
the bearer would dance and sing, and resume her work when
the sobbing ceased.

The Indians lived harmoniously together, holding their goods
in common, and hence having little subject for dispute. They
disdained the haggling of the French merchants, who would
bargain for an hour to beat down the price of a beaver skin.
"You are richer than we," they said, "and so should give liber-
ally of what you have." Such logic was to the French ridiculous
but unanswerable.

In their quarrels they did not fight with fists, but wrestled
and pulled hair in a terrible fashion. Their disputes were mostly
mild and anodine, not the brooding hatreds of the French. "For
to see any assembly of French people without reproaches,
slights, envy, and quarrels with each other is as difficult as to

1 1 1

see the sea without waves, except in monasteries and convents, where grace triumphs over nature."

Of the little decencies of life they had no inkling. Their table manners left everything to be desired. They never washed their hands nor their utensils; they divided their meat by tearing it under their muddy moccasins; they wiped their hands, when monstrously foul, on their hair or on a dog's back. They yielded pleasurably to every corporal impulse reproved by civilized etiquette.

Tobacco was their joy and solace. They inhaled the smoke and expelled it through the nostrils, thus warming the brain and drying up its humidity. The smoke likewise, says Lescarbot, opens the bowels, calms the passions, and induces sleep. Some of the French were so bewitched by the drug that they would no more be without it than without meat and drink.

The Indians loved feasting, music, the dance, and storytelling. The old men told endless tales of ancient gods and talking beasts. Says Nicolas Denys: "When they made their holiday feasts, after being well filled, there was always somebody who told a story so long that it required all the day and evening with intervals for laughing. They are great laughers."

They were great dancers too, always eager to find a pretext for a ritual or ceremonial performance. An orator spoke for two or three hours; for further hours the dancers marched round and round, stamping the ground, springing up, contorted, in a half leap, making frightful faces, waving their fists threateningly above their heads. A chief singer, man or woman, led the chorus, beating time against a tree with a stick. "All the rest dance and say *heh*, *heh*, like a man breathing hard; and at the end of every song, they all make a loud and long exclamation, saying *heeeee-e-e*." Lescarbot, with his precious inquisitiveness, listened outside a wigwam to some singers and noted down the words and music. This is, I am sure, the earliest transcription of North American music. The musicologist will find it in the Champlain Society's noble edition of Lescarbot.

The Indians made war, not for land, but for honor or revenge. Their art of war was all ambushes, night surprises, and such subtilities. They took scalps and carried off prisoners, but unlike the Iroquois, they did not torture and eat their captives.

They had no knowledge of God and no form of worship, but their medicine men were friends to the devil. Their faith was a universal pantheism. An Indian tapped a shattered, worn-out iron kettle; it answered with no sound. "Ha!" he said; "it does not speak, because it is dead, and its soul has gone to the land where the souls of kettles are accustomed to go."

Champlain and Lescarbot were troubled by the natives' ignorance of God. The French had no cleric with divine authority to teach, nor did they possess the language well enough to expound the Christian mysteries. They saw, however, the need and the opportunity for evangelization. Lescarbot was touched to watch the chief Secoudun, with a crude cross on his breast, imitate the pious formulas of the French, lifting his eyes to heaven and crossing himself before eating. His soul seemed to be crying for instruction. Lescarbot went so far as to recommend that the Mass should be said in the native tongues, in the interest of savage salvation. "I am driven to think that the lack of devotion which is seen throughout almost the whole Church springs from no other cause than lack of understanding of that for which one prays."

(In fact, in later times the Church departed from its almost universal rule and permitted the American Indian to hear the sacred drama in his own tongue. At Caughnawaga, just outside Montreal, you may still hear the Mass sung in Mohawk.)

So through the winter and spring the French fraternized with the Indians and learned to know their ways. Old Membertou and other chiefs were guests at the high table, awe-struck spectators of the ceremonies of the Order of Good Cheer. Never before had Champlain associated with the natives on such familiar terms. Never hitherto had he been brought to define the rightful and advantageous relations of French and Indian.

A few years before, in Mexico, he had felt and stated his pity for the oppressed American natives, and had hoped that their bodies might be preserved in this world and their souls in the next. In Port Royal he learned to regard the natives as individuals, each with his own character. He recognized the human virtues of his new companions: their friendliness, gaiety, courage, hardihood; and their faults: improvidence, volatility, superstition. They seemed to him no longer mysterious hostile halfmen, dancing apes; they were true men and women, each with a soul, to be saved or damned. They could be friends and helpers of the French, or they could be murderous enemies. Which they would be depended entirely on the French. He saw at Port Royal the working of the system of friendship, and there he learned the rudiments of his own colonial policy.

Not only did he come to like the Indians, he came to respect them. The contrast with his own people was striking. Deprived of their supplies from home, the French were helpless, doomed to death. But the Indians, with their few primitive tools and weapons, could defy cold, heat, hunger, and disease. If the French were inclined to scorn the Indians, these had reason to scorn the visitors, innocent babes in the wilderness. They had a low opinion of French timorousness, quarrelsomeness, and stinginess. One of their chiefs heard M. de Poutrincourt say (this was four or five years later) that his King, Louis XIII, was young and unmarried. "Perhaps," said he, "I may let him marry my daugher. But according to the usages and customs of the country, the King must make me some handsome presents, namely, four or five barrels of bread, three of peas or beans, one of tobacco, four or five cloaks worth one hundred sous apiece, bows, arrows, harpoons, and other similar articles."

Not long after Champlain's time a missionary had occasion to listen to a revealing harangue by an Indian chief at Ile Percée on the Gaspé.[2] "You tell us of your French houses," said the simple savage. "Why do men who are five or six feet high need houses sixty to eighty? Have you as much cleverness and ingenuity as we, who carry our houses with us, so that we may lodge wherever we please, independently of any seignior? We are at home everywhere, because we set up our wigwams wherever we go, without asking permission of anyone. You tell us of the riches and abundance of France, a very paradise in comparison with our little hell. But we are much happier than you, for we are content with the little that we have. If France, as you say, is a terrestrial paradise, why did you leave it? Why abandon wives, children, relatives, and friends? Why risk your life and property every year to come to this poorest

[2] Chrestien Le Clercq: *New Relations of Gaspesia* (Toronto, Champlain Society, 1910), 103.

and least fortunate country of the world? We shall hardly take
the trouble to go to France, since its natives leave it every year
to enrich themselves on our shores. We believe that you are
much poorer than we, seeing that you glory in our old rags
and in our miserable suits of beaver which can no longer be of
any use to us, and seeing that you find among us, in the cod-
fishery, the wherewithal to comfort your misery and the poverty
which oppresses you. As to us, we find all our riches and our
conveniences among ourselves, without trouble and without
exposing our lives to the dangers in which you find yourselves
constantly through your long voyages. And, while feeling compassion for you in the sweetness of our repose, we wonder at
the anxieties and cares which you give yourselves night and
day in order to load your ship with fish. We see also that all
your people live, as a rule, only upon cod which you catch
among us. It is everlastingly nothing but cod—cod in the morning, cod at midday, cod at evening, and always cod. Now tell
me this one little thing, if you have any sense: which of the
two is wiser and happier—he who labors without ceasing and
only obtains, with great trouble, enough to live on, or he who
rests in comfort and finds all that he needs in the pleasure of
hunting and fishing? Learn now, my brother, once for all, that
there is no Indian who does not consider himself infinitely more
happy and more powerful than the French."

Such suggestions as these must have been presented in the
long after-dinner sessions at Port Royal. Champlain himself was
a slow, tenacious thinker, but Lescarbot's agile lawyer's mind
delighted in novel ideas, surprising contentions, paradoxes. At
the beginning of his book he considers the question whether
the Europeans have any right to occupy American soil, so evidently the property of the Americans themselves. Though he
decides, on the grounds of true religion's rights, in favor of
Europe, the mere presence of the question in his mind is remarkable enough. It will hardly occur to any other white settler
until the time of the high-hearted Roger Williams.

The winter passed, not without profit to Samuel Champlain.
He worked at his maps, brought his written record up to date,
hunted and fished. And he had time to think, to organize his
views. It was now clear to him that this great unspoiled conti-

nent could be a source of incredible wealth to France. The wealth was not in gold and jewels, but in furs, fish, and the future products of the soil. To make this wealth available it was necessary to colonize determinedly and lavishly. Such meager enterprises as those of de Monts and Poutrincourt were too weak and precarious to succeed. The French government itself must support the colonization, and on a great scale. This is the essential policy he was to pursue for the rest of his life, however he might accept expedient compromises.

The spring came in March, thought better of it, and returned finally in May. Everyone, gentleman and commoner, cleared the gardens and sowed his seeds, and the virgin soil responded gratefully. There was great rivalry in matching the heights of shoots, great affection for one's own peas, beans, and lettuces. The Paris apothecary Louis Hébert showed a singular love of the soil and gentle power over it. He also sought the woodland herbs and tried to find their medical properties. Lescarbot remembers: "I have never done so much bodily work, through the pleasure which I took in digging and tilling my gardens, fencing them in against the gluttony of the swine, making terraces, preparing straight alleys, building store-houses, sowing wheat, rye, barley, oats, beans, peas, garden plants, and watering them, so great a desire had I to know the soil by personal experience. So much so that the summer days were too short for me, and very often in the spring I was still at work in the moonlight." Everything throve mightily, rejoicing the city farmer. Never had he been so happy, arguing about other folks' money before the bar of Paris.

On May 24 came word from home. Says Lescarbot in his high style: "The sun did but begin to cheer the earth and to behold his mistress with an amorous aspect, when the Sagamos Membertou came to give us advertisement that he had seen a sail upon the harbor." The pinnace came offshore; to the sound of cannon a young man, the new captain of the old *Jonas*, disembarked.

He brought bad news, almost the worst of news. The fur-trading monopoly of de Monts and his partners had been suddenly annulled. The company was in great financial difficulties.

It could no longer support a colonizing venture. The settlers were directed to return home.

The reasons for the annulment were evident. Under the monopoly fur prices had risen sharply. The powerful Hatters' Corporation of Paris complained to Finance Minister Sully, who had no faith in colonies. There were rumors of bribes in high places. Sully brusquely cancelled the monopoly, though it still had seven years to run. The company could not bear the expense of a colony without the monopoly; it suffered already from contraband trading by French and Dutch.

At this news bitter resentment burned in the hearts of Poutrincourt and his chief men. They must, then, admit the failure of their enterprise and return to France. However, there was no particular hurry. The *Jonas* would spend the summer in the Canso region, fishing and fur trading. Poutrincourt determined to remain in his seigniory, to harvest his crops and take home evidence of the bountiful fertility of New France.

The first excitement of the summer was the departure of Membertou and his braves for a war with the Almouchiquois of Maine.

The exploring trip of the previous autumn had been marked by "incidents." Then in November one of Membertou's warriors, on a trading journey, was killed at the mouth of the Penobscot. His companions brought his embalmed body to Port Royal. All the tribesmen painted their faces black and howled for a week. They then burned all the victim's possessions, including his dogs, thus providing a wholesome lesson for the French, with their lust for inheritances. Then they put him in his grave, sitting upright, and everyone gave him a present—furs, weapons, knives—for his convenience in the other world.

During the winter, preparations for war went on. The young men built a play fort, and the women besieged it. If the women captured the fort and beat and stripped the defenders, this was a good omen. Messengers were sent forth, as far as Gaspé, to make pacts and to bring in allied expeditionary forces.

On June 1 the war canoes set forth from Port Royal, amid cheers and cannonading from the French.

Soon after, Lescarbot accompanied a trading party to the New

Brunswick shore. He had a happy journey, for he was a happy man. He visited the abandoned settlement of Sainte Croix and found it little damaged. "The court was there, full of whole casks, which some ill disposed mariners did burn for their pleasure; which thing when I saw, I did abhor, and I did judge, better than before, that the savages were (being less civilized) more humane and honester men than many that bear the name of Christians, having during three years spared that place, wherein they had not taken so much as a piece of wood, nor salt, which was there in great quantity, as hard as a rock." The party returned in good hap to Port Royal, arriving "at the very point that fair Aurora began to shew her ruddy cheeks upon the top of our woody hills."

Champlain, meanwhile, went with Poutrincourt to the head of the Bay of Fundy in a last vain effort to discover the fabled copper mine. On the tremendous tides of Minas Basin they passed the long rhinoceros snout of Cape Split and landed among the greasy red clay banks of the shore. They found, probably in Parrsboro Harbor, a very old cross covered with moss. Christians had been there long before. Champlain did not know who they were, nor do we.

On July 12 Ralluau arrived in a shallop from Cape Breton with specific orders from de Monts for the return of the colony.

On July 30 the main body of the colonists, including Lescarbot, set off in four small boats to join the *Jonas*. Lescarbot celebrated the departure fittingly, with a Pindaric ode, complete with strophe, antistrophe, and epode, with invocations to Neptune and the Muses, and with an appeal to King Henry to bring religion to the benighted peoples of the New World. He began also, but had to finish and polish at sea, a poetic *Farewell to New France*, which includes a long catalogue of the wild life and products of the country. As poetry it may rasp the sensitive ear; as a catalogue it has its value, and as an expression of the character of Lescarbot, its charm. His gusto is strong in it, his delight in the visible world, in the beauty of hummingbirds, in the rich color and shape of his darling vegetables.

The small boats must have passed, in fog or darkness, Raleigh Gilbert on his way to plant a colony in Maine. He was

From Champlain's original water color in the John Carter Brown Library, Providence.

SPANISH BURNING MEXICAN INDIANS
FOR THE INQUISITION.

From the Cornell University Library.

THE BATTLE OF CHATHAM, 1606.

The explanations are Champlain's own. "A. The place where the French were making the bread. B. The savages surprising the French by discharging arrows at them. C. Frenchmen burned by the Indians. D. French, larded with arrows, fleeing to the boat. [The letter is missing in the picture.] E. Troops of savages burning the Frenchmen they had killed. F. Mountain above the harbor. G. Indian lodges. H. Frenchmen on the shore charging the savages. I. Indians defeated by the French. L. Shallop in which were the French. [The presence of Indians conflicts with the text.] M. Savages around the shallop, who were surprised by our men. N. The Sieur de Poutrincourt's pinnace, O. The Harbor. P. Small stream. Q. Frenchmen fallen dead in the water while trying to reach the off Cape La Have on July 30 and passed Cape Sable on August 4.

The party arrived safe at Canso. There Lescarbot made the acquaintance of a sterling old sea captain named Savalet, from Saint-Jean de Luz. He told Lescarbot that this was his forty-second voyage to these coasts, and that he had a profit of ten thousand francs in his hold. Heaven, or Neptune, had been kind to him.

The main party waited at Canso for Poutrincourt, Champlain, and seven others who remained in Port Royal to await the ripening of their grain.

On August 10 Membertou and his men returned triumphant from their war. Lescarbot has left us a vivid account of it, in the form of a long heroic-epic poem. Nature was wholeheartedly on the side of the Micmacs; at any setback the heavens groaned and the river shores echoed with despair. There are fine descriptions of treachery and countertreachery; *"et trompant, les trompeurs trompeusement il trompe."* There is a long account of the decisive battle, in the best tradition of Ariosto. According to Lescarbot, the war was won with the aid of French muskets, as well as steel-tipped arrows. Are the French, then, to be blamed for first putting firearms in the hands of the natives? Almost certainly not. Such weapons were far too precious to be yielded to the fickle indigenes. Lescarbot is here to be treated with caution. He had all his information at second hand. He wrote his poem to beguile the Atlantic passage:

> *Cherchant dessus Neptune un repos sans repos,*
> *J'ai façonné ces vers au branle de ses flots.*

One knows what poets are when Apollo sends his divine frenzy but not sufficient documentation.

The joy of Membertou and his triumphant returning warriors turned to woe at the news that their French friends were about to leave them. To their wails and pleas Poutrincourt promised that in the following year he would send settlers to dwell there permanently and to teach the Indians the white man's secrets, "which promise did in some sort comfort them."

Now the rear guard delicately harvested their wheat, equal to the best of France, and other specimens of Acadian abundance.

These were carefully packed for transport. Champlain wrapped his precious charts and documents in tarpaulins. On August 11 he bade his last farewell to Port Royal.

On the way to Canso he made an excellent map of the Atlantic shore.

The *Jonas* set sail, with all her passengers, on September 3. She made a good crossing, sighting the Scilly Isles on the 29th. On October 1 she arrived in St. Malo.

Champlain set foot again on French soil after three years and seven months of absence.

What reckoning did he make of these years?

He had made an ample and accurate survey of the coast of New England, New Brunswick, and Nova Scotia, and had drawn up immeasurably the best set of maps made in all this early period. He had explored almost all the area accessible by water. In his three winters he had learned how to combat the worst foes of the adventurer: cold and hunger. He had learned how to disarm the third foe, the savage, by sympathy and understanding.

It is not his habit to tell us what was in his mind. But it is clear that he had come to love this clean, wild, beautiful land, or he would not have volunteered to remain year after year. Naturally he sought wealth there, but his greed for gain was not immoderate. He was more interested in his charts and soundings than in the illusory copper mine. Naturally he would have liked power and authority, but he accepted without a murmur his position as a specialist, a supernumerary, while others ruled the little colony. No, the dominant in his spirit was the desire to know, the westward urge of the explorer.

He was never again to see Port Royal and the Atlantic coasts of Acadia. Let us therefore briefly resume the history of that country and of some of our old companions.

Poutrincourt, on landing in France, repaired promptly to court and laid at the feet of King Henry his offerings of Canadian wheat, rye, barley, and oats, as fine as that of the French garden land of the Beauce. He presented also a dozen live Canada geese, and the King had much joyance therefrom. And a caribou, which soon died miserably in a moat at St. Germain. Poutrincourt asked permission to return to his domain of Port Royal, to fulfill his promise to old Membertou, and to answer an obscure need in his heart. But there were many delays and difficulties. Before he could set out, Champdoré, the pigheaded pilot, captained a trip for de Monts in 1608. Champdoré found Membertou serenely waiting in Port Royal. The Indians had harvested the French grain and filled seven hogsheads for themselves and one that they had saved for their white friends. Champdoré explored some part of the interior of New Brunswick and returned with a profitable cargo of furs.

Poutrincourt, meanwhile, had difficulty in obtaining backing. Against his will he made a bargain with Queen Marie that, for a handsome sum, he would take out two Jesuits. He was long delayed, and finally sailed in 1610, giving his Jesuits the slip but enlisting a zealous parish priest. They arrived at Port Royal in June and were ecstatically received by Membertou and his people. The priest worked with such miraculous zeal that he converted and baptized Membertou and twenty others within three weeks of his arrival. This was the beginning of the great missionary work of France in the New World. A somewhat clouded beginning, indeed, for the conversion was far too speedy to be quite regular or convincing. It was designed, apparently, to prove that the Jesuits were as little needed as they were wanted. The Jesuits arrived, none the less, in the following year and found that the mass baptisms had had no effect on the baptized.

A noble patroness had bought for the Jesuits from de Monts all of North America from Florida to the St. Lawrence, except for Poutrincourt's fief at Port Royal. How the Jesuits labored and suffered, how they colonized Mount Desert Island in Maine, how they were wiped out by Governor Argall of Virginia, is a wonderful story, but it may not be told here.

Poutrincourt and his two sons maintained themselves in Port Royal until 1613, when their settlement was blotted out by the English from Virginia. Most of the survivors were brought back to France in the following year; a few lingered precariously in Acadia. Poutrincourt was killed in France, gallantly fighting for his King, in 1615. His son Biencourt, who best spoke the language of the Micmacs and best knew their ways, tried in vain to promote new colonizations. He died in 1623.[3]

Young Pontgravé returned to Port Royal with Biencourt. He got into trouble, fled to the Indians of New Brunswick, and lived happily their life. He is one of the first of the *coureurs du bois*, the Frenchmen who found savagery more congenial than civilization.

The Indians at length discovered that the conveniences of European culture—the knives, kettles, and wine—must be paid for, and not in furs alone. The French brought rats, which multiplied and upset the economy of the wild, attacking the Indians' provisions, thieving in their wigwams, destroying dead game left in the snow. The French brought also terrible diseases: tuberculosis, measles, dysentery, quinsy. Even in 1613 the Jesuits noted that the natives were dying off, the population decreasing.

Good Membertou died of dysentery, apparently in 1611. Devoutest of the converts, he made an edifying end and was given a solemn Christian burial. "This Sagamore was in every respect a great man," said the Jesuits, "not only in the opinion of his own people but in ours; and the good God seems to have raised this man's excellent nature high above the ordinary character of the Canadians, in order that He might gather him to Himself as the first fruits in righteousness of his race."

And Lescarbot, our sprightly Lescarbot, on returning to France immediately set to work on his book. It appeared in 1609 and ran through several editions. In that year he was briefly jailed, being involved in some anti-Jesuit agitation. He spent two years in a minor diplomatic post in Switzerland and wrote an agreeable book on that country. He married in 1619, and six years later he was in the court in a dispute about his wife's property.[4] Thus he disregarded his own advice: to flee the vanities and chicaneries of civilization and to seek peace in the bosom of nature.

[3] He has often been confused with a cousin of the same name, who was director of a fashionable riding academy in Paris. See Adrian Huguet: *Jean de Poutrincourt* (*Mém. de la Soc. des Antiquaires de Picardie*, XLIV, 1932), 470 *et seq.*

[4] Huguet: *Jean de Poutrincourt*, 468 *et seq.*; P. de l'Estoile: *Mémoires-Journaux* (Paris, 1881), X, 88; *Catalogue des Factums* (Paris, 1902), VI, 238.

His book is now reckoned one of the classics of exploration. In its time it had its own effect. It portrayed the life of the colonist in pleasing colors; it laid down a program for the development of a French overseas empire, to be built not on mines nor serfdom, but on the patient labor of French peasants tilling new and fertile fields. This was the program that Champlain strove to put into effect, the program that the French government later adopted, and that lies at the base of all the greatness of French Canada. Lescarbot also pictured for his French readers the Indian as a man of shrewd wit and fundamentally virtuous instincts, whose friendship could be won for France, whose soul must be won for God. This picture in French minds went far to support the magnificent missionary effort of the seventeenth century. His picture of the noble savage lingered on, to reappear in Rousseau, in Chateaubriand, and the romantics. In its place it lingers on today.

CHAPTER IX

The Fourth Voyage—Quebec

WHEN IN OCTOBER 1607 Champlain saw the defiant walls and the gray clustering houses of St. Malo, his heart was filled with the choking joy of the homing man. But he had surely the normal experience of the emotional traveler ready to embrace his mother country. The mean exactions of boatmen and porters, the perfunctory interest of acquaintances in his far adventures, their absorption with local politics and scandal, checked his effusions and replaced them by resentment. Even the little satisfactions of civilization were somehow unsatisfying. A French dinner was not so good as he had imagined it to be. Perhaps, like Cabeza de Vaca emerging from his eight years in the wilderness, he quitted his soft bed to sleep on the ground.[1]

The crowding of men in their narrow towns made him uneasy. The Indians had been filthy enough, God knows; but their filth was somehow less revolting than that of city dwellers, huddling in their foul alleyways, half street, half sewer. His fine new clothes were splashed with the reeking sulphurous mud of Paris, which seemed to burn what it touched. In Canada he had learned to drink pure water; if he demanded water in the capital he was given a rank fluid drawn in buckets from amid the floating offal of the Seine.

[1] Morris Bishop: *The Odyssey of Cabeza de Vaca*, 153.

1 2 4

He strolled in the garden of the Tuileries on its open days, in the fashionable Cours-la-Reine, which has become the Champs-Elysées. He idled on the Pont-Neuf, watching the perpetual shows of the charlatans and mountebanks. He noted with approval that the curled gallants wore broad-brimmed beaver hats, though the bourgeois still clung to his hood. He stopped in at the fashionable hatter's, Costar's, "The Sign of the Striped Ass," on the Pont Notre-Dame, thumbed his beavers, and was respectfully listened to. But in the throngs of Paris he saw no friendly faces. He was alone, more alone than he had ever been in the endless wild.

He had been too long away. He was a stranger in his own land. His secret love now went to his own New France, serene and cold, treacherous and lovely. His heart was given to Canada, and there all the best of his life was to lie.

His first act was to seek out de Monts, to lay before him his report, with its set of precious maps and charts. He found his chief in deep discouragement. De Monts had lost over 100,000 livres in his enterprises and was on the edge of ruin.[2] Under the new system of free trade he could think no more of planting colonies.

Champlain summoned up all his eloquence. The settlement in Acadia, as he had thought from the first, was a mistake. In that country were few furs, few minerals, and, as he had proved, no entry by water to the interior, no passage to the South Sea. The thing to do was to return to the St. Lawrence, the great channel of the fur trade.

Now here was the idea. The French regularly set up their summer trading post at Tadoussac. They forced the Indians from the far lakes to make a round trip of two thousand miles in their birch-bark canoes. The Indians naturally charged high for the difficulties and dangers of transport. The thing to do was for a company of traders to establish a permanent warehouse and colony upriver. Where? At the strong point of Quebec. The colony would be a fort to protect the river against the raids of the terrible Iroquois. Thence the company's traders could go in summer up to the great rapids, get the first choice

---

[2] *Champlain's Works*, III, 324. The sum seems enormous. Perhaps it is an error for 10,000 livres.

of furs, buy them cheap, and bring them downriver in security.

Yes, but a colony would be expensive. Our monopoly is gone. Would we not simply pay to open the river to all the interlopers, the shysters, who will bear no part in our expenditures?

Let us go and see King Henry personally. He will receive us, old companions of his wars. Perhaps he does not know what Sully and the Council have been doing in his name.

Champlain and de Monts called upon the King and were warmly greeted. After, no doubt, some happy reminiscence of the wars and a bottle of white Gascon *piquepoult*, they laid their complaint, and their proposal, before the monarch.

King Henry was much interested. He had observed that the Dutch East Indies Company was paying dividends of seventy-five per cent; that the English had established lucrative trading posts in India, and that they were now preparing a settlement in Virginia. He agreed that France too should have its colonies. He regretted the injustice done by his Council in canceling de Monts's monopoly. But *que voulez-vous*, the commercial pressures were strong—

In the end he proposed a compromise. He would restore the monopoly, but for one year only, for the season of 1608. In return de Monts and Champlain would found their permanent colony in Canada.

Duly, on January 7, 1608, the King published an edict annulling the action of his Council, extending de Monts's monopoly of the fur trade for one year, and warning all infringers that their vessels and cargoes would be confiscated.

De Monts immediately set to work. Somehow he raised the money to equip three vessels. One, under Champdoré, went back to Port Royal and the New Brunswick coast. One was under the command of our old friend Pontgravé. His orders were to spend the summer trading in the St. Lawrence and to return in the autumn. The third ship, probably the *Don de Dieu*, Captain Couillard, carried Champlain and a little band of artisans with supplies for a northern winter, trade goods, and plenty of guns and ammunition.

Champlain was appointed lieutenant of M. de Monts. This,

we may notice, was his first recorded experience in command.
He had passed his fortieth year.

Pontgravé sailed from Honfleur on April 5, and Champlain
followed him on the thirteenth. He made a good crossing, and
anchored off Tadoussac on June 3. He lowered the longboat to
go ashore. On the way he met a shallop steered by a Basque
sailor, with Pontgravé's pilot, Captain Testu, amidships. He
had the look of a prisoner.

The pilot poured forth an angry tale. Pontgravé, arriving at
Tadoussac, had found a Basque whaler busily trading for furs
with the Indians, contrary to all the King's orders. When Pontgravé commanded him to cease and desist, the Basque's answer
was to open fire with cannon and musket. Pontgravé and two
of his men were severely wounded, and one was killed. The
Basques then boarded his vessel, and carried off all his cannon
and muskets. They would return the armament, they said, when
they were ready to sail for France, for, King's orders or no
King's orders, they were going to buy furs.

"And what are you doing here?" said Champlain to the
Basque.

"I come on behalf of our master, Captain Darache. We have
no quarrel with you. We want only assurances from you that
you will not interfere with us."

"I will say nothing until I have seen Pontgravé," said
Champlain.

The messenger seemed conciliatory. "We'll be glad to help
you out in any way we can, if you're reasonable." There was
a good deal of talk, says Champlain.

He went ashore and found Pontgravé, very sick, in the shack
used for a trading post. Pontgravé, who had had experience of
Basque pugnacity, said that if Champlain's ship entered the
harbor, there would be a battle, and that one or both ships
would be put out of commission, and there would be an end to
any hope of establishing a colony upriver.

Moderation and compromise were congenial to Champlain's
nature. He paid a formal call on Captain Darache. "After a good
deal of discussion, I made peace between Pontgravé and him,
and made him promise that he would undertake nothing against

Pontgravé, nor against the King's interest nor that of the Sieur de Monts. That should they do the contrary, I would regard my promise as null and void." The argument as to the furs the Basques had taken would be referred to the French courts on their return.

It was a victory for the turbulent Basques. They went on trading, little concerned about what the French courts would do to them. They would sell their furs long before any legal action could be taken. What if some day a court should render a decision against them? Let the bailiffs try to catch a Basque whaler!

Champlain let them have their victory. He was more concerned with establishing his colony than with enforcing de Monts's monopoly. He was slow to wrath, no hothead, tenacious of his essential purpose.

He set his carpenters to work fitting out the thirteen-ton pinnace for the journey up the St. Lawrence. In the meantime he went some distance up the Saguenay, finding the country most disagreeable. He heard interesting tales of the Indian tribes who inhabited the far north, near the salt sea, forty or fifty days' journey distant. "I have often desired to explore up the river, but have been unable to do so without the natives, who have been unwilling that I or any of our people should go with them."

He set out from Tadoussac in the pinnace on the last day of June and arrived at Quebec on July 3, 1608. This, then, is our historic date for the founding of Quebec, the first settlement north of Florida which has been continuously occupied (for there are gaps in the history of Port Royal, and Jamestown, Virginia, was long abandoned).

Champlain selected as his home some shelving land a little above the water's edge, protected in the rear by towering cliffs. His "Habitation" stood approximately on the site of the present church of Notre-Dame des Victoires, by a quiet little square in the old town. The alignment of his structures may be recognized, vestigially, in that of the rue St. Pierre and the rue Notre-Dame. The promenaders of Dufferin Terrace, the tourists at the windows of the Château Frontenac, look down on the history of three and a half centuries.

Champlain put his men to work and drove them hard. Some cleared the ground and dug cellars and ditches. Some sawed planks for the first building, the warehouse. The sailors went back to Tadoussac in the pinnace to bring another load of supplies.

The workmen, sluggish with long idleness at sea, grumbled in the summer heat of the St. Lawrence valley. They were tormented by flies by day, by mosquitoes at night. "No skin is proof against their sting, and everyone pays his blood as tribute," says a Jesuit Father. "I have seen persons so swollen after being stung by them that one would think they would lose their eyes, which can scarcely be seen."

Leader of the grumblers was Jean Duval, locksmith. We have met him before, if you remember. He was in the scapegrace crew that came out with Poutrincourt in 1606, and he was one of the unruly five who disobeyed orders and remained on shore on Cape Cod and were attacked by Indians. He was the only one of the five who survived, though he was wounded by an arrow. After a winter in Port Royal and a winter in France he signed on for another year in the New World. Probably he had good reason for leaving his native country. He was a man of violence, and a troublemaker.

Duval sounded out four of his companions whom he knew to be of like kidney to himself. One was Antoine Natel, another locksmith; the profusion of locksmiths in young Canada is extraordinary. They should rise and cast off tyranny, said Duval. After corrupting the other workmen, one by one, they would give a false alarm some night and shoot Champlain as he came out of his hut. And then they would make overtures to the Basques and Spaniards at Tadoussac, and sell them the new fort, and go back to Europe very rich. (So there were Spaniards too at Tadoussac! What price de Monts's monopoly!)

Duval bound his fellows by great oaths; the first who should divulge a word would be stabbed.

But while the malcontents were working on their mates, the worthy pilot, Captain Testu, arrived from Tadoussac in the pinnace. Antoine Natel, no longer able to bear the weight of his secret, broke down and confessed all to the captain. Testu took Champlain into the woods and told him the whole story.

Champlain summoned Natel, "all trembling with fear lest I should do him some harm. I reassured him and told him not to be afraid; that he was in a place of safety and that I forgave him all that he had done with the others, provided he told the whole truth on every point, and the reason which had moved him to do this. He said there was no reason, save that they had imagined that, in handing over the place to the Basques or Spaniards they would become very rich, and that they did not wish to go back to France."

Champlain sent him back to his work. He then arranged that a trusty sailor on the pinnace should invite the conspirators on board to enjoy two bottles of wine, which Champlain provided. At ten in the evening, when the plotters were carousing below decks, Champlain and the faithful sailors appeared, well armed, and commanded them to surrender. Taken by surprise, they dared not stir. The sailors bound them well, with sailors' knots.

Champlain then roused his whole company and told them that he would forgive all if they would tell the entire truth about the affair. While the smith made handcuffs for the accused, Champlain took depositions from all his colonists. "They were very glad, according to their statements; for they were living in constant fear of one another and particularly of the four scoundrels who had misled them. Since then they have lived in peace, satisfied, according to their deposition, with the treatment they here received."

Pontgravé, his ship's officers, and even a part of his crew were summoned from Tadoussac to help judge the case.

"We had the prisoners confronted [by their accusers], and all that had been stated in the depositions was reaffirmed, without any denial on the part of the prisoners, who confessed that they had acted wickedly, and deserved punishment, unless mercy should be shown them; and they cursed Jean Duval for being the first who had led them into this conspiracy as soon as they sailed from France. The said Duval was unable to say anything, except that he deserved death; and that everything contained in the depositions was true, begging for pity for himself and for the others who had sided with him in his wicked intentions."

The jury of ship's officers and sailors deliberated with Champlain and Pontgravé. They voted to put Duval to death, as a

punishment and as an example. The three others were condemned to be hanged, but their sentence was suspended. They
were to be sent back to France in irons and turned over to the
Sieur de Monts, "to receive fuller justice, according as he might
decide, with all the papers and the sentence upon Jean Duval
before him."

So Duval was strangled and hanged at Quebec, and his head
was placed on a pike and set up in the highest spot of the fort.
"He did not have the patience to wait his normal time, but
must needs gain Heaven by scaling the walls," sighs Lescarbot.

It would be interesting to know what the Indians made of
this peculiar behavior of the Christians.

In this affair Champlain acted with the utmost forbearance.
If he had hanged his prisoners after a summary court-martial
no one would have blamed him; indeed, he admits that his loyal
workmen were discontented, fearing that he would forgive the
criminals, who would wreak vengeance on the taletellers. But
Champlain insisted on something in the nature of a jury trial.
By this means he protected himself against protests at home,
and against the reproach of his own conscience.

He demonstrates once more his prudence, his ponderation.
He was a lover of moderate means and a hater of bloodshed.
And yet one may feel in his actions a certain hesitancy, a certain
reluctance to act with decision and speed.

On September 18 Pontgravé left Quebec with the three
prisoners in irons. It appears that they were eventually pardoned. Champlain remained with twenty-three men. Now that
the troubling element was gone, all set to work with a will to
make their winter home.

This home Champlain called his "Habitation." It consisted
of three huddling buildings, each nineteen by thirteen feet and
two stories high, and a single-storied warehouse of the same
ground dimensions, with cellar. There was also a separate dove-
cot. Around the continuous wall of the buildings, above the
ground floor, ran an exterior gallery for defense. Outside the
wall was a moat with drawbridge; outside the moat, raised
platforms for cannon; and then an exterior palisade. Beyond
the palisade were the gardens. Atop the structure were a great
sundial and a flagstaff, flying the lilies of France.

When his buildings were tight against the weather, Champlain put some of his men to clearing the gardens and to planting wheat, rye, and native grapevines.

The friendly Montagnais gaped and wondered.

The Indians were very busy from mid-September to mid-October catching eels, which resorted here in incredible numbers. The women summarily cleaned and smoked the surplus for winter use. This is the single example of Montagnais providence. When the run of eels ended, they went off for two months to hunt beaver.

On November 18 a heavy fall of snow came down.

In this month a sailor and Antoine Natel, the repentant locksmith, died of dysentery. The cause, opines Champlain, was eating badly cooked eels.

In mid-December the Indians returned. They had caught few beaver, because of high water. They settled down to an exclusive diet of smoked eel.

Before the end of January the eels were finished. Famine came. The Indians ate their dogs, though commonly the Montagnais had no liking for dog meat. They gnawed at their moccasins, at their fur robes. The children died first, as their mother's milk dried up. (The lactation period of Indian mothers in this grim country was likely to be three years.) But the Indians bore their familiar sufferings with wonderful fortitude. They would lie sick in the snow for hours, uncomplaining.

In February "some Indians made their appearance on the other side of the river, and shouted to us to go to their aid, but this was out of our power, on account of the large amount of ice which was floating down the river. So hungry were these poor wretches, that being at their wits' end, they, men, women, and children, resolved to die or cross the river, in the hope that I would succor them in their dire need. Accordingly having taken this resolution, the men and women seized the children and got into their canoes, thinking they would reach our shore by an opening in the ice which the wind had made; but no sooner were they in the middle of the river than their canoes were caught between the ice floes and broke into a thousand pieces. They maneuvered so well that they jumped with their

children, whom the women were carrying on their backs, upon
a large block of ice. While they were on it, we could hear them
screaming so much that it was pitiful; for they expected nothing
less than death. But fortune favored these poor wretches so much
that a large ice floe struck the side of the one upon which they
stood with such force that it threw them upon the land. They,
seeing such a favorable turn of events, went ashore with as
much joy as they ever experienced, in spite of the famine they
had endured.

"They came to our settlement so thin and emaciated that they
looked like skeletons, most of them being unable to stand. I
was astonished at their appearance, and at the way they had
crossed the river, seeing them so weak and faint.

"I ordered bread and beans to be given to them. They could
not wait for these to be cooked before eating them. To cover
their wigwams I lent them also some bark, which other Indians
had given me. As they were making their wigwams they
noticed some carrion which about two months previously I had
thrown out to attract foxes. This carrion was a sow and a dog
which had lain there through the hot and cold weather. When
the weather was mild it stank so strongly that one could not
stay near it. Nevertheless they took it and carried it off to their
wigwam, where they devoured it half cooked, and never did
meat seem to them to have a better taste. I sent two or three
men to warn them not to eat any of it, if they did not wish to
die. As these men came near to the Indians' wigwams, they
smelt such a stench from this half cooked carrion, of which each
of them had a piece in his hand, that they almost vomited, so
that they did not stay there long. These poor wretches finished
their banquet.

"I did the best I could to furnish them with supplies, but it
was little in comparison with their large numbers. In a month
they would have eaten up all our provisions, such hearty eaters
are they. For when they have food, they lay nothing by, but
eat their fill day and night, and then starve. And they did
another thing as disagreeable as the first. I had had a bitch hung
in a tree-top to serve as a bait for martens and birds of prey;
and the thing interested me, inasmuch as the carcass was often
attacked by them. These savages went to the tree, and not being

able to climb up it on account of their weakness, they felled it, and at once carried off the dog, which was now only skin and bones, with the head stinking and rotten, and immediately devoured it."

Here was hunger such as the French had never conceived. It must have caused them a thrill of terror, at the thought how precariously they were supported by their own supplies from France.

The Indians' hunger was so needless! All summer they reveled in abundance of fish and game, but they laid almost nothing by. "I consider," says Champlain, "that if anyone were to show them how to live, and how to till the soil, and other things, they would learn very well; for there are many of them who have good judgment, and reply pointedly to the questions put to them. But they have bad points: they are revengeful and awful liars, people whom one must not trust too far, but rather judiciously, and with force in one's hand. They promise readily, but perform badly. They are people the majority of whom, so far as I have been able to see, respect no law, but have plenty of false beliefs. I asked them what sort of ceremonies they used in praying to their God. They told me that they had no other than this, that each one prayed to God in his heart, just as it suited him. That is why there is no law among them, and why they do not know what it is to pray to and worship God, living as they do like brute beasts. I believe they would soon be brought to be good Christians, if one were to live in their country, as the majority of them desire."

Champlain observed the natives with interest. He learned of their trial-marriage system: a girl, at fourteen or fifteen, tries out a series of suitors, and after half a dozen years, settles on a husband, with whom she lives chastely. He watched the curious burial ceremonies. They hung their dead, frozen, to trees, to be buried in the spring. He found exasperating their faith in dreams, devil-sent visions. A dream of the enemy would send the whole band clamoring in the night to the Habitation's walls. Champlain would send out a few men to search the woods, and would then lecture the Indians on their folly. "But these admonitions were of small avail, and they used to say that we knew better than they did how to protect ourselves in every way, and

that in time if we were to come and live in their country they
would be able to learn these."

In his description of the primitive Montagnais, Champlain's
kindly spirit breathes. He pitied them; their trust moved him,
and their appeals for his aid and mercy. He was fond of them,
as one is fond of children, excusing their perversities, pardoning
their candid filth. He felt even a paternal affection. Indeed, who
was there for him to love? He had hardly seen his parents for
years. There was no woman waiting in France, and no children
of his own getting. His need to love found its outlet among
these simple people of the wild.

How did he communicate with the Montagnais? How did he
question them on such subjects as their belief in immortality?
Their Algonquin tongue is appallingly difficult, as the Jesuits
discovered. (Their Latin was child's play in comparison.) Champlain had brought no interpreter; he himself was a poor linguist.
I suspect that he learned a smattering of recurring words, as
the Montagnais learned a smattering of French, and that he
developed to a high degree the language of sign and gesture.
He had also two bright boys with him: Étienne Brûlé, about
fifteen, and Nicolas Marsolet, a little older. Without method,
without labor, they picked up the language. They adapted themselves to native life, joined the Indians in hunting moose through
the snow, in fishing through the ice with nets. They learned to
bear cold and hunger stoically, to endure the reek of the wigwams, the acrid smoke, the indiscriminate dogs. They learned
how to follow a true course through strange forests, how to
sleep through a freezing night and not freeze, how to make
slitted wooden goggles against snow blindness. They adopted
native habits, like clapping their mouths as a sign of astonishment. They adopted also some of the natives' less commendable
customs, in the easy promiscuity of the Indian youth.

The winter wore on. If it was a normal Quebec winter (some
were abnormal: the season of 1646-7 was so mild that it hardly
froze all winter), the snow lay four or five feet deep about the
palisade; during cold spells the trees split with a sound like
musketshots. The wine, the ink, and the medicines froze. A
colonist, a little later, lost all the skin off his tongue by in-
cautiously licking the snow from his axe.

Champlain surely filled some idle hours in sketching the Canadian flora and fauna, the Indians, the white landscape. Once a sketcher always a sketcher. Nothing of his work in Canada survives, save in the form of engravings in his published works. How wonderful it would be to happen some day on a bundle of Champlain's water colors, forgotten in some ancient Norman attic!

In February the scurvy came. Eighteen of the twenty-two men contracted it, and of the eighteen, ten died. Three more died of dysentery, in addition to the two dead in October. The surgeon died. Every man was down with one disease or the other.

Champlain was apparently smitten with the scurvy for the first time in four years. He pondered upon this chief menace to colonization in the north. "It is my view," he says, "that it comes altogether from eating too much salt food and vegetables which heat the blood and corrupt the inward parts." He noted that an Indian who spent the winter in the fort changed his diet to salt meat, caught the scurvy, and died. Had Champlain stopped there, we should applaud his etiology. However, he adds other contributing causes: the winter, which corrupts the blood, and the infectious vapors of the earth. He observed that the disease attacked the clean as well as the dirty. The only cure he could propose was good bread and fresh meat.

Had he then no fresh meat? You may have noticed that he had put out a dead sow as fox bait. Lescarbot says outright that de Monts sent him some cows, "but for want of some village housewife who understood taking care of them, they let the greater part die in giving birth to their calves. Which shows how necessary a woman is in a house, and I cannot understand why so many people slight them, although they cannot do without them. For my part, I shall always believe that in any settlement whatsoever, nothing will be accomplished without the presence of women."

Cows? And calves? Then there was a bull? Cows would have been trouble enough in a thirteen-ton pinnace; but a bull? And how about fodder for the winter? No, I think Lescarbot was misinformed.

Before long the settlers learned to slaughter animals when

winter set in hard, and to hang the frozen meat in an icy cellar. This was the system of northern Indians and Eskimos, the system of commerce today. We shall hear little more of scurvy.

On April 8 the snow suddenly melted. Trees and bushes began busily to put forth their green. The survivors nibbled at new shoots, answering their cravings. Little by little the scurvy disappeared.

On June 5 a shallop arrived, with the Sieur des Marais, son-in-law of Pontgravé. He had hurried up from Tadoussac, where Pontgravé lay safe in port, fresh from France.

Of the twenty-four men who had stood on the shore in Quebec and waved farewell in the previous September, eight remained, and four of these were still tottering with illness. The eight were the pilot Laroute; the two boys Étienne Brûlé and Nicolas Marsolet; and four others whose names we do not know. And Champlain—hardy, indomitable Champlain.

CHAPTER X

The Fourth Voyage—Lake Champlain

On June 7, 1609, Champlain left Quebec to consult with Pont-gravé at Tadoussac.

The news from France was not too bad. De Monts's monop-oly had expired, but negotiations were forward to bring him some sort of compensation for his pioneer work. He had had a good year in 1608. He was ready to continue his support of the Quebec colony, unless things took a turn for the worse. He ordered Champlain to return at the end of the summer to report.

"And now," said Pontgravé, "what is to be our plan for the summer?"

This, I conclude from Champlain's course of action, was his reply:

"If there is to be no monopoly, we can best serve de Monts and the company by forestalling the free, unlicensed traders with the Indians. We have already gone far in this direction by establishing our permanent post in Quebec. The next thing to do is to push farther upstream, to meet the Indians from the interior nearer to their hunting grounds, and thus get the pick of the furs. The obvious place is the great rapids, where the Ottawa joins the St. Lawrence.

"The trouble, of course, is that this region is too exposed to the marauding Iroquois from the south. As we haven't enough

men to protect our Indian clients from raids, the thing to do is
to take the offensive, to make a raid into the hostile land. A
dozen men with muskets would be the equal of an Iroquois army.
We could teach them a lesson they would remember. And I
would have a chance to see that country, of which I hear most
interesting stories."

"Is it necessary, do you think, to take sides? Wouldn't it be
better to remain neutral, to keep out of the Indian quarrels, and
to buy from both parties?"

"No, that wouldn't work. The Indians don't understand
neutrality. We have been telling them that we are their friends
and that we want to help them. They understand this to mean
that we are going to help them in their wars. We have already
promised to do so, and the Indians expect people to keep their
promises. And it's in our interest to do just that. The Algonquins and the Hurons control the fur supply. The Iroquois, in
their warmer country, have only second-rate furs. There is no
point in our making concessions to them."

"Then it is in our interest to—ah—put them out of business?"

"No. We don't want to destroy them or enslave them or take
over their territory. All we want is peace, so that the Indians
from the west can bring in their furs without loss and without
fear. If we could make peace by a treaty, that would be the best
thing. But if we made a treaty, we would have to buy off the
Iroquois somehow, and we can't afford to do that. Anyhow, I
doubt if we could make a treaty. This war has been going on
for generations, and our fellows seem to rather enjoy it. I don't
think we could make any treaty that would hold. The only thing
to do is to back up our own side and give the Iroquois a good
scare."

"But isn't there some danger in provoking these fighting
Iroquois?"

"Possibly. Still, they are our enemies now, because they are
the enemies of our friends. They would have attacked Quebec
already if it weren't so far from their range. But we needn't
worry about the Iroquois danger. What we have to fear is our
friends. Look at our situation a couple of months ago. We were
eight white men, alone in Canada, all of us sick. Suppose one
of the Indians had had a dream about us; they might have

burned the Habitation to the ground or tomahawked us all in our beds. Or suppose that a medicine man had got jealous of us. Or simply suppose that the local Indians should get the idea that we are favoring their enemies or that we don't keep our promises. Our lives wouldn't be worth a sou. No, the only course for us is to make an alliance with our friends and to keep the terms of the alliance."

Such, no doubt, was the conversation that took place in the cabin of Pontgravé's ship at Tadoussac.

Champlain returned to Quebec in a shallop with twenty men. He paused there briefly and continued upstream. At Batiscan, seventy miles on, he found an encampment of two or three hundred Indians, Algonquins and Hurons. "These were on their way to Quebec, to help us in our discoveries in the country of the Iroquois, with whom they are in mortal conflict, and they spare nothing belonging to these enemies."

This was Champlain's first meeting with the Hurons, who are to play a great part in his life.

The word "Huron" is French, not Indian. The first French who saw them were struck by the ridge of coarse black hair they wore on their skulls. *"Quels Hurons!* What wild boar's heads!" cried the French. The casual remark clung to the race forever, and so came to be written large in the geography of North America.

The Hurons were Iroquoians, not Algonquins. They were a handsome race, taller than the French. They were markedly intelligent, possessing the largest cranial index of any Indian tribe. A missionary said that they were the aristocrats of Canada, the Algonquins the bourgeois, the Montagnais the peasantry.

They first appear in our history when Cartier found them on the sites of Quebec and Montreal. They were at that time engaged in a permanent war with their kinsmen the Iroquois Five Nations. By 1603 they had migrated to their Huronia, in the southeast corner of Georgian Bay. Whether they removed from choice or under pressure is not clear.

In Huronia they became a great rich race of traders. They sold corn, tobacco, and fish to other tribes, and bought furs, which they sold to the French or to intermediaries for European

goods. In the early years of the seventeenth century they built
a great trading empire in the fastnesses of the northern forests.
Early in the spring they would meet the hunting Indians from
Lake Superior and the west and buy their furs. They would
then set off to meet the French. There were three routes. The
easiest, the southernmost, was across Lake Nipissing, down the
Ottawa to the rapids, down the St. Lawrence to Tadoussac.
This is a mere thousand miles, with about fifty portages. The
middle route turned north at Mattawa, continued through a
maze of lakes to the St. Maurice, and down that river to its
junction with the St. Lawrence at Trois Rivières. The northern-
most route took them as far as Lake Mattagami, only a hundred
miles or so from James Bay, then over a cruel portage to the
streams flowing into Lac St. Jean, and so down the Saguenay
to Tadoussac. On their way they exchanged various products,
Indian and French, for the furs of the nomad hunting tribes.
The furs they sold at handsome profit to the French fishermen
and traders. Loaded with a fresh supply of French trade goods,
they would then embark, by the southern route, for Georgian
Bay, arriving home in the autumn.

All this effort, fatigue, and danger, this mighty journey of
two or three thousand miles, to carry a few hundred pounds of
furs to the trading post! Think of the labor, in driving the canoe
over stormy lakes and up turbulent rivers, in carrying the
bundled furs through the tangled growth of wild watersheds!
Think of the hunger, for these merchants could spare little time
for hunting and fishing and little cargo space for supplies; and
in the spring they would find few roots and berries by the way.
How often must their frail canoes have been wrecked in boiling
rapids! And how often their entire precious burden swept away!

In this year of 1609 the Huron trading empire was still
a-building. But Champlain knew well the commercial importance of the race. He was glad to welcome their representatives
and to entertain them, as from time immemorial merchants have
entertained visiting customers.

There were solemn greetings and exchanges of presents.
Champlain smoked in ritual silence with the chiefs, Ochateguin
of the Hurons, Iroquet of the Algonquins. After proper reflection Iroquet made a loud harangue to his people. His son, he

said, had come ten months since to visit Champlain, and Champlain had then told him that he and Pontgravé wished to help the northern tribes against their enemies. Iroquet had therefore asked the Hurons to meet the Christians, whom they had never seen. These Hurons were skilled in war and full of courage, and knew the country and rivers of the Iroquois country. And now he proposed that they should all visit the wonderful house of the white men at Quebec, and should then set off on the warpath together. "They also asked as a token of great friendship and rejoicing to have muskets and arquebuses fired off, whereat they would be much pleased. I did so and they uttered loud shouts of astonishment, especially those who had never heard or seen the like."

So, surely to Champlain's annoyance (like the annoyance of other merchants entertaining clients), the whole party repaired to Quebec, and there feasted and danced for five or six days. At length the war party set out for the land of the Iroquois. With Champlain in his shallop were Desmarais, Pontgravé's son-in-law, the pilot La Route, and nine men. They ascended the bountiful river, Champlain observing details he had overlooked on his journey of 1603. They traversed broad Lac St. Pierre and arrived at the mouth of the River of the Iroquois, the Richelieu, which debouches into the St. Lawrence at the present Sorel. Here there was a dispute; a number of the Indians went back to their own country with the goods they had obtained by barter. Why should they risk the profits in hand?

The Richelieu was broad and bland. The Indians assured Champlain that in his shallop he could sail up it to the Lake of the Iroquois. (Perhaps there was a misunderstanding; or perhaps they were tempting him on.) But when Champlain reached the roaring rapids at Chambly, he found no passage for his shallop and no possibility of cutting a road for it through the dense woods. "I was particularly sorry to return without seeing a very large lake, filled with beautiful islands, and a large, beautiful region near the lake, where they had represented to me their enemies lived. Having thought it over well, I decided to proceed thither in order to carry out my promise and also to fulfill my desire." The "desire" is the lust of the explorer, to see the yet unseen, first of any men of his race.

Champlain called for volunteers. Two stepped forward; their names we do not know. The others quailed at the prospect of the adventure; "their noses bled," says Champlain. He let them go, sending them back to Quebec in the shallop.

Now (it was July 12) the sincere warriors, white and red, held a review above the Chambly Rapids. There were twenty-four canoes with sixty Indians, a mingling of Hurons, Montagnais, and Ottawa Algonquins. Champlain and his two Frenchmen carried, for all their baggage, their heavy arquebuses, powder, match, and shot. They wore steel corselets, half armor. (You may see an authentic example in the museum at Fort Ticonderoga.)

Champlain had an old soldier's interest in the routine of the warpath. On making camp, the Indians built wigwams and felled trees for a barricade. The riverbank was left open, to permit escape by canoe. The chief sent three canoes upriver to scout for evidence of the enemy. "All night long they rely upon the explorations of these scouts, and it is a very bad custom; for sometimes they are surprised in their sleep by their enemies, who club them before they have time to rise and defend themselves. Realizing this, I pointed out to them the mistake they were making, and said that they ought to keep watch as they had seen us do every night, and have men posted to listen and see whether they might perceive anything, and not live as they were doing like silly creatures. They told me that they could not stay awake, and that they worked enough during the day when hunting."

So these Indians were at the same time stoic and soft, grim-purposed and capricious, cunning and silly, like the rest of us.

On the march, a troop of scouts went first, watching for the marks on trees which were messages from friends or indications of enemies. The main body followed; parties of hunters fanned out on the flanks.

Every night the *pilotois*, the medicine man, was called upon for an augury. He built a wigwam covered with beaver-skin. "When it is made, he gets inside so that he is completely hidden; then he seizes one of the poles of the tent and shakes it, whilst he mumbles between his teeth certain words, with which he declares he is invoking the devil, who appears to him in the form

of a stone and tells him whether his friends will come upon their
enemies and kill many of them. This pilotois will lie flat upon
the ground, without moving, merely speaking to the devil, and
suddenly he will rise to his feet, speaking and writhing so that
he is all in a perspiration, though stark naked. The whole tribe
will be about the tent sitting on their buttocks like monkeys.
They often told me that the shaking of the tent which I saw was
caused by the devil and not by the man inside, although I saw
the contrary. . . . I often pointed out to them that what they
did was pure folly, and that they ought not to believe in such
things."

In accordance with the forecasts of the oracle, "the chiefs
take sticks a foot long, one for each man, and indicate by others
somewhat longer their leaders. Then they go into the wood,
and level off a place five or six feet square, where the headman,
as sergeant-major, arranges all these sticks as to him seems
best. Then he calls all his companions, who approach fully
armed, and he shows them the rank and order which they are
to observe when they fight with the enemy. This all these
Indians regard attentively, and notice the figure made with
these sticks by their chief. And afterwards they return from that
place and begin to arrange themselves in the order in which
they have seen these sticks. Then they mix themselves up and
again put themselves in proper order, repeating this two or
three times, and go back to their camp, without any need of
a sergeant to make them keep their ranks, which they are quite
able to maintain without getting into confusion."

The trouble with this sort of battle practice, which used to
be called in our own army a "dry run," is that it may be totally
forgotten in combat.

On July 13 the party paddled cautiously up the broad Richelieu. The hunters brought in abounding game: stags, fallow
deer, fawns, roebuck, bear. By nightfall the party stood where
the waters broaden out, at or near Rouses Point, to form a
shining lake.

Champlain and his two companions were the first known
white men to set foot on the soil of New York State.

Now for two weeks (if Champlain's chronology is at all
exact, and indeed it is often sadly at fault) the party felt its way

prudently south along the lake. Champlain noted the beautiful islands and rivers. His mention of a grove of chestnuts places him in Burlington, Vermont, for there alone are they known to have stood by the lake. He observed to the eastward "very high mountains on the tops of which there was snow." This is amazing indeed. Perhaps, say the commentators, he was deceived by white marble outcroppings on the Green Mountains. Still, an experienced explorer should not have been so easily deceived.

He was still a little credulous. The Indians gave him the piglike snout of a five-foot garfish. Some, they said, are eight or ten feet long. This fish "shows marvellous ingenuity in that, when it wishes to catch birds, it goes in amongst the rushes or reeds that lie along the shores of the lake, and puts its snout out of the water without moving. The result is that when the birds come and light on its snout, mistaking it for a stump of wood, the fish is so cunning that, shutting its half-open mouth, it pulls them by their feet under the water." It couldn't have been a crocodile?

Champlain looked across the lake to the blue humps of the Adirondacks. The Indians told him that there they would meet their enemies. They would pass a rapid ("which I afterwards saw"); then they would enter another lake, ten leagues long [Lake George], then go by land two leagues to a river [the Hudson], which descends to the coast of Norumbega, adjoining that of Florida.

This information is pretty accurate. Champlain's knowledge of Algonquin and the Algonquins' knowledge of French were sufficient for the communication of geographical facts.

Now, as the party was in hostile territory, it traveled by night, hiding by day in the deep woods. The Indians asked Champlain anxiously about his dreams. In fact, he says, he dreamed that he saw the Iroquois drowning in a lake; he tried to rescue them but was prevented by his companions, who said the Iroquois were all bad men and should properly drown. This dream gave great encouragement to his allies.

For Champlain it was an intoxicating journey. He was stirred by the beauty of the summer nights on this lovely lake, winding among monstrous mountains. He watched the strange fireflies, drawing bright lines in the velvet darkness; he heard the enormous purr of unknown insects, happy in the heat. This lake, he determined, would be his own. He would call it by his own name.

At ten o'clock on the evening of July 29, the invaders, paddling softly southward, came to a cape on the westward shore. It was, almost certainly, the rounded promontory below Fort Ticonderoga, rich with its memories of later wars. Some spots on this earth seem destined to be battlefields; they smell of blood.[1]

Out of the dark came loud shouts and cries. It was a war party of Mohawk Iroquois, heading north in their heavy, clumsy, elm-bark canoes.

The Iroquois, recognizing their inferiority on the water, pulled in to shore and immediately built a barricade, chopping down trees "with the poor axes they sometimes win in war, and with stone axes."

The invaders lay off the shore, tying their canoes together with long poles.

Two Iroquois canoes paddled out for a parley, "to learn from their enemies whether they wished to fight, and these replied that they had no other desire, but that for the moment nothing could be seen and that it was necessary to wait for daylight in order to distinguish one anther. They said that as soon as the sun should rise, they would attack us, and to this our Indians agreed."

This then was the etiquette of warfare: a parley and an agreement on the hour of battle. This war had much of the character of an organized sport. The later wars, for commerce and survival, had no such courtly air.

All night the Iroquois danced on the shore. The allies in their canoes sang songs of insult. Both sides shouted boasts of victory and scurrilous depreciation of the opponent, as in the ritual of modern baseball.

In the first dawn the allies went ashore unhindered by the Iroquois. It was no doubt thought unsporting to interfere with a landing operation. The three Frenchmen with their arquebuses were carefully hidden from the enemy's view.

[1] See Appendix E: "The Site of the Battle of 1609."

The allies formed in battle array. At the agreed time the Iroquois marched solemnly out of their barricade. There were two hundred of them, strong, robust men. They outnumbered the allies by more than three to one.

"They came slowly to meet us with a gravity and calm which I admired; and at their head were three chiefs. Our Indians likewise advanced in similar order, and told me that those who had the three big plumes were the chiefs, and that there were only these three, whom you could recognize by these plumes, which were larger than those of their companions; and I was to do what I could to kill them. I promised them to do all in my power, and told them I was very sorry they could not understand me, so that I might direct their method of attacking the enemy, all of whom undoubtedly we should thus defeat; but that there was no help for it, and that I was very glad to show them, as soon as the engagement began, the courage and readiness which were in me.

"As soon as we landed, our Indians began to run some two hundred yards toward their enemies, who stood firm and had not yet noticed my white companions who went off into the woods with some Indians. Our Indians began to call to me with loud cries; and to make way for me they divided into two groups, and put me ahead some twenty yards, and I marched on until I was within some thirty yards of the enemy, who as soon as they caught sight of me halted and gazed at me and I at them. When I saw them make a move to draw their bows upon us, I took aim with my arquebus and shot straight at one of the three chiefs, and with this shot two fell to the ground, and one of their companions was wounded who died thereof a little later. I had put four bullets into my arquebus. As soon as our people saw this shot so favorable for them, they began to shout so loudly that one could not have heard it thunder, and meanwhile the arrows flew thick on both sides. The Iroquois were much astonished that two men should have been killed so quickly, although they were provided with shields made of cotton thread woven together and wood, which were proof against their arrows. This frightened them greatly. As I was reloading my arquebus, one of my companions fired a shot from within the woods, which astonished them again so much that, seeing their chiefs dead, they lost courage and took to flight, abandoning the field and their fort, and fleeing into the depths of the forest, whither I pursued them and laid low still more of them. Our Indians also killed several and took ten or twelve prisoners. The remainder fled with the wounded. Of our Indians fifteen or sixteen were wounded with arrows, but these were quickly healed."

So at Ticonderoga, on the green shore of Champlain's lake, was fired the first musket shot in a war that was to continue, in effect, for two hundred years.

The battle was won, as, we are told, wars are usually won, by the New Weapon. This new weapon was to transform completely the wars of red men and white, and red men and red. The battle of Ticonderoga was fought by two massed groups in close order. We shall not see such another. The Indians soon threw away their useless shields, revised their tactics, and resorted to a strategy of raids and surprises.

What we have seen was a Stone Age battle, half war, half sport. It was a noble dance of death, a bloody ballet, performed according to accepted rules. Champlain, with his new weapon, violated the rules.

The resentment of the Iroquois was bitter. (The resentment is always bitter on the part of those "unfairly" defeated by mechanization, air raids, atomic bombs, bacteria.) Champlain's arquebus inspired among the Iroquois a tradition of French treachery never to be forgotten.

And Champlain's arquebus has, of course, been blamed by modern writers. A policy of neutrality, they say, would have been loftier, worthier, than this disloyal warfare. Had Champlain come as an unpolitical explorer, not as a partisan, he might have passed through the Iroquois country and down the Hudson; and Henry Hudson (who was due in New York on September 3 of this year) would have found the lilies of France waving on Manhattan Island.

Yes, but neutrality, as I have tried to show, was vain, if not impossible. Except as an ally with an arquebus, Champlain could not have penetrated as far as Ticonderoga. He could not have done other than he did. Had he insisted on neutrality, he must have remained in a fortified trading post on the lower St.

Lawrence. In fact his policy of alliance opened up to him and to the French the great north and the great west. To gain his end he accepted, as a calculated risk, the hostility of the Iroquois.

After the battle the victors danced, sang, and feasted for three hours on the abandoned corn meal of the Iroquois. Meanwhile Champlain inspected the outlet of Lake George and regretted that his exploration was at an end. For the allies had no thought of pursuing their enemy, clinching the victory. They had sufficiently proved their valor and had taken live prisoners for their amusement.

The flotilla headed northward. "Having gone about eight leagues, the Indians, towards evening, took one of the prisoners, to whom they made a harangue on the cruelties which he and his friends without any restraint had practised upon them, and that similarly he should resign himself to receive as much, and they ordered him to sing, if he had the heart. He did so, but it was a very sad song to hear.

"Meanwhile our Indians kindled a fire, and when it was well lighted, each took a brand and burned this poor wretch a little at a time in order to make him suffer the greater torment. Sometimes they would leave off, throwing water on his back. Then they tore out his nails and applied fire to the ends of his fingers and to his privy member. Afterwards they scalped him and caused a certain kind of gum to drip very hot upon the crown of his head. Then they pierced his arms near the wrists and with sticks pulled and tore out his sinews by main force, and when they saw they could not get them out, they cut them off. This poor wretch uttered strange cries, and I felt pity at seeing him treated in this way. Still he bore it so firmly that sometimes one would have said he felt scarcely any pain. They begged me repeatedly to take fire and do like them. I pointed out to them that we did not commit such cruelties, but that we killed people outright, and that if they wished me to shoot him with the arquebus, I should be glad to do so. They said no, for he would not feel any pain. I went away from them as if angry at seeing them practise so much cruelty on his body.

"When they saw that I was not pleased, they called me back and told me to give him a shot with the arquebus. I did so, without his perceiving anything, and with one shot caused him to escape all the tortures he would have suffered, rather than see him brutally treated. When he was dead, they were not satisfied. They opened his body and threw his bowels into the lake. Afterwards they cut off his head, arms, and legs, which they scattered about; but they kept the scalp, which they had flayed, as they did with those of all the others whom they had killed in their attack.

"They did another awful thing, which was to cut his heart into several pieces and give it to a brother of the dead man to eat and to others of his companions who were prisoners. These took it and put it into their mouths, but would not swallow it. Some of the Algonquin Indians who were guarding the prisoners made them spit it out and threw it into the water.

"That is how these people act with regard to those whom they capture in war. And it would be better for them to die fighting and be killed at once, as many do, rather than to fall into the hands of their enemies."

This was Champlain's first view of Indian torture, its horror and its ghastly humor.[2] He was revolted, as any decent man must be. He had seen cruelty enough, in the wars of religion, in Mexico, in the chances of his hard life among hard men in a brutal time; he had never seen such delight in agony. He now learned what it would mean for a white man to fall into the hands of redskin enemies, or what it would mean for a white man to anger his capricious redskin friends.

Notice that he had no authority over the allies. With all his prestige, he did not order them to cease their torturing; he merely turned away with such evident disgust that his hosts permitted him, as a personal favor, to shoot the victim. He was

---

[2] The most gruesome thing about the Indian tortures was the broad comedy that accompanied it. Champlain could not understand the witticisms; Father Lemercier, a little later, did. "What was most calculated to plunge the victim into despair was their raillery, and the compliments they paid him when they approached to burn him. One would say to him: 'Here, uncle, I must burn thee!' and then this uncle found himself changed into a canoe. 'Come,' said he, 'let me calk and pitch my canoe; it is a beautiful new canoe I have just bought; I must stop all the leaks well;' and meanwhile he was passing the firebrand all along his legs. Another one asked him: 'Come, uncle, where do you prefer that I should burn you?' and the poor sufferer had to indicate some particular place. In the midst of this heat, there were some who tried to make him believe that he was cold. 'Ah, it isn't right,' said one, 'that my uncle should be cold; I must warm

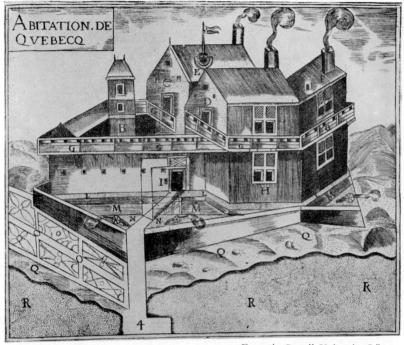

THE HABITATION OF QUEBEC.

"A. The warehouse. [Letter missing in illustration.] B. Dove-cot. C. Building for munitions, and for lodging workmen. D. Another building for workmen. E. Sun-dial. F. Another building for the forge, and for lodging artisans. G. Gallery making circuit of buildings. H. Lodging of Sieur de Champlain. I. Entrance door, with drawbridge. L. Promenade around Habitation, ten feet wide to edge of moat. M. Moat encircling Habitation. N. Platforms, as tenails, for cannon. O. The Sieur de Champlain's garden. P. Kitchen. [Letter missing in drawing.] Q. Open space in front of Habitation, on river-bank. R. The great river of St. Lawrence."

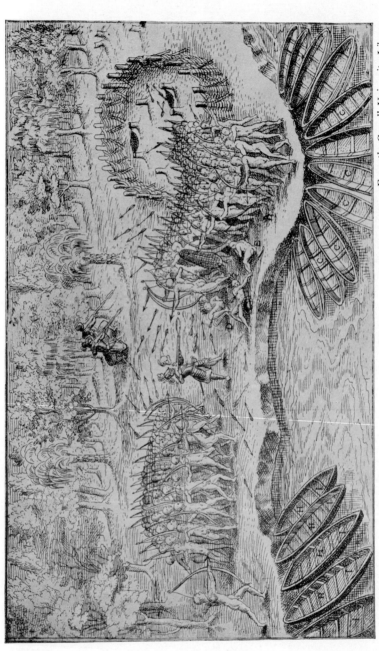

THE BATTLE OF TICONDEROGA, 1609.

"A. The Iroquois fort. [Letter missing in illustration.] B. The enemy. C. The enemy canoes of oak-bark, each holding 10, 15, or 18 men. D, E. Two chiefs killed, one wounded by an arquebus-shot of Sieur de Champlain. F. The Sieur de Champlain. G. Two arquebusiers of Sieur de Champlain. [Letter missing.] H. Montagnais, Hurons, and Algonquins not a commander, only a visiting specialist. Another man in his place might have tried to assume authority, to order a stop to the torture; he might even have succeeded. This was not Champlain's way. He gained his ends by courtesy, diplomacy, understanding. Such was his character, such his weakness and strength.

The expedition made all haste northward, traveling at the rate of sixty to seventy-five miles a day. At Chambly Rapids the Hurons and Algonquins left with their share of the prisoners. "We all separated with great protestations of mutual friendship, and they asked me if I would not go to their country, and aid them continually like a brother. I promised them I would."

Whether or not the Indians took their own vague invitation seriously ("Do come and see us the next time you're around Georgian Bay"), Champlain made careful note of it. He had every hope of accepting.

In two days the Montagnais covered the 120 miles from the mouth of the Richelieu to Quebec. They announced their victory to their friends on shore by beating their paddles against the canoes, singing, and shouting in unison as many times as the number of their captives.[3]

Finding all in good order at Quebec, Champlain continued downstream to Tadoussac to see the ceremonies of victory. "Approaching the shore each took a stick, on the end of which they hung the scalps of their slain enemies with some beads, singing meanwhile all together. And when all were ready, the women stripped themselves quite naked, and jumped into the water, swimming to the canoes to receive the scalps of their enemies, which were at the end of long sticks in the bow of

---

thee.' Another added: 'Now as my uncle has kindly deigned to come and die among the Hurons, I must make him a present, I must give him a hatchet;' and with that he jeeringly applied to his feet a red-hot hatchet. Another one likewise made him a pair of stockings from old rags, which he afterward set on fire; and often, after having made him utter loud cries, he asked him: 'And now, uncle, hast thou had enough?' And when he replied: 'Yes, nephew, it is enough, it is enough,' these barbarians replied: 'No, it is not enough!' and continued to burn him at intervals, demanding of him every time if it was enough." A horrid detail is the fact that ears of corn for supper were roasting in the same fire that heated the steel hatchets for torture. (*Jesuit Relations*, XIII, 66–8.)

[3] The Iroquois painted heads on their canoes indicating the number, age, and rank of their dead victims and live captives. Just like a fighter plane today.

their canoes, in order later to hang them around their necks, as if they had been precious chains. And then they sang and danced. Some days afterwards they made me a present of one of these scalps as if it had been some very valuable thing, and of a pair of weapons belonging to their enemies, for me to keep to show to the King. And to please them I promised to do so."

So the war of 1609 ended. It bound the French openly and irretrievably with the Huron-Algonquins, in enmity with the Iroquois. Henceforth the French were committed; there could be no drawing back. At best there could be only uneasy truces.

As it turned out, Champlain had joined the losing side. The Iroquois, excellent warriors, well organized, were destined to exterminate the Hurons and discomfit the Algonquins.

His declared hostility to the Iroquois closed the door to any advance by the French up the St. Lawrence above the Lachine Rapids, the natural highway to the interior. But in fact this highway was already closed to the Hurons. The French could probably not have used it by making a mere declaration of neutrality. They would have had to join the Iroquois against the Hurons. And all the interests of commerce and security bound them to the Huron-Algonquins, not to the Iroquois.

The war marks the introduction of firearms into Indian warfare. From now on, the dearest desire of every Indian will be to obtain, by barter, theft, or murder, one of these "thunder tubes." In the American wilderness death had found his best friend.

The war had another result for Champlain personally. It established his reputation among the Indians and the French as a brave man who went forward when others went back. Only two years later a French Jesuit in Acadia, who did not know him, referred to him as "Champlain, renowned for valor." Not only was he renowned for valor and fortitude, he was renowned for his fidelity to his promise. The Indians learned to regard him as the man who kept his word.

But Champlain was unconscious of all this. He busied himself for the rest of the summer with the fur trade and with work on the Habitation, so that its occupants might spend the winter in good health and at ease. As he was himself summoned to France to report to de Monts, he put in charge of Quebec a worthy sea captain, Pierre de Chauvin (not to be confused with the Pierre Chauvin who was in these parts in 1600, and who was now dead.) Second in command was a gentleman, the Sieur du Parc. Fifteen others formed the garrison.

Champlain sailed with Pontgravé from Tadoussac on September 5 and arrived safe in Honfleur on October 15.

He took the post to Fontainebleau to see de Monts, who was camped outside the King's palace. He waited upon His Majesty and told him the story of the war by Lake Champlain, "wherein he took pleasure and satisfaction." He presented to the King a belt of porcupine quills, two scarlet tanagers, and the skull of the monster garfish from Lake Champlain. He does not mention the Iroquois scalp.

And then to business.

CHAPTER XI

The Fifth Voyage

AND HOW HAD THINGS GONE, Champlain asked de Monts.

None too well, none too well. In the previous winter his
monopoly had expired. To be sure, the council had thrown him
as a sop an indemnity of 6,000 livres. But he was to collect this
indemnity himself from the traders of the seaport cities. And
how was he to inspect the eighty or more fishing vessels to
determine which ones had brought back some bales of furs in
the hold? You might as well try to drink up the sea. He had
sent an officer to St. Malo demanding payment on pain of imprisonment, and the Malouin officials, bubbling with suppressed
mirth, told him that he had got hold of the wrong names and
they could not discover the right ones. De Monts had spent
more than he had collected.

There was another bit of funny business. The King, for all
his bluff and open ways, was not above a little duplicity. In
April 1609 he had tried secretly to hire the Englishman Henry
Hudson to colonize for France. That looked as though he was
dissatisfied with de Monts's efforts.

On the other hand, Pontgravé had brought back a profitable
cargo. Perhaps all was not yet lost.

De Monts now made a new appeal to the King for a monopoly
of the fur trade in the interior of Canada, the regions opened

by his initiative and the courage of Champlain. "This he could not obtain," says Champlain, "although his requests and proposals were just and reasonable. And although he saw that it was hopeless to obtain this commission, he did not cease to pursue his project, from his desire that everything should turn out for the good and honor of France."

The constancy of de Monts, a necessary complement to the fortitude of Champlain, has been too little recognized. The only memorial to him that I know is a spring on Mt. Desert Island, where he never set foot.

De Monts consulted with his partners, Collier and Le Gendre of Rouen. Free trade along the upper St. Lawrence would certainly cut down their profits, and they would have to bear all the expense of the Habitation of Quebec. On the other hand, the mere possession of that post gave them a considerable advantage in trade. An advantage as great, or greater, was Champlain's friendship with the natives of the interior and his prestige among them. And there was always the chance that he might penetrate farther into the interior, to the mysterious Salt Sea, perhaps even to China!

The partners decided to carry on for at least another season and to continue the Habitation for one more winter.

Champlain made an effort in another direction. Father Cotton, the Jesuit confessor of the King, had an ambition to establish his order in the New World, and some wealthy and pious ladies were ready to contribute the needful funds. Champlain made him a proposition: for 3,600 livres his missionaries could join the settlement at Quebec, convert the heathen, and have (apparently) some share in the fur business. The Sieur de Monts, in authorizing this proposal, did some violence to his Huguenot convictions, but he was a businessman first of all. However, Father Cotton refused. He wanted a free hand, and so he sent his Jesuits to Acadia and Maine, where they met nothing but calamity.

Groaning, de Monts and his partners found the money to equip two ships. Pontgravé would devote himself to trading; Champlain would carry out a cargo of supplies to support the Habitation through another winter. Eleven artisans were enlisted, no settlers, no real colonists with their families.

After sailing from Honfleur, Champlain was laid low by a serious illness. Fortunately his ship was forced back by storms and bad lading. "During this time I recovered my health fairly well, and although somewhat weak and debilitated, I nevertheless re-embarked."

He arrived at Tadoussac on May 26. Here he discovered several ships, which had appeared there as early as May 18. "Such a thing had not been seen for sixty years, according to the reports of old seamen who sail regularly to these parts." On such casual phrases as this we build our theory that French traders visited the St. Lawrence from the mid-sixteenth century onward.

In Tadoussac, Champlain found the Sieur du Parc, who had wintered in Quebec. Everyone there was well, he said, and only a few had been slightly ill. They had had scarcely any winter, and fresh meat nearly all the time. Their greatest trouble had been boredom.

Champlain was triumphant. "This winter shows how in future those who undertake such enterprises ought to act, since it is difficult to make a new settlement without labor, and without incurring ill fortune the first year, as has been the case in all our first settlements. And in truth by doing without salt provisions, and having fresh meat, one's health is as good there as in France."

The Montagnais were happy to see Champlain and immediately reminded him of his promise to accompany them on the warpath. Certainly, he said, he would keep his promise. However, there must be a bargain. As soon as the war was over, the Indians must fulfill their own promise; they must lead him from Trois Rivières up the St. Maurice northward, "as far as a place where there is such a large sea that they had not seen the end of it [Hudson Bay], and that we should then come back by way of the Saguenay to Tadoussac. I asked them whether they were still willing to do this. They said they were, but it could only be done next year. This answer pleased me, but I had also promised the Algonquins and Hurons to assist them in their wars, and they had promised to show me their country and the great lake [Lake Huron], and some copper mines and other things which they had mentioned to me. Hence I had two strings to my bow, and if one failed the other might stay taut."

Here spoke the explorer, the dreamer. Pontgravé or any others of the French would have made a commercial bargain; an administrator would have asked for power and rule. Champlain asked only the privilege of a heartbreaking journey through cold and hungry lands, to discover and to see.

Champlain ascended the stream to his Habitation. He found everything in good shape and all the comrades hale and hearty. Captain Pierre de Chauvin was clearly an efficient commander.

Some local chiefs were at Quebec eagerly awaiting their warrior friend. A war party of sixty valiant Montagnais soon arrived. A banquet-conference was held. The Indians, in an after-dinner flow of eloquence, put to Champlain a delicate question. "There are many Basques and Mistigoches [for so they call the Normans and the people of St. Malo] who say that they will accompany us on the warpath. What do you think of it? Do they speak the truth?"

"No, they do not. I know well what they have in mind. What they say is merely a pretext to obtain possession of your goods."

"You have spoken truly! They are women, who wish to make war only on our beavers!"

Champlain told his friends to meet him at the agreed rendez-vous at the junction of the Richelieu and the St. Lawrence, where the Hurons and Ottawa Algonquins had promised to join him. He loaded four pinnaces with trade goods and set off upstream, pursued by several rival traders, scenting profit.

An Algonquin messenger met him on the way, with news that his chief Iroquet, two hundred Algonquins, and two hundred Hurons were heading for the rendezvous. "He drew out of a sack a piece of copper a foot long, which he presented to me. It was very fine and pure. He gave me to understand that the metal was abundant where he had obtained it, which was on the bank of a river near a large lake. He said that it was taken out in pieces, and when melted was made into sheets and smoothed out with stones. I was much pleased with this gift although it was of small value."

This copper came surely from the outcrops along the southern shore of Lake Superior, copper that was passed from Indian hand to hand throughout the interior of the continent. Champlain is mistaken, however, in supposing that the Indians melted it. The copper was soft enough to be worked cold.

Champlain's flotilla arrived at the mouth of the Richelieu, at the present Sorel, and lay to below an island, probably St. Ignace. The French interlopers hovered about, ready to seize any rewards from under the nose of the pathfinders. The Indians chopped down trees, not for defense, but to clear a space for dancing.

An Algonquin canoe grounded on the island. A messenger leaped ashore, crying out that the Iroquois were close by; they had built a barricade beside the Richelieu. The allies must attack immediately, to gain the advantage of the offensive.

The Indians were in the mood; they decided immediately to attack, without, however, proper reconnoitering or planning of the battle. "They made such haste that instead of getting ahead they kept things back. They came to our pinnace and to the others, begging me and my companions to accompany them in their canoes, and they urged me so strongly that with four others I embarked with them. I asked our pilot, La Route, to stay in the pinnace, and to send me four or five more of my companions, should the other pinnaces send shallops and men to our assistance; for none of the pinnaces would go with the Indians except that of Captain Thibaut who came with me. The Indians shouted to those who stayed behind that they were woman-hearted, and knew no other fighting but the war on peltry."

The Indians crossed the river, took their weapons and shields, and hurried to the battle so hastily that they soon lost the five volunteers. The five, exasperated, weighed down with armor and ponderous arquebuses, followed the Indians' track as best they could through tangled woods and marsh, with water to their knees. Their pikemen's corselets were intolerable, with sweat trickling and tickling inside, with unattainable insects hunting under the steel. "The hosts of mosquitoes were so thick that they hardly allowed us to draw our breath, so greatly and severely did they persecute us."

One could not have blamed the French for abandoning their heedless allies in disgust. But they caught sight of two Indians of their side and ordered them to act as guides.

They soon met a messenger, who brought news that the
allies had impetuously attacked the Iroquois barricade and had
been thrown back with many losses. They had then decided to
await the arrival of the wonder-working thunder tubes. "Hardly
had we gone an eighth of a league before we heard the howls
and shouts of both parties, flinging insults at one another, and
continually skirmishing whilst waiting for us. As soon as the
Indians saw us they began to shout so loud that one could not
have heard thunder.

"I directed my companions to keep behind me and not to
leave me. I approached the enemy's barricade to reconnoitre it.
It was made of strong trees, placed one upon another, in a
circle, which is the ordinary form of their forts. All the Montagnais and Algonquins also approached the barricade. Then
we began firing many arquebus-shots through the branches;
for we could not see them as they could see us. As I was firing
my first shot close to their barricade, I was wounded with an
arrow which split the tip of my ear and entered my neck. I
seized the arrow which was still in my neck and pulled it out.
The point was tipped with a very sharp bit of stone. At the
same time one of my companions was also wounded in the arm
by another arrow, which I pulled out for him.

"My wound did not hinder me, however, from doing my
duty, and our Indian allies also did theirs, and the enemy too
fought well; so much so that one could see the arrows flying
on all sides as thick as hail. The Iroquois were astonished at the
reports of our arquebuses, but most of all because the bullets
pierced better than their arrows. And they were so frightened
at the execution done by the bullets, having seen several of their
companions fall dead and wounded, that out of fear, thinking
these shots to be irresistible, they would throw themselves upon
the ground when they heard the report. Besides, we hardly
missed a shot, and fired two or three bullets each time, and for
the most part had our arquebuses resting on the side of their
barricade.

"When I saw that our ammunition was beginning to fail, I
said to the Indians that they must carry the place by storm, by
breaking down the barricades. To do this they must take their
shields, and covering themselves therewith, must come near

enough to fasten strong ropes to the posts which supported the barricade and by main strength pull them down, and so make an opening wide enough to let us into the fort, and that meanwhile by means of our arquebuses we should keep the enemy back, should he attempt to hinder them. I said also that a number of them should fell certain large trees which were near the barricade, in order to make them fall upon the enemy and crush him, and that others with their shields should keep the enemy from hurting the choppers. All of which they carried out very promptly."

(Champlain must now have gained some competence in the native speech, to have made such orders comprehensible in the heat of battle.)

"As we were on the point of completing this, the pinnaces, which were a league and a half away, heard the sound of our fighting, the echo of the firing being carried to them, with the result that a courageous young man of St. Malo, named des Prairies, who, like the others, had brought his pinnace to barter furs, said to those who had stayed behind that it was disgraceful of them to see me fighting in this way with savages without going to my help, and that for himself he held his honor too high for anyone to reproach him with such a thing. Thereupon he decided to come and join me in a shallop with some of his men, and some of mine whom he brought with him.

"As soon as he arrived, he went towards the Iroquois fort, which was on the bank of the river. Here he landed and came to look for me. When I saw him, I made our Indians cease breaking down the fort, so that the newcomers might have their share of this pleasure.

"I requested the Sieur des Prairies and his companions to fire some arquebus volleys before our Indians stormed the place, as they had decided to do. They did so, and fired several shots, wherein each conducted himself very properly. And after sufficient firing had been done, I spoke to our Indians, inciting them to finish their work. At once they approached the barricade as they had done before, having us on their flanks to shoot at those who should try to prevent them from pulling it down. They behaved so well and so bravely that, thanks to our volleys, they made an opening, which nevertheless was difficult to get through, for there still remained a part as high as a man, as well as branches of felled trees, which impeded us greatly. Still, when I saw that there was a pretty fair opening, I gave orders for the firing to cease, which was obeyed. At the same moment, some twenty or thirty, both Indians and whites, went in, sword in hand, without meeting much resistance. Immediately all who were able began to flee, but they did not get far, for they were laid low by those about the barricade, and any who escaped were drowned in the river. We took some fifteen prisoners, the rest having been killed by arquebuses, arrows, and swords.

"When all was over, there arrived another shallop with some of our companions, but it was too late, although in time to carry off the booty, which was small. There were merely some beaver skins, and dead bodies covered with blood, which the Indians would not take the trouble to strip, and made sport of those who did so, who were the people in the last shallop. The others refused such a nasty task. In this way, by God's grace, was victory won, and the Indians gave us much praise on that account."

The scene of the battle was named Cap de la Victoire, and so it has been known ever since.

Here the Iroquois learned a new lesson: that the white man's terrible weapons, properly supported, could carry even barricades. They learned also that the end of a battle now meant, not the flight of the victor with a few captives, but the extermination of the vanquished.

The native allies of the French learned, beside these lessons, the cowardice of some white men, and the greed of some, who tore the bloody garments off dead Indians on the battlefield. They learned to meet the white man's scorn with their own. And they learned that they must look well to recognize their friends among these pale faces. Their best friend, tested in venture and battle, was Samuel Champlain.

The Algonquin and Montagnais losses were three dead and fifty wounded. While musket bullets pierce and kill, arrowheads discharged at any distance are blunted in man's flesh and merely wound.

The Indians scalped the Iroquois dead and, singing, carried off their prisoners. The long-haired scalps fluttered on sticks at the bows of the canoes, like foxes' tails on the radiator caps of our country dandies. One canoe was ornamented with a dead body cut in quarters, to be eaten in the ritual of triumph.

On the island of St. Ignace the victors danced and sang to the music of pebble-filled drums and tortoise-shell fiddles. The vanquished, tied to stakes, sang their own songs of defiance. Their nails were pulled out, lingeringly, to prevent their picking at their bonds. They were burned bit by bit, hour by hour. I have had enough of these sickening tortures and skip to the moment of death. "As soon as one would fall to the ground, they would pound the body violently with clubs; then they would cut off arms, legs, and other parts of the body, and amongst them no one was esteemed worthy who did not cut off a piece of flesh and give it to the dogs. Such is the courtesy which prisoners receive. Nevertheless, they endure all the tortures inflicted on them with such constancy that those who see them are struck with astonishment."

After Champlain had his wound dressed by the surgeon, he had to look at the festival of torture. It was evident that he he could not check it. The best he could do was to obtain the gift to him of an Iroquois prisoner as his personal prize. "It was no small service I did him."

The French merchants spread out their wares on the shore and did good business, heedless of the death songs and the smell of burning flesh. The interlopers carried off the best part of the furs. "It was doing them a great favor to search out for them strange tribes, in order that they might later on carry off the whole profit without running any risk or hazard."

On the following day the Algonquin chief Iroquet and the Huron chief Ochateguin, old friends, arrived with eighty men. They were much disappointed to have missed the battle.

Champlain had a proposal to make. He had a likely youth of seventeen, who had survived two winters at Quebec, who spoke Montagnais pretty well, who knew how to take care of himself in the woods. This was, almost certainly, Étienne Brûlé. He had himself asked to spend a winter with the Ottawa Algonquins, to learn their language, of the same stock as the Montagnais dialect. "Certainly," Champlain had said, "but I want you to do more. I want you to observe the country, its rivers and communications; find out about minerals and other resources; if possible, make your way westward to the great lake [Huron]; keep your eyes open, and on your return make a good report of what will be useful to us." Brûlé delightedly accepted.

Now Champlain proposed to Iroquet that he should take young Brûlé back with him and return him in the following year. "He promised me to do so, and to treat him like his own son, saying that he was much pleased thereat." However, his followers objected, fearing that some accident might happen to the boy, which might provoke a war.

Champlain asked a powwow with the chiefs. His account of it well illustrates his manner of dealing with the Indians. "I asked them why Chief Iroquet, whom I considered to be my friend, had refused to take the youth with him. I said that it was not like a brother or a friend to deny me a thing which he had promised me, and which could only bring good to them all. If I wished them to take this youth, it was for the purpose of increasing our friendship with them and their neighbors beyond what it had been."

(His real purpose was hidden by these high phrases. He was merely using the language of diplomacy, which the Indians certainly recognized as such.)

"Their hesitation, I said, gave me a bad opinion of them, and if they would not take this lad with them, as Chief Iroquet had promised me, I should never have friendship with them, for they were not children, that they should break this promise. Then they told me that they were quite satisfied to take the youth, but they were afraid that, if he changed his diet, and were fed less well than he had been accustomed to, some harm might befall him, at which I might be angry, and this, they said, was the sole cause of their refusal.

"I answered them that as to the life they led and the food they ate, the lad could well adapt himself to these, and that if from sickness or the fortune of war any harm should happen to him, this would not prevent me from being kindly disposed toward them, for we are all liable to accidents which we ought to bear patiently. But I said that if they should ill-treat him, and any misfortune happened to him through their fault, I should indeed be displeased. However, I did not look for such from them, but for the contrary.

"They said to me: 'Since, then, you have this desire, we will take him along, and will treat him like one of ourselves. But you must take a young man in his place, who will go with you to France. We shall be very glad to have him report to us all the fine things he has seen.' I gladly accepted the proposal and took the young man." The Indian chosen was a Huron, who acquired the name of Savignon.

Thus on St. Ignace Island was inaugurated the system of the *coureurs du bois*, who carried French influence to Hudson Bay, to the Rocky Mountains, to the Gulf of Mexico. Obscure, illiterate men, they have left no more mark on history than the rude cross with which they signed their names. "For over two centuries the student of North American exploration is often forced to admit that the great names belong to 'path-finders,' whereas the 'trail-makers' are unknown. Usually, of course, the natives made the trails and established the routes, but wherever these avenues were integrated in some white man's design, there is the chance that lurking in the background of anonymity was some *voyageur* who was almost one with the natives." [1]

Here on St. Ignace Island was inaugurated also the system of exchange students, which flourishes mightily in the universities of our world.

Champlain now proposed a rendezvous for the following year below the Great [Lachine] Rapids, on the island of Montreal. By setting the trading point so far upstream he might give his rivals the slip; he would also defer to the Hurons and Algonquins by shortening their journey while lengthening his own.

Now the year's business was done. Champlain returned to Quebec and supervised the building of a new palisade around the Habitation. The gardens were doing well; the corn, wheat, rye, and barley promised excellently, though the grapevines had died for lack of proper cultivation. An annoying thing happened: the Iroquois prisoner, too loosely guarded, escaped. We shall hear more of this next year.

[1] John Bartlet Brebner: *The Explorers of North America*, 159.

Champlain put the Sieur du Parc in charge of Quebec, with a garrison of sixteen men. Regretfully he said farewell. This strong house by the Canadian river was his home; in France he was rootless, a sojourner.

There was bad news in Tadoussac. Free competition in the fur trade had resulted in loss for everyone. Too many people had rushed into the business. A number of ships lay in harbor with half their cargo of trade goods still aboard. "Many will long remember the loss they sustained that year," says Champlain; and Lescarbot: "So great was the greed of the merchants for beaver that three quarters of them, thinking they were on their way to win the Golden Fleece without striking a blow, did not even win fleeces of wool, so great was the number of Argonauts."

There was more bad news, bad indeed. Late arrivals from France brought word that King Henry had been assassinated. Champlain and de Monts were bound to Henry, and he to them, by memories of old companionship in the wars. He had favored their purposes in Canada and had revoked adverse decisions of his council. Now the ruler of France was a nine-year-old boy, Louis XIII. The regent would be his foreign mother, Marie de Medicis. Who would care for the past services of old Champlain now? Who would care for Canada?

On August 13 Champlain set sail from Tadoussac. He had as passenger the Huron youth Savignon. The only remarkable incident of the voyage was that the ship passed over a sleeping whale, cut a wide wound near its tail, and awakened it very quickly. The ship arrived in Honfleur on September 27.

CHAPTER XII

The Sixth Voyage

THE TAVERNKEEPERS of Honfleur were well used to reporting a summer's news to thirsty patrons home from the sea. Here is what Champlain learned in the end of September 1610.

Good King Henry had been stabbed on May 14 by a certain Ravaillac, who, it was whispered, was in Jesuit pay. The regency was assumed by his queen, the fat Italian busybody, Marie de Medicis. All King Henry's projects had immediately gone by the board; the Queen's one purpose was to get at her spouse's treasure: the war reserve of six millions stored in the Bastille. The old ministers were powerless; effective control was in the hands of the Queen's fantastic *femme de chambre*, la Galigaï, and her scoundrel husband, Concini. *Une belle équipe!* The nobles were restless, were said to be plotting in their castles. One was going to see some sad times, my dear sir.

Heavy-hearted, Champlain went to make his report to de Monts. Financially it was not brilliant. Thanks to their special relations, he and Pontgravé had brought back decent cargoes. But free competition had raised costs. One used to give a couple of knives for a prime beaver; now one had to pay fifteen or twenty. And competition in the French market was forcing down prices in Paris; really, the trade was hardly worth the labor and risk. But the Habitation was well equipped for the winter; young

Brûlé on the Ottawa might bring back some good news. And
the bonds Champlain had knit with the Hurons and Algonquins
were certain to prove profitable. It would be foolish to renounce
these advantages, so painfully won, to surrender all future rewards to greedy merchants who had never spent a sou nor struck
a blow.

De Monts and his partners, reluctant, complaining, agreed
to carry on for another year. No doubt they enjoyed the feeling
that they were masters of a colony in a far, romantic country,
the feeling that they were explorers by proxy. No doubt they
liked Champlain and hated to dash his dreams, his high and
perilous enterprises. Perhaps, even, they were honestly patriotic
and proud that they were advancing the might and majesty of
France.

Now Champlain had another bit of business to attend to:
He wished to marry.

He was forty-three years old. His father had died (when we
do not know). If his mother still lived, in Brouage, he could
hardly have seen her for years. He was alone in the world and
beginning to feel his loneliness.

He made a surprising choice. He found a girl of twelve,
Hélène Boullé, daughter of a Paris functionary, Nicolas Boullé,
secrétaire de la chambre du roi. The well-to-do bourgeois family
is said to have been Huguenot, but it must have turned Catholic,
or at least have permitted the daughter's conversion, for the
marriage was celebrated in one of the most important Paris
churches.

The contract was signed on December 27, 1610. The wit-
nesses on Champlain's side were de Monts himself, his secretary, Jean Ralluau, who had made at least two trips to Acadia,
and Lucas Legendre, one of de Monts's Rouen partners. All
Champlain's friends were business friends; he had wandered too
much to cultivate the long intimacies of normal men.

The contract contained the usual provisions for marriage
portions. M. Boullé agreed to provide 6,000 livres, Champlain
only 1,800. Since usually the two parties matched their sums,
there is a suggestion here that Champlain made up for the
difference by his prestige and prospects. He was a desirable
parti.

The contract contains an unusual provision. In consideration of the tender age of the said Hélène Boullé, the marriage should not be consummated until two years should elapse, "unless it be deemed advisable and be decided between them, their relations and friends, to proceed earlier to the completion of the said marriage."

There is another item to be noticed. Champlain is denominated *"noble homme Samuel de Champlain, sieur dudict lieu* [Brouage]." His father is referred to as the late Antoine de Champlain, Captain in the Navy. Observe the *de*, the *particule*. Hitherto our Champlain had signed himself merely Samuel Champlain; henceforth he will always insert the *de*, which conveys a hint of honorable rank, a hint at least of landownership. Perhaps Champlain inherited land in Brouage at his father's death; or perhaps the *de* was adopted merely for the gratification of Hélène and his new family. The appellation *"noble homme"* means as little. The notaries called almost any respectable person *"noble homme,"* as we write on envelopes the indiscriminate "Esq." Champlain's official post as *"lieutenant du roi"* in the New World was probably a charge that carried with it a certain social dignity.

It snowed heavily on the day the contract was signed. The boy King amused himself in the courtyard of the Louvre by making snowballs. Champlain told his little spouse of other and greater shows she was destined to see.

Three days later the church ceremony took place in imposing St.-Germain-l'Auxerrois, facing the old Louvre. It was the parish church of the Kings of France, where they made their Easter duties.

What impelled Champlain, so wise and sure, to marry this child, this baby?

He would be amazed and offended at our prurient curiosity. A French bourgeois of his time did not bring his wife into public view. Champlain barely mentions her in his work; it would not occur to him that she should be mentioned. A man has a right to his private life.

But the dead have no privacy. When we are interested in a man, we want to know all about him, what he conceals as well as what he tells. If he is a ghost who haunts posterity's imag-

ination, by a happy return we—posterity—are ghosts who
haunt his mind and house, peering into beds in locked rooms,
interrupting his thoughts. If he hides from us, we will surmise,
we will guess.

Champlain, in his wandering life as sailor, campaigning
soldier, explorer, had known few women. He was timid with
them, ill at ease; their games and jokes, their pretty small talk,
made him feel foolish. He was happier with a band of men, in
a ship's wardroom, in a forest cabin. He dreamed of women's
kindness and love, but he had no strong physical need for their
caresses; he was not *porté sur la chose*, or he would not have
chosen the explorer's life, the life without women. His tender-
ness, as I have already suggested, found its outlet in affection
for the savages, ferocious, trusting children. His need to love
had become a paternal need. Remember that he was forty-three,
and that a man of forty-three was then older than he is today.
Think of Molière's Arnolphe; think of the unchecked progress
of arthritis, gout, anemia, diabetes, malaria; think that half the
accidents our surgeons repair would then have caused permanent injuries; think of the loss of teeth (where we have a filling,
a man of the old days had a gap).

So when Champlain sought a bride, he recoiled from the lush
and bouncing daughters of his friends. When he saw the beautiful child of twelve, his heart spoke. But his emotion (I am sure)
was no unseemly lust; it was the repressed desire for fatherhood.
What if the consummation of the marriage was postponed for
two years? Champlain had his pleasure merely in taking his
child bride by the hand to see the sights of Paris, to watch the
pomp of Notre-Dame, a carrousel in the Louvre, the free shows
of the tooth drawers on the Pont-Neuf. The bystanders supposed the pair to be a burgher with a beloved daughter, and
Champlain, I think, was pleased at their error.

The winter of 1610–11 was given to preparation for the trade
of the coming summer, and to the delightful instruction of
Hélène. Meanwhile Champlain supervised the education of his
other charge, the Huron youth Savignon. I like to think that
the three took their outings together: the proud little bride
between the ruddy, uncomfortable savage and the kindly Champlain, wearing the finest beaver hat in Paris. Alas, there are

no documents in support; they have been swept down history's drain. But Lescarbot saw Savignon in Paris, very scornful of the French. "Often when he saw two men quarrelling without coming to blows or killing one another, he would mock at them, saying that they were naught but women, and had no courage." He had a sight of the ten-year-old King and probably an audience.

In the last days of February, Champlain said farewell to his bride, for there could yet be no thought of taking her to Canada With Savignon he went to Honfleur. He found there the free traders, rivaling in haste to be off, to be first in harbor at Tadoussac.

He set sail with Pontgravé on March 1 and soon ran into bad weather. Near the Banks he met icebergs, two hundred, two hundred and fifty feet high. Fog came down so thick one could hardly see the length of the ship. At one moment a berg loomed directly ahead. "And as each one committed himself to God, thinking we should never escape the danger of that iceberg, which was already under our bowsprit, we shouted to the helmsman to bear off. The great mass of ice was driving before the wind so fast that it passed close to our vessel without striking it, but the ship stopped as if to let it go by. Although we were out of danger, yet each one's blood cooled down slowly from the fright we had had; and we praised God for having delivered us from this peril."

Feeling its way among the bergs, the ship crossed the Grand Bank and approached the Nova Scotian coast. Before the voyagers loomed a great bank of ice, extending as far as eye could see. They found what appeared to be a passage, and penetrated it for some ten leagues. At nightfall they discovered it to be a blind alley. "There seemed no possible way for us to return whence we had come. Still, after due reflection, we decided to make an effort to find the opening by which we had entered, and this we set about to do; but with night came on fog, rain, snow, and such a high wind that we could hardly carry our mainsail, and we lost all bearings of our route. For when we thought we could avoid the ice and pass through, the wind had already closed the passage." They made short, desperate tacks among the floes. "More than a score of times we thought we should not come off alive. The whole night was spent amid difficulties and labors. Never was the watch better kept, for nobody had any desire to sleep, but rather to struggle to get out of the dangerous ice. The cold was so great that all the ship's running rigging was so frozen and covered with big icicles that we could not work it nor stand upon the vessel's deck."

Day brought only fog. The captain tried to lie to in the lee of a cliff of ice, under bare poles. When the ship drifted away he hoisted sail and returned to the sheltering lee. He repeated this maneuver for a day and a night. Then, the fog lifting a little, he tacked timorously to and fro and found himself in a great walled pond.

"We remained four or five days in this extreme danger, until one morning as we looked about us in all directions, we saw indeed no passage, but a place where we judged the ice not to be thick, and where we could easily pass through. We made for this spot and passed many *bourguignons*, which are pieces of ice separated from the great masses by the violence of the winds. On reaching the bank of ice, the sailors armed themselves with great bars and other pieces of wood to ward off the *bourguignons* we might meet, and in this way we cleared the bank, but not without striking smaller pieces, which did no good to our vessel, although no great harm was done to us. Being outside, we praised God for our deliverance."

The deliverance was only temporary. The ship rounded the enormous floe, and headed toward Cape Breton. Then she met another great ice bank, extending as far as the eye could see. "And when you saw it, you thought it was land, for it was so level that you would have really said it had been made so on purpose. It was more than eighteen feet high, with twice as much under water."

And Champlain says, in a magnificent anticlimax: "These frequent encounters with ice annoyed us very much."

At last, on April 27, land was sighted: Cape Canso, where Cape Breton Island is set off from the Nova Scotia mainland. The ship headed out to sea, to round Cape Breton and enter the Gulf. She ran into ice and more ice, and at one point was nearly lost. "We were on the point of launching our boat. Even had we escaped on this ice the only result would have been that we should all have starved miserably to death. As we were deliberating whether to launch our boat, a light breeze sprang up, which pleased us greatly, and by it we escaped from the said ice."

The fog came down for another night and day. "Yet we failed not to attempt to set sail in order to get out of the ice. But though we thought to free ourselves, we found ourselves so hemmed in that we did not know which way to tack. And once again we were forced to lower sail and to let ourselves drift until the ice made us hoist sail, and we tacked a hundred times from side to side and several times just escaped destruction. Here the coolest would quite lose his head, as well indeed as the greatest astrologer alive."

The following morning a strong wind arose, chasing the fog. Under the bright sun they saw themselves in a pond of ice, less than a league and a half in circumference, with the island of Cape Breton in plain view. "We saw also a small bank of ice astern of us and beyond it the open sea, which made us decide to pass through the ice-bank which was loose. We accomplished this quite dexterously without losing our vessel, and put out to sea for the night, heading to the southeast of the icebergs."

The next day was the first of May, when, according to sea custom, the crew assembled and fired a salute for the captain. This they certainly did with a will. On this day they met and spoke another vessel floundering amidst the ice. She was commanded by a son of M. de Poutrincourt, on his way to join his father in Acadia. He was already three months out, and far off his course. He had as passengers two Jesuits, who have left an account of their terrible journey. "In some places appeared prodigious icebergs, two hundred and fifty feet high, as big as if you would join several castles together. It was as if Notre-Dame de Paris with a part of its island, with houses and palaces, should go floating on the water."

At last, on May 3, Champlain's ship passed Cape Ray and entered the open water of the Gulf. On the thirteenth, two and a half months out from France, she dropped anchor off Tadoussac. The country was still covered with snow.

In harbor, Champlain and Pontgravé found three French

vessels, independent fur traders. Their early arrival had done them little good. The Indians, though wretched and hungry after a hard winter, were holding their furs until more ships should arrive and competition should send prices up. "Thus those people are mistaken who think that by coming first they can do better business, for these Indians are now too sharp and crafty."

The independents watched Champlain's every movement. They were feverishly building pinnaces, ready to follow him anywhere. They knew well that he had appointed a meeting place and time with the Hurons and Algonquins; they were determined to be there too. But Champlain gave them the slip and sailed in his pinnace to Quebec.

Here he found the Sieur du Parc and his men all in good health. They had had good hunting in the snows and had not been touched by sickness.

Champlain endeavored in vain to persuade the Montagnais to take him for a journey of exploration up the St. Maurice. "Next year," they said. Their reluctance was probably due to their interests as middlemen. They did not wish the French to made direct contact with the hunting tribes of the north. Champlain's longing to see new lands was rebuffed but unappeased. "I put the matter off till the first opportunity that should present itself."

Champlain, in his pinnace, stole away from some annoying pursuers and went upstream to the Great Rapids, landing there on May 28. None of his Indian friends from the interior had arrived. He occupied himself, therefore, in choosing a site for a permanent settlement, a second Habitation. With Savignon for companion, he explored the island of Montreal, passed the rapids by land, and inspected the Lac Saint-Louis and the Lac des Deux-Montagnes. He chose finally a welcoming spot beside the St. Lawrence, with good soil and open meadows where cattle could be grazed. He noted the abundant vines, butternuts, plums, cherries, and strawberries, and a white sweet fruit tasting like bananas (probably the snowberry).

This chosen spot he called the Place Royale. It was on, or near, the site of the present Customs House of Montreal, just back from the row of piers where the great ships lie.

He had the ground cleared, ready for building. He sowed seeds as a test, and they prospered well. To try the clay, which seemed suitable for brickmaking, he built a wall, to see how it would endure the winter. He noted that a stronghold could be established on a pleasant island in midstream. This he named the Ile Sainte-Hélène, for the patron saint of his little wife. Her island, still bearing her name, is now a public park. Above it rise the noble arches of the Jacques Cartier Bridge.

Thus Champlain planned for the future. In fact he was never to see in being the colony he proposed. Not until 1642 were laid the permanent foundations of Ville-Marie de Montréal.

Impatient for the coming of his Huron and Algonquin friends, he sent Savignon, a Montagnais chief, and a French youth named Louis to make contact with them on the Ottawa. Four days later Savignon returned alone.

This was his story. The canoe proving unseaworthy, the three had turned back. They had observed in the midst of the Great Rapids an island swarming with herons. (Still today it is known as Ile Héron.) Louis insisted on visiting it. They reached it safely and had their fill of hunting. But when they tried to descend the roaring waters by the north shore, the canoe turned over, and Louis and the Montagnais were drowned. Savignon, however beaten and buffeted, clung to the canoe and saved himself. He returned in great fear, "lest vengeance should be visited upon him, as is usual amongst the Indians. He told us this sad story, which filled us with sorrow."

Champlain went to look for the bodies of the lost men. "I assure you that when he showed me the spot my hair stood on end to see such an awful place, and I was astonished that the victims had been so lacking in judgment as to go through such a frightful place, when they might have gone another way; for it was impossible to go through there, on account of seven or eight waterfalls which tumble from ledge to ledge, the lowest of which is three feet high. All this made a remarkable noise and whirl, and part of the rapid was completely white with foam, which indicated the worst spot. There was a noise so loud that one would have said it was thunder, as the air rang from the sound of these cataracts."

This murderous fall and the lake above were then named for

Louis, or for his patron saint, which is the same thing. (Although one may think that St. Louis has too much honor, for letting his votary drown.) Henceforth the French called the great rapids the Saut St. Louis, until they were renominated Lachine, the China Rapids. The Lac St. Louis still bears the name of the hapless boy.

Day after day passed, and the Indians did not appear. Meanwhile the traders from the lower river found their way to the rendezvous. At least thirteen pinnaces of various owners lay in the lee of Windmill Point. Pontgravé was there with the others, but the advantage of monopoly trading was lost.

At last, on June 13, the Indian convoy of two hundred men, mostly Hurons, arrived. Champlain jumped into a canoe with Savignon and paddled toward them. He recognized his friends Ochateguin the Huron and Iroquet the Algonquin. The Indians shouted in unison. A chief stood up and made a speech, applauding the French for keeping their promise. The Indians uttered three more solemn shouts. The French replied with a volley of musket shots from the pinnaces. "This astonished them so much that they begged me to ask that there should be no more firing; for, said they, the greater number had never seen Christians nor heard thunder of that sort, and were afraid it might hurt them."

The exchange students greeted their own people. Savignon gave his Hurons a vivid and laudatory account of the wonders of civilization. Brûlé, dressed entirely in Indian skins, walking pigeon-toed, made his report in French which came a little haltingly. He had been well treated by his Algonquin hosts; he had been happy.

The Indians encamped and held a council. They summoned Champlain and Brûlé, "who had learned their language very well." Brûlé translated from French to Algonquin; another, perhaps Iroquet, translated from Algonquin to Huron and back again. The Indians said that they wished to form a close alliance with Champlain, and that they were sorry to see all the pinnaces present. Savignon reported that he did not know these traders nor what was in their minds. "They saw clearly that it was only love of gain and avarice which brought these people thither, and that when the Indians should need their help they would give none, and would not do as I had done, who used to offer to go with my companions into their country and to help them, of which I had given them proofs in the past.''

(I think they said all this, certainly. But I think Champlain emphasizes it in his book, to show his superiors and the French public the error of free trade, the desirability of a monopoly for his company, and the wisdom of his warlike policy.)

They feared the armed men in the pinnaces, said the chiefs. There were rumors that the free traders acted with treachery, violence, and a high hand. "I assured them that the others would not do so, and that we all served one King, whom our Indian had seen, and that we were all of the same nation, but that business was a private affair. And I said that they ought not to be afraid, for they were as safe as if they were in their own country."

(I confess I am a little suspicious here, Champlain seems to be carrying fair-mindedness to unreasonable excess. I suspect that this passage is intended to prove to interested readers that the royal provisions for free trade were being carried out with scrupulous exactness.)

The chiefs had some unpleasant news for Champlain. The Iroquois prisoner whose life he had saved the year before, and who had escaped from Quebec to his own country, had spread the report that Champlain had given him his liberty with the mission of making an alliance with the Iroquois. Champlain, he said, proposed to go to the Great Rapids with six hundred Iroquois, to lie in wait for the northern Indians and kill them all. The spreading of this tale had so alarmed the Algonquins and Hurons that four hundred men who had planned to make the trading trip had changed their minds.

Champlain protested, of course. Indeed, the constancy of his actions was disproof enough of the story. But the episode shows the power of rumor among the Indians and its extraordinary diffusion, across hostile lines, through a thousand miles of forest.

Champlain questioned his friends at length concerning the geography of the upper St. Lawrence and the Great Lakes. Four of them assured him that they had seen a sea, far from their country, difficult of access. They meant Lake Superior, or possibly Lake Michigan. "They told me also that during the preceding winter some Indians had come from the direction of Florida, beyond the country of the Iroquois, who were familiar with our ocean." These were probably the Andastes, who dwelt along the Susquehanna. What travelers these Indians were! "They spoke to me of these things in great detail, showing me by drawings all the places they had visited, taking pleasure in telling me about them. And as for myself, I was not weary of listening to them."

Presents were formally exchanged. Champlain received a hundred beaver skins and matched them with shining hatchets and other trade goods. Then the barter with the merchants began. "Each pinnace carried off its share. We had had all the trouble and risk; others, who did not worry about discoveries, had the profit, which is the only motive that moves them, since they invest nothing and risk nothing."

The next day the Indians barricaded themselves, both on the side of the woods and on that of the French boats. At nightfall the chiefs summoned Brûlé, who had gained their utter confidence, and Savignon. At midnight Champlain was sent for. He followed the messenger through the dark woods, putting himself entirely in the Indians' hands. "I found them all sitting in council, and they made me sit down beside them, saying that their custom was, when they wished to meet to discuss some matter, to do so at night, in order not to have their attention diverted by any objects; for at night one thought only of listening, whilst daylight distracted the mind by the objects seen. But it seemed to me that, having confidence in me, they wished to tell me their desire in secret. Moreover, they were afraid of the other pinnaces, as they gave me afterwards to understand; for they told me they were displeased at seeing so many Frenchmen, who were not very friendly towards one another, and that they would have much liked to see me alone. They also said that some of their people had been beaten; that they were as kindly disposed toward me as to their own children, and had such confidence in me that they would do whatever I told them, but that they much mistrusted the others. Furthermore that should I return, I was to bring as many people as I liked, provided they were under the leadership of one chief; that they had sent for me to assure me again of their friendship, which would never be broken, and that they hoped I should not be angry with them. They said, moreover, that knowing I had resolved to visit their country, they would show it to me, at the risk of their lives, assisting me with a good number of men who could go anywhere, and that in future we should have the same confidence in them as they had in us."

(Remember that these words were communicated by single or double translation, that no notes could be taken upon them, that Champlain reconstructed them next day or months later. Still, the substance is probably correct. Here, for his French readers, and indeed for us, is his justification of his alliance with the Hurons and Algonquins, and of his military aid to them in the previous year. Alliance opened to him the rich, mysterious west, while the strictly business policy of the free traders would result only in distrust or hostility on the part of the natives.)

The chiefs then presented to Champlain fifty beaver skins and four wampum belts, as precious to them as gold chains. These, they said, were the gifts of distant chiefs, and were to be shared by Champlain and his "brother," Pontgravé. They protested their friendship. "If there were any Frenchmen who wished to go with them, they would be more pleased than ever in order to maintain a firm friendship between us.

"After much conversation I proposed to them that, since they were willing to show me their country, I should humbly request His Majesty to assist us, to the extent of forty or fifty men, equipped with arms and implements necessary for the expedition, and that I should embark with these men on condition that they, the natives, should provide us with provisions during our journey, but that I should bring them what was required to make presents to the chiefs of the regions through which we should pass, and that we should then return and spend the winter at our settlement. Furthermore, if I discovered the country to be good and fertile, I promised to establish several settlements there, whereby we should have communication with one another, and live happily in the fear of God, whom we should make known to them. They were much pleased with this proposal, and urged me to see to it."

(And here we have the clear statement of Champlain's policy, which he was to propose in France, which he was to follow all the rest of his life. One may distinguish in it four headings: alliance with the trading Indians, and military aid if necessary; exploration, in the hope of finding a Western sea and a passage to the Orient; colonization, with the establishment of permanent posts in the far interior; and religious instruction, leading to Christianization. Each of these purposes was necessarily linked to the single purpose of his masters: the development of the fur trade. The commercial purpose justified the others; the others supported the commercial purpose, and enlarged it to a dream of illimitable wealth.)

It was daybreak when the council came to an end. The Indians said they were going off to hunt beaver, which Champlain knew to be unlikely at that place and season.

On the second night following, he and Brûlé were again summoned. They went eight leagues overland to a new encampment, apparently on the shore of the Lac des Deux Montagnes. Champlain was greeted with a formal banquet of meat and fish. This he choked down, though he had just dined well on the way. Savage etiquette admitted no excuses. The braves withdrew for a conference in the woods, and Champlain killed time by regarding the scenery, which, he says, was very agreeable, and indeed it still is.

The two were then bidden to the council. All smoked long in silence. The *compliments d'usage* followed, the protestations of affection and trust. The Indians would have been much hurt, they said, if they had been unable to make a proper farewell to their good friend. (The savage sensibility, the woodland courtliness!) Their surreptitious departure from the trading area had been caused only by a rumor that the independent merchants planned to kill them. "They felt that I could not defend them against the others, who were much more numerous, and so they had used this craftiness, in order to get away quietly. Had there been only our two pinnaces, they would have stayed a few days longer. They begged of me, when I returned with my companions, not to bring any other people. I told them that I had not brought these, but that they had followed me without my asking them, and that in future I should proceed in a different fashion from what I had done in the past, at which declaration they were highly pleased."

(Another lesson for the members of the King's Council, who would read this report in the way of business.)

Impressed by the services of Brûlé among the Algonquins, these Hurons asked that a Frenchman be delegated to winter with them. Champlain said he would be glad to send one who would volunteer. The Indians said that a rival trader named Bouvier was trying to persuade them to take a youth back with them. Would Champlain approve?

"We are not enemies," replied Champlain. "You have seen us talking together. But so far as trade is concerned, each of us does what he can. Bouvier probably wishes to send this youth, as I sent mine, hoping for future advantage. Still, it is your duty to decide to whom you owe most and from whom you expect most."

This was fair, and the Indians recognized the fairness, as Champlain knew they would.

"There is no comparison," they said, "between what we owe to the two of you, for you have given us much assistance in our wars, and have offered your personal help for the future. Since we have always found you truthful in such matters, everything now depends upon your good pleasure. But Bouvier is offering some very fine presents."

"It is a matter of indifference to me whether you take this lad or not. But he must stay with Iroquet."

So it was settled. But notice the final provision: the rival youth was to learn Algonquin, not Huron. Champlain already had Brûlé, Marsolet, perhaps others, who knew Algonquin or its Montagnais dialect. He had no interpreter for Huron except Savignon. He would permit no competitor to gain a special advantage among the Hurons.

One thing more, said the chiefs. One of their men, who had been three times a prisoner of the Iroquois, and who had three times escaped, had resolved to go with nine others on the warpath to avenge his mistreatment. All the chiefs had begged him not to undertake so desperate a venture; they hoped that Champlain would remonstrate with him more effectively. (Notice how little authority the chiefs had over their willful braves.) Champlain argued with him, but in vain. "Showing me his hacked-off fingers, as well as the great cuts and burns on his body, where they had tortured him, he replied that it was impossible for him to live unless he killed some of his enemies and took vengeance upon them. He said that his heart told him that he must set off as soon as possible, and he did go, firmly resolved to fight bravely."

When a warrior's heart spoke, all authority must defer. We never hear of this brave little band again: probably the Iroquois completed the formula of torture.

Now the council broke up. Champlain took formal leave of his friends. He had a moving farewell with Savignon, most disconsolate at quitting the French and returning to the hard life of the woods. But Champlain was glad to be rid of the responsibility for Savignon; any mishap to him would be imputed to French treachery. Among the Hurons he would be most useful as a living witness to French fair dealing.

Brother Sagard saw Savignon in Huronia a dozen years later. He had the fate of others who have seen wonders. When he told his companions about the French King's rolling golden cabin drawn by eight moose without horns, and about a machine that proclaimed the hours of the day, his companions laughed at him. He asked in vain to return to France. Could he buy a wife there for three beaver skins, he inquired.

(A century and a half later Voltaire wrote a philosophical tale about a Huron's visit to France and his naïve impressions of civilization. Had Voltaire, who read everything, read of our Savignon? At least he knew the name of Brother Sagard.)

Now Champlain, having said his farewells, prepared to return to his pinnace by the woodland path. "But no!" said the Indians. "We shall take you back by a speedier way; by the rapids!"

Champlain demurred to the limit of courtesy, for he could not swim. The Indians insisted, and he recognized that an outright refusal of their offer would be put down to cowardice, the unforgivable fault. The Indians stripped naked; Champlain, trained to French decency, wore his shirt. Eight canoes made the descent, "for it often happens that some are lost in running the rapids. Consequently they keep close together, in order to give prompt help, if a canoe should happen to capsize. They told me that if unfortunately my canoe should upset, since I did not know how to swim, I ought under no circumstances to let go, but to keep hold of the small pieces of wood in the center of the canoe, for they would easily rescue me. I assure you that even the bravest people in the world who have not seen nor passed this place in small boats such as theirs, could not do so without great apprehension."

What an understatement! Go to the Lachine Rapids today; watch the water, smooth, quiet-flowing, terrible, speeding down to the belt of rocks where it leaps white and high; you will feel a sense of calamity, of death. There is something uncanny in the fierce hurry of the flood down to a wide horizon, lying below the normal level of the world's edge. It is a brave man, however stout a swimmer, who will shoot these rapids in a little boat. Our Champlain gives once more the fullest proof of his fortitude, embarking for the journey in a birch-bark canoe, only in order not to lose face with his Indians.

He came through without mishap. He was the first white man to run the Lachine Rapids and survive.

On the following day the Indians set off for their homes. The Hurons took with them Étienne Brûlé, unsated with Indian adventure. He was thus the first white man to see Lake Huron.[1] Captain Bouvier's young man accompanied Iroquet, for a winter on the lower Ottawa.

Since a large party of Algonquins was reported on its way to the rendezvous, Champlain lingered on, as did the independent traders, who had little to show for their enterprise. They waited three tiresome and hungry weeks. At last the Indians arrived. They were Algonquins from Allumette Island on the upper Ottawa. The chief, one-eyed Tessouat, was an old friend of Champlain's. The two had met at Tadoussac back in 1603.

[1] Champlain does not give the name of the youth who accompanied the Hurons, and it seems curious that he does not identify him with the young interpreter who sat beside him at the ceremonies of the trading fair. Still, the chances are it was Brûlé who made the western journey. In 1615 he accompanied Champlain as Huron interpreter; he carried out a diplomatic mission alone to the Andastes, who spoke an Iroquoian tongue, closely allied to Huron. When and where did he learn the Hurons' difficult speech, if not in the winter of 1611–12?

They brought no great cargo of furs. They presented ten beaver skins to each captain, with apologies for the scant number. To Champlain they were most deferential. "You are not like the others," they said. "They are well disposed toward us only on account of our beaver skins. But you have always assisted us, and are not double-tounged like the others."

The words gave pleasure to kindly Champlain, who loved rectitude, and who liked to have his rectitude recognized. But he felt it his duty to defend the traders, who, despite their commercial rivalry, were making a common cause with him in penetrating the country. It would be dangerous to set all the French at each others' throats.

"All those you see assembled are your friends," he said. "Perhaps, should opportunity arise, they will not fail to do their duty. We are all friends; you should continue to be well disposed toward us. I hope that all will trade in peaceable fashion."

The chiefs made Champlain secretly a present of forty beaver skins. They said they were happy that he planned to make a settlement at the rapids. Champlain brought up again a proposal that he should explore to the northward. The Indians were evasive; but they offered to take one of Champlain's youths and treat him like one of their own children. Champlain picked a young man named Nicolas du Vignau. "I gave him a very particular memorandum of the things he should observe." We shall hear more of Nicolas du Vignau.

A second party of Algonquins arrived. The first comers greeted them with a dance, performing military evolutions to music, weapons in hand. The newcomers sang and did a seated dance, gyrating in their canoes. Then they proceeded to barter their few poor furs.

Finally the leave takings took place. The great trading fair of 1611 was at an end.

I have reported this gathering in detail, since it serves as an example of the ceremonial typically observed. First the formal opening of the fair, with organized shouts and speeches of welcome. Then a conference, with a policy committee bringing in its report. Then the main business of the assembly, the trading, the haggling over prices, the shopping from merchant to merchant. Meanwhile, many a private meeting in smoke-filled glades, propositions, deals, and confidences. Then a full assembly, at which the program for the coming year was discussed. And diversions: banquets, songs, even a dance.

It was more than a trading fair; it was a trade convention. The ritual, as it is observed today in our great hotels, has changed only in unessentials.

The result of this fair was that the Hurons and the Ottawa Algonquins were knit by ever tighter bonds to the French. The Indians promised more and better furs; Champlain promised military aid. He was opening the way for an exploration to the west on a large scale. He had gained his end in Canada; now it remained for him to gain his end in France, to persuade his superiors, or the government, to fulfill the promises he had made.

On July 18 he left the rapids and arrived at Quebec in two days. He made some repairs at the Habitation and planted some rosebushes. He arranged to leave a garrison for the winter; the captain he does not name. He then slipped down the river to Tadoussac and informed Pontgravé that he had decided not to winter in Canada, but would return to France. His reason is clear. He alone could hope to persuade those in place to send him back to Canada with fifty good men, ready to fight the Iroquois, ready to push westward to unknown lands.

He took ship with a Captain Thibaut of La Rochelle. After an uneventful journey of just a month, he landed in the captain's home port on September 10.

CHAPTER XIII

The Seventh Voyage

TODAY LA ROCHELLE is one of the most picturesque cities of France, a somnolent ancient port, with covered galleries along its streets, with richly carved façades, memories of wealth and pride. For Champlain, to whom the concept "picturesque" would have been difficult, La Rochelle was merely the great Protestant business city, thriving with unholy prosperity.

In the merchants' offices he had some good news. De Monts was in the near-by city of Pons, of which (if you remember, if you have been reading with steadfast attention) he was governor. This was a bit of luck for Champlain. He bought a horse, *un malheureux cheval*, a sorry creature. He set off for Pons; and (but this is supposition) he made a short detour to visit his old home of Brouage. He was warmly greeted, for Brouage was aware of the Western world and proud of Champlain's achievement. Among the welcomers (but this is supposition on supposition) was Louis Houel, royal secretary, and director of the Brouage salt works. Houel recounted Champlain's visit (and this is supposition cubed) to the Recollect monks in their Brouage monastery, and troubled certain bored solitaries with dreams of missionary adventure in the New World.

Champlain rode on to Pons. He urged his jade into the court of the château, which still stands nobly poised above the little river. M. de Monts welcomed him heartily with the inevitable treasured bottle (for this is great wine country, only a dozen miles from Cognac).

Champlain presented his report. He dwelt at length on the importance of the alliance he had formed with the Hurons and Algonquins, on the presumed wealth of the interior, on the discoveries waiting to be made. He spoke of his promise to return in the following year with a force of fifty men. The Company must not let him down; he must not lose face with his friends. Surely the government could be persuaded to provide such an insignificant army to win an empire for France!

De Monts's imagination took fire. "I must attend to this myself. It will need influence and wire-pulling at court. As soon as I can get away, I shall go to Fontainebleau. I shall meet you there."

Cheerily Champlain parted from his friend, and cheerily took the great western highway toward Paris. But on the way his horse stumbled, fell, and rolled on its rider, nearly killing him.

Champlain lay long in some roadside inn, through an interminable autumn, probably through an interminable winter.

What an infuriating experience! He had survived the Atlantic storms, dodged the fog-wrapped icebergs; he had shot the St. Louis Rapids in a birch-bark canoe; he had put himself in the hands of hundreds of bloodthirsty savages and had had an Indian arrow in his neck; he had journeyed six thousand miles in tiny boats, only to fall under a wretched horse on a French highway a few short leagues from home! His little bride awaited him; important business summoned him; and he must groan on a bed, alone, in a dismal inn!

When at length he was well enough to ride on to Paris, he found plenty of news awaiting him. De Monts had seen his partners from Rouen, and they, in a fury at the sight of the balance sheet, had refused to have anything more to do with New France. Free trade, they said, would be their ruin. The business forever promised, never returned a decent profit.

But constant de Monts still had faith. He bought out the shares of his partners and became sole owner of the business.

In the spring of 1612 he sent out Pontgravé with a few men to carry on the settlement at Quebec. Champlain was unable to accompany them, whether because of his injury or because de Monts needed him in Paris. Champlain grieved to think of the disappointment of his Indian friends, who would come to the rendezvous expecting to see him at the head of a little army. Well, *tant pis*; there was nothing to be done.

Champlain had a proposition to make. Since free trade was destroying the business, and since there was little chance of a renewal of de Monts's monopoly, the solution would be to form the responsible traders into a common company. Each would pay in a fixed sum, for the support of the Habitation, for exploration to the west, for the establishment of posts in the interior. Nonmembers would be forbidden to engage in the fur trade. This association was, as Professor Harold A. Innis of Toronto points out, in fact a trust, and Champlain was America's first trust promoter.

Although de Monts saw in the proposal the annihilation of the great sums he had already paid out, he consented to it. Let us admire the constancy of good de Monts, his faith in his old companion's dreams, his faith in Canada.

But de Monts was distracted by urgent affairs from promoting the interests of the new company. He turned over to Champlain the whole duty of obtaining its authorization at court.

Champlain, who has hitherto been only the trusted agent, the specialist, now for the first time assumes a leading role in the business concerns of New France. He finds that the conduct of great affairs is not so difficult after all. One needs only to see clearly the purpose, to seek the means, never to be distracted, never to surrender.

He had an interview with President Jeannin, superintendent of finance. Jeannin, old, wise, and cynical, approved the scheme heartily. But (if we may read a little between the lines) he said to Champlain:

"My dear sir, your project is a sound one, and useful to France. But powerful interests are opposed to it. If we should grant this monopoly to a restricted group of merchants, a great outcry would go up from every seaboard city that we are throttling trade and that we have certainly been bribed. We are unpopular enough already without giving our enemies such a weapon. Now I will tell you what to do. Put yourselves under the protection of some great nobleman. He will exert pressure on us, and we will yield, with apparent reluctance. And he will have to take all the blame and the unpopularity."

"Whom would you suggest?"

"This is off the record? Then why not the Comte de Soissons? He is a prince of the blood and governor of Normandy. And he is the head of the most powerful cabal in France."

"Mm, the Comte de Soissons. I knew him in the wars. But, if I may be permitted to say so, he is vain, fickle, not very intelligent, and extremely avaricious."

"Precisely. Give him a good share of the future profits, and he will do anything for you. We will drop him a hint; he will demand the post of viceroy of New France, and we will grant it to him. Reluctantly, of course, very reluctantly."

President Jeannin laid his finger along his nose, and Champlain chuckled with appreciation.

Champlain called on the Comte de Soissons. "I pointed out to him," he says, "the importance of the matter, and showed him the way to regulate it, as well as the harm which confusion had already produced, and the complete ruin with which it was threatened, to the great dishonor of the French name, unless God stirred up someone who would set it on foot again and would give some hope of accomplishing some day the result expected from it."

The Count was persuaded, with financial arguments that are not revealed.

Champlain presented a petition to His Majesty and the lords in Council. A decree of October 8, 1612, appointed the Comte de Soissons viceroy of New France. A week later Champlain was officially named his lieutenant in that country. He immediately prepared to have the King's commission published in all the ports and harbors of France.

And on November 1 the Comte de Soissons died of the smallpox.

Champlain turned desperately to the Prince de Condé, nephew of the Comte de Soissons, greedier, meaner-minded than his uncle. In six years, says Cardinal de Richelieu, Condé extorted 3,660,000 livres from the Queen. De Monts's company could offer him little in comparison to his other gains, but he was anxious for that little, especially for the annual gift of a horse worth 1,000 crowns.

Condé was appointed viceroy of New France, by an act of November 22, 1612, and Champlain was confirmed in his lieutenancy. According to the terms of the act, any French merchant could engage in the fur trade by joining the company and paying to it the proper fees, which were no doubt high.

The merchants, who had no stomach for paying fees without any sure return, made the expected outcry. And, as was foreseen, the might of Condé silenced the grumblers.

Champlain's commission is an interesting document, containing various provisions that Champlain certainly asked to have inserted. He is instructed to live in Quebec, to construct and garrison other forts at need, to subject all the peoples of New France to the authority of His Majesty, to instruct them in the knowledge of God and of the Catholic faith. He is given the right to commission officers, to establish a system of justice, to make alliances and treaties with native princes, and, if the treaties be broken, to make war. He is instructed to make explorations and discoveries, particularly in the St. Lawrence area, in order to find the easy road to China and the East Indies. He is ordered to seek for gold and other minerals. And he is given the right to seize and apprehend the vessels of any unlicensed merchants trading above Quebec, to confiscate their goods and transport the masters to France for trial.

With this document in hand, Champlain becomes the effective ruler of New France.

While these affairs were in course, the ships that had been out to Canada for the summer returned.

Pontgravé reported on the season's business, the last under the system of free trade. A swarm of independents had appeared at the St. Louis Rapids, and none had made any proper profits. Two hundred Indians had come down from the interior. They were much annoyed not to find Champlain and his promised army. Pontgravé had made every apology, assuring them that Champlain would certainly return in the following year, and insisting that they must be on hand to meet him. But the independents were telling the Indians a different story. Champlain, they said, was dead; he would never come again. "Thus does jealousy steal into bad natures in opposition to worthy objects," says Champlain. "They only want people to run a thousand risks in order that they may keep the profits and the others the hardships. It is unreasonable when one has caught the sheep for another to have the fleece. Had they been willing to share our explorations, use their resources, and risk their persons, they would have shown that they possessed honor and a love of renown; but on the contrary they show that they are driven by pure malice to seek to enjoy equally with us the fruits of our labors."

(But possibly there is some excuse for the merchants. After Champlain's accident he was laid up for a long time. Perhaps he did not appear in Paris till the spring; perhaps the merchants actually thought him dead.)

Among the passengers on Pontgravé's ship was the youth Nicolas du Vignau, who had spent the winter of 1611–12 with Chief Tessouat and the Algonquins of the upper Ottawa. He brought exciting news.

"I have seen the northern sea," he said. "The Ottawa River comes from a lake which has an outlet northward into that sea. In seventeen days one can go from the St. Louis Rapids to that sea and back again. On the shore of that sea I saw pieces of the wreck of the English ship. I was told that there were eighty men on this ship. These Englishmen tried to take the Indians' food from them by force, so the Indians killed them all, except a boy whom they are keeping for you. I have seen the scalps of those Englishmen."

Champlain was delighted. He knew that Henry Hudson had wintered in James Bay in 1610–11. Nicolas's story seemed reasonable enough. It justified Champlain in making a serious attempt to find a good overland route to this Northern sea. France must make a proper claim to the northland, rich in furs; she must check any English effort to divert the fur trade to Hudson Bay. Nothing would spur the lords in Council so much as a suggestion of English commercial rivalry.

There was, however, something vaguely suspect in Nicolas's words and manner. "Tell me all the truth, so that I may inform the King," said Champlain. "I warn you that if you are telling a lie, you are putting a rope around your neck. But if your story is true, you can count on being well rewarded."

Nicolas took the greatest of oaths that his story was completely true, and even drew up a written account of his adventures. Champlain reported the matter to President Jeannin and the other eminences, who told him that he should certainly look at the northern sea. They did not, however, offer any subsidy for the expedition.

Now, as the time draws near for Champlain's departure, let us look for a moment into his private life.

When he returned to Paris in the winter or spring of 1612, he found his thirteen-year-old bride waiting, happy to see again the adventurous husband of whom she had boasted to her girl companions. He brought her, in his saddlebags, curious souvenirs, beaded moccasins, baskets of sweet grass adorned with porcupine quills. For her elders, perhaps more gruesome presents: an Iroquois scalp, a tobacco pouch made of the skin of a human hand with the fingernails intact.

In the intervals of business the two walked the streets of Paris together, Champlain in the sober black of the well-to-do bourgeois, Hélène in her black fur-trimmed mantle and white coif. They attended, certainly, the great three-day festival in the Place Royale (now the Place des Vosges) celebrating the betrothal of the young King to a Spanish princess. They saw the Chevaliers de la Gloire defend the Palais de la Félicité against the attack of the Chevaliers du Soleil. They saw a moving mountain spouting fire from its top and water from its sides. Champlain criticized the costume of dancers dressed as savages in one of the ballets. In the evening they watched the torchlight procession through Paris, which set only two serious fires.

I think this was the happiest period of Champlain's married life.

But soon it was time to be off for New France.

The new company had met plenty of opposition. The hostile merchants of the coast bitterly objected to joining the association. The Parlement of Rouen refused to publish the King's commission. Champlain had to make three journeys to Rouen with home, with an assurance of the good treatment they would receive and of the quantity of fine goods which were at the Rapids, as well as of my desire to help them in their wars."

He obtained from the Indians, with much difficulty, two canoes and a guide. He loaded the craft with food, arms, and presents for strange chiefs he would encounter. He carried his precious copper astrolabe, with which to take the latitudes northward to the icy sea. He had with him four Frenchmen, sturdy paddlers. One was an interpreter, Thomas (probably Thomas Godefroy). Another was the youth Nicolas du Vignau, who had been to Hudson Bay in the previous year. Or so he said.

Champlain's distrust of this shifty young man was mounting. When his men were assembled at St. Helen's Island for the leave taking, Champlain said to Nicolas that if his story was not true, he should now make his confession and thus spare them all a dangerous journey. Nicolas swore, on peril of his life, that all he had said was the exact truth.

On May 27 Champlain put his loaded canoes into the water. His mates fired a farewell salute with their small arms. He was very happy. He was off again, into the west, into the unknown. He would have no more concern with mean merchants, with pettifogging councilors. He must trust henceforth only to strong arms and courageous hearts.

The party made the long and very difficult portage around the rapids, "which is no small labor for those who are not used to it." They traversed Lac St. Louis, where the St. Lawrence and the Ottawa meet. "This lake is filled with fine large islands, which are like meadows, where it is a pleasure to hunt, venison being found there in abundance, as well as wildfowl and fish. The surrounding country is filled with great forests." At day's end the party built a barricade against prowling Iroquois and kept a good watch through the night.

Next day they portaged past the swift waters dividing Montreal Island from Ile Perrot, where today Galipeault Bridge carries an endless stream of unregarding motorists. They entered the ample, coruscating Lac des Deux Montagnes, the delight of summering Montrealers. Gradually the lake narrowed, the water shoaled, the paddlers labored hard against the current. They began to meet long, furious rapids. They unshipped their goods, carried, it seemed, forever, and re-embarked in placid reaches.

They came to Chute à Blondeau, today a green village by roaring narrows, pleasing to the tourist's eye. "Here we had much labor, for so great is the swiftness of the current that it makes a dreadful noise, and, falling from level to level, produces everywhere such a white foam that no water at all is seen. This rapid is strewn with rocks and in it here and there are some islands covered with pines and white cedars. It was here we had much difficulty, for being unable to portage our canoes on account of the thickness of the woods, we had to track them, and in pulling mine I nearly lost my life, because the canoe turned broadside into a whirlpool, and had I not luckily fallen between two rocks, the canoe would have dragged me in, since I could not quickly enough loosen the rope which was twisted around my hand, which hurt me very much and nearly cut it off. In this danger I cried aloud to God and began to pull my canoe towards me, which was sent back to me by an eddy such as occurs in these rapids. Having escaped, I gave praise to God, beseeching him to preserve us. Later on our Indian came to my help, but I was out of danger.

"One must not be surprised that I was anxious to preserve our canoe; for had it been lost, we must have prepared to remain there or wait until some Indians came along, which was a poor prospect for those who have nothing to eat, and are not used to such fatigue. As for our Frenchmen, they did not fare any better, and several times they were nearly lost. But God's mercy preserved us all."

Champlain continued upstream to the mild and cheery level lands above Hawkesbury. Here he met a party of Indians, who were surprised indeed to see him. He held a council with them and told them that if they were resolved to go to war, he and his men would join them. Thereat they were much pleased. When he asked for a guide to the upper river the Indians tried to dissuade him. "The way is bad," they said; "hitherto you have seen nothing like it." Champlain persisted and obtained a good guide, a strong paddler. The weakest of his Frenchmen he sent back to the St. Louis Rapids.

He pushed on against the stream, through a clean, attractive

country, with good soil and fine open woods. On June 4 he came
to the site of Ottawa, where the Rideau flows in from the south
and the Gatineau from the north. He admired the superb fall
of the Rideau, throwing its waters forward clear of the cliff to
make a curtain (*rideau*). The Indians passed behind the waterfall
for amusement, barely wetting themselves. Champlain was
captivated by this beautiful spot, where one day was to rise the
towered capital of all his realm.

Here the Ottawa River thundered over a barrier with a noise
that could be heard two leagues away. The Indians called the
fall Asticou, the boiler, and so it is now known by the French
translation, Chaudière. But today the wild waters are enslaved
and work humbly in factories.

After a very difficult portage over sharp rocks the travelers
came to a long lake with fine wooded islands. This is the Lac
Deschênes, basking in its wide, rich alluvial valley. Then past
the long rapids of the Chats. The labor of carrying became intolerable for the French. They cached most of their food and
superfluous clothing. They wondered at their two tireless Indian
helpers, bearing their great burdens swiftly through the tangle
along the shore. So we soft white men in the north still wonder
at our guides.

They entered now the long Lac des Chats, passing the site of
marbled Arnprior. Points of grim, banded gneiss, outcrops of
the Laurentian shield, thrust down from the north. The land
of the red cedar began. On an island, probably near Braeside,
Champlain set up a high cross with the arms of France.

The river narrowed again, flowing swiftly, leaping high and
white over granite boulders. They had reached Portage du Fort.
"Above here," said the Indians, "river very bad. Rapids very
bad. We make long portage to west. Find chain of lakes. Much
better."

"Not at all," said Nicolas du Vignau. "Stick to river. River
all right."

"You tired of living!" said the Indians.

Champlain looked at young Nicolas with increasing suspicion.
A hard canoe trip is a good test of character. And Champlain
remembered that Nicolas had said that the Northern sea was
only eight days' journey from the St. Louis Rapids. The party

was now ten days out and had not yet reached the land of King Tessouat. Though they were not, of course, traveling at the pace of Indians, they had proved Nicolas's calculations false.

Champlain began to wonder if Nicolas was not trying to impede his progress, to prevent him from arriving anywhere. He suspected, even, that Nicolas was hoping for a fatal accident to his master in some thunderous fall.

He took the Indians' advice. Ahead of them lay a seven-mile portage over high, heavily wooded ground. They cached all their provisions and packed for the carry. Champlain's share was three arquebuses (have you ever lifted an arquebus?), three paddles, his cloak, and his astrolabe. Before starting he took the latitude, making, in his agitation, a mistake of a full degree.

It was a cruel carry. The men suffered more from mosquitoes than from their burdens, says Champlain, for as one struggles through the brush, sweat pours down, mosquitoes assemble joyfully, and one has no hand free to deal with them.

They came at length to Olmsted Pond, near Haley. Here they camped and immediately built a smudge to drive away the mosquitoes. "Their importunity is so remarkable that it is impossible to give any description of it." The travelers set their nets and caught some fish. This was their first food in twenty-four hours.

The next day they made a portage "through more difficult country than we had yet seen, on account of the wind having blown down pine trees one on top of the other, which is no small inconvenience; for one must go now over and now under these trees."

While floundering among these trees Champlain lost his astrolabe. Where it fell, it lay for two hundred and fifty-four years. It was then picked up by a sharp-eyed fourteen-year-old boy; and now it is safely ensconced in the collections of the New York Historical Society.

The party set down their loads on the bank of Muskrat Lake. Here they found a tribe of agricultural Indians. Their chief, Nibachis, was much astonished that Champlain and his companions, loaded with gear, could have come so far. "You must have fallen from the clouds," he said. "It is clear that your reputation is merited; you are the sort of man who carries out all he sets his heart upon." He made the French a most welcome present of fish. Champlain then had Thomas the interpreter tell him and his chiefs that he had come to assist them in their wars, and that he wished to push on further to see other chiefs for the same purpose. At this they were very glad and promised to help him.

Nibachis was as good as his word. He lent Champlain two canoes and an escort, which guided him to the north end of Muskrat Lake and over an easy portage to the Ottawa River again, near Perretton.

Here he found an old friend, Tessouat, the one-eyed King of the Allumette Algonquins. Champlain had met him first at Tadoussac ten years before and had seen him dance naked in solemn celebration of victory.

Tessouat could not believe his single eye. "I am dreaming!" he cried. He welcomed Champlain with shouts of incredulity and delight.

He took Champlain to visit his village and stronghold on Morrison Island, in midstream of the Ottawa, with swift rapids on either side. The situation was a strong one, safe from attack. It had another advantage: it was a tollgate on the river highway.

Shrewd King Tessouat and his sagacious people had worked out a commercial racket, simple and profitable. They commanded the rapids and the portage routes by their side. Though they numbered only four hundred warriors, they were able to enforce the payment of customs duties by all the native traders bound for the St. Lawrence with cargoes of furs. They became haughty and insolent, and even dared, a little later, to seize and abuse priests for attempting to travel free. Brother Sagard, in 1624, found them the most churlish, arrogant, and uncivil of the tribes he had seen. It was one of these Islanders who gave Champlain the supreme example of barbarity. Says Father Le Jeune: "When Monsieur de Champlain went to help them in their wars, and saw one of them treat roughly a woman prisoner or a child, he tried to make them understand that such barbarity was foreign to the kindness natural to man. An Island Savage, upon hearing this, said to him: 'See what I shall do, now that thou speakest of it;' and he took by the foot a nursing child, and struck its head against a rock or tree."

The wickedness of their hearts was belied by their fine exterior. Sagard calls them "the best clothed and painted and the most prettily bedecked of any, as if finery were inseparably combined and bound up with arrogance, vanity, and pride, as the nursing mother of all the rest of the vices and sins. The young women and girls seem to be nymphs, so well dressed are they, and hinds, so fleet of foot are they."

Champlain was struck with the elaborate tombs of their cemetery, painted red and yellow, decorated with wood carvings, including the sculptured portraits of the deceased. These Indians made much of their cult of the dead and turned their grief to profit. "They ought to be very rich this year," said Father Le Jeune in 1636. "A Captain of the Island having died this year, and their tears being not yet dried, no strange Nation can pass by there without making them some gift, to make them more easily swallow, as they say, the grief occasioned by the death of their Chief."

Champlain noted the poverty of the soil. "Why do you waste your time cultivating this poor region?" he said. "There is much better land to be had at the Great Rapids."

"We are forced to take refuge here, to be safe from our enemies," said Tessouat, making no mention of the commercial advantages of his home. "But if you will make a settlement of Frenchmen at the St. Louis Rapids, we will leave our home and come to live near you, for our enemies can do us no harm if you protect us."

"This year," said Champlain, "we shall prepare wood and stone. Next year we shall build a fort and plow the land." At this the Indians gave a great shout in sign of approval.

On the following day a formal banquet was held. "All the guests came, each with his wooden bowl and spoon, and sat down on the ground in Tessouat's cabin without observing any rank or ceremony. He served out to them a sort of stew, made of maize crushed between two stones, mixed with meat and fish cut into little pieces, and all cooked together without salt. There was also meat roasted on coals, and boiled fish, which he also distributed. As for myself, since I wished none of their stew, because they are very dirty in their cooking, I asked them for some fish and meat to prepare in my own way, and they gave me some. For drink we had fine clear water. Tessouat, who gave the banquet, conversed with us without eating himself, as is their custom.

"When the banquet was over, the young men, who are not present at the speeches and council-meetings, and who during banquets remain at the doors of the wigwams, left. Then each of those who had stayed began to fill his pipe, and several offered me theirs, and we spent a full half hour at this ceremony, without uttering a word, as is their custom."

Champlain then addressed the council, through his interpreter. "The object of my journey," he said, "is to assure you of my affection, and of my desire to aid you in your wars. The reason I did not come last year is that my King kept me otherwise employed. But now he has commanded me to visit you, and to reassure you regarding his purpose. I have now come to observe the nature of your country. It is my desire to visit the nation of the Nipissings, who dwell six days' journey to the west. I wish to invite them also to go on the warpath. I request of you, therefore, four canoes and a crew of eight men, to make this expedition."

The elders smoked sullenly and muttered to one another. Tessouat spoke for them. He began with diplomatic compliments. "You are more kindly disposed towards us than any Frenchman we have seen, and you have proved it by the toilsome journey you have just made." And then the diplomatic reproaches. "You did not come last year, and we sought you in vain at the rapids, trusting in your promise. Some of the Frenchmen there treated us very badly, and we decided to go no more to the trading fair. Most of our warriors have gone on the warpath, counting no more on French aid. So I suggest that we make plans for a great expedition against the Iroquois next year. In the meantime, we shall alert all the tribes of this region.

"Now as for your proposal to push westward and visit the Nipissings, we advise you against it. The way is hard. Those tribes are sorcerers; they have killed many of my people by magic and poisoning. They are cowardly, and would be useless in our war."

Champlain recognized in Tessouat's words the commercial motive, the age-old opposition of the middleman to the direct contact of producer and consumer. Nevertheless, as he says, "my one desire was to see these tribes, and to make friends with them, in order to view the northern sea."

He protested that he was ready to make the journey, however hard; that he was proof against spells and sorceries; that his only purpose was to unite the tribes in friendly bonds.

The Indians yielded. They would lend him the four canoes! "Thereat I was much pleased, and forgot all my past troubles in the hope of seeing that much desired sea."

Champlain then left the council to its deliberations and went for a walk in the gardens, inspecting the first shoots of the pumpkins, beans, and French peas. (This is our first indication that European seeds were in the hands of the Indians, soon to alter their economy.) After a time the interpreter Thomas, who had been listening to good effect, came to find him, with word that the council was in the mood to revoke its promise.

"This news grieved me greatly, and at once I went off to find them, and told them that till then I had held them to be men and true to their word; but that now they were showing themselves children and liars, and that if they did not wish to keep their promises, they should not pretend to be my friends; however, if they felt inconvenienced by giving me four canoes, they could give me but two, and only four Indians."

Champlain was able to take the high hand, at need, with the Indians, whose thought and behavior he had come to know so well.

The chiefs sulkily repeated their objections. They were trying to discourage him for his own good.

Champlain played his trump. He pointed to young Nicolas du Vignau. "This youth," he said, "has been in that country; he did not notice all the difficulties you speak of, nor did he find those tribes so evil as you say."

The chiefs stared at the hangdog youth. Tessouat said to him: "Nicolas, is it true that you have said you were in the Nipissing country?"

After a long silence Nicolas spoke. "Yes, I was there."

All the chiefs rose to their feet, shouting. They rushed upon him, "as if they would have eaten him or torn him asunder."

"You are a liar!" cried Tessouat. "You know very well that

every night you slept alongside of me and my children, and every morning you got up in the same place. If you went to those tribes, it was in your sleep. How have you been so impudent as to tell lies to your chief, and so wicked as to try to risk his life among so many dangers? You are a scoundrel; he ought to put you to death more cruelly than we do our enemies. I am not surprised that he importuned us so much on the strength of your words."

Nicolas, silent, hung his head.

"Nicolas," said Champlain sternly, "what is your answer? You must make a reply to these accusations. What evidence have you of your journey?"

Nicolas remained silent.

Mastering his fury, Champlain pulled him out from the Indian lodge. "Nicolas," he said, "you must tell me the truth. If you have seen the northern sea, say so, and you will get your reward in due time. If not, in God's name admit your lies, so that we won't risk our lives any farther."

"I was there," said Nicolas, and made a great oath in support of his word. "I was there, and if the Indians will give us canoes, I will prove it to you."

"Good," said Champlain. The two re-entered the lodge. As the Indians perceived Nicolas they all shouted "Liar!" together. "Put him to death! Let him name the person who took him to the northern sea! Let him name the lakes, rivers, and trails on the way!"

"I have forgotten the name of my guide," said Nicolas. "I have shown the route on the map I gave to the Sieur de Champlain."

Champlain drew out Nicolas's map and showed it to the Indians. They questioned Nicolas regarding it. He would make no reply, but, says Champlain, by his sullen silence manifested his wickedness.

Champlain withdrew to think things over. As a matter of principle he should accept a Frenchman's word against that of the natives. It was hard to believe that Nicolas had invented the whole elaborate story. "It was more likely that he had seen these things but that his ignorance did not allow him to reply to the questions of the Indians." His statements agreed with the news from England about the explorations in Hudson Bay.

"Now while the canoe was being got ready, I sent for him to come before his companions, and I told him that the time for dissimulation was past, and that he must tell me whether or not he had seen the things he had related. I said that I wished to seize the opportunity that presented itself, that I had forgotten all that had happened, but that if I had to proceed farther, I should have him hanged and strangled without any mercy. After some reflection he fell on his knees and asked me for pardon, declaring that all he had stated regarding this sea both in France and in this country was false; that he had never seen it, and had never been farther than Tessouat's village; and that he had related these things in order to return to Canada.

"In a transport of rage at this I had him removed, being no longer able to endure his presence, and I gave Thomas orders to inquire carefully into the whole affair. To Thomas he persisted in saying that he had had no idea I would undertake the expedition, hoping some difficulty might arise which would prevent me from going farther, such as this with these Indians, who had refused to give me canoes. In this way he hoped the journey would be put off for another year, while he on reaching France would secure a reward for his discovery. Moreover that if I would leave him in this country he would go on until he had found this sea, even if he should die in the attempt. These are his words as reported to me by Thomas, and they did not give me much satisfaction; for I was astonished at the effrontery and wickedness of this liar."

Here were all Champlain's hopes and plans dashed, and the labors of an entire summer spent for nothing. He was enraged at the lying youth, and enraged also at himself, at his own gullibility, his failure to judge character, his inability to distinguish a liar from a truthteller.

"Shortly afterwards and very sorrowfully I went and informed the Indians of the deceit of this liar, telling them that he had confessed the truth to me. At this they were much pleased, but reproached me with having had so little confidence in them, who were chiefs, my friends, and men who always spoke the truth. 'This very wicked liar must die,' said they; 'do you not see that he wanted to kill you? Give him to us, and we promise you he will tell no more lies.' And because they were all howling to get at him, and their children still more loudly, I forbade them to do him any harm, and made them also keep their children from doing so, inasmuch as I wished to bring him back to the Rapids to show him to those gentlemen to whom he was to bring salt water; and I said that when I got there, I should consider what was to be done with him."

In this passage, I think, we may read Champlain's genuine nobility of character. He had been meanly deceived as never before, as never again. The lies of Nicolas, his perjuries under sacred oaths, had led him on a hard and fruitless journey, ending in loss of face before the natives. Nicolas had hoped, had weakly striven, for Champlain's death. If ever, under these pioneer conditions, a man deserved execution, Nicolas did. Champlain had but to nod, to lift a finger, and the youth would have met his merited fate. But no, Champlain mastered his anger. He recognized in it, no doubt, a share of self-condemnation, an impulse to punish another for his own folly in trusting one unworthy of trust.

Champlain, quelling the Indians' anger and his own, gives proof that he has attained true fortitude of the spirit.

"My journey in this direction having ended, and without any hope of seeing the sea in those parts except by surmise, there remained to me nothing but the regret of not having made better use of my time, as also the troubles and fatigues which nevertheless I had to suffer patiently. Had I proceeded in a different direction, relying upon the reports of the Indians, I should then have made a beginning of an affair which must now be postponed until another time."

What affair? Possibly one of the explorations he has previously projected, up the Saguenay, up the St. Maurice to the north. But I think it more likely that he dreamed of mounting the St. Lawrence to the great shoreless inland seas.

At any rate, there was no point in going farther up the Ottawa. He urged the Indians to come down to the St. Louis Rapids, where they would receive good treatment from the company traders. He set up a high cross of white cedar, bearing the arms of France, on the river shore. (The painted fleurs-de-lis were certainly his own handiwork.) He told the Indians that harm would befall anyone who touched it. They promised him that he would find it standing on his next visit.

On June 10 he took leave of Tessouat, vowing that if God kept him in good health he would come in the following year, ready to go on the warpath with his friends. Tessouat promised to collect great numbers of Indians for that enterprise.

Forty canoes, well loaded with furs, set off downstream. They took the river route, past present Waltham and Fort Coulonge, instead of the hard portage route by which Champlain had come. They negotiated a series of very bad rapids. "I saw clearly that had we come up that way, we should have encountered many more difficulties and should barely have got through, and that it was not without reason that the Indians opposed our liar, whose one object was my destruction."

When the fleet reached the Chaudière Falls at Ottawa the Indians performed a ritual observance. Here stood a fantastic rock resembling a man's head and raised stumps of arms. This, they said, was a powerful divinity. A chief took up a collection of tobacco on a wooden plate. The plate was put in the midst of the company, and all danced and sang about it. "Then one of the chiefs makes a speech, pointing out that for years they have been accustomed to make such an offering, and that thereby they receive protection from their enemies; and that otherwise misfortune would happen to them, as the devil persuades them. When he has finished, the orator takes the plate and throws the tobacco into the middle of the boiling water, and all together utter a loud whoop. These poor people are so superstitious that they would not think they could have a safe journey, unless they had performed this ceremony there."

(Superstition? I in my time have sacrificed tobacco in the Chaudière Falls, and I had a very prosperous journey.)

They came, in fact, safely to the St. Louis Rapids. Here Champlain found the eager merchants, including three newcomers who presented licenses from the Prince de Condé. Champlain checked these and found them in order, and gave the holders permission to trade. With his new authority he was able to supervise the trading and prevent any of the abuses that had so discredited the merchants in the previous year. The season was, in fact, a profitable one.

Now there was an act of justice to be done. Champlain assembled all the responsible Frenchmen and the Indian chiefs. Nicolas du Vignau was haled forth. A Frenchman acting as prosecutor questioned him on his actions. He confessed that he had never seen the northern sea, and that he had lied because he wished to make the journey. He asked only for pardon. If Champlain would leave him in Canada, he said, he would work so hard that he would make good his fault, and would visit this sea, and in the following year would bring back definite news concerning it. On this condition Champlain granted him his pardon.

We never hear of him again. Did he in fact attempt to fulfill the condition and find the icy sea, and did he venture into the great northern waste and there obscurely die? I doubt if he was of such mettle. He was despised by the Indians as a liar, by the French as a marplot. The Indians would not receive him. "We left him in God's keeping," says Champlain. He must mean that French and Indians turned him into the woods, to fend for himself. Probably he did not survive long.

The Indians accepted, however, two honest and truthful youths to be educated in their language and in hardihood. Their names we do not know.

As Champlain's business was now ended, he went down to Quebec, and then to Tadoussac. He took the first homeward-bound vessel, and after a speedy passage, arrived in St. Malo on September 26.

CHAPTER XIV

The Eighth Voyage—The Journey to Huronia

WHEN CHAMPLAIN set foot on French soil in September 1613, he put off the explorer to become the businessman. Before even proceeding to Paris, he called on the chief merchants of St. Malo to point out to them the advantages of joining the new company, the trust.

The summer's operations had, indeed, been profitable to the company members. The independents came to recognize that the only safe way to share in the fur trade was to buy into the company. By the end of the year the merchants of St. Malo, reluctantly persuaded, divided the control with those of Rouen. The La Rochelle dealers, though invited, failed to pay their assessment within the specified time.

In Paris, Champlain made his report to the Prince de Condé and to his owners. They were pleased with the prospects; they decided to carry on in accordance with the terms of their concession. "The Company" became the recognized power of New France, regarded with respect in the old country, with awe in the new. It was referred to, briefly, as the *"compagnie des marchands,"* or the *"compagnie de Rouen."* But soon its commonest appellation was the *"compagnie de Champlain."* This widespread use of Champlain's name denotes his dominance of the company's spirit, if not of its finances.

In this autumn of 1613 Champlain had a delightful business in train: the preparation for the press of his second published book, the *Voyages du Sieur de Champlain.*

It is a handsome book, in large format, on fine paper, with maps and illustrations. Author and publisher co-operated to make it a featured volume of the publishing season. It opens with dedicatory letters to the King and to the Queen Regent. Since normally an author dedicated his volume only by permission, the presence of King and Queen Mother in the liminary matter was a guarantee of the book's importance. The dedications are followed by two poems. The first, calling upon the French to carry their country's standard into the new lands, is signed by l'Ange of Paris. This may have been the Sieur l'Ange who made a trip to Canada in 1613; he was certainly not a literary man. The second poem was by Nicolas Motin, now vaguely remembered as a producer of dirty verse for a special trade. His stanzas for Monsieur de Champlain are pure enough, though one may note his insistence on the nakedness of the savages, and on naked Andromeda, who is brought in merely for decoration.

Are we to conclude that Champlain was now moving in the literary circles of Paris? I think not; the publisher could have bought Motin's praise for a few crowns.

Champlain's *Voyages* tells the story of his adventures from 1604 to 1613, from his landing in Acadia to his penetration of the Ottawa country. In organization and in style it marks an improvement on his *Des Sauvages* of 1603. He is less bound by the day-to-day entries in his journal; he responds more skillfully to the interests of the general reader. He recounts dramatic episodes, such as the unmasking of Nicolas du Vignau, with admirable vividness. His style has become easier, more fluent; he has dropped a certain legalistic formality, and tells his story without elegance indeed, but with the rhythms of the spoken language. He wrote, certainly, as he talked. One would say that he talked well.

He intended his book to be useful. For the mariner, he included two maps, one a chart adjusted to the variation of the magnetic needle. He supplied also charts of the Atlantic harbors newly discovered. For the general reader, the adventure stories, the descriptions of the curious native customs, gently but repeatedly enforced the constant theme: the necessity of active governmental support, to capture the fur trade, to exploit the great riches of the interior, to ward off competition from other colonial powers, to bring the natives to the knowledge of Christ, and to find a passage to the boundless wealth of the Orient.

His book is embellished with illustrations, spirited, awkward, and sometimes puzzling to the student. Some commentators, struck by obvious impossibilities, have discounted their value. For instance, he depicts the Habitation of Port Royal, which must have been crudely built of logs, as a typical French farmhouse, trimly boarded, neatly gabled. However, we cannot, for such criticism, dismiss the illustrations as fanciful. Doubtless Champlain made some of his dainty sketches for the engraver, and the engraver prettified and improved, according to the conventions of his trade. But Champlain must have seen them in proof and passed them for publication. In design, composition, and significant detail, the illustrations should be taken as Champlain's own work.

His *Voyages* had a good sale, if one may judge by the number of copies that still survive. It did not, however, take the imagination of his contemporaries by storm. One looks in vain for references to the book in the memoirs and journals of the time. The French were too concerned with the intrigues of the nobles, with the spendthrift policies of the court, with taxes and the cost of living, to waste much attention on savages beyond the seas. Champlain was probably disappointed; but then, authors always are.

In the midst of the happy business of correcting proofs, Champlain had another task in hand. More and more he regretted the absence of any missionary effort among his Indian friends. "They were living without faith or law," he said, "without God, without religion, like brute beasts. So I came to the conclusion that I would be doing very wrong if I did not work to find some means to bring them to the knowledge of God."

He was sincere, certainly. His faith, once offhand enough, was deepening with the years. Yet it must also have occurred to him that competent missionaries would pacify, with Christian principles, the turbulent tribes near his settlement. They would also serve as envoys to distant tribes, and would provide information useful to the explorer and the fur-merchant.

In 1610 (you remember) he had besought Father Cotton, the King's Confessor, to send a Jesuit mission to the St. Lawrence, and had set 3600 livres as the necessary subsidy. Father Cotton had chosen instead to send his Jesuits to Acadia. From this experience Champlain preserved a certain resentment against the Jesuits.

"I exerted myself," he says, "to find some good friars, with zeal and affection for the glory of God, whom I might persuade to come with me to this country to plant there the faith."

The good friars were soon found. His friend the Sieur Houel of Brouage, whom he had seen, as I suppose, in 1611, informed him that certain Recollect friars of Brouage were eager to carry the message of Christ into the wilds.

The Recollects, Franciscan Minorities, Brothers of the Strict Observance, were extremists among the monks. They sought to fulfill the grimmest injunctions of St. Francis, accepting perfect poverty, the rudest of garments, the extreme of self-abnegation. They were called Recollects because of their devotion to *recollectio*, an untranslatable word combining self-gathering, self-communion, meditation.

The trouble with *recollectio* is that the lively human spirit fights undaunted against the orders of the will, and *acedia*, black boredom, melancholia, may ensue. A prison is no less a prison if one has locked oneself in and tossed the key out the window.

The Recollects of Brouage found their meditations disturbed by the fame of their fellow townsman. Visions of the sea's perils, of sweet sufferings in far glittering lands, of holy martyrdoms, intruded upon the subjects set for *recollectio*.

The Sieur Houel visited the monastery, expounded his idea, and asked if any would volunteer to go to Canada. Every monk in the chapter volunteered.

The difficulty was that the enterprise would be expensive, and that the order's vow of poverty was strictly kept. Two of the Brouage monks walked to Paris, obtained papal authorization for their purpose, and interviewed Champlain. He liked the Recollects because they came from his home town and were probably acquaintances, and also because they were "without ambition." There is a suggestion in his words that the Jesuits possessed this quality in excess. He offered to do his best to raise money for a Recollect mission.

We are now in the summer of 1614. Champlain was still in town; he had been prevented by urgent business from making his annual trip to Canada. (But to this I shall return in a moment.)

An opportunity for missionary fund raising was presented by the assembling of the States-General. Representatives of the Church, nobility, and bourgeoisie met in conclave—for the last time, as it turned out, for 175 years. The Provincial of the Recollects addressed a meeting attended by all the cardinals and bishops, and by the Prince de Condé. He asked for contributions; Champlain carried on by interviewing the prelates separately. By these efforts 1,500 livres were raised, too small a sum to be much credit to the prelates' generosity, but sufficient to buy food and equipment for four missionaries, vestments, a portable altar with its furniture.

Now we turn back to the commercial record of 1614. There were endless business troubles, obscure and of little interest. Condé obtained from the King a renewal of the Company's monopoly, to run eleven years from November 14, 1613. He obtained likewise an extension of his control from Quebec down to the Gaspé peninsula. In a heated meeting at Fontainebleau the merchants of Rouen and St. Malo agreed to take out six families of colonists each year. Champlain was to have at his disposal, for military purposes, four men from each vessel on the river. He was also to receive a proper salary. The merchants of La Rochelle, who had disregarded the summons to the meeting, were excluded from the trade.

The supervision of these arrangements was of such importance that Champlain dared not depart for the trading journey of 1614. It was, apparently, a profitable season for the merchants. However, the Indian chiefs to whom Champlain had made the formal promise to return with an army for the Iroquois war and to build a fort at the St. Louis Rapids, were disappointed and angered. This was the second time he had failed them. There were many mutterings around the campfires.

In this summer of 1614 the Habitation of Quebec, formerly

the property of de Monts, came officially under the control of the Company (in which, of course, de Monts was an important shareholder.)

In Paris, Champlain carried through his program and countered the attacks upon it. Certain disgruntled merchants of St. Malo succeeded in inserting a proposal for freedom of the fur trade in the agenda of the States-General. The proposal was to be slipped through by influence. Champlain got wind of it and informed the Prince de Condé, whose greater influence overwhelmed the lesser influence of the merchants. Thus the Prince de Condé earned his salary.

Now, in the first months of 1615, the annual expedition was prepared. It was to be an important year. Champlain knew that he must fulfill his promise to aid his allies in the Iroquois war, if he was not to lose face with them irremediably. Though he had been unable to get a detachment of the royal army, he could make a draft of four men from each of the licensed trading vessels. If not trained soldiers, they would be good tough, resourceful fellows, who had already made some acquaintance with Canada and the Indians.

And at last Champlain could realize his dream of missionary work among the natives. Four Recollects arrived with their equipment: Father Denis Jamet, who was in charge; Father Jean d'Olbeau; Father Joseph le Caron; and Brother Pacifique du Plessis. We know little of their background, not even for certain whether any of them were the high-hearted dreamers of the Brouage monastery. Brother Sagard, himself a Recollect, says that Joseph le Caron had, before entering religion, taught the young King Louis XIII the first rudiments of the Christian faith, but I can find no corroboration of this statement. Whether true or a rumor, it implies at least that Father Joseph was a gentleman, who might naturally have his entree at court. His monastic purpose of self-abasement would be dramatically fulfilled by his passing from the scented Louvre to the filthy frozen camps of Canada.

Though Champlain had his missionaries and his little levy of armed men, he had no proper colonists. The provision for six families of settlers a year was blandly ignored by the merchants.

Champlain and his party left Honfleur on April 24 on the

Saint-Étienne, with Pontgravé in command. She was a fine big ship of 350 tons, a veteran of the Canada trade. She had brought supplies out to Acadia in 1605.

The *Saint-Étienne* made a very quick trip, arriving at Tadoussac on May 25. The passengers transshipped to small boats and ascended the river to Quebec. Father d'Olbeau and Brother Pacifique immediately began the building of a little chapel and dwelling. Father Le Caron, eager to see the savages whom he was to change from wolves to sheep, hurried on to the St. Louis Rapids. Champlain, Pontgravé, and Father Jamet followed, after they had seen to necessary business in Quebec. Champlain was pleased by Father Jamet's exclamations of delight at the beauty of his new country, clothed in the tender green of early June.

A little below Montreal Island, Champlain encountered Father Joseph le Caron, heading downstream in a company pinnace. Father Joseph was filled with joy and ardor. He had met the Hurons at the Rapids and had found them splendid people, simple, honest, cordial, and most clearly possessed of immortal souls. Their ignorance cried to him for enlightenment, their desperate state for the means of salvation. He had determined to return with them to winter in their western land, to bring them one by one to the knowledge of Christ and the hope of Paradise. He was now bound for Quebec to fetch the furniture for the Mass.

"Not so fast!" said Champlain. "You are new to this country. You have no woodcraft; you are not toughened for a season in the wilds. I advise you to winter in Quebec, preparing yourself. Next spring you shall go to the Hurons, and I shall accompany you."

Champlain records his splendid reply. "It is necessary for me to go there, to better learn the character of these people, and to learn their language more easily. People warn me about the difficulties of dealing with them. But I am sure I can overcome all the difficulties and bear the trials, and adapt myself cheerfully to their bad food and to the hardships, through the grace of God, of which I am certain and assured. For the service of God is at stake, and it is for the glory of His name and for the preaching of His holy gospel that I freely undertook this journey, with the assurance that He would never abandon me in such an effort. As for temporal comforts, it doesn't take much to content a man who had vowed himself to perpetual poverty, and who seeks only Heaven, not so much for himself as for his brothers. For it isn't consistent with the rule of our Order that one should have any other ambition than God's glory, when one has made up one's mind to suffer and support for the glory of God all necessities, pains, and toils which may present themselves."

This was the right spirit. Perhaps his zeal and the grace of God would carry him through. "I would no longer seek to turn him from his purpose," says Champlain. "He set out with this determination to be the first to proclaim among the Indians the name of God, through His holy grace, with great pleasure that an opportunity presented itself for him to suffer for the name and glory of our Savior Jesus Christ."

The happy Father went singing on his way to Quebec, and Champlain, perhaps jealous of such joy, continued upstream to the rapids.

He found his Indian friends expecting him and demonstratively pleased at his return. In the intervals of trading they exposed the situation. Iroquois raiders were becoming increasingly active and bold as the Huron trade developed. The Huron losses in men and goods were more and more serious. The Dutch on the Hudson encouraged the Iroquois warriors, paying well for captured furs from the cold north. It was high time that the Hurons and Algonquins should strike the enemy in his own country. They earnestly prayed that Champlain would fulfill his oft-repeated promise to give them substantial aid.

Champlain consulted with Pontgravé. "We came to the conclusion that it was very necessary to assist them, both to engage them the more to love us, and also to provide the means of furthering my enterprises and explorations which apparently could only be carried out with their help, and also because this would be to them a kind of pathway and preparation for embracing Christianity. For which reason I resolved to go and examine their territory, and to help them in their wars, in order to induce them to let me see what they had so often promised me."

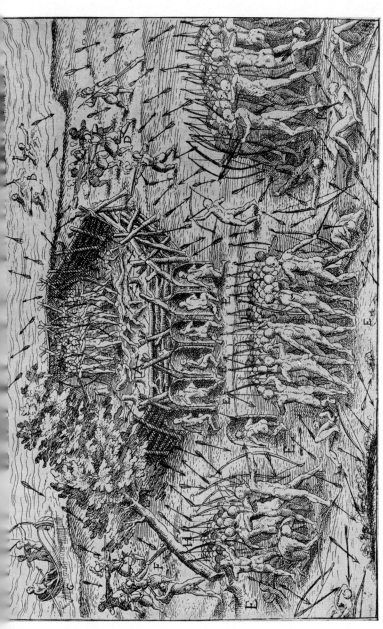

THE BATTLE OF SOREL, 1610.

"A. The Iroquois Fort. B. Iroquois jumping into the river to escape, pursued by Montagnais and Algonquins, jumping in after to kill them. E. All our savage friends. F. The Sieur des Prairies of St. Malo with his companions. G. The Sieur des Prairies' shallop. H. Great trees cut down to demolish the Iroquois' fort."

THE BATTLE OF ONONDAGA LAKE, *1615.*

(Notice the familiar trinity of purposes in Champlain's mind: business, exploration, and Christianization.)

Champlain announced his decision at a general assembly. The chiefs were overjoyed. They promised to raise an army of 2,500 warriors, "who would do wonders." Champlain proposed to bring as many men as he possibly could. "I explained to them the means we must employ in fighting, wherein they took especial pleasure."

Opportunely, Father Joseph le Caron arrived from Quebec with his equipment. On the shore of the St. Lawrence, in the presence of the gaping savages, he and Father Denis Jamet celebrated Mass, the first in the St. Lawrence country. It was June 24, 1615. (The first celebration in Quebec took place on June 25.) The Indians "were in admiration at the sight of the ceremonies used and of the ornaments which seemed to them so beautiful, the like of which they had never beheld." Thereafter, a solemn Mass became an inevitable feature of the annual trading fair.

Champlain was now obliged to revisit Quebec to make arrangements for the governing of the colony during his absence on the warpath. He was held in Quebec only a fortnight; but meanwhile the Indians left the rapids for their home countries, much aggrieved because he had not more promptly returned. They thought he must be dead or captured by the Iroquois. But Father Joseph le Caron and twelve Frenchmen (the apostolic number) accompanied the Hurons. "This news troubled me a little, seeing that had I been there, I should have ordered many things for the journey which I was now not able to do, both in respect to the small number of men and also because there were not more than four or five who knew how to handle fire-arms, seeing that in such an undertaking the best are none too good. All this, however, did not make me lose courage for proceeding with the expedition, by reason of my strong desire to pursue my explorations."

On July 9 he set off from the St. Louis Rapids on the long journey to the Huron land. He had with him Étienne Brûlé and "his own man," probably Thomas Godefroy, the interpreter of Algonquin. He had ten Indians. But he had only two canoes.

That means six men in one canoe, seven in the other. That means that they could carry only their arquebuses, a too scanty supply of powder, match, and shot, some trade goods, a minimum of clothing, the barest provision of food. It means too the grossest discomfort for the travelers. Poor Brother Sagard, in similar case, had to crouch with bent head for hundreds of miles, to avoid being rhythmically prodded by the paddle.

The two canoes headed up the Ottawa River, taking the course Champlain had followed two years before. Then he had been able to set his own pace; now he was subject to the demands of his Indians, hurrying to escape the terrible raiders from the south.

Champlain does not describe the journey. He seldom complains; he takes hardship and hunger as a matter of course, rather enjoying such tests of manhood. But the missionaries Sagard and Brébeuf tell us what the ascent of the Ottawa meant to the paleface.

Their remembrance is all of pain and toil. They sat hunched in a canoe so crowded, so cranky, that any shift of position was forbidden. Their faces were pressed against Indians' bare bodies, unbelievably foul-smelling. (There seems to be a difference, and a mutual repulsion, in racial sweat.) The long and frequent portages were heartbreaking. The priests' water-soaked cassocks chafed their legs; their sandaled feet were bruised by the rocks and torn by the brambles. "There are portages of one, two, and three leagues," says Father Brébeuf. "For each several trips must be made, no matter how few packages one has. In some places, where the current is not less strong than in the rapids, the savages get into the water, and haul and guide by hand their canoes with extreme difficulty and danger; for they sometimes get in up to the neck and are compelled to let go their hold, saving themselves as best they can from the rapidity of the water, which snatches their canoe from them and bears it off."

On the way they watched for the caches which had been made on the downstream journey. These consisted invariably of parched corn in birch-bark cartons. "It astonished me greatly," says Brother Sagard, "how they could identify so accurately all the places where they had hidden it, without making any mistake, although sometimes it was far away from the trail and in the depth of the woods or buried in the sand."

As evening approached they looked for a good camp by the shore, where dry wood was at hand. Each had his task. One collected wood, one put up a flimsy shelter, one prepared the meal, one made fire, revolving a pencil of wood in a wooden slot until the friction kindled tinder. If time permitted, some would fish, setting nets in the river. Often, too, they would troll during the day, trailing behind the canoe a hook baited with frog skin.

The cook hung a kettle of water on the fire, laid his parched corn on a skin, pounded it with flat stones, and set it on to boil. If fish or meat was available, it was thrown in, half cleaned or not cleaned at all. This was the *sagamité*, a kind of corn mush. It was commonly full of dirt and refuse from the pounding stones, of ash and cinders, of insects. Water flies were, indeed, esteemed as flavoring. "Besides, the bowls could hardly have a pleasant smell," says Sagard, "for when the Indians were under the necessity of making water in their canoe they usually used the bowl for the purpose; but on land they used to stoop down in some place apart with a decency and modesty that were anything but savage."

No wonder the poor French had indigestion. According to one Jesuit, they were forced to rise four or five times every night, what with the food and with sleeping on the bare ground.

And so to bed, with only a screen of birch bark against the rain, with a stone for pillow, with one's wet gown for cover. The mosquitoes, the deer flies, the no-see-ems came to the feast. Sagard says he would have been blinded had he not worn a veil over his eyes, and there were some who lost their sight for several days. These Europeans had not yet been immunized against American insect poisons; their first mosquito bites caused a swelling like a half lemon. And so while the Indians slept, the French would lie awake all night in torture, amid the evil stench of the Indians' bodies.

There could be no hanging back. The Indians on the march ruthlessly abandoned any, even of their own kin, who could not keep the pace. Brébeuf tells of an Algonquin who burned himself in a campfire. His tribesmen killed him, for fear he might be an inconvenience in the canoe. The Europeans were always in special danger, for their possessions—knives, awls, fishhooks, beads—were very tempting.

And yet suddenly, inconsequently, the wild men would turn kind. "When they saw me for several days unable to eat their sagamité, so dirtily and badly cooked," says Sagard, "they had some compassion for me and encouraged and helped me as well as they could, and what they could was not much." His host let him share his bear's skin when it rained at night, and even prepared for him a bed of soft branches and a reed mat. "In compassion for my difficulties and weakness he would not let me row or wield a paddle, and this was no small labor from which to relieve me, in addition to doing me the service of carrying my things and my bundle at the rapids, although he was already well laden with his own goods and with the canoe, which he carried on his shoulders over the vexatious and painful trails."

With such a routine of his days, Champlain and his men ascended the course of the Ottawa. They made again the hard, long carry of Portage du Fort. (But the second time such a labor seems easier.) They were greeted, banqueted, and provisioned by old friends: Nibachis and Tessouat. On leaving Tessouat's kingdom, in the region of present Pembroke, Champlain headed west into new country.

The Ottawa narrowed day by day, amid the grim granite of the Laurentian shield. The travelers portaged endlessly around rapids, where the coppery water leaped white over enormous boulders. Then they would come to long peaceful bights in the lee of evergreen mountains, and would camp on sandy beaches exuding red ocher. Great fish leaped from the water; vast blue herons labored heavily into flight. The French fell asleep to the long two-toned rattle of the tree toad and the insane laughter of the loon. It was a very disagreeable region, says Champlain, a barren wilderness, uninhabited save for a few primitive fishermen. "It is true that God appears to have been pleased to give this frightful and abandoned region some things in their season for the refreshment of man and of the inhabitants of these parts; for I can assure you that along the streams there are such a great quantity of blueberries, which is a small fruit very good to eat, and many raspberries and other small fruits, that it is marvellous. The people who live here dry these fruits for their winter supply, as we in France do prunes for Lent."

Thus they came to Mattawa, where the pathway of the Ottawa leads northward. Here, notes Champlain, the eastbound Huron traders may turn north and find their way through an endless series of lakes and little rivers to the system that leads down through Lac St. Jean to the Saguenay and Tadoussac. The mere thought of such a journey may send a twinge through our civilized muscles.

At Mattawa, Champlain's party left the Ottawa and headed west up the Mattawa River, too violent to permit much paddling. They traversed serene hillbound lakes: Lake Talon, Trout Lake, still the resort of earnest anglers, forever disappointed, never despairing. From Trout Lake a portage of only three miles took them over the watershed that divides the basin of the Ottawa from that of Lake Huron. From here on the streams flow westward, down to the Freshwater Sea.

So on July 26, seventeen days out from the St. Louis Rapids, Champlain set down his canoe on the shore of Lake Nipissing. He stood in the heart of the present city of North Bay, where now the fishermen of a continent come to dance and dine in Top-Hat Taverns, to gape at quintuplets.

Champlain, looking across the ample surface of the lake, blending into sky, felt that he had at last conquered the barrier of the west.

Here he was cordially greeted by the Nipissing Indians, the Sorcerers, of Algonquin stock. There were seven or eight hundred of them. They were a prosperous people, great traders. In midwinter their buyers went west to Sault Ste. Marie to exchange their European trade goods for furs brought by tribes from Lake Superior and Lake Michigan. In the spring a party made a forty-day journey to Hudson Bay for the same purpose. In the autumn they visited the Hurons of Georgian Bay, selling dried fish from Lake Nipissing for a winter's supply of corn. They were too busy to have much time for agriculture.

They were sorcerers, holding intimate converse with the

devil. Their ability to cast spells and inflict diseases was notorious among the neighboring peoples. "But," says Sagard, "apart from their magic spells and communications with demons I found them very kindly and polite."

They were very proud of their country, regarding it as the most beautiful in the world. When a French agent was sent to live with them, they assumed that France was very ugly, since the Frenchman had quitted his country for theirs. And indeed it is a lovely land of water and meadow, as Champlain, usually sparing of admiration, remarks.

After two days of rest and canoe repairing he was again on the move. His boatmen headed southwest across the lake, passing the Manitou Islands, then approaching the southern shore, reddish sand topped by evergreens. They found the granite entrance gates to the French River, the lake's outlet. Now again they were in the harsh country of impervious, unwasting stone, where only hardy trees may grow in crevices and hollows. Though to us, fresh from our cities, it is a beautiful, pure, everlasting realm, to Champlain it was merely disagreeable. "I did not find in all its length ten acres of arable land, but only rocks and a country somewhat hilly."

So down the French River, past falls and rapids, as the plane of the Laurentian shield gradually inclines till it meets the level of Lake Huron, and the lake water pries into innumerable gaps in the rumpled shore, and the granite hillocks of the shield become capes, and islands, and bare stone humps, and finally reefs, as they step down into the wide water. Here at last was the Freshwater Sea, of which Champlain had first heard in 1603, twelve years before, of which he had dreamed ever since.

He was not the first white man to see Lake Huron. Almost certainly Étienne Brûlé came here with the Hurons in 1611; and certainly Father Joseph le Caron and twelve French improvised soldiers preceded Champlain by only a week.

Near the mouth of the French River Champlain met a party, three hundred strong, of Indians whom he named the *Cheveux relevés*, the High Hairs, "because they have their hair elevated and arranged very high and better combed than our courtiers, and there is no comparison in spite of the irons and methods these latter have at their disposal." Their bodies were elaborately tattooed, their faces painted, some with a lacy pattern, some with one side green, the other red. They had this singularity, or this coquetry: they wore no breechclouts at all. When good Brother Sagard saw them, he tried desperately and vainly to avert his eyes. He notes, however, that the women and girls dealt with the males as offhandedly as with gentlemen properly dressed; male nudity, he was astonished to record, did not entail female immorality.

These Indians were later known as the Ottawas; they were the ancestors of the Chippewas and Pottawatomies, and of Pontiac the Prophet. Their home was apparently on Manitoulin Island.

Champlain gave their chief a hatchet. "He was as happy and pleased with it as if I had made him some rich gift. Entering into conversation with him, I asked him about his country, which he drew for me with charcoal on a piece of treebark. He gave me to understand that they had come to this place to dry the fruit called blueberries, to serve them as a manna in the winter when they can no longer find anything."

Now Champlain turned southeast along the shore of Georgian Bay, rounding numberless rocky points where the waves beat high, treading numberless bewildering channels in the lee of islands. It is a drowned country, with over 95,000 charted islands. Some are mere stony whalebacks, some wide and ample areas. Tortured scrub and cedar cling to the granite's gaps; inland, noble spruce and firs rise, all bending eastward, their branches flung like blown hair by the wild wind.

The Indians bent furiously to their paddles, covering 175 miles in less than three days. They were hungry for home. A Jesuit who came later reports that on the last day, on Lake Huron, his Indians paddled from 1 a.m. to midnight.

On August 1 Champlain came to shore in Huronia. His canoemen entered broad, green-ringed Matchedash Bay, picked up familiar landmarks, and grounded their craft on the west side of Penetanguishene Bay, about four miles north of present Penetang. At their shouts the braves of a near-by village appeared, with many a welcoming "Ho, ho, ho!" which seemed to be drawn from the stomach's pit.

Champlain and his men had made a journey of seven hundred

miles from the St. Louis Rapids, half of it up the tumultuous Ottawa, in twenty-two paddling days, making an average of thirty-two miles a day.

Huronia was, and is, a happy country. It lies in the present county of Simcoe, mostly in the townships of Tiny and Tay, so named (with adjoining Floss) for the lap dogs of the wife of eighteenth-century Governor Simcoe. It is a region of comfortable rolling hills, of rich forests of maple, oak, and elm, tall and straight. In 1615 the woods were a network of baffling trails. Here lived some 30,000 Hurons, in villages surrounded by cleared lands, whereon they grew excellent corn, beans, and squash. They were beginning to cultivate peas double the size of the French seeds brought from Quebec and planted in this eager soil. "This district seemed to me very pleasant in contrast to such a bad country as that through which we had just come," says Champlain.

With his escort he paid formal visits to the chiefs of two villages and was most cordially received. Nay more; "On the second night, having gone outside the lodge to escape the fleas, which were very numerous and a great pest to us, a shameless girl came boldly up to me, offering to keep me company, which I declined with thanks, sending her away with gentle remonstrances; and I passed the night with some of the savages."

One may draw from the incident what lessons one pleases, moral, physical, or psychological. The fact that Champlain reported the episode at all shows that it impressed him, though the carefree promiscuity of the Huron girls was hardly news. Perhaps he was publicly recording his fidelity to his distant girl bride. But I think that he was a man of genuinely high principle, as rough, lonely men so often are. I think, too, that his habits were molded by his sense of his responsibility, of the necessity of preserving the white man's prestige, of the importance of setting an example to his men. I think finally that he was not much tempted by the casual sinful lusts of the flesh.

On his second day he came to the village of Carhagouha, fortified with a triple wooden palisade thirty-five feet high. The Hurons already lived in fear of Iroquois raids on their homeland. Carhagouha stood a little northwest of the present village of La Fontaine.

Here Champlain found Father Joseph le Caron and his twelve Frenchmen. There were effusive greetings. "And what sort of a trip did you have, Father?"

Father Joseph shuddered. He said (and this I take from a letter he wrote home): "I can hardly tell you the fatigue I suffered. I had to keep my paddle in hand all day long, and row with all my strength with the Indians. More than a hundred times I walked in the rivers over the sharp rocks, which cut my feet, in the mud, in the woods, where I carried the canoe and my small baggage, in order to avoid the rapids and the frightful waterfalls. And the hunger! We had only a little saga-mité, which was dealt out to us morning and evening. Yet I must avow that amid my pains I felt much consolation. For alas! when we see such a great number of infidels, and nothing but a drop of water is needed to make them children of God, one feels an ardor which I cannot express to labor for their conversion and to sacrifice for it one's repose and life."

He had suffered not only because of his European softness. His Franciscan garb, gray undyed wool, bound with a knotted cord, his flat-soled, open-topped sandals, were ill adapted to forest and stream. His gown soaked up water like a sponge, and when he stepped into a canoe, it sprinkled water and sand, to the Indians' fury. His bare feet, puffed with mosquito bites and thorn scratches, were tortured by the sandal thongs, wet or dried stiff. He had all the burden of the Mass vessels, cruci-fixes, communion wine, breviary. He had no time for his daily religious duties. And he must endure the strange agony of un-comprehending silence, for, alone with the sweating paddlers, he had no words to express his simplest needs or desires.[1]

"And now?" said Champlain. "You are picking up a little of the language?"

Father Joseph sighed. It was a dreadful language, all vowels

[1] A few years later the Jesuits printed a little set of rules for the behavior of missionaries bound for the Huron country. They are very illuminating, suggestive of a hundred woeful errors. Here are some examples: "You must have sincere affection for the savages. . . . To conciliate the savages, you must be careful never to make them wait for you in embarking. You must provide yourself with a tinder box or with a burning mirror, or both, to furnish them fire in the daytime to light their pipes, and in the evening when they have to encamp. These little services win their hearts. You should try to eat their sagamité or salmagundi in the way they prepare it, although it may be dirty, half cooked, and very tasteless.

2 2 3

and grunts. Point to a tree, and one person will tell you one word, another, another. You begin to recognize words, but every time you hear them they have different endings. You can never know when an Indian is making a joke, telling you with a straight face some horrible obscenity when you ask the word for, say, the sacred chalice.

"How are my men behaving?"

"Badly. Very badly. The Huron girls are utterly shameless, and some of our French are more shameless then they. A few of the men are making surprising progress in the language, but I fear by unholy means. They have accommodated themselves quickly to the filth and sloth of the Indians, and spend their days hunting, fishing, and idling about the village."

As to the other numerous things which may be unpleasant, they must be endured for the love of God, without saying anything or appearing to notice them. . . . You must be prompt in embarking and disembarking; and tuck up your gowns so that they will not get wet, and so that you will not carry either water or sand into the canoe. . . . It is not well to ask many questions, nor should you yield to your desire to learn the language and to make observations on the way. . . . You must try to be, and to appear, always cheerful. Each one should be provided with half a gross of awls, two or three dozen little knives, a hundred fish-hooks, with some beads of plain and colored glass, with which to buy fish or other articles when the tribes meet each other; and it would be well to say to them in the beginning: 'Here is something with which to buy fish.' . . . Be careful not to annoy anyone in the canoe with your hat; it would be better to take your night-cap. There is no impropriety among the savages. Do not undertake anything unless you desire to continue it; for example, do not begin to paddle unless you are inclined to continue paddling. . . . Finally, understand that the Savages will retain the same opinion of you in their own country that they will have formed on the way; and one who has passed for an irritable and troublesome person will have considerable difficulty afterwards in removing this opinion of him. . . . When you meet savages on the way, as you cannot yet greet them with kind words, at least show them a cheerful face, and thus prove that you endure gayly the fatigues of the voyage. . . . This is a lesson which is easy enough to learn, but very difficult to put into practice; for, leaving a highly civilized community, you fall into the hands of barbarous people who care but little for your philosophy or your theology. All the fine qualities which might make you loved and respected in France are like pearls trampled under the feet of swine, or rather of mules, which utterly despise you when they see you are not as good pack animals as they are. If you could go naked and carry the load of a horse on your back, as they do, then you would be wise according to their doctrine, and would be recognized as a great man; otherwise not. Jesus Christ is our true greatness; it is he alone and his cross that should be sought in running after these people, for, if you strive for anything else, you will find naught but bodily and spiritual affliction." (*Jesuit Relations*, XII, 117–23.)

"Ah well, let them have their little vacation. We'll be on the march again soon."

In Carhagouha the Indians built for Father Joseph a bark-roofed cabin, which he called a chapel. On August 12 he celebrated Mass and on the spot set up a cross. In our own times a greater cross has been erected on the presumed site to commemorate the first Mass said in the present province of Ontario.

Champlain waited impatiently for the Indian war party to assemble. The season was passing; if they were to invade the Iroquois country, it was high time to be gone.

He visited five of the chief villages of the region, exhorting the chiefs, through his interpreter Brûlé, to hurry. On August 17 he arrived at the chief village, Cahiagué. It stood, according to conclusions from recent investigations, near the village of Warminster. Here was held a council of the chiefs, and here the great campaign of 1615 was planned.

CHAPTER XV

The Eighth Voyage—The Invasion of Iroquoia

THE CHIEFS, assembling in council at Cahiagué, greeted Champlain with great delight. Ochateguin was there, whom he had known since 1609. And Darontal, to whom he took an immediate liking. And others, each representing a clan of the Huron nation.

"We thought you were dead or captured by the Iroquois!" they said to him. "And so we gave up the idea of an invasion of the Iroquois country."

Champlain recognized well the dilatoriness and capriciousness of the Indians. He must inspire them; he must provide the hard core of purpose. "It is not too late," he said. "With my fourteen men and their fourteen guns we can attack the enemy stronghold. We can bring terror into their country, as they have into ours."

The chiefs smoked and nodded. "The time is propitious," they said. "We have received word from our brothers the Carantouans that they wish to swear friendship with us, to make an alliance, and to contribute five hundred good men for a common war on the Iroquois."

"Who are these Carantouans?"

"They are of our race and tongue. They dwell three days'

2 2 6

journey to the south of the Iroquois stronghold. Though they
have only three villages, they hold their own against more than
twenty villages of their enemies. They love the French by
reputation, and they hate the Iroquois and the Dutch who aid
and supply the Iroquois. Indeed, last year they captured in war
three Dutchmen who were helping the Iroquois, but as
they had never before seen a' Christian, they supposed these
palefaces to be French, and so in courtesy let their prisoners
go."

(These potential allies were in fact the Andastes, or Susque-
hannas, an Iroquoian tribe established on the upper Susquehanna
and Chemung Rivers. Their headquarters was a large village
on Spanish Hill, in South Waverly, Pennsylvania, just across
the New York State line. Dutch sources corroborate the capture
and release of the three Hollanders, who gave us our first map
of the Susquehanna region.)

Champlain was delighted to hear of these allies, so strategi-
cally placed. "We must immediately send envoys to them, with
instructions as to the time and place where they shall meet us,"'
he said.

"Immediately, yes. But first we must dance, and feast, and
sing."

These Indians were infuriating. When once under way they
could proceed at a killing pace, never pausing or seeming to
tire. But they would waste days and weeks, sunk in sloth and
frivolity, before making up their minds to start. The failure of
timing usually caused their plans to go awry. How the European
soldier longed for discipline!

While Champlain watches the week-long dances, impassive
but chafing with bored impatience, we may pause to consider
why he held so strongly to this invasion of Iroquoia. What
concern was it of his?

His concern was chiefly commercial. The Iroquois raids on
the Ottawa River highway were increasing as traffic upon it increased. Every Iroquois wanted a steel tomahawk and knife for
himself, an awl and needle for his wife. The brave with an old
stone hatchet was shamed before his fellows. The easiest way
to get a set of the new equipment was to ambush a Huron

canoeful of treasures. Almost as good was the capture of a cargo of furs bound for the trading fair on the St. Lawrence. These could be carried to the Dutch market at Fort Nassau, today's Albany, and bartered for the precious trade goods.

For behind the Iroquois stood the Dutch. Their demand was always for furs, more furs, fine, heavy beaver from the frozen lands. The Iroquois country of central New York provided only second-quality furs, with relatively few beaver. Its local supplies were soon exhausted. The Iroquois looked jealously to the well-organized fur trading systems of the far north.

In these circumstances Champlain argued from his European military experience. With his handful of men he could not guard the commercial routes. His strategy must be, then, to carry the war into the enemy's country, to destroy his cities, to put him on the defensive, so that he would perforce abandon the offensive and desist from his raids.

In fact, the savage art of war was not so simple a problem of the application of force. Where there are no battle lines, no wealthy cities to be defended, no munitions factories, no G.H.Q., a raid on enemy territory would not check retaliatory raids; quite the contrary indeed. In theory both sides could continue raiding until both sides were annihilated.

Champlain recognized that the real, eventual enemy was the Dutchman in Fort Nassau and New Amsterdam. Naturally he says nothing so impolitic in his book, which the Dutch ambassador might read. (He says merely that he was anxious to make contact with the Andastes, since they were only seven days' journey from the Dutch headquarters.) But I think it is pretty obvious that he regarded this expedition into enemy country as a reconnoissance of the Dutchman's protectorate. Sooner or later the French of Quebec would have to fight it out with the occupiers of Fort Nassau and the Hudson.

It has often been said, and written, that Champlain's attack on the Iroquois made this vengeful race everlasting enemies of the French. But this statement simplifies things too much. The ancient, traditional hostility of Iroquois and Hurons expressed itself in raids by either party, tests of the young braves' gallantry, in which the raiders' purpose was to take a few scalps as trophies and a few prisoners for torture by the home fires. The element of sport was strong in these wars, and indeed the sporting attitude has not entirely disappeared from our own grim conflicts.

Champlain's espousal of the Huron cause helped to transform the war from the supreme form of sport to a struggle for commercial advantage. By allying himself with the Hurons he automatically made the French enemies of the Iroquois. But by putting the war on a commercial basis he altered its nature, its ideology. A change in commercial interest could change the line-up of combatants, transform hostility to alliance. In fact, the Iroquois resentment was not insuperable. Nine years later Champlain made a peace between Hurons and Iroquois and enforced it for several years. The peace could not last, because the commercial interests of the two parties were directly opposed and were irreconcilable.

By joining the Hurons, Champlain merely recognized that the French could not be neutral and remain in the fur trade. In the circumstances, and according to the code of his times, and of most times, Champlain's policy was fully justified. It was, in fact, the only reasonable policy.

At length the feasts and dances came to an end. The assembled warriors numbered only five hundred, not the twenty-five hundred who had been promised. Champlain had his interpreters, Brûlé and Thomas, and the twelve Frenchmen who had come to Huronia with Father Joseph.

The war party moved to the narrows near Orillia, where Lake Simcoe empties into Lake Couchiching. Here another council was held. Twelve stout Indians were selected as an embassy to the Andastes. Their instructions were to bid the Andastes to come on a fixed date to the Iroquois stronghold and there to join in a common assault. The embassy was a dangerous one, for it would have to pass through enemy country.

Étienne Brûlé, hardy, reckless Brûlé, asked permission to accompany this expedition. Although Brûlé was his only competent interpreter of Huron, Champlain agreed, "since he was drawn thereto of his own inclination, and by this means would see their country and observe the tribes that inhabit it."

Brûlé and the painted ambassadors departed, paddling swiftly south across Lake Simcoe. Champlain was not to see his interpreter again for four long years.

It was now September 8. Frost was at hand; soon the leaves would begin to fall, and it would be too late for a successful forest war of ambush and surprise. Champlain was in a passion of impatience.

Finally the expedition got under way. It coasted down the eastern shore of Lake Simcoe, then made the long carry across the watershed dividing the basin of Lake Huron from that of Lake Ontario. The Indians were following approximately the line of the present Trent Canal, which meanders aimlessly among the meadows of Ontario.

The Indians put down their canoes in Balsam Lake, ringed with graceful firs. With assurance they took the shortest course among the puzzling points and islands to the obscure outlet. They carried into Cameron Lake, then past the rocky gorge of Fenelon Falls into long, tranquil Sturgeon Lake, then Pigeon Lake, Buckhorn Lake, Stony Lake. (What maps these Indians carried in their minds!) Past Burleigh Falls and its rapids, down dwindling Katchiwano Lake, down the Otonabee River, where proud Peterborough was destined to rise, and after much winding through a flat and fertile land, into wide Rice Lake. Then past the falls of Campbellford, through placid Percy Reach, and so down the Trent River, now dammed and ample, once flecked with roaring rapids, to the peaceful Bay of Quinte.

It was a rich and cheery country, says Champlain. "Along the shores one would think the trees had been planted for ornament in most places." He notes the vines, the walnut trees, the abundant fish. All this lovely region was completely uninhabited, for its Indian population had abandoned it in fear of Iroquois raiders.

The army amused itself, and lost precious time, by hunting deer and bear. The five hundred men would make a great circle in the woods, drive the animals down to water, and there kill them with arrows and with sword blades fastened to sticks. "I took a peculiar pleasure in watching them hunt in this manner, watching their skill." The French wasted their ammunition by shooting the deer, and unfortunately also shot a savage (perhaps the first tragedy of white deer-hunters in Canada.) "At this a great clamor arose among them, which nevertheless subsided upon the gift of some presents to the wounded man, which is the ordinary method of allaying and ending quarrels."

Somewhere in this region the Hurons were joined by a detachment of Algonquins under Chief Iroquet. He had fought beside Champlain at Ticonderoga in 1609; he had taken young Brûlé with him for a winter's education in 1610. He was one of Champlain's old and excellent friends, and was clearly fond of war and excitement. As his homeland was on the lower Ottawa, near Hawkesbury, one must suppose that he was summoned to meet the Hurons at some recognizable rendezvous in Ontario.

Now the expedition was in the placid reach of the Bay of Quinte, zigzagging fifty miles to the open water of Lake Ontario. This is our first clear record of the sight of the lake by a white man. But certainly Étienne Brûlé, who had first (probably) seen Lake Huron, had crossed the western end of Ontario three weeks before on his way to the Andastes. Brûlé was, however, not a man to concern himself with history's records.

The party emerged from the inner channels, left the willowed, pebbled shore typical of the Great Lakes, and headed south to the False Duck Islands. Here they turned east, across thirty miles of open water, guided by the steppingstones of Duck Island, Galloo Island, Stony Island. They had a calm day, we hope, for this crossing of Ontario, for its waves can quickly become too high and wild for crowded canoes, however skilfully manned. Champlain, who could not swim, may well have felt some qualms.

They landed on the New York shore under the high bluff of Stony Point, probably to the south of it. They were now in enemy territory, and it behooved them to proceed cautiously. Hiding their canoes in woods near the water, they marched directly south along the lake shore, on sandy spits beside reedy lagoons. The passage of the lagoon openings was troublesome for the nonswimmers, and the safe transport of guns and powder, delicate. The country was well forested, with many chestnut trees.

The party came to the mouth of the Salmon River, by the present Selkirk Shores State Park, and turned inland. They marched silently, in single file, each man setting his foot in the print of the man ahead. They headed south, along the route of our U.S. Highway 11, to the outlet of Oneida Lake at Brewerton. They were moving cautiously; it took them four days to cover fifty miles, if Champlain's reckoning is correct (and of this I am not at all convinced.)

It was October 9. At this season the leaves are falling fast in northern New York.

At Brewerton the scouts brought in eleven prisoners: three men, four women, three boys, a girl. They were Onondagas from the stronghold, who had come to fish in these well-populated waters.

Chief Iroquet, preluding, catlike, the tortures to come, amused himself by cutting a finger off one of the women's hands. Champlain was outraged. "This is not the deed of a warrior," he said, "to behave cruelly to women, who have no other defense but tears. We should treat women with humanity, because of their helplessness and weakness. Your act shows a base and brutal heart. If I see any more of these cruelties, you will not encourage me to help you in your war."

Iroquet stared open-mouthed. "Our enemies treat us in the same way," he grumbled. "But since our ways displease you, I won't do anything further to the women. Just to the men." The Indians were sulky at Champlain's interference, his spoiling of their sport.

Champlain and the chiefs now made their battle plan. They would creep up on the enemy fort, ten miles distant, post themselves in the woods for the night, and attack at dawn.

The next day the army slipped warily through the forest. They came close to the fortified village at about three in the afternoon. It stood (I think) within the present city of Syracuse, where sluggish Onondaga Creek flowed into Onondaga Lake. But the site of the stronghold is bitterly disputed. If you would judge of the arguments you must read Appendix F.

As the attackers drew near the fort some of them were surprised by Onondaga braves. The others, bursting with ardor and disregarding all their orders, ran to the rescue of their comrades. The battle was on, the plan of attack forgotten.

Champlain and the French came up and let fly with their arquebuses. The Onondagas, unlike the Mohawks at Ticonderoga, knew an arquebus when they heard one. They quickly gathered up their dead and wounded and retreated to the imposing shelter of their stronghold.

Champlain made a quick reconnoissance of the fort. It was large enough to contain a village of long houses; it was protected on one side by open water, on two sides by running streams. It was walled with stout palisades thirty feet high, says Champlain, but I suspect his memory has added a few feet. The palisades "were interlaced together with not more than half a foot between them, and supported galleries like a parapet which they had fitted with double timbers, proof against our shots."

His illustration shows the general construction, and other Iroquois forts give us supporting information. It would seem that there were two palisades. The builders constructed them by driving a double row of tree trunks into the ground, inclining each pair so that they would cross, perhaps fifteen feet from the ground. The space between was filled with logs. The upright tree trunks were bound together at their crossing and projected upward, making a series of V-shaped pockets. Horizontal logs were laid along this series of V's to make a precarious runway, which was screened with bark on the outer side. Rough ladders, mere notched poles, along the inner face, gave archers, stone throwers, and fire fighters access to the gallery.

Champlain recognized that this fortress could not be carried immediately by storm. Furious that the advantage of surprise was lost, he called a council of his chiefs. "I used some very hard and unpleasant words, in order to incite them to do their duty; for I foresaw that if everything went according to their caprice and under the guidance of their counsels, evil alone would result, to their loss and destruction."

He drew upon his experiences in the siege of Breton towns in the far days of the civil wars of France. "The thing to do," he said, "is to construct a cavalier, a movable tower overtopping the walls of the fort, from which we may fire down on the defenders. At the same time we shall make wooden mantelets,

2 3 3

or screens, impervious to arrows, and we shall move them forward against the fort. With such protection we shall be able to set fires along their palisade, and thus make a breach."

The chiefs protested. "Would it not be better to await the arrival of the five hundred men promised by the Andastes?"

Not at all, said Champlain. "Perhaps our envoys never reached the Andastes. Perhaps the Andastes have been waylaid on their journey here. Anyway, the numbers your ambassadors promise have an unaccountable way of diminishing. Look; the men in the fort are busy strengthening their walls. A relieving army of Iroquois may arrive. And the leaves are falling fast. Time, my friends, is on the side of the enemy."

The chiefs were persuaded. At dawn on October 11 the Hurons set to work to make their cavalier. They chopped down tall, slim trees, high enough to overtop the thirty-foot walls of the fort. These were fixed in position by crosspieces. Other long trees were lashed to the base to serve as carrying poles. At the top of the structure a rude platform for sharpshooters was fitted, with heavy breastworks on the enemy's side.

It sounds like a crazy contrivance, topheavy and insecure. Champlain's illustration shows a fine carpentered tower, built of neatly squared timbers, securely nailed, with a large firing platform of smooth planks with rectangular loopholes cut out with a saw. But all this is the engraver's license. The Hurons had no tools but hatchets, knives, and stone clubs. They had no nails, no adze, no saw. Their cavalier was built only of tree trunks and branches, with its members bound together with grapevines or withes, or fitted into insecure notches and loose slots. It was at least a triumph of primitive engineering.

Champlain says the cavalier and the mantelets were finished in four hours. This I find hard to believe.

"We advanced to attack this village," he says, "having our cavalier carried by two hundred of the strongest men, who planted it about a pike's length in front of the village, and I ordered three of the arquebusiers to mount upon it, where they were well protected from the arrows and stones which might be shot or thrown at them. Meanwhile, the enemy did not on that account cease to shoot a great many arrows which did not miss their mark, and they threw a great quantity of stones over their palisades. Nevertheless, the incessant arquebus fire compelled them to dislodge and to abandon their galleries, in consequence and by virtue of the cavalier which overlooked them, and they durst not appear nor show themselves, and fought under cover. Now when our men were carrying the cavalier, instead of bringing up the mantelets according to orders, including the one under cover of which we were to lay the fire, they abandoned them and began to shout at the enemy, shooting arrows into the fort, which in my opinion did no great harm to the enemy. But they must be excused, for they are not warriors, and moreover they will not submit to discipline nor correction, and do only what they like. This is why one of them thoughtlessly set fire to the wood placed against the enemy's fort, but quite in the wrong place and in the lee of the wind, so that it produced no effect.

"When this fire went out, most of the savages began to carry wood against the palisades, but in small quantity, so that the fire, so poorly fed with fuel, could produce no great effect. Moreover confusion unexpectedly arose among these people, to such a degree that one could not make oneself heard, which troubled me greatly. In vain I shouted in their ears and showed them as best I could the danger they ran through their lack of intelligence, but they heard nothing on account of the great noise they were making."

Champlain was probably shouting in a mixture of Algonquin and French, for he could have had only a small stock of Huron words. No one had time to interpret. He recognized that he was merely adding to the confusion, not dominating it.

"Seeing then that it was troubling myself to no purpose to shout, and that my remonstrances were useless, and being unable to make head against this confusion nor to do anything more, I determined with my own people to do what I could and to fire at those we could discover and see. Meanwhile the enemy took advantage of our confusion to go for water and poured it out so plentifully that one would have said streams were falling from their spouts, so much so that in no time they completely put out the fire, and this without on that account ceasing to shoot their arrows, which fell upon us like hail. Those on the cavalier killed and maimed many of them. We were engaged in this fight about three hours. Two of our principal chiefs were wounded, to wit, one named Ochateguin and another named Orani, and some fifteen others of ordinary rank were also wounded. The rest on their part, seeing their men wounded, including some of their leaders, began to talk of retreating without further fighting, to wait for the five hundred men, who ought not to be much longer in coming, and so they withdrew, heeding only this disorderly whim. Moreover the chiefs have no absolute control over their men, who follow their own wishes and act as their fancy suggests, which is the cause of their confusion and spoils all their enterprises. For having decided upon something with their leaders, it requires only some good-for-nothing fool, should the fancy seize him, to make them give up their resolve and decide upon a new plan. Thus they do nothing in cooperation, as may be seen by this expedition.

"But we withdrew into our fort, I having received two arrow wounds, one in the leg, the other in the knee, which gave me great trouble, besides considerable and extreme pain. And when we were all assembled I addressed several complaints to them for the confusion which had occurred, but all my discourses availed as little as if I had been silent, and moved them in no way; for they said that many of their people had been wounded, myself included, and that this would cause much fatigue and inconvenience to the others to carry them as they retreated, and as for turning against their enemy again as I proposed they should do, there was no possibility of it. However they said they would wait another four days for the five hundred men who were expected, and that when these had come, they would make a second attempt against their enemies and would carry out my commands better than they had done in the past. There the matter ended, to my great regret."

The matter ended, one would say, with the demonstration that the Onondagas were better organized and commanded than the Hurons. This battle by the lakeside, under the red and gold of the maples, proved to the Indian world that stout defenders in a well-built fort could defy attackers armed with arquebuses and aware of the devices of European siege warfare. The advantages of the arquebus—range, accuracy, and penetration— were largely lost in an assault on a strong point. At close quarters, the quick-firing Iroquois arrow was a match for the slow-firing arquebus.

Indian awe of the new weapon faded. The prestige of Champlain and of the European dropped sharply, both among the Iroquois, reviewing the battle over their council fires during the following winter, and, what was far worse for Champlain, among the Hurons and the Algonquins.

"On the following day a violent wind arose which lasted two days, very favorable for setting fire anew to the enemy's fort; whereupon I urged them strongly, but they would do nothing, as if afraid of being worsted and moreover recalling to mind their wounded."

This was our familiar high northwest wind, interspersed with pelting squalls, bringing the cold, bringing acutely bright air purged of moisture, and scattering down the wasted leaves.

"We were encamped until the sixteenth of that month, during which time some skirmishes took place between the enemy and our men, who for the most part were cut off by the enemy rather through their own imprudence than from lack of courage; for I assure you that every time they went out to attack, we had to go and fetch them and disengage them from the press, since they could only retreat under cover of our arquebusiers, whom the enemy greatly feared and dreaded. For as soon as they caught sight of one of our arquebusiers, they quickly withdrew, saying to us by manner of persuasion that we should not interfere in their battles, and their enemies had very little courage to call us in to assist them, with very many other discourses on this subject to influence us."

Here speaks a resentment that was to grow as the Iroquois pondered the case and fed their vengeance. The French had provided a clear moral justification for Iroquois reprisals. They had intervened, without warning, in an old-established native war. Worse, they had done so with the new weapon, flouting all ancient custom. They had wantonly broken the rules of the Indian war game.

It was apparently two days later, on October 18, that the invaders gave up the hope that the Andastes reinforcements would arrive, and set out on the long retreat. Flurries of hail and snow were coming down. It was such a day as we know well in this country, with a high, pure west wind and occasional black clouds, full of whipping snow, marching across the lake and level land.

Four years later Champlain learned what had happened to the Andastes.

Étienne Brûlé and his twelve Huron companions had left the camp on Lake Simcoe on September 8. They debarked in Cook Bay, and made the twenty-eight-mile carry to Lake Ontario, following a well-marked trail along the Humber, just to the west of Toronto. From here on, their course is entirely conjectural. Very likely they carried up the Dundas valley, and over the high ground to the Grand River, below Brantford, and then slid down the Grand to Lake Erie. (Another first for Brûlé.) Champlain's map of 1632 marks their journey with a dotted line, but not much may be deduced from it, save that the mission went well south, to avoid the Senecas, and then east to the Andastes village at Waverly, near Elmira. Their route is hotly argued by historians on the basis of fragile probabilities and likelihoods. I would suggest, with no assurance at all, that they cut across narrowing Lake Erie, left their canoes at the mouth of Cattaraugus Creek, went up the stream and east to the Canisteo near Hornell, then down along the Canisteo and the Chemung. Says Champlain: "They had to pass through the country and territory of their enemies, and to avoid any evil plot they sought a more secure path by traversing woods, forests, and dense and difficult thickets, and by marshy swamps, frightful and unfrequented places and wastes, all to avoid the danger of an encounter with their enemies. In spite of this great precaution, Brûlé and his companions, in traversing a plain, met with some hostile savages returning to their village, who were surprised and defeated by our savages, four of the enemy being killed at once and two taken prisoner, whom Brûlé and his companions brought along to the town of Carantouan, where they were received by the inhabitants of that place very affectionately and with gladness and good cheer, to the accompaniment of dances and feasts."

The Andastes met in council, heard the ambassadors, and decided to send their five hundred warriors to the Onondaga fort, three short days' journey distant. They were, however, very slow in their preparations. Nothing could persuade them to abridge the ritual feasts and dances. They set forth at length for the rendezvous, dodging the Iroquois villages on the way. Their route we do not know, but a glance at the map will show that they might easily have passed through Ithaca, Auburn, Cortland. Brûlé, first in so many places, was probably the first white man to look on the Finger Lakes.

When the Andastes arrived at the Onondaga fort they read in messages on the trees that the Hurons had left two days before. At this the Andastes returned homeward.

The remainder of Brûlé's adventures may be left to a later date.

We now rejoin Champlain and his allies. On their last day in camp the Indians were busy making some curious harnesses for the transport of the wounded. They resembled the carrying frames for papooses. A frame of hickory or elm rested against the carrier's back; at right angles to the frame a seat projected. This was held in place by straps of hide or of the plaited inner bark of the elm. The frame and its burden were supported by a tumpline over the carrier's brow. The wounded man sat on the precarious seat, his back to the bearer's back. His legs were hunched under his chin and tightly bound in this intolerable position.

"It was impossible to move any more than a little child in its swaddling clothes," says Champlain, "and this causes the wounded great and extreme pain. I can say this indeed from my own case, having been carried for several days because I was unable to stand, chiefly on account of the arrow-wound I had received in my knee, for never did I find myself in such a hell as during this time; for the pain I suffered from the wound in my knee was nothing in comparison with what I endured tied and bound on the back of one of our savages. This made me lose patience, and as soon as I gained strength to stand, I got out of that prison, or rather hell."

Remember that Champlain was forty-eight years old, and at his age the muscles and the spirit have lost some of their young resilience. His swollen, suffering knee was violently compressed to make him huddle, embryolike, on the carrying frame. His war enterprise, so long promised, so long desired, had failed. As he was tossed and buffeted, helpless, on his bearer's back, whipped by branches, beaten by snow, half immersed in forded streams, he had need of all his fortitude.

The party retraced its course northward in all haste, covering sixty miles in two days. When they reached Stony Point they found, to their great relief, that their canoes were still intact.

They prepared to recross Lake Ontario to the relative safety of the north shore.

"Now," said Champlain to the chiefs, "I must ask you to let me have a canoe and a crew of paddlers. It is of the utmost importance that I return to my settlement for the winter. I should say it is only two hundred miles from here down the St. Lawrence to the St. Louis Rapids. I could be there in four or five days."

Champlain's glance met the impassive faces he knew so well. "We cannot spare any men," said the chiefs.

Champlain was prepared for this. "I have obtained four volunteers, who will happily spend the winter with me in Quebec."

"We cannot spare a canoe," said the chiefs.

Champlain restrained his fury. In his own words: "This hardly afforded me satisfaction, but on the contrary upset me greatly, making me suspect some ill will, since they had promised me when the war was over to bring me back and conduct me as far as our settlement; moreover I was very badly equipped for spending the winter with them, or otherwise I should not have minded. And not being able to do anything, I had to resign myself to be patient. But some days later I perceived that their plan was to detain me with my comrades in their country, both for their own safety and out of fear of their enemies, and that I might hear what took place in their council and meetings, and decide what should be done in the future against their said enemies in the interest of their own security and preservation."

Here I think Champlain is a little disingenuous. The Hurons had been confident of a miracle, and the miracle had not taken place. When an allied expedition fails, soldiers always blame their allies for its failure. The Hurons blamed the French. And if these Hurons were like all other soldiers, they whispered of sabotage, of treachery. They whispered that Champlain had lost the battle because he wished to lose it. They were a fickle people anyway; remember that in 1611 they were ready to believe the wild tale that Champlain was plotting with the Iroquois against them. And now that he proposed to leave his allies and undertake a journey through country controlled by the enemy, the Indians muttered that he was planning to join the enemy.

It was the moment when Champlain should have asserted his white man's ascendency. He should have demanded that he and his thirteen French companions be returned to Quebec. He should have imposed his demand by ringing words, by force of will, by power of personality, by threats. After all, the French still had their arquebuses.

But no, Champlain protested in vain, and then accepted the decision of the chiefs. There was in him, I think, a certain unsureness, self-doubt, in emergencies. He was unable to dominate, to impose his will on stubborn united wills. He was too sympathetic, too understanding of others' minds. Conceding an evident justice in the arguments of his adversaries, he could not bring himself to overwhelm them by a demand for the execution of his own purpose. We need not blame him. It was not in his character to be a Moses, a Cortés, a Lawrence of Arabia.

As an honest man, he had some reason to reproach himself. The failure of his expedition had lowered the prestige of the French with friend and enemy. Far from ending the threat of raids on Huron fur traders, it encouraged the Iroquois to attack. It gave the Iroquois a moral justification, a battle cry. It helped to change the character of the war from one of gallant but pointless raids for scalps to a grim commercial war of extermination.

The battle of Hurons and Iroquois by Onondaga Lake in 1615 has been called one of the decisive battles of American history. Had the Hurons won, it is said, the French would have imposed their influence on all the Iroquois, and Iroquoia would have become tributary to the French instead of to the Dutch, and the course of colonial history would have been changed. This, I think, is going much too far. If the Hurons had captured the Onondaga fort, they would have been defeated at the next Iroquois fort, for the alarm was given and the arquebusiers had used most of their ammunition. And even if, by a miracle, the Hurons had won all the battles, the handful of French in distant

Quebec could not have brought the Iroquois into their sphere of influence. The Dutch in Fort Nassau were too near; the Iroquois furs would continue to flow there, to be exchanged for Dutch trade goods. No, history would have been changed only by a French victory over the Dutch.

Humiliated, almost disregarded, Champlain took his place in the canoe. He headed west, away from Quebec, four hundred miles distant. By way of Huronia, it was twelve hundred cruel wilderness miles to his Habitation. He had no clothing, no equipment for the winter. Ammunition was short. Wounded and in pain, he could walk only with difficulty. The nights were bitter cold; he must sleep without a blanket on wet ground or in snow. He felt old and tired. A deep discouragement was in his heart, and yet he does not complain, for his body and his spirit were schooled and tempered in fortitude.

CHAPTER XVI

The Eighth Voyage—Winter in Huronia

THE DEFEATED HURON ARMY, homeward bound, crossed Lake Ontario at its northeast corner. Champlain's record is here loose and puzzling. It is likely that the voyagers dared not affront the open lake, still whipped by the west wind, and that they crept along the New York shore and crossed by way of Wolfe Island to the neighborhood of Kingston. They went twelve leagues up a river, the Napanee or the Salmon. They visited a lake (Loughborough?) swarming with swans, bitterns, Canada geese, ducks, teal, thrushes, larks, snipe. At a famous rendezvous of the deer, they built a semipermanent camp, making cabins of wood chinked with moss and covered with bark. Champlain was taken into the lodge of his friend Darontal. Now it was the Indians who were doing favors to the troublesome French.

A party of twenty-five Indians engaged in a great deer hunt, like those of European princes. "They went into the woods near a little grove of firs, where they made a triangular enclosure, closed on two sides, open on one. This enclosure was made of great wooden stakes eight or nine feet in height, joined close together, and the length of each side was nearly fifteen hundred paces. At the extremity of this triangle there is a little enclosure, getting narrower the farther it goes, and partly covered with branches, with only one opening five feet wide, by which the deer were to enter. They did so well that in less than ten days their enclosure was ready. When everything was completed, they set out half an hour before daybreak to go into the woods about half a league from their enclosure, keeping about eighty paces apart, each having two sticks which they strike together, walking slowly in that formation until they reach the enclosure. The deer, hearing this noise, flee before them until they reach the enclosure, which the savages force them to enter. Then the latter coming together towards the opening of their triangle, the deer steal along the said palisades until they reach the extremity, whither the savages pursue them hotly with bow and arrow in hand, ready to shoot. And when the savages reach the extremity of their said triangle, they begin to shout and to imitate the cry of wolves, whereof there are many that devour deer. The deer, hearing this terrifying noise, are forced to enter the retreat by the small opening, whither they are very hotly pursued with arrows, and when they have entered, they are easily caught in this retreat, which is so well enclosed that they can never get out of it. I assure you that one takes a peculiar pleasure in this mode of hunting, and they did so well that in the 38 days that we were there they captured 120 deer, with which they made good cheer, keeping the fat for the winter and using it as we do butter, and a little of the meat which they carry home for their feasts. They have other devices for catching deer, such as traps wherewith they cause the death of many. This is how we passed the time, waiting for the frost in order to return more easily, inasmuch as the country is marshy."

During the hunts Champlain got himself perilously lost in the woods. He caught a glimpse of a bird that seemed strange to him, as well it may have, for it was as big as a hen, yellow, with a red head and blue wings, and with a beak like a parrot. This remarkable bird lured him into the forest, making short successive flights like a partridge, and when he was well lost, it flew away. It has never since been seen. Possibly it was the Devil.

Champlain floundered in the dark woods, in the rain. He spent the night in what shelter he could find. Next day he shot three or four birds. "My meal over, I began to ponder what I ought to do, praying God to give me the will and courage to bear my misfortune patiently, should I have to remain abandoned in these wilds without other counsel or consolation than the divine goodness and mercy, and at the same time exerting myself to return to our hunters. And thus committing all to His mercy, I gathered more courage than before, going this way and that the whole day without perceiving any track or path except those of wild beasts, whereof generally I saw a good number."

Let him smile who has never been lost in silent woodlands, with help only a mile or two away. Champlain knew that save for the Huron hunting parties there were no Indians in all this vast web of lake and forest. Winter was at hand; his wounded knee still troubled him; he had only eight or ten charges for his arquebus and no other weapon. This was a dark moment for even the most valiant spirit.

He spent a second night in the open. On the next day he encountered a stream and followed it down, in the hope of finding the hunters' camp. The stream grew to a river; he discovered the marks of a canoe carry and knew that he had seen this spot before. After a third night he rejoined his friends, "with great satisfaction, both on my part and theirs; for they were still in search of me and had almost lost hope of seeing me again. They begged me not to wander away from them any more, or always to carry with me my compass and not forget it; and they said to me: 'If you had not come back and we had been unable to find you, we should not have gone down to the French any more for fear they should accuse us of putting you to death.'"

Thereafter Champlain's host and good friend Darontal always sent an Indian with him when he went hunting.

By December 4 the lakes were well frozen. The Indians made snowshoes and toboggans for their loads of deer hides and choice cuts of tender meat. They headed for home and journeyed for nineteen days across Ontario. There were frequent long carries through the woods. Champlain, with his bad knee, found his twenty-pound pack burdensome, but the Indians carried each a hundred pounds and sometimes even kindly added Champlain's burden to their own. They had four days of thaw "which gave us much trouble and discomfort, for we had to pass through fir woods full of streams, ponds, marshes and swamps, with many fallen trees lying one upon another, giving us a thousand troubles, with obstacles which brought us great discomfort on account of always being wet even above the knee."

Father Le Jeune, who wintered with the Montagnais in 1634, vividly describes the distresses of travel in such circumstances. "If it happened to thaw, O God, what suffering! It seemed to me I was walking over a road of glass, which broke under my feet at every step. The frozen snow, beginning to melt, would fall and break into blocks or big pieces, into which we often sank up to our knees, and sometimes to our waists. If there was distress in falling, there was still more in pulling ourselves out, for our snow-shoes were loaded with snow, and became so heavy that when we tried to draw them out it seemed as if somebody were tugging at our legs to dismember us. I have seen some who slid so far under the logs buried in the snow that they could not pull out either their legs or their snowshoes without help. Now imagine a person loaded like a mule, and judge how easy is the life of the savage."

On December 23 the Hurons came at last to their village of Cahiagué. They found there other detachments of the great expedition, among them Chief Iroquet and his Algonquins, who for some reason had decided to winter with the Hurons. With Iroquet was his son, who had been badly mauled by a bear. The presence of these foreigners caused the troubles usual among idle allied soldiers in cantonments.

For three weeks Champlain rested in the long house of Darontal. He describes the structure as 150 feet long and 6 feet wide. (But archæologists now working on the site find the normal dimensions 80 by 30 feet.) It swarmed with Indians, and also with mice, fleas, and lice. In its length were twelve fires giving off an acrid smoke that found no outlet, and caused general eye trouble, even, occasionally, blindness.

Champlain soon regretted the pure though bitter cold of the open. He decided to profit by his stay to explore the country beyond, to find new nations, new lands.

On January 4 he left Cahiagué.[1] He went first to Carhagouha to see Father Joseph le Caron.

---

[1] Champlain's dates are, as so often, specific and clearly wrong. I adopt the rectifications of Laverdière.

THE GREAT INDIAN DEER HUNT.

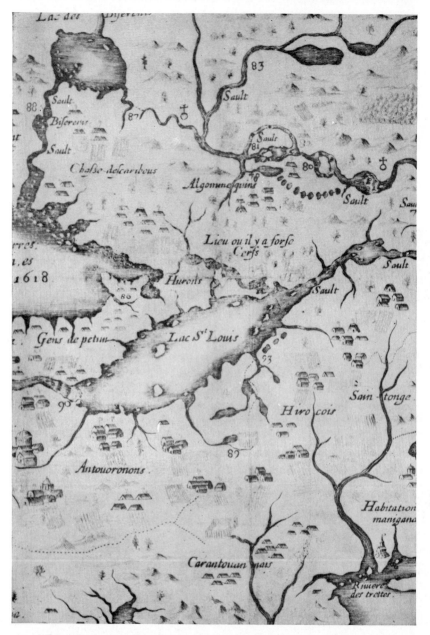

SECTION OF CHAMPLAIN'S MAP OF 1632 SHOWING
PRESENT ONTARIO AND CENTRAL NEW YORK

Lac St. Louis: Lake Ontario	86. Huronia
Lac des Biserenis: Lake Nipissing	87. Portage, Mattawa chain to Lake Nipissing
78. Muskrat Lake	88. French River
81. Morrison Island	89. The Iroquois fort
82. Ottawa River	90. Niagara Falls
83. Upper Ottawa River	93. Salmon River, N. Y.

He found the missionary in his little cabin, still full of zeal but somewhat depressed. The privations he could bear; his cross was the difficulty of turning God's word into Huron. He was making progress; he had compiled a little dictionary of recurring words, and he was even beginning to get some glimmer of the organization of the langugage, the barbarous grammar. But like Father Biard in Acadia, he played the clown for an hour, trying to elicit such words as think, believe, remember, forget. How could you teach the mysteries of sin and salvation to people who had no word for sin, salvation, redemption, grace? He could never be sure whether the Indians were telling him, straight-faced, dirty words for holy things. To be sure, they were in a way revenging themselves on the French sailors on the St. Lawrence, who taught the Indian women to utter innocently in French the most frightful blasphemies and indecencies.

The Indians' impieties, however horrible, were somehow pathetic. They wished, even, to borrow Father Joseph's chasuble to use as a war banner.

Father Joseph delightedly accepted Champlain's proposal that they should make a visit to the Indians to the west.

The two set off in mid-January with a party of Indian guides. In two days they reached the country of the Petuns, the Tobacco Indians, along the shore of Nottawasaga Bay, in the neighborhood of present Meaford and Owen Sound. These were an Iroquoian people, closely related to the Hurons and speaking their language. They were sedentary and agricultural, growing great crops of tobacco, corn, beans, sunflower, hemp. They were dependent on the Hurons, who held the monopoly of their trade. They welcomed the visitors most warmly with a mighty feast of meat and fish. Champlain, risking the displeasure of the Hurons, urged them to come down to the fair at the St. Louis Rapids with their furs.

Somewhere hereabouts Champlain and Father Joseph found the tribe of High Hairs, *Cheveux relevés*, whom he had met during the previous summer at the mouth of the French River. These were of Algonquin stock, merely wintering among the Iroquoian Tobacco People. No doubt they came here from the stony north to enjoy the abundant food and fish, for which they would pay with furs. These were the people whose braves disdained breechclouts. Champlain notes that they were the cleanest of all the Indians in their lodges, that they were great warriors, and greater feasters. They begged him to join them against their enemies the Fire People, the Mascoutins, who lived to the west of the Detroit River. Champlain replied that, to his regret, he did not for the moment have the necessary means. He repeated his usual request that they should come down to the rapids for trade. Obviously his purpose was to establish friendly relations with the most distant clients of his employers, the French merchants.

He now proposed to visit the Neutrals, an Iroquoian people who lived along the north shore of Lake Erie from Niagara to the Detroit River. He was discouraged by the Petuns, who told him a long story of a murder, of strained relations, of danger. In fact the French missionaries found a little later that every obstacle was put in the way of their visiting the Neutrals, certainly because the Hurons were jealous of their own status as middlemen in the fur business.

Everywhere among these tribes Champlain inquired about their knowledge of the west. He was told that in that mysterious country were peoples white like the French; a fair-haired scalp had even been seen. Champlain was excited. These peoples must be of superior civilization, he opined. "One would need to see them to know the truth of it, but one would have to have help. Only time and the courage of some persons of means, who can or will undertake to assist this project, can decide, in order that one day a full and complete exploration of these parts may be made in order to obtain certain knowledge of them." His appeal, throughout his lifetime, was unheeded.

Champlain and Father Joseph turned back, with the intention of visiting a tribe of Nipissing Indians who were wintering in this well-fed country. Champlain had a new project. These were the Indians who made annually a forty-day journey to Hudson Bay to buy furs. Champlain proposed to accompany them to fulfill his purpose balked in 1613. No thought of hardship could diminish his desire to see and know.

But on his way to the Nipissing village he had had news from Cahiagué. The Hurons and Algonquins there were at violent odds.

The Hurons had presented an enemy prisoner to Chief Iroquet of the Algonquins, in the expectation that he would be correctly tortured and eaten. But the Algonquins were a little less ferocious than the Hurons. Iroquet took a liking to his prisoner, sent him hunting, treated him with fatherly kindness. The Hurons were revolted at such impropriety; they sent an emissary, who killed the prisoner in the presence of the Algonquin headmen. These, outraged, immediately killed the emissary. The Hurons responded by attacking the Algonquin settlement, pillaging and wounding. Then the Hurons imposed reparations, as victorious aggressors do, to the extent of six hundred feet of wampum, fifty wampum belts, a large number of kettles and hatchets, and two females. "This news troubled me greatly, for I pictured to myself the awkward situation that might arise both for them and for us who were in their country." Awkward, indeed; this was the sort of thing that might develop into a long racial war. The Algonquins commanded the highway of the Ottawa; they could easily block the fur trade entirely. And, to take the short view, they could regard Champlain and his companions as friends of their enemies and could prevent their return to Quebec.

On his way to Cahiagué, Champlain stopped at the Nipissing settlement in the hope of arranging his expedition to the north. He learned, however, that Iroquet had just been there to gain support in the threatened conflict with the Hurons. Iroquet had paid the Nipissings well with wampum to abandon their northern journey and to assemble their strength at Cahiagué. "If anyone was sorry it was I; for I had quite expected to see in that year what in many preceding years I had sought for with great solicitude and effort amid much toil and risk of my life." He hoped that the trip was merely postponed; he collected much positive information about the northland and inspected trophies from that country, including buffalo skins.

Arriving at Cahiagué, he found the situation very tense. At the request of the Indians he assumed the role of judge or arbitrator. His interpreter assembled depositions from both sides. At a council of representative chiefs, Champlain took the floor. He urged peace, pointing out the dangers of division when the common enemy, the Iroquois, were aroused. He dwelt on the benefits of the fur trade to the Indians, while thinking, as he admits, of the benefits of that trade to the French. "Several speeches were made on both sides, and the conclusion was that I should give them my opinion and advice, seeing by their speeches that they referred the whole matter to my decision, as to their father, promising me if I did so that in the future I could dispose of them as seemed good to me, referring the whole settlement to my discretion."

Champlain then expressed the proper, politic sentiments: grief at the unhappy contretemps; esteem for both parties; a warning of the disasters that a war between allies would bring from the Iroquois; a hint that if they should go to war the French would have to seek out other tribes with whom to trade. "Since we love one another like brothers, let us leave to our God the punishment of those who deserve it."

He summoned all his eloquence. For the death of one man they were endangering the lives of thousands and rendering the survivors liable to perpetual slavery. "While in truth a man was of great consequence, they ought to consider how he had been killed and to take into consideration that it was not deliberately and in order to start a civil war among them."

He reviewed the case, pointing out that when the Huron aggressor had stabbed the Onondaga prisoner in the belly, the victim had pulled out the knife and stabbed his attacker; so that the blame for the Huron's death could not be clearly laid to the Algonquins. The Algonquins had then eaten the Onondaga, thus showing that they had no undue affection for him. The Algonquins had paid sufficient reparations. "Since they had promised me to submit everything to arbitration, I begged both parties to forget all that had taken place between them, and never to think of it more, nor to bear hatred or ill will toward one another, and to remain good friends as before. Should they do this, they would constrain us to love them and to assist them as I had done in the past. But on the other hand, should they not be pleased with my advice, I begged as many of them as could to come down to our settlement, where in the presence of all the ships' captains this friendship would be further cemented and we could concert measures to protect them from their enemies, to which they ought to be giving thought."

This conclusion, which answered, on the whole, the desires of both sides, was applauded. The two parties separated with at least outward indications of amity.

We have seen Champlain at work, resolving astutely a delicate and ominous situation. An essentially reasonable man, he appealed by instinct to the reason of his hearers, whether princes of the French court or savages squatting in Canadian snows. The method of reason and reasonableness was successful. Another would have been less deferential, would have assumed a high tone, and might have daunted these stubborn wills by his own more stubborn will. Such a one might have attained his immediate ends more readily than did Champlain. But Champlain, little by little and year by year, gained the respect and love of the natives of all Canada, because of his reasonableness, because of the recognizable integrity of his spirit. Already, and for the first time, the Indians call him their father.

Now, awaiting the spring, Champlain retired to the house of hospitable Darontal in Cahiagué. He lived the life of his hosts and made notes and sketches, to give us our first description of the life of an Iroquoian people.

To escape the foulness of the long house he wandered about the fortified village, which contained nearly 2,000 people. The spoiled Indian children followed him, mocking his beard, for all Indians regarded hair on the face with horror. Insolent, whining dogs, ignorant of the bark, came too. Unreproved, they thrust their noses into any cooking pot, little foreseeing their own destiny: to end in such a pot.

In a stout cage in the village lived some bears, being fattened for food. And in the woods round about, animals abounded, black foxes, flying squirrels, and such small deer. And skunks, which the Indians called "Devil's brats." (Father Le Jeune, in Quebec, took the creature as a symbol of sin. "No sewer ever smelled so bad," he says. "I would not have believed it if I had not smelled it myself. Your heart almost fails you when you approach the animal. I believe the sin smelled by Saint Catherine of Siena must have had the same vile odor.")

The winter food of the provident Hurons was abundant and relatively varied. Corn and beans were their staples. These they pounded to flour in wooden mortars, then they mixed the flour with dried berries or deer fat and baked loaves of bread in the ashes. One type of corn bread was called "chewed bread," for the kernels were stripped from the ear by the teeth of the women and children. The commonest dish was migan, or sagamité: corn with various additions boiled in earthen pots. Champlain found its taste as bad as its smell, especially when compounded with fish that the cooks did not bother to clean. A revolting delicacy was corn on the cob buried in mud under water for several months until well rotted and then boiled with meat or fish. "I assure you that nothing smells so bad as this corn when it comes out of the water all covered with mud, yet the women and children take it and suck it like sugar-cane, there being nothing they like better." They also consumed much squash, roasted or boiled, and this Brother Sagard found his chief solace in Huronia. They had no salt, but the French became accustomed to the lack and did not suffer from it. The Hurons' starchy diet, and the grinding sand in their food, rotted their teeth. Archæologists find thirty per cent of their teeth decayed and a high incidence of mastoid infections and other sequelæ.

During the winter they had little meat except an occasional dog for a feast. Sagard tells us that after one's first disgust is conquered, one finds a dog tasty, like good pork. Fish from Lake Huron abounded. Champlain joined the Indians in fishing through the ice, with nets dropped through a ring of holes.

When stored supplies failed, the Indians had many resources, such as the yellow lily root. They would suck cornstalks, in the conviction that thus they gained strength. Or they would defeat hunger with tobacco, which they dried and pounded to the dimensions of our coarse cut.

The winter duties kept everyone comfortably busy. The men fished and hunted, made bows and arrows, canoes, nets, and snowshoes, and repaired the fortifications. The women carried on the routine work of the village, spun and wove, molded and baked pots on open fires, and endlessly ground corn to supply the expeditions of the following summer.

Champlain inquired in vain about their system of laws. He could not discover that they had any, only customs. Matters of general concern were settled in councils of the elders and headmen. Every year a national assembly was held, including

representatives of all the clans. Decisions were reached by
majority vote. No particular chiefs held absolute command,
though the eldest and bravest received common respect. "As to
punishments, they employ none, nor positive commands either,
but everything they do is by entreaty of the elders, and by dint
of speeches and remonstrances they accomplish something."
Even war was conducted in this haphazard way, as Champlain
had learned to his cost.

Their lack of religion was shocking. They adored no god,
but had indeed some regard for the Devil. Champlain reflected
that to bring the Hurons to the knowledge of God it was not
sufficient to send friars; French settlers also were necessary, to
set an example of an upright and godly life. "Inhabitants and
families are needed to keep them to their duty and by gentle
treatment to constrain them to do better and by good example
to incite them to correct living. Father Joseph and I have many
times conversed with them on our belief, laws, and customs;
they listened attentively in their councils, saying to us sometimes: 'You say things that pass our understanding and that
we cannot comprehend by words, as something beyond our intelligence; but if you would do well by us, you should dwell in
our country and bring women and children, and when they come
to these regions we shall see how you serve this God whom
you worship, and your mode of life with your wives and children,
your way of tilling the ground and sowing, and how you obey
your laws and your manner of feeding animals, and how you
manufacture all that we see proceeding from your invention.
Seeing this we shall learn more in one year than hearing your
discourses in twenty, and if we cannot understand, you shall take
our children who will be like your own; and thus judging our
life wretched by comparison with yours, it is easy to believe
that we shall adopt yours and abandon our own.' Their speech
seemed to me natural good sense, showing their desire to know
God.

"It is a great pity to allow so many men to be lost and see
them perish at our doors without succoring them, which can
only be with the aid of kings, princes, and ecclesiastics, who
alone have the power to do this. For, also, they alone ought to
win from other nations the honor of so great a work, to wit,

planting the Christian faith in an unknown and savage country, being told by these people, as we are, that their one wish and desire is to be fully instructed about what they ought to follow and avoid. It is therefore the task of those that have the power to attend to it and to contribute toward it of their abundance; for one day they will answer before God for the loss of so many souls whom they leave to perish by their neglect and avarice, for these are not few but in very great number. Now this shall take place whenever it please God to give them grace to that end. As for myself I desire this result rather today than tomorrow, from the zeal I have for the advancement of the glory of God, for the honor of my King, for the welfare and reputation of my country."

Here, in the midst of his sober record, speaks Champlain's ardent spirit; here he sets down his dream. Certainly he was a competent businessman, scrupulously serving his employers, the French fur merchants. The interests of the fur trade came first, for without the fur trade, there would be no settlement and no exploration. But the fur trade was only a means to greater ends: the extension of French dominion to all the barbarous continent, and the extension of Christ's dominion to bring all these pitiable souls out of their darkness to salvation.

The Devil's agent, the Oki (continues Champlain), is doctor as well as priest. In case of illness he and his aides, with bearskins over their heads, dance about the patient. The neighbors, bringing gifts, gather, and all sing together, beating with sticks on dry tree bark. After an hour or two of dancing, the sick person is inspired to rise and join the dance. "But others really sick are not readily cured by such playing and dancing and goings-on. Sometimes they make such a noise and din, from morning till two o'clock at night, that it is impossible for the patient to bear it except with great difficulty."

The Oki and his adepts work themselves up to a hysterical frenzy. "They become like lunatics or madmen, throwing fire about the cabin from one side to the other, swallowing red-hot coals, holding them for a time in their hands, also throwing red-hot ashes into the eyes of the other onlookers, and on seeing them in this state one would say that the Devil, Oki, or Manitou, if such we must call him, possesses them and torments them in that manner. And when this noise and din is over, they withdraw each to his own quarters. Those who have a great deal of trouble at this time are the wives of those possessed, and all who belong to their cabins, for fear lest these mad folk should burn up everything inside their houses, and this leads them to take away everything in sight, for when they come in they are quite mad, with eyes flashing and frightful to see. Suddenly a whim will seize one, and, laying hold of anything he finds and meets with in his path, he will throw it from one side to the other and will then lie down and sleep some little time, and waking up with a jump will take fire and stones and throw them in all directions, without any precaution. This madness passes after sleep which comes upon him again, and then he will fall into a rage in which he summons several of his friends to sweat with him, which is the remedy that serves them best for keeping well, and while they sweat, the kettle works hard to satisfy their hunger. They remain sometimes two or three hours enclosed with big pieces of tree bark, covered with their robes, and having in their midst a great number of stones which have been heated red-hot in the fire. They sing all the time they are in the rage. Many jugfuls of water are given them to drink, since they are very thirsty, and after all this the demoniac or devil-possessed madman becomes sober. However, it sometimes happens that three or four of these sick persons get well, rather by happy accident and chance than by science, which only confirms their false belief, so that they are persuaded they have been cured by these ceremonies, not bearing in mind that for two who get cured ten others die from the noise and great din and the blowings they make, which are more fitted to kill than to cure a sick person. But that they should expect to recover their health by this noise and we on the contrary by quiet and rest, shows how the Devil does everything the wrong way about.

"There are also women who go into these rages, but they do not do so much harm; they walk on all fours like beasts. Seeing this the Oki begins to sing, then with some grimaces blows upon her, ordering her to drink certain waters and immediately to give a feast either of fish or of flesh, which must be found, even if it be scarce at the time; nevertheless this is done at once. When the shouting is over and the banquet finished, they return each to his cabin until the next time he comes to pay her a visit, blowing upon her and singing, with several others summoned for that purpose, holding in their hands a dry tortoiseshell filled with little pebbles which they rattle in the ears of the sick woman, ordering her to make forthwith three or four feasts, and a singing and dancing party, at which all the girls appear decked out and painted."

The French missionaries, soon to come, give us much additional information about the Okis, their ceremonies, their herbs and other remedies for the sick and insane. Brother Sagard reports with horror one curative process. About a sick woman's couch were crowded all the youths and maidens of the village, and there they devoted themselves to a night of tumbled love, while an Oki at each end of the house sang and rattled his tortoise shell from dusk to dawn. "May God be pleased to put an end to such a damnable and wicked ceremony."

Champlain could not but be impressed by the activity of the Indians' emotional lives. The girls began taking paramours at any time from their eleventh year on, receiving presents of wampum necklaces, girdles, and bracelets. "They continue this plan of action until they make a satisfactory union. Some girls spend their youth in this way, having had more than twenty husbands, and these twenty husbands are not the only ones who enjoy the creature, however much married they may be; for after nightfall the young women run about from one lodge to another, as do the young men for their part, who possess them wherever it seems good to them, yet without any violence, leaving all to the wishes of the woman. The husband will do the like to his woman neighbor, no jealousy arising among them on that account, and no disgrace or injury being incurred, such being the custom of the country. Now the time when they do not leave their husbands is when they have children. The previous husband returns to her, to show her the affection and love he bore her in the past more than to any other, and testifies that the child she will have is his, and of his begetting; another will say the same to her, and finally it is a contest to see who shall win and have her for wife. And in this way it is the woman's choice and option to take and accept whoever pleases her most, having in these courtships and amours gained much wampum and, besides, this choice of a husband. The woman remains with him without leaving him again, or if she leaves him it must be for some very good reason, other than impotence, for he has given his proofs on this head. Nevertheless while with this husband she does not cease to give herself free reign, but she remains and dwells always in his household, keeping up a good appearance; so that the children they have together, being born of such a woman, cannot be sure of being lawful." Because of this universal uncertainty, inheritance did not pass from the father to his putative children. A man's property and honors were conferred upon his sister's offspring.

Poor Brother Sagard was constantly shocked by the proposals of Huron girls, naïve in iniquity, who wished to marry him for a night or week. He labored to explain to them, in halting Huron, his dedication, and to describe the modesty of French maidens. His work was largely undone by his soldier-companions, who, for their own evil purposes, told the Huron belles that French girls were twice as licentious as they, which moved them to appalling emulation.

Huron life had many pleasures. Besides the sport of hunting and fishing, the young men played a kind of hockey, and especially lacrosse. The Okis would often ordain a game of lacrosse between villages as a cure for some patient. It was played with such a will that broken limbs and death sometimes resulted, and a net increase in business for the Oki.

The Indians were great gamblers. Their best games were a kind of jackstraws and the game of dish, in which six plum stones, black on one side, white on the other, were tossed in the air. The players, and even whole villages, would wager and lose all their possessions. One Huron, stripped of everything, put up his hair and his little finger. A woman staked herself and, losing, went into slavery. A chief's son, ruined at dish, hanged himself to a tree. (He seems, however, to have been a victim of *Todestrieb*, for he told a little girl that someone within him was always saying: "Hang thyself! Hang thyself!")

The Hurons painted and ornamented their utensils, not unskillfully, with the forms of men and beasts. Their music was elaborate and followed rigorous forms, but it gave the French no pleasure.

The chief of their delights was the ritual feast. The missionaries describe them in great detail: the feast of farewell, the feast of thanksgiving, the feast of the mad, the eat-all feast, the war feast, the marriage of the fish net to two virgins. These were often combined with elaborate dances and masquerades lasting for days. Everyone was disguised; Father Brébeuf saw some dressed as devils with horns, some naked with bodies whitened, some wearing sacks on their heads, others stuffed with straw to imitate a pregnant woman. Brother Sagard witnessed a dance of naked men and women, with accompaniments too dreadful to report.

The treatment of the dead was ruled by ceremonial customs. The bodies were laid in temporary tombs or in huts high above ground, out of reach of prowling animals. Every ten or twelve years a feast of the dead was held. The skeletons were cleaned and transported to a rendezvous where the Hurons met the neighboring peoples. In democratic councils, and in banquets and the dance, the bonds of alliance were strengthened. The bones of all the dead were put in a common grave, while orators proclaimed that similarly the living should be united in friendship and harmony. Much food was interred with the remains, and many rich presents, necklaces, wampum chains, tomahawks, kettles, sword blades, knives. Champlain did not himself see this ceremony, but the Jesuit Fathers were interested spectators.

In his full year among the Hurons, Champlain came to know them as none, save Brûlé, had known them before. He found much to praise. He admired the superb physique of the men and the beauty of the young women. "Their breasts hang down very little except when they are old." He was impressed by the Indians' acuteness of sense, their magnificent, uncomplaining endurance, their courage, their stoicism in pain. Brother Sagard tells how they would burn a tuft of pith on their arms without changing face. Indeed a swaggering Frenchman suffered a test of manhood with a Huron. They bound their arms together at wrist and elbow, laid a burning coal between, and each blew upon the coal until it was consumed. Both passed the test with honor; but Sagard sighs that the Frenchman would not have done as much for the love of God.

The Hurons showed an exemplary hospitality and were often

unexpectedly kind. Harmony commonly reigned among them; Father Brébeuf calls their gentleness and affability almost incredible among savages. They were fond of laughter, and they were great jokers, though their humor often took the primitive form of making the priests say bad words unwittingly. They were faithful to their oaths; they had a punctilious sense of justice.

They had plenty of bad qualities too: cruelty, vengefulness, vaingloriousness, insubordination, volatility. Their taciturnity made a striking contrast with French vivacity.[2] They were accomplished thieves, filching as skillfully with their feet as with their hands. "To steal and not be discovered is a sign of superior intelligence among them." And of course they were unbelievably filthy, with hardly the most elementary rules of hygiene. A long house in winter was to the missionaries a small foretaste of hell.

Yet there was much in this existence to attract certain hardy young Frenchmen among Champlain's companions. They were the sons of peasants or artisans, accustomed to endless toil from sunup to sundown. They knew grinding poverty, cruel exactions, the contempt of their betters, hunger, cold, and every hardship. They had lived in peasant huts, chimneyless, windowless, pell-mell with the domestic animals. They were well inured to filth and foulness. But among the Huron braves they could give their days to fishing and hunting, bringing down even the noble stag. In France only the King and his court

[2] "If a Frenchman returns from the chase, he is hardly in the house before it is already known whether or not he has captured anything. Even if he has not, he can hardly wait until the table is set for the meal, having the appetite of a hunter. If he returns from some journey, although he may be quite tired out, they cannot wait till he has rest before having him tell all the news he knows. Our Savages are far removed from this animation. Here is what I have very often seen among them. A Savage, returning from the chase, will sometimes throw outside the cabin what he has brought back with him. Having entered, he does not say a word, neither does anyone address him. He sits down near the fire and undresses; his wife takes his leggings and shoes, wrings them out if they are wet, and puts them to dry; he throws a robe over his shoulders and warms himself, this all taking place in silence. If his wife has saved him anything to eat, she presents it to him on a bark plate without saying a word; he takes it and eats it in silence. After eating, he smokes, and when he has finished smoking, he begins to talk. If no one has looked outside to see what he has brought back, he informs them that there are some beavers or some porcupines." *Jesuit Relations*, XI, 211. (Father Le Jeune.)

might chase the deer, while a peasant could be hung for killing a rabbit robbing his own garden. The French in Huronia lived in sober truth like lords. And when the day of sport and idleness was over, there was the welcome of the Huron girls, arch and artful.

For Champlain the conclusion was not so simple. This was his only protracted stay among the natives, as a lodger, not as a fêted guest. He observed and meditated. "With all their wretchedness, I consider them happy," he says. Like Sagard, he found them in many ways superior to civilized men. Unlike Sagard, he did not fear that the French would corrupt their simple virtues. He roundly favored the planting of French agents among them, to consolidate the interests of the two races and to instill French ideals among the natives. Later he spoke openly in favor of miscegenation. He did not feel that the Indians were inferior; they were merely different.

This is the relativism that runs through French thought, from Montaigne to our own times. Life is not an affair of absolutes, right and wrong, virtue and vice. Our ideals, our actions, our doctrines, are determined by circumstances. "Truth on this side of the Pyrenees, error beyond."

In his dreams he could see a great race, Christian French and Christian Indian, occupying this interminable land. It would guard the way to the western ocean, to the Orient. And all of it would acknowledge allegiance to his own God, to his own King, to France.

The winter passed, and the spring. On May 20 the expedition to the St. Louis Rapids set out. Champlain, the interpreter Thomas, Father Joseph, and the twelve Frenchmen—for apparently none but Brûlé had been lost—took their places in the canoes.[3] Champlain's friend Darontal was among the Huron chiefs.

The return journey, along Lake Huron, through Lake Nipissing, down the Ottawa, was a leisurely one, consuming forty days. No doubt some time was spent in barter with the trading tribes in the Lake Nipissing area. There was plenty of time to fish and hunt.

---

[3] Father Leclercq says that Sagard found in Huronia, in 1623, five or six Frenchmen who had gone native. But I find no such statement in Sagard.

At the end of June the party reached the St. Louis Rapids. Champlain found here good old Pontgravé, "who had almost despaired of seeing me again, from the bad news he had heard from the savages, to the effect that I was dead."

A week later Champlain left for Quebec, taking Darontal with him to repay the hospitality he had received in the wilds. He bade farewell to the other Indians, assuring them of his affection, promising to return loaded with presents, and adjuring them to forget their internecine quarrels. This they promised to do.

In Quebec there was a moving meeting between the French of the Habitation and those who had returned unexpectedly from the silent wilderness. Father Joseph celebrated a solemn Mass of thanksgiving. Champlain had the pleasure of displaying his imposing home to Darontal, who wondered and admired. "He told me privately that he would never die content until he had seen his friends, or at least a good part of them, come and make their abode with us in order to learn to serve God and to follow our mode of life, which he considered supremely happy in comparison with theirs." He urged Champlain to make a settlement at the St. Louis Rapids to protect the trade route. If this should be done, many of the Hurons would come to live there as the Frenchmen's brothers. Champlain promised to found such a settlement as soon as he possibly could.

This is the last time that Champlain refers in his works to his darling project for an establishemnt at the rapids. Had he succeeded in this design he might have been able to defend the trade route from the Iroquois incursions, and to spare the Hurons and the French innumerable woes. In fact not for thirty years was Montreal destined to be founded.

At the Habitation, Champlain found a delightful novelty: a Frenchwoman. Her name was Marguerite Vienne; she was the wife of a Frenchman, probably a company clerk. We cannot, alas, erect in her honor a shining memorial to the first white woman in Canada. That distinction must go to certain nameless, branded hussies, no better than they should have been—not nearly so good—who came out with Roberval in 1542, and by him were soundly whipped.[4]

[4] N.-E. Dionne (*Samuel Champlain*, II, 125) and Benjamin Sulte (*Mélanges historiques*, 17, Montreal, 1930, 24) say that Abraham Martin, company clerk,

Marguerite Vienne was ill, poor thing, and she died on July 19, just before the departure of the homeward-bound Frenchmen. She had at least the melancholy distinction of first receiving in Canada the sacrament of extreme unction.

Darontal, burdened with presents, left Quebec for the long journey home. Champlain actively superintended the enlargement of the Habitation. An addition was securely built of native stone and lime, proof against attack by fire. Champlain chose from the prospering gardens and orchard fine specimens to show in France.

Father Joseph le Caron and Father Jamet decided to return home, in order to bear witness to the possibilities for Canadian missionary work and to raise funds. Father d'Olbeau and Brother Pacifique would remain in Quebec for a second winter.

Champlain and his two priests made their farewells. At Tadoussac they found Pontgravé waiting. They set sail on August 3 and, borne by fair winds, reached Honfleur on September 10. "Here on our arrival we gave praise and thanks to God for His great care of us in preserving our lives, and for having as it were snatched and plucked us out of the many perils to which we had been exposed, and likewise for having brought us safe and sound back to our country. We prayed him also so to influence the heart of our King and of the lords of his council that they would contribute what was required of them to better the condition of these poor savage people and to bring them to the knowledge of God, the honor whereof will accrue to His Majesty, the greatness and growth thereof to his estate, the profit to his subjects, and the glory of all these undertakings and toils to God alone, the author of all perfection; to whom be honor and glory, Amen."

came out in 1613 with his wife, Marguerite Langlois, and that Nicolas Pivert brought out his wife, Marguerite Lesage, in 1614. Dionne includes them in his annual census of the colony. Now it often appears that Canadian historians have access to genealogical material that escapes us. (How do they know, for instance, that Etienne Brûlé was born in Champigny?) But in this case the failure of Champlain or Sagard to mention the presence of women in Quebec before 1616 casts doubt on the modern allegations. There is a reasonable solution: Martin and Pivert came out alone; after they had determined that life in Canada was tolerable for women, they sent back to France for their wives, or their childhood sweethearts, who arrived after 1616.

CHAPTER XVII

The Ninth Voyage

BAD NEWS INDEED greeted Champlain on his arrival at Honfleur! Just nine days before, on September 1, the Prince de Condé, Viceroy of Canada, had been arrested, in the very Queen's audience room of the Louvre, and was imprisoned. He had carried his greed and rebellion a little too far.

Champlain pulled a long face. "Our enviers will not be slow in spewing forth their venom. They will do what they have not hitherto dared, for when the head is sick, the members cannot be in good health."

He was, of course, entirely right. The Marquis de Thémines, who had personally arrested Condé, and who had immediately been rewarded by a marshalship of France, laid claim to the viceroyalty of New France. Condé had been paid annually with a horse worth 1,000 crowns; Thémines demanded one of 1,500 crowns. The Queen Mother, as Regent, granted his request. Condé protested from his prison. The matter was appealed to the Parlement, then to the King's Council. In a tangle of plots and subplots Thémines won the viceroyalty and the horse. No one gave a thought to the needs of the colony or to Champlain's dream of an expedition in force to the western land.

The friends of Canada did their best. They pointed out the precarious state of the Quebec settlement, the urgent need for supplies and soldiers, and especially for genuine colonists, to till the soil, feed the inhabitants, and set an example to the Indians. M. de Monts, constant in good works, drew up a two-year plan to render the colony self-supporting. But the merchants thought only of their profits, and the new Viceroy was concerned only for his 1,500-crown horse.

The Recollects, Fathers Joseph le Caron and Denis Jamet, pathetically passed from hand to idle hand a memorial they had drawn up in Quebec. To convert the Indians, they alleged, it was necessary first to make them men, and then Christians. To civilize them, it was essential to increase the colony, "the greatest obstacle to which was on the part of the gentlemen of the Company, who, to monopolize trade, did not wish the country to be settled, and did not even wish us to make the Indians sedentary, without which nothing can be done for the salvation of these heathens."

The Recollects continued that Protestants, who held the best share of the trade, nullified their missionary efforts by showing open contempt for the mysteries of the faith. To advance the Catholic cause, the Company must endow more laborers for this vast vineyard. The good work could not progress "unless the colony is increased by a greater number of settlers, mechanics, and farmers. Free trade with the Indians should be permitted without distinction to all Frenchmen. Huguenots should be excluded. It is necessary to render the Indians sedentary, and to bring them up to our manners and laws."

The Recollects' zeal smote vainly against the buffers of indifference. The gentlemen of the Company politely agreed, and did nothing. "Very zealous for their trade, they cared little to deserve God's blessing by contributing to the interests of His glory," says Leclercq, a Recollect historian of that century.

The high prelates and the public took small interest in the fantastic dreams of two obscure barefoot friars. The best the petitioners could obtain was free passage for two missionaries. It was decided that Father Joseph should return to Canada with a new recruit, Father Paul Huet. Father Jamet would remain in France, to collect funds and make friends for the conversion of Canada.

At least, Champlain gained one triumph. He found a genuine, a bona fide settler, with wife and family.

This was his old friend Louis Hébert, the Paris apothecary who had come out to Acadia in 1606, had wintered at Port Royal, and had made two more journeys thither, in 1610 and 1614. His wife had joined him there in 1611, sharing with Mme de Poutrincourt the distinction of being the first white women in Acadia. The Héberts loved the soil and its fruits and wonders; Canada spoiled them for a life of compounding drugs in a sunless Paris shop. Urged by Champlain, they sold everything and signed on with the Company on reasonable terms. But when in the spring of 1617 they arrived in Honfleur to embark, the Company disavowed its agreement. *Tant pis*; they would go anyway. They took ship with their two daughters and small son.

Champlain, preparing to join the party, was served with a writ by a particular enemy, Boyer of Rouen. This document, issued by the Parlement of Rouen, claimed to revoke his lieu-tenancy of New France. Clearly, it had to be contested.

And now there is a very funny business to consider. Champlain says in his edition of 1632 (not in the 1619 edition): "I embarked for the voyage of the year 1617, on which nothing happened worthy of note." No contemporary mentions his presence on this voyage or in Canada. Now on July 22 Champlain signed in Paris an engagement before a notary to hire a servant girl for his wife for a four-year term. Therefore Champlain did not go to Canada in 1617. His statement is false. Historians have counted one journey too many.

Is he lying? Was there some business reason why he wanted to establish, contrary to the facts, an absence from Paris?

No, the explanation, I think, is merely that he forgot. Revising his book for the 1632 edition, he wondered why he had failed to mention the 1617 voyage. Remembering nothing clearly about that summer, he assumed that he must have made the trip and that nothing happened worthy of note. Too often the painstaking reader of his works finds patent errors and indications that the more uncertain he was, the more specific he became.

The Canada ship set sail on March 11 without Champlain.

She was commanded by Captain Morel, an old North Atlantic hand, who had taken Champlain to Acadia in 1604. It was a long, stormy, three months' passage. The passengers consumed most of the supplies destined to feed Quebec during the following winter. Had Champlain been on board, we may be sure he would have better protected the interests of his colony.

Arriving thankfully in Tadoussac, the voyagers constructed an evergreen chapel, and Father Huet celebrated Mass, with two sailors at his side to whisk away the flies and mosquitoes, while the ship's cannon boomed for the elevation. The heretic Protestants, says Sagard, grumbled between their teeth.

The pinnace took the settlers to Quebec. The hungry garrison welcomed them enthusiastically. Great was their distress when, for all their supplies, one man carried ashore on his shoulder a single barrel of bacon.

The commandant, du Parc, reported that they had had a hard winter, otherwise not greatly eventful. But two men, a locksmith and a sailor, had mysteriously disappeared.

The Hébert family were the wonderment and delight of the colony. Their marriageable daughter caused a great refurbishing of shaving tackle. Louis Hébert set to and cleared some gardens, traditionally on the site of the present rue Sous-le-Fort, beneath the cliff. All his work had to be done with spade and pick; not for years did he have a plow and draft animals.

The trading fair took place at the St. Louis Rapids. The tribes were disappointed not to find Champlain, not to see any preparations for the promised fort. There was vague talk of more war with the Iroquois, but nothing was done.

Captain Morel's ship returned to France, bearing Father d'Olbeau, who planned to influence the great and rich to aid the good work. Silence, a hungry silence, settles down again upon Quebec.

Champlain, in Paris, labored against intrigue and indifference. France was too concerned with her intermittent civil war to lend him much attention. The people had no emotion to spare after the assassination in the Louvre's court, by order of the fifteen-year-old King, of Concini, now the Maréchal d'Ancre, the Queen Mother's darling. The ravening populace took possession of the fallen favorite's body and obscenely tore it to bits. One man ripped out the heart, grilled it, and ate it. Champlain may well have seen this horrid sight, and if so, he must have reflected on the mockery of civilization's self-pride.

In the interests of Canada he struggled against the noble grafters of the court, against the shysterism of unlicensed merchants, trying to inveigle themselves into the Canada trade without taking responsibility for settlement, against the merchants of his own company, demanding only quick profits, heedless of the long-term interests of the colony. More and more Canada seemed to him a land of repose for the spirit, a land where men's actions were clear and simple, where life was purified by the wilderness air.

He appealed direct to the King and the lords of his Council, hoping to kindle a spark in some tindery spirit.

"The peoples of New France," he wrote, "have given me so faithful a report of the north and south seas that one cannot doubt but that this would be the means of reaching easily to the Kingdom of China and the East Indies, whence great riches could be drawn." Did the Council realize even the extent and importance of the actual trade with New France and the imminent danger of its loss? For if the settlement should be abandoned, the envious English and Dutch would pounce upon it and would prevent more than a thousand French vessels from engaging in the fishing and whaling industries.

He proposed, therefore, that the Chamber of Commerce of Paris take an active hand in the development of this trade, and for its convenience drew up a memorial.

"Firstly, His Majesty will establish the Christian faith among an infinite number of souls. . . .

"Secondly, the King will make himself master and lord of a country nearly 1800 leagues in length, watered by the fairest rivers in the world and by the greatest and most numerous lakes, the richest and most abundant in all varieties of fish that exist, and full also of the greatest meadows, fields, and forests. . . .

"Thirdly, the Sieur de Champlain undertakes to discover the South Sea passage to China to the East Indies by way of the

River St. Lawrence, which traverses the lands of the said New France, and which river issues from a lake about 300 leagues in length, from which lake flows a river that empties into the said South Sea, according to the account given to the said Sieur de Champlain by a great number of people. . . .

"That his Majesty would derive a great and notable profit from the taxes and duties he could levy on the merchandise coming from the said country, as likewise from the customs duties on the merchandise that would come from China and from the Indies, which would surpass in value at least ten times all those levied in France, inasmuch as all the merchants of Christendom would pass through the passage sought by the Sieur de Champlain, it if please the King to grant them leave to do so, in order to shorten the said journey by more than a year and a half, without any risk from pirates and from the perils of the sea. . . .

"Furthermore the said Sieur de Champlain proposes to build at Quebec a town almost as large as St. Denis, which shall be called LUDOVICA, in the center of which will be built a fair temple, dedicated to the Redeemer, and called the Church of the Redeemer, as a memorial and commemoration of the good that it shall please God to do to these poor people, who have no knowledge of His holy name, to incline the will of the King to bring them to the knowledge of the holy Christian faith and to the bosom of our holy mother Church. . . ."

He then describes the proper fortification of his city. He proposes immediately to transport thither fifteen Recollect friars and three hundred families.

"And inasmuch as all existing states are supported politically on four buttresses, which are force, justice, trade, and husbandry, it is necessary to add force, which will consist of three hundred good men well armed and disciplined, and who nevertheless will have to work by turns at whatever will be necessary, as it is inexpedient in founding colonies to carry thither people, whatever their quality may be, who are incapable of earning their living.

"And it will be well to consider that, should the said settlement at Quebec not be kept up and strengthened by settlers against attack, the English or the Flemings, who are our neighbors, will drive us out, as they have already done the Jesuits [of Maine] and the Sieur de Poutrincourt, whose settlements they have captured and burned.

"The Flemings are settled in a place where they permit no one to go save those of their nation, which place is not very far from us. The English are settled in Virginia, where they permit no Frenchman to enter, as likewise in the north, where the said English have established themselves, permitting no foreigners save of their own nation to engage in the whale fishery. . . ."

Champlain then promises, on his honor and life, that if he receive reasonable aid, he will so establish the French on the St. Lawrence that no human force need be feared.

He looked at his memorial with satisfaction. His dream of the future of Canada seemed reasonable enough to him, and indeed, barring a certain error in geography, it seems reasonable to us.

He appended, for the instruction of the Chamber of Commerce, an estimate of the potential wealth of his country, in fisheries, whale oil, forest and agricultural products, dyes, hemp, mines of silver and iron, textiles, furs, building stone, and hides. He added up the annual value of these exports to reach the astounding total of 5,400,000 livres.

This was too much. No hardheaded business man could be expected to take such figures seriously.

The Chamber of Commerce transmitted the memorial to the King, on February 9, 1618, approving it and praying that the King grant Champlain funds for colonization. The Chamber then forgot the whole matter, and so did everyone else, except Champlain.

He made just one convert. This was his own brother-in-law, Eustache Boullé, a likely youth of eighteen, two years younger than Hélène de Champlain. Listening open-mouthed to fireside tales of far adventures, of manly pleasures in the wilds, he revolted against the prospect of a life of pettifoggery in the Paris courts. After, no doubt, a family scene, he obtained permission to try his luck in Canada.

Champlain and Eustache set out in March 1618. They boarded Pontgravé's ship in Honfleur. Father d'Olbeau was on board with a new Recollect recruit, Brother Modeste Guines. They had a long and hard crossing and reached Tadoussac on June 24.

Here they had their news of the winter in Quebec. It had been a difficult one indeed, full of famine and sickness. But only one man had died, and he a Scotch Huguenot, who had refused conversion on his deathbed and had gone direct to Satan's realm. Life went on. Father Joseph had performed the first marriage in Canada, uniting young Anne Hébert and a Norman named Étienne Jonquest. The Héberts were not discouraged about their purpose of tilling Canadian soil, though the merchants' factors put every obstacle in their way. "Oh God!" cries Sagard. "Everywhere the big fish eat the little ones!"

The chief news was ominous. The two Frenchmen who had disappeared in 1616 returned, dead, to cry of murder, to demand vengeance. Their skeletons were found by the river shore, bound together by withes. The skull of one was beaten in, as by a stone hammer. It was evident that their bodies had been sunk in the river, and that God had willed that the crime should be known and had removed the weights.

The French found an informer among the Montagnais and learned the facts. One of the dead Frenchmen had beaten an Indian. He, with a companion, had tracked down his tormentor and had taken vengeance. The second Frenchman had died only because he was a witness.

The Montagnais met in council and professed themselves ready to make proper reparation in the form of valuable furs. No, said the French; this is not French justice; you must deliver up the two malefactors for punishment. This seemed very silly to the Montagnais. Nonetheless they yielded, and one of the murderers presented himself at Quebec, formally attired in his ceremonial finery. A common meeting was held, with a great deal of speechmaking, each side trying to explain to the other the correct principles of justice. At length the murderer, bored by the interminable discussion, asked to be put to death without further talk. No, said Father Joseph, that would be most irregular. He must be properly tried.

The French recognized that this was a ticklish situation. They examined the case. "First, we were weak, considering the numbers of the savages outside and inside our factory, who, vindictive and revengeful as they are, might have fired it everywhere and put us to rout. The second reason was that there would be no more security in intercourse with them [if we should execute the murderer], and we should live in perpetual mistrust. Thirdly, trade might be injured and the King's service impeded." It was decided, then, to parole the murderer in charge of his father, to require him to serve the French henceforth, and to demand friendship of the Indians in return for the murderer's life.

This weak decision was far from pleasing to Champlain and Pontgravé. They concluded that the case must be re-opened in conference with the Indians.

With some foreboding Champlain ascended the river to Quebec. He found his dear Habitation intact, though no work had been done on it since his departure, two years before. The gardens, thanks to Hébert, were in fine shape, with excellent grain growing in the manureless soil, the French vines thriving, and the gardens blessed with cabbages, radishes, lettuce, purslane, sorrel, parsley, squash, cucumbers, melons, peas, and beans.

As soon as possible Champlain went upriver to the trading fair. It was held this year at Trois Rivières, halfway between Quebec and the St. Louis Rapids. Its location marks a triumph for the French traders, for their journey was reduced while that of the Indians was correspondingly increased. The triumph was perhaps a vain one. The Iroquois menace to the Indians' trade route was growing, particularly since the Dutch on the Hudson had just completed a formal alliance with the Iroquois confederation.

At the fair, Champlain found many old friends from Huronia. They embraced him, one after another, with loud shouts: *"Ho, ho, ho!"* He warmly greeted representatives of other tribes he had interviewed in their far homelands. Having come to the fair at his urging, they were much honored by the French and rewarded with rich presents.

At the general council the Indians begged Champlain for military aid against their enemies. Champlain was forced to be vague, for he had no soldiers and no munitions. He tried to throw the blame on the Indians for their own failure to appear in sufficient number. And he made a great grievance of the murder of the two Frenchmen. He would, however, ask his King for men, money, and supplies for a war expedition in the following year.

He took up the question of the murder. "The matter must be taken very seriously," he said privately to Pontgravé. "Otherwise the savages may feel free to do the same again, or even something worse, for they are people governed by example. They may accuse the French of lacking courage. If no further mention of it is made, they will judge that we are in fear and terror of them. If we let them off so easily they will become more insolent, bold, and unbearable, and ready to engage in more serious and deadly designs. Moreover the other savage tribes which have heard or will hear of this deed, and that it remained unavenged or avenged only by a few gifts and presents, may boast that to kill a man is no great matter, since the French make so little account of seeing their comrades killed by their neighbors that they eat and drink with them, and they walk and converse familiarly with our people, as may be seen."

"On the other hand," (this seems to be Pontgravé's reply) "the savage folk are without reason, difficult of approach, easily estranged, and are very quick to take vengeance. If we insist on their doing full justice, there will be no security for those who may undertake explorations among them."

Champlain yielded, as he yielded too often. "To tell the truth," comments Sagard, "we are more afraid of discontenting the savages, because of the fur-business, than we are of offending Frenchmen."

The matter ended in an anticlimax, in a few solemn warnings. The French traded in peace with the murderers and their people. As Champlain foresaw, the Indians were surprised at French softness; they learned a new insolence and arrogance in their dealings with the merchants.

The episode of the murder is not yet closed; it is postponed to a later year.

Among the Hurons was one figure as swarthy as they with sun and dirt, and dressed in their embroidered skins. It was Étienne Brûlé.

Champlain greeted him warmly. "I thought you were dead! Where have you been? And why did you and the Andastes not meet us at the Onondaga fort?"

Étienne told him the story that has already been summarized in its place.[1]

"And after you returned to the Andaste village?"

"I tried to get some guides to take me back to Huronia. But no one would move in the winter through the enemy land, when one can be seen from afar and tracked through the snow. So to kill time I explored to the south. I followed a river [the Susquehanna] which discharges on the coast of Florida, where there are many powerful and warlike tribes which make war one upon another. The climate there is very mild, and there is a great quantity of animals and game, but to reach this country one must have much patience on account of the difficulties in passing through most of its wastes. I continued along this river to the sea, past islands and the coasts near them, which are inhabited by several tribes and numerous savage peoples, who nevertheless are well disposed and love the French nation above all others. But as for those who are acquainted with the Dutch, they complain much of them, because these treat them too harshly. It very seldom snows there, and even when it does snow, it is not a foot in depth and melts on reaching the ground."

(Brûlé reached, then, Chesapeake Bay and went far enough along it to be convinced it was the sea, with its tides and brackish water. Perhaps Baltimore. One more record for this triumphant explorer.)

"Then I came back to the Andaste village, to find some companions to take me back to the Huron country. After some stay, five or six of the savages decided to make the journey. But on our way we met a great band of our enemies. They attacked us so fiercely that we were scattered and separated. I had run off in the hope of escaping. I could no longer retrace my steps nor find the trail nor any sign so as to retreat, and thus I wandered through the woods for some days without eating and almost despairing of my life, through hunger.

"At last I came on a little path which I determined to follow no matter where it might lead, whether towards the enemy or

[1] See page 238.

not, preferring to place myself in their hands, trusting in God, than to die alone so miserably.

"I hadn't proceeded far when I discovered three savages, laden with fish, who were returning to their village. I ran after them to join them, and I began to call to them, at which call they turned around, and, in fear and apprehension, prepared to flee and leave their burden. But I spoke to them, reassured them, and bade them lay down their bows and arrows in token of peace, and I laid down my arms too, though I was very weak and feeble on account of not having eaten for three or four days. On coming up with them I told them of my mishap and my wretched state, and we sat down and smoked together. They had pity and compassion on me, and offered me every assistance. They brought me to their village and entertained me and gave me something to eat.

"But as soon as the people of the place heard of it, that an Adoresetouy had arrived, for so they called the French, which name means 'iron men,' they came crowding in great numbers to see me, and took me to the lodge of one of the principal chiefs, where I was questioned. They asked me who I was, whence I came, what had driven me and led me to this place and how I had got lost, and further whether I was not one of the French nation which was making war on them. I replied that I belonged to another better nation that was desirous only of their acquaintance and friendship. This they refused to believe and they rushed upon me, and tore out my nails with their teeth, burned me with red-hot firebrands, and plucked out my beard hair by hair, though this was contrary to the wish of the chief.

"In this emergency one of the savages spied an *Agnus Dei* hanging about my neck. On seeing it, he asked what it was, and tried to seize it and tear it off, but I said to him in a resolute voice: 'If you take it and put me to death, you shall see that immediately afterwards you and all your house will die suddenly!' The savage paid no attention, but pursuing his evil purpose tried to seize the *Agnus Dei* and tear it from me. All together were prepared to put me to death, after first making me suffer many pains and tortures. But God who had mercy on me would not permit it, but in His providence caused the sky

which had been clear and fine suddenly to become overcast and
to be filled with thick heavy clouds, which ended in thunder and
lightning so violent and continuous as to be something strange
and awful. This storm so frightened the savages, because it was
unusual and they had never known the like, that it distracted
them and made them forget their wicked intentions. They left
and forsook me, yet without unbinding me, for they dared not
approach me. This gave me an opportunity to use gentle words
with them, calling to them and representing the harm they were
doing me without any reason, making them understand how
angry our God was with them for having thus ill-treated me.
Then the chief approached me, unbound me and brought me
into his lodge, where he cleaned and doctored my wounds. After
this, there were no dances and feasts to which I was not summoned."

(Maybe so, maybe so. It could have happened, and I do not
like to abate the world's wonders. But the sudden thunder-
storm, unique in the weather-wise Indians' experience, seems
a little too pat, and the terror of the Indians excessive. If this
was not a miracle, it was a miracle story of a familiar melo-
dramatic type. Inscrutable as God's ways are, I find it hard to
believe He would have performed a miracle for Brûlé, who had
become almost a pagan savage. The Recollects looked upon him
askance for his glad indulgence in every Indian vice, and especially for his lack of piety. He was far from devout; once when
in peril of death he could remember no Christian prayer but the
Benedicite. Worse, when he came to the falls at Ottawa he
solemnly sacrificed tobacco to the Indian god, and, he alleged,
was repaid by having an excellent journey. The story of the
wonder-working *Agnus Dei* sounds like a shrewd fabrication to
prove the teller's piety and the particular favor of the Frenchman's God. It sounds even like a joke on gullible Champlain.
Sagard, recounting the miracle, can only sigh: "God works his
marvels often through the worst persons.")

"After some time with these savages," continued Brûlé, "I
determined to withdraw to our quarters and settlement. And
taking leave of them I promised to make them friends with the
French and their enemies, and to make them swear friendship
for one another, and with this object I would return to them as

soon as I could. On my departure they conducted me four days journey from their village, whence I came to the country of the Hurons." As it was the summer of 1616 the French had already departed.

"There I remained some time. Then resuming my journey to the French I passed along the Freshwater Sea [Lake Huron], and went by boat some ten days along its northern shores, and I would have gone farther, according to your instructions, only for a rumor of war preparations among them. I will carry out this exploration ere long, with God's aid, and will guide you thither."

Such a proposal was most fitted to warm the heart of Champlain, as Brûlé well knew. Champlain promised that his services would be recognized, and encouraged him to behave himself until the following summer, when, it was to be hoped, the exploration might be undertaken.

Brûlé then took his leave, to return to Huronia with his wild companions, to whom he was much more kin than to the men of his own blood.

The trading fair ended, an uncommonly profitable one for the Company. Champlain returned to Quebec and saw to the repair and strengthening of the fortifications. What he did not do, no one did.

In Quebec was held the first religious jubilee in Canada, by special permission of the Pope. As the French visited the stations set up in the woods, the Indians followed, imitating, comically and pathetically, the genuflections of the faithful.

Champlain then went downriver to Tadoussac. He arranged that a party, including a priest, should winter there among the Montagnais. He embarked, with Father Huet and Brother du Plessis, on Pontgravé's ship, which was laden with a most noteworthy cargo for the owners.[2] They reached Honfleur on August 28, after a passage of less than a month, "with a favorable wind and to everybody's satisfaction."

[2] Jacques Lecointe: *Histoire du règne de Louis XIII* (Paris, 1716), III, 262.

CHAPTER XVIII

The Tenth Voyage

ARRIVING IN FRANCE in this autumn of 1618, Champlain found that he had merely exchanged the squabbles of Indian chiefs for the intrigues of French merchants and courtiers.

The Marshal de Thémines, Viceroy of New France, received his annual 1,500-crown horse from the merchants and gave Canada no further thought. But Condé, from his prison, vociferated that if the merchants paid the usurper Thémines, they would eventually have to pay twice. In the spring of 1619, Thémines made the bad mistake of killing in a duel the brother of the Bishop of Luçon, a rising young man soon to make his mark as the Cardinal de Richelieu. Thémines's star waned and went out. Condé was released from prison, and demanded and obtained his back pay from the merchants. The merchants wrung their hands and vowed they were ruined; they could not spare a penny for colonization, fortification, or exploration. Condé made a present of 500 livres to the Recollects, and this was his only contribution to the welfare of Canada. He then sold the viceroyalty to the young Duc de Montmorency, Admiral of France, for the substantial sum of 11,000 livres.

The fur trade had become, in fact, a very nice business. Fifteen to twenty thousand beaver skins were shipped annually;

in one year, twenty-two thousand. The monopoly held the prices paid to the Indians down to the barest minimum, and by astute control kept the selling price in Paris high.

Such profits were very tempting to enterprising businessmen. Unlicensed adventurers crept up the St. Lawrence, bought furs along the shore, and got away, though sometimes, through their unfamiliarity with the river and by the mercy of God, they were wrecked.

The merchants of Brittany, not members of the trust, slipped an authorization for free trade through the King's Council. Champlain went into action, obtained an injunction, and after great dispute, a revocation of the act. But all this haggling, of which you may read at length in Champlain's books, seems pretty dreary today, as indeed it seemed to Champlain, chafing to achieve greater ends.

In the course of the dispute the Company was sharply criticized for its failure to send out colonists and to support religion. The Company's reasons were obvious: first, a horror of spending money; and second, a fear that a resident agricultural population would absorb the furs, and that sedentary God-fearing Indians would cease to hunt and trap in order to obtain trade goods. And third, there was the chronic unwillingness of the influential Huguenot members to aid the Church.

Disturbed by criticism, and harried by Champlain, some of the Company merchants drew up a project of settlement for 1619. It was modest enough. It provided for only eighty men for Quebec. But even this timid proposal had no success. In the end two families were sent out, without Champlain's approbation. The head of one was a butcher, the other a needlemaker. Both were entirely the wrong sort.

As Champlain was preparing for his summer in Canada he was curtly informed by the Company that Pontgravé would be in charge of the settlement, and that Champlain would have authority only over exploration. And of course no men or equipment were provided for exploration. We must conclude that Champlain's plans and projects irritated the businessmen; they wanted an agent single-minded in his devotion to the fur trade.

Champlain protested vigorously. As Lieutenant of the King, appointed and paid by His Majesty, he was in command of the settlement and could not be removed by the merchants. The royal representative must rule Quebec and the Company's agents in residence there. Champlain had no personal grievance against Pontgravé; "I was his friend, and his years would lead me to respect him as I would my father; but to consent to the assignment to him of what belonged to me by right and reason, that I would by no means suffer."

He carried his protest to the King's Council and was amply sustained, and the intriguing merchants were condemned. But while this was going on, Pontgravé had sailed for Canada, and Champlain was left in Paris. Perhaps this was the merchants' idea in the first place.

He had at least the leisure to see through the press his third published volume, his *Voyages and Discoveries Made in New France, from 1615 to 1618,* by the Sieur de Champlain, Capitaine Ordinaire for the King in the Western Ocean. It is a handsome quarto, with illustrations showing savage life and the high points of Champlain's own adventures. The dedication, to the King himself, by his gracious permission, breathes the hope that His Majesty will encourage colonization and evangelization, so that the Indians "with the French speech may also acquire a French heart and spirit."

It is a propaganda volume, of course, an answer to French curiosity about savage life, an appeal to French imagination, missionary zeal—and cupidity; and also a defense of Champlain's own dealings with the Company. However, he is sparing in criticism of the merchants. He is too closely associated with them to tell all. He hardly suggests, for instance, the bitter opposition between Protestant and Catholic within the colony.

During the winter he strengthened his position for the disputes he foresaw in Canada. He was appointed Governor of New France, with complete authority over the settlement, except for the merchants' warehouse. But this exception was an important one. The Quebec factor of the merchants ruled within his warehouse and had control of most of the able-bodied men. In the long winter controversies the factor could, and did, oppose Champlain's measures for security, for building, for clearing and tilling the land. The factor also had his hand on most of the supplies.

In the spring of 1620 Champlain sailed once more. And now he had with him the best of recruits—his wife.

Hélène, a spirited and high-minded girl, had had enough of tormented widowhood in Paris. She would see this fabulous country of Samuel's, and she would rule there as Governor's Lady. She brought three waiting-women to keep the Governor's mansion in suitable style.

There were other passengers: Father Jamet and a new Recollect, Father Le Baillif. And a rather enigmatic person, the Sieur Dolu. He was sent out as the personal agent of the new Viceroy, the Duc de Montmorency, with orders to make a close inspection and to report.

Champlain happily displayed to his wife the routine of life at sea, the excitement of storms, the charms of calm, when the sailors danced together on the deck. When they reached Canada he pointed out the familiar landmarks, such as the Bird Rocks, a cloud of fluttering wings. And so they came to Tadoussac and pulled ashore, to the lee of the everlasting mountains. There, down from Quebec, was Eustache Boullé, Hélène's brother. "He was greatly pleased, and she and I were still more so."

The news? Why, the Habitation was in good order. Pontgravé, as commander, had given the colony a jolly winter, with plenty of drink, song, and play. Gambling with an Indian, he had won his clothes, wife, and children, and then, roaring with laughter, had given them back. But Brother Pacifique du Plessis had died, and Hébert's daughter, Mme Jonquest, in childbirth, and the child too. Interlopers from La Rochelle were trading on the river, and they had sold the savages a large supply of firearms, with powder, match, and ball—a very bad business. Champlain shook his head.

The governor and his lady re-embarked in a pinnace and made haste to Quebec. The whole population, white and red, cheered on the bank, till they were suddenly hushed at the sight of beautiful Mme Champlain, and then they cheered twice as loud. Two peculiar passengers were put ashore—a pair of asses. These, on setting foot in their new continent, brayed enormously. The Indians turned and fled into the woods. "Have the French brought these furious beasts to devour us?" they said. "Or to rejoice us with their musical airs?"

Champlain, his lady, and Dolu inspected the settlement. (Pontgravé was absent upriver at the trading fair.) To give thanks for their safe arrival they walked half a league, a little unsteadily, to see the tiny convent and chapel of the Recollects. It stood on a pleasant spot above the St. Charles, where today rises, appropriately, the great bulk of the General Hospital.

They returned to the Habitation. "I found the settlement in such an abandoned and ruinous condition that I felt grieved. The rain was coming in everywhere; the wind blew through all the crevices of the planks, which had shrunk as time went on; the store-house was on the point of tumbling down; the courtyard was in such a dirty and disgusting state, one of the dwellings having fallen to pieces, that the whole looked like some poor abandoned settlement in the fields, which soldiers had occupied. Greatly astonished was I at the state of affairs."

And the governor's Lady and her ladies-in-waiting were certainly in tears.

Louis Hébert's ten-acre farm, on the site of the present arch-bishopric, was in good condition. He complained that every obstacle was put in his way by the Company agents. They forbade him to trade with the Indians, and set a ruinous monopoly price for his farm products. He was not discouraged, however; he loved this country and was not going to be forced out.

The two other settlers, the butcher and the needlemaker, had done absolutely nothing in the course of a year, had not even cleared an acre of land. They had spent the winter hunting, fishing, sleeping, and drinking. Champlain gave them a sharp reproof and a warning.

Dolu, inscrutable, made his notes.

Pontgravé returned from the trading, and in midsummer set out for France. Dolu, carefully guarding his papers, embarked with him.

Autumn came, and winter. Champlain was busy, and happy, building a fort on the cliff overlooking the Habitation, "though none of the shareholders of the Company had been able to appreciate the necessity of having a fortified place for the protection of the country and of their own property." The stronghold he named Fort St. Louis, in honor of the King.

Hélène was less happy. She would not be familiar with Mme

Hébert, a mere apothecary's wife, and still less with the families of the drunken needlemaker and butcher. Except for her husband and brother, the inhabitants were all workmen, traders' clerks, priests. She turned in boredom to the Indians, and these, worshipping her beauty and kindness, wanted to make a goddess of her. She carried a little mirror on a chain, according to the Paris style of 1620. The savages, seeing their reflection, supposed, prettily, that she had their image in her heart.

The ships arrived from France early, in mid-May of 1621. They evidently brought some domestic animals, though no horses.

In Champlain's sealed bag of mail was a letter from the King promising arms and munitions. And a sensational message from the viceroy, Montmorency.

Dolu had turned in to his chief a damning report on the conduct of the colony. Only Champlain figured in it creditably. Montmorency acted with decision. He doubled Champlain's salary, raising him to 200 crowns a year. He annulled the Company's monopoly, forbade the old merchants to trade with Canada, and granted the sole rights of the fur business to Guillaume and Emery de Caen, Huguenot merchants of Rouen, for a period of eleven years. He ordered Champlain to confiscate and hold all the goods of the old company in the warehouse.

Now this was all very well. But how was Champlain to confiscate the Company's goods? He had only one trustworthy aide, Eustache Boullé, in the settlement of sixty souls.

With as much bluster as he could command, he served his summons on the Company's agent. The agent, who had been reading his own letters, refused to surrender his goods unless Champlain should produce an order signed by the King himself. This, as the agent well knew, Champlain did not have.

Champlain yielded. He had good reason; the trading season was on, and if the merchants could not or would not trade, all the good will of the Indians, so carefully cultivated, would be lost. He announced that he would make no changes until the Sieur de Caen should arrive with a royal decree.

At this juncture Pontgravé, representing the old company, appeared at Tadoussac, as if nothing had happened. The old company had not taken Montmorency's decree lying down. It had carried the dispute to court, in a snow of stays and injunctions. Champlain, lacking sure information, was bewildered. He compromised and compromised, and apparently infuriated every one.

Not until July 15 did word come of Guillaume de Caen's arrival at Tadoussac. He brought letters that justified Champlain's moderation, for the King announced that he had decided to permit both companies to trade for this year of 1621 only, and required that both should contribute equally to the support of the colony. This makeshift settlement was unsatisfactory to all concerned. De Caen had arrived too late to do much trading; to recoup himself he prepared to seize Pontgravé's ship while its master was upriver.

Champlain and Pontgravé hurried down to Tadoussac. Champlain heard both sides, and found both unreasonable, but de Caen the most. He then took formal possession of Pontgravé's ship on behalf of the viceroy; de Caen, unimpressed, led a party to board her. And Champlain says: "Before the Sieur de Caen boarded Pontgravé's vessel, I weighed anchor on the twelfth of August and slipped past the Saguenay, so as not to be present when de Caen made the seizure."

I have no right to blame Champlain, and I do not blame him. But I must note again that he reveals a certain lack of dominating force. He did not stand and fight and die for his decision; he slipped away so as not to be present. Though fearless in battle and dauntless in danger, he was not resolute to the end in dealing with angry businessmen. He was too reasonable a person, perhaps.

When all was quiet again, Champlain returned. He took delivery of the arms the King had promised. The shipment consisted of just four arquebuses, two petards, and some miscellaneous gear, lead, pikes, halberds, armor. Champlain was horrified. Was this all? He suspected, no doubt with good reason, that the supplies had been pilfered on the way.

De Caen at length patched up his quarrel with Pontgravé, selling him supplies at a thumping price. The two captains then sailed for France, taking with them most of the men of the old company, including the incompetent butcher and needlemaker, with their families. Peace—the peace that Champlain loved— came again to Quebec.

On October 24 was born the first French child in Canada. He was the son of Abraham Martin, pilot, called "the Scotchman," and his wife Marguerite Langlois. The name of Abraham Martin is preserved in the Plains of Abraham, famed in history and in song.

In this year also Guillemette Hébert was married to Guillaume Couillard, an exemplary settler and destined to be the founder of a great line in Canada. He joined his father-in-law to work the little farm on the plateau above the river.

The snows came, and the bitter glittering days, and the crackling nights. Champlain worked at his fort with the few men at hand. He worried about his enemies: the Iroquois, even the shifty Montagnais, who might attack the settlement from hunger or because a chief had dreamed a dream of omen. He worried too about the English, planting their colonies in Massachusetts, growing in power and boldness along the coasts. His stores of beaver would be a dainty plum for some English pirate.

To bind his Indians in a closer alliance, for defense against the Iroquois and against white raiders from the sea, he conferred on a Montagnais chief the title of Captain. In return the Indians promised to clear the land and plant corn, and guaranteed to keep peace with the French. Thus Champlain sought to solve the problems of security and food supply.

But the spring passed without incident. In June the traders arrived from France, with news that the commercial troubles had been appeased by the grant of shares in the new company to reputable members in the old.

At the same time two Iroquois braves appeared at Trois Rivières, making proposals for a general peace. The Montagnais were wholeheartedly in favor; "they were sick and tired of the wars they had had, which had lasted over fifty years." Champlain himself no less heartily favored a peace that would enable the Hurons and Algonquins to bring down their furs in security and confidence. He insisted, however, that sufficient guarantees be given to guard against duplicity.

The two Iroquois were escorted to Quebec, and a mighty

festival was held, with day-long dances. Champlain discovered that the visitors had insufficient credentials from their own people; the proposal of peace was unauthorized by any Iroquois council. He therefore arranged that four Montagnais ambassadors, fully empowered to treat, should be sent to the Iroquois.

Champlain has been accused of organizing and fomenting the Indian wars in order to keep the fur trade in French hands. Notice, now, that when an opportunity presents itself for peace, he eagerly furthers it. Such a course was consonant with mere good sense. Peace might permit the Dutch to gain some share of the fur trade; but the French felt they could hold their own in fair competition. Peace would put a stop to the serious depredations of the Iroquois, and would remove the unfailing threat to the very existence of the French on the St. Lawrence.

By summer's end the traders departed, all save old Pontgravé, who remained in Quebec as chief factor for the new company. His gout troubled him so that he did not leave the Habitation throughout the winter. His presence was a solace to Champlain; the two had a quarter century of common memories of adventure. But Mme Champlain probably found him coarse.

Champlain superintended the household tasks of the settlement, especially the autumn and spring sowing. "I took a singular pleasure in the work." And so another peaceful season went by. And in the summer the French traders, headed by Guillaume de Caen, came again.

They brought with them a precious passenger, Gabriel Sagard, a Recollect lay brother summoned to missionary labors in the wild. He has left us one of the classics of the rich literature of exploration, from which I have delighted to quote. Ever inquisitive, observant, yet somehow naïve, simple-hearted, he lets his garrulous pen take its own course. His picture of life in the French settlement and among the Hurons is the most detailed that we possess. His eye caught the vivid scene, the revelatory action, the grotesque contrast, more readily than did the matter-of-fact mind of Champlain, to whom the picturesque had become commonplace. On every page Sagard reveals his happy, pious, ingenuous mind. The genial gusto of his style gives his book the art above art, the art unconscious of itself.

At the moment when the French arrived, trouble weighed upon Champlain's mind. He had heard from a friendly Indian that the Montagnais murderer of 1616 was stirring up the Indians to attack and destroy the French at Quebec and Tadoussac. His admiring fellows had made him a chief. A dangerous situation, clearly.

Champlain, Guillaume de Caen, Brother Gabriel Sagard, and others went up to the trading fair at the mouth of the Richelieu. Here they found the sulky murderer. De Caen urged that he be publicly pardoned in the interests of peace. "To this I could not agree," says Champlain, "remembering the perfidy of which he had been guilty in the assassination of our men." Nevertheless, under pressure he did agree to the pardon. Once again he yields to the blustering voices of men less judicious and worse informed than himself.

The murderer was then persuaded to make a public confession of his crime and a plea for grace. He asked that the deserved penalty be remitted. Champlain and de Caen took a bared sword, and solemnly cast it into the St. Lawrence. De Caen was pleased, but Champlain reflected bitterly that the Indians concluded that the pardon was granted "through lack of courage on our part, and because we did not dare to put him to death, although he deserved it; and indeed it gave them a very poor opinion of us that we had not shown anger at the crime." This conclusion was fully corroborated by Sagard, who reported later that "our Hurons, who are adepts at dissimulation and who kept an unmoved countenance while this was going on, turned the whole ceremony into ridicule and made a mock of it when in their own country again, saying that all the Frenchmen's anger had been drowned with this sword, and that henceforth for killing a Frenchman one would get off at the cost of a dozen beaver skins."

We hear nothing more of the peace treaty with the Iroquois in the course of this summer. Champlain has been roundly accused of breaking up the negotiations for peace. Some color is given to the accusation by a statement of Sagard's. He says that when he tried to bring about a peace between the Hurons and the Iroquois, he was warned off by some gentlemen of the Company, who told him that if peace should reign, the Iroquois would bring the Hurons to trade with the Dutch. The Jesuit Charlevoix, writing more than a century later, goes farther. He asserts that Champlain heard that the Hurons were planning to make peace with the Iroquois, and so sent Sagard and his companions to Huronia to break up the project.

But no, this evidence is not good enough to offset Champlain's own record of his labors to make and preserve general peace. Nor does it upset the mere argument of common sense: that peace was more advantageous to the French than war. But let us get on, and relegate this question to Appendix G.

The trading fair of 1623 came to its end. Father Joseph le Caron, Father Nicolas Viel, and Brother Gabriel Sagard embarked in Huron canoes for the journey to Huronia, to the land where Father Joseph had begun his ministry with Champlain in 1615. Eleven French laymen accompanied the clergy. One, the Sieur du Vernet, was one of those mysterious and fascinating people of whom we get only tantalizing glimpses. A nobleman, he had already lived among the savages of Brazil; he enlivened the Huronian winter with many a wild tale and piquant comparison. He was the uneasy man, the adventurer, who belies the facile generalization that the French are a stay-at-home people. Étienne Brûlé was in the party too, and two other Frenchmen, detailed to winter among the Algonquins. One sees how Champlain was carefully planting his agents and interpreters. Each received a hundred pistoles annually—a considerable sum—to hold the savages to their allegiance and to insure their appearance at the trading fair.

By the end of August, de Caen, Pontgravé, and the summer visitors left Quebec, and the guiet, golden, happy autumn came in. Champlain busied himself and his men by laying foundations for a new warehouse, strengthening Fort St. Louis on the summit, and building a practicable road up the cliffside. This was probably the lower part of the present rue de la Montagne.

The winter came and went. Hélène Champlain was, no doubt, bored beyond endurance by the petty routine of her days. Was she a solace to her husband? Courteously, modern writers so assume, but we have, in fact, no hint from contemporaries. I suspect that she found the snowbound Habitation intolerable after a life spent in the heart of Paris under the very walls of the Louvre. I suspect that her complaints wore on Champlain's nerves. At their marriage she was a child of twelve, and her endearing childishness had appealed to his longing for fatherhood. Now she was a spirited young woman of twenty-five, and he was an oldish gentleman of fifty-six. He felt himself neither proper father nor proper husband. Her background was that of the purse-proud, class-conscious Paris bourgeoisie; his, that of a lowborn fisherman, sailor, soldier, adventurer. They were made for mutual incomprehension. I suspect there were stormy scenes in the crowded common room of the Habitation, and in the Governor's bedchamber.

But Champlain was happy as ruler of the little house, the capital of his enormous realm. He loved his dark subjects, and the great assaults of winter, and the defeat of winter by the uprising spring. With delight he noted the stages of the spring's conquest: on May eighth, the cherry trees opening their buds, the hepatica springing; on the ninth, the raspberries budding; on the tenth, the first leaves of the elder bush; on the twelfth, white violets; on the fifteenth, the winter wheat a span high, and the chervil ready to cut, and the sorrel in the woods two inches high; on the eighteenth, the swollen buds of oak, apple, and plum; and on the thirtieth, the strawberries and the fruit trees all in flower, and the Indian corn beginning to show.

In June the French traders arrived, and the active business of the summer began.

The peace between the Montagnais and the Iroquois had been ratified, despite the fact that a crazy Montagnais had killed an Iroquois. To the peace Champlain gave his hearty approval and support.

Thirty-five canoes filled with Iroquois bringing furs to trade arrived at the rendezvous. They were cordially welcomed by the French and by the other Indians. Thanks to Champlain's careful dispositions, no inflammatory incidents occurred. In a feast of friendship, peace between the Iroquois and the Algonquins, Hurons, and Montagnais was formally celebrated.

The Hurons came down to Quebec, bringing Father Joseph le Caron, Brother Gabriel Sagard, and other Frenchmen, including Brûlé, who was back from the mysterious western Great

Lakes. Father Nicolas Viel, with a few companions, was remaining for another winter in Huronia.

All the settlement gathered to hear the story of the Huronian winter from Brother Gabriel. Playing with his pet muskrat, which slept every night in the wide sleeve of his habit, he told wonderful tales: of his frightful and amusing adventures, of his vain efforts to explain the way of salvation to the Hurons, of native behavior, comic, horrible, and touching. But all this he has set down at great length in his charming book, and it need not delay us now.

To Champlain privately, Sagard reported that the interpreters, Brûlé and others, had been most un-co-operative. They had made an agreement not to teach the native languages to the clergy. They did not wish the Indians to settle down, abandon the fur-trade for agriculture, learn to lead moral lives. Brûlé especially was very vicious in character and "much addicted to women." He gave the natives a deplorable impression of French morals. But undeniably he was an excellent explorer. He had gone west along the Freshwater Sea and past some great rapids (Sault Ste Marie) to another enormous inland ocean (Lake Superior). Sagard had heard also reports of strange civilized races, far to the west, near the Chinese Sea.

After the meeting, Brother Gabriel invited some of his Huron friends to a banquet in the Recollect convent. He gave them presents; to the captain of his canoe, a big house cat, a creature hitherto unknown in Canada.

"This good Captain thought the cat had a rational mind, seeing that when he was called, he would come and play with one, and so he conjectured that the cat understood French perfectly. After admiring this animal, he asked us to tell the cat that he should let himself be carried home to his country, and that he would love the cat like his own son. 'Oh Gabriel!' he cried, 'he will have plenty to live on at home! You say that he is very fond of mice, and we have any amount of them. So let him come freely to us!' So saying, he tried to embrace the cat; but that wicked creature, who did not understand his way of caressing, immediately thrust out all his claws and made him let go quicker than he had grasped him.

" 'Ho, ho, ho!' said the good man. 'So that's the way he treats me! Ongaron, ortiscohat! He's ugly, he's bad! Speak to him!' Finally, having got the cat with a great deal of trouble into a birch-bark box, he carried him off in his arms to the canoe, and fed him through a little hole with bread that he had received at our convent. But when he tried to give the cat some sagamité, to his despair the cat escaped and flew up on a tree and they could not get him down again. And as for calling him down, nobody home [*personne à la maison*]; he didn't understand any Huron, and they didn't know how to call a cat in French, and so they were forced to turn their backs on him and leave him in the tree, very unhappy at losing him, and the cat very worried about who was going to feed him in the future."

Brother Gabriel was bidden to return to France, with Father Joseph le Caron, to report on the spiritual state of Canada. It was beginning to be clear, even to the Recollects, that their order was too weak and poor to bear alone the burden of converting a continent.

Champlain resolved to return also, with his wife. They had spent four winters in Quebec, amid innumerable trials. It was high time that Champlain should renew contact with his superiors; who knew what was being plotted in his absence? And it was high time that homesick Hélène should see again the dear, dark streets of her beloved Paris.

Champlain made a final inspection of Quebec. The new warehouse was nearly completed, all but the roof; the fort needed only fascines and outworks. A little more labor would put everything in order.

He left in command Emery de Caen, chief clerk, nephew of Guillaume de Caen. The settlement numbered fifty-one persons: men, women, and children.

Champlain and his lady made their farewells on August 15, 1624. On October 1 they arrived in Dieppe, praising God for bringing them safe to land.

CHAPTER XIX

The Eleventh Voyage

ON RETURNING to Paris in October 1624, Champlain's first act was to reunite his wife with her tearful and thankful family. He then found a home suitable to his distinction, in the rue de la Marche, the present rue de Saintonge, in the ancient, swarming quarter of *le Temple*.

His chief, the Duc de Montmorency, conducted him to the King's presence to make his report. Hopeful ever, he poured his projects, his dreams, into the unheeding royal ear.

Montmorency was hardly more helpful than the King. He confessed to Champlain that he was bored to death by the merchants and their endless squabbling over money. "It's more bother being Viceroy of New France," he said, "than being Admiral of Old France." Not long after he announced with satisfaction that he had sold the viceroyalty to his nephew, the Duc de Ventadour, governor of Languedoc. (The French had by this time developed the abusive system by which the holder of a government post could dispose of it like any other property, subject only to the King's approval.)

The transfer was in fact the outcome of behind-the-scenes ecclesiastical deals. The Recollects in Canada, after nine devoted years, were forced to recognize that the results of their missionary work were pitiably small. They had performed only a few baptisms, mostly of dying children, who could be assured of heaven only if assured of death. The ignorance, light-mindedness, and venality of the Indians made every conversion suspect; "they would be baptized ten times a day for a glass of brandy," says Father Leclercq. The Recollects were too few and too poor to do the good work properly. It could be accomplished only by a strong, wealthy, numerous order. The Recollects decided to invite the Jesuits to share the task.

Their invitation came to the Jesuits, literally, as an answer to prayer. The Jesuits, who had gone out to Acadia and Maine in 1610, and whose efforts had ended in disaster, longed to re-enter the great missionary field of Canada. Some of them had formed, to this end, a league of prayer. When the Recollects appeared, the prayer was exactly fulfilled, and the Jesuits understood that God's blessing was upon the enterprise.

The Jesuits, knowing by what earthy instruments God's will is performed, have always made a specialty of politics. They knew the right people to see. In this case the right person was the Duc de Ventadour, a young man of most exemplary piety. Indeed, he was destined, five years later, to quit his eighteen-year-old bride and enter the priesthood.

The Jesuits soon persuaded the young duke to buy the vice-royalty from his uncle, and thus to promote their interests in Canada, which were obviously identical with God's interests.

The King proclaimed Ventadour's appointment in the spring of 1625. The new viceroy arranged to send out six Jesuits at his own expense. Among them were three of the great names in Canada's history; Charles Lalemant, Ennemond Massé, and Jean de Brébeuf, martyr.

Champlain was confirmed as lieutenant of New France. His commission permits him to make war at need, and requires him to make explorations, to discover the easiest way to the kingdom of China and the East Indies.

He did not join the Canada expedition of 1625, whether because he felt himself entitled to a long vacation in Paris or, as is more likely, because he served Canada better by remaining in France, influencing the mind of the new viceroy and arousing the embattled merchants to a higher sense of their duties and opportunities.

The Jesuits went out in the spring to found their mission in Quebec. They soon learned that the enemies of their purpose were not so much the Indians as the French. The Huguenot merchants hated them on principle, and even many of the Catholic traders opposed evangelization as a possible hindrance to the fur trade. When the Jesuits arrived in Quebec, Protestant Emery de Caen refused to allow them to disembark, on the ground that he had no orders to receive them and no place to lodge them. The kindly Recollects came to the rescue, sheltering the Jesuits in their little convent. The Jesuits set vigorously to work, and laid the foundations of their great missionary center, Notre-Dame des Anges. It stood just to the east of the St. Charles, between the small streams of Lairet and St. Michel. The motorist crossing the Dorchester Street Bridge faintly troubles its shades.

In this summer the Recollect Father Nicolas Viel was returning from Huronia after two years of toil, suffering, and discouragement. His Huron guides wantonly drowned him, for his few pitiful possessions, in the Rivière des Prairies just above Montreal. He was the first martyr in Canada. Ever since, the place of his death has borne the name of *"le saut du Récollet."*

When Guillaume de Caen returned to France from the summer's expedition, he found himself in the miidst of the usual broils of discontented stockholders. He was also in trouble with the new viceroy. The regulations permitted Protestant psalm singing as far as the Newfoundland Banks but no farther. Now Ventadour, acting on information from the priests, accused de Caen of permitting the Protestant zealots to roar their heretic psalms on the undefiled reaches of the St. Lawrence, and even to trouble the Mass at the trading fair, to the scandal of the faithful and the perturbation of the Indians.

The disputes, commercial and religious, were carried to the King's Council. There it was ruled that de Caen should again have the concession for 1626, on condition that he pay interest of forty per cent on 60,000 livres, and that he appoint a Catholic as ship's captain.

During the winter Champlain was putting some of his private affairs in order. A recently discovered document gives some hint of it.[1] In this document Champlain is designated as *escuyer*, esquire. The appellation marks one more step in Champlain's ascension toward dignity and social consideration.

The spring of 1626 came in, and with it the old restlessness in Champlain's heart. He was nearly sixty, a man of standing, well married to a young, attractive, high-minded wife. She must have begged him to take his ease at last, not to leave her for the dangers and discomforts of the wild. There were surely many tears and much anger in the rue de la Marche.

According to the pious chronicles it was at this time that she began to feel a religious vocation. ("A girl might as well be a nun!" I can hear her cry.) She proposed that she should take up her residence in a convent. Champlain objected, but offered to live henceforth in continence, an easy sacrifice for a man of sixty. Perhaps with some spite in her saintly aspiration, Hélène meditated on the charms of conventual peace. But for Champlain peace dwelt only in Canada.

In April he embarked at Dieppe on the *Catherine*, a fine ship of 250 tons. He was accompanied by his faithful brother-in-law, Eustache Boullé, now commissioned Lieutenant.

On board, Champlain found his old friend Father Joseph le Caron. What memories they awakened together of hardship and adventure in far Huronia! This was better than to spend one's life discussing the price of meat, the choice of falbalas, in swarming, clattering Paris!

After a journey of over two months, marked by bad weather, even a hurricane, they reached Tadoussac. The Protestant sailors were strictly enjoined against psalm singing on the St. Lawrence, whereat they murmured much.

Then up the river to Quebec. Old Pontgravé hobbled out to meet the pinnace. It had been a terrible hungry winter, he said. And he had almost died of the gout, proof enough that meat and brandy were not the cause of his ills.

---

[1] On December 29, 1625, he made over to a good friend, Charles Lebert, sieur du Carlot, engineer and royal geographer and sergeant-major in Brouage, a donation he had received in Cadiz in 1601 from Guillaume Hellaine of Marseille. See A.-Léo Leymarie: "*Inédit sur le fondateur de Québec,*" in *Nova Francia,* I, 80–85, 1925.

Eagerly Champlain inspected his settlement, his home. The Habitation looked exactly as he had left it a year and a half before. The construction material, including 1,800 hand-sawed boards, lay about in rotting piles. Two or three families, too indolent to build a dwelling, were crowded in a single room. All Champlain's instructions had been disregarded; his absence had been a long holiday.

He climbed the path to the fort. Its gates stood wide open. Some chickens squawked the alarm, and two women appeared, the only garrison of Fort St. Louis.

He had a long talk with his old companion honest Hébert. Pontgravé, in command through the winter just ended, had been decent enough, but he was too old and sick to manage the colony. Emery de Caen, who had ruled through the winter and summer of 1625, had used every means to discourage Hébert, to force him back to France in disgust. De Caen had bought the little farm's produce at the lowest rates of French markets and had sold European supplies at fantastic prices. He had countermanded Hébert's order for a plow. Hébert was soon bankrupt. Étienne Brûlé, open-hearted and open-handed with his friends, offered him a loan of a hundred crowns without interest. De Caen stepped in to forbid the accommodation. De Caen alone could be banker; he made the loan at twenty-five per cent interest.[2]

We may well surmise the fate of Quebec without Champlain.

After his first moment of discouragement he recognized once more that he must alone supply all the planning and the driving force. He put all the men hard to work. He rebuilt the fort larger and stronger. He erected a stable and two dwellings for cow-herds at Cap Tourmente, thirty miles downstream. He gave good advice on forest architecture to the Jesuits; but these, fortunately, were independent, for they had brought out twenty good workmen to build their chapel and living quarters of Notre-Dame des Anges.

Champlain had been dubious about the Jesuits at first. Perhaps he remembered his own fruitless arguments with Père Cotton, the King's confessor, back in 1609. Now their energy, ability,

[2] *Au Roy sur la Nouvelle France*, 7–19. (Pamphlet of 1626, of which the only known copy is in the John Carter Brown Library.)

and steadfast purpose removed his doubts. He took, indeed, the saintly Père Lalemant as his own confessor.

The summer's trading passed off without incident. Apparently the Iroquois came again to market, for they were at war with the Mohicans, who barred the way to Fort Orange. A party of Dutchmen was aiding the Mohicans, contrary to their own commercial interest, one would say.

At the end of August the French traders, with groaning Pontgravé, made their farewells and sailed for home. During the bright, happy days of autumn Champlain was disturbed only by the scanty supplies in store for the winter. Well, he must pray that the ships would return betimes next year.

The winter came early and lasted late, until the end of April. The snow at Quebec lay nearly five feet deep. Rations were uncommonly short, but were eked out by a pair of moose, the present of the Indians.

The community was saddened by the death of Louis Hébert, Canada's first *habitant*. The natives wept him as much as the French, says Sagard, for they lost in him a true foster father, a good friend, and a zealous advocate of their conversion. On his deathbed he made a touching exhortation to his family on the vanity of this life, the treasures of heaven, and the merit to be acquired by labor for one's fellows. "I die happy," he said, "since it has pleased Our Lord to do me the grace of seeing converted savages die before my eyes. I crossed the seas to come and succor them, rather than from any private interest, and I would die happily for their conversion, if such should be God's good pleasure. I beg you to love them as I have loved them, to assist them according to your power. God will thank you for it and reward you in Paradise. They are rational creatures like ourselves, and they could love our God if they had knowledge of Him, and to this end I beg you to aid them by your good example and your prayers. I exhort you also to peace and love, for therein you will fulfill the law of God, founded on charity. This life is brief, the life to come is for eternity. I am ready to go to the presence of God, my judge, to whom I must render an account of all my past life. Pray to Him for me, that I may find grace before His countenance, and that I may be some day numbered among His elect."

He raised his hand and gave to all his benediction, and rendered up his soul in the arms of his Creator on January 25, 1627, the day of the conversion of St. Paul.

During the winter some of the Montagnais visited the Dutch on the Hudson. They reported that the Dutch asked them to join an alliance with the Mohicans against the Iroquois. Despite the solemn peace between the northern coalition and the Iroquois, this seemed to the Montagnais a splendid opportunity to exterminate the ancient enemy. When the project was made known to Champlain, he vigorously opposed it, "for there was more to take into account than the destruction of the Iroquois, considered as enemies of the Dutch, since the whole question involved much more serious consequences, of which I shall say nothing."

What does he mean by this mysterious phrase? Why, this, I suppose: that the extant peace with the Iroquois insured the security of the northern fur trade and brought Iroquois furs to the French trading fair; that the ruin of the Iroquois would mean a rise in importance of the Dutch and their Mohican allies, and keener competition between Fort Orange and Quebec; that the eventual enemy of French Canada was the European rival who held the Hudson. Besides, Champlain had learned that for business purposes any peace was better than any war.

Champlain lectured his Indians on the advantages of peace and of their new security from fear. He sent Boullé to an Indian council at Trois Rivières to persuade the Indians to keep the peace. Though Boullé's mission was successful, there were, as usual, some young Indian hotheads who would not be bound by any conclusions of their moderate elders. These made a surprise raid on the Iroquois in June, murdered some, and brought back prisoners for leisurely torture. Champlain hurried up the river to the mouth of the Richelieu and used all his eloquence to persuade the Indians to release the prisoners and make their apologies to the Iroquois. His plea for good sense carried the day. A peace-making deputation to return the prisoners was dispatched to the Iroquois. But the deputation was unfortunately constituted. It included the Montagnais who had murdered the two Frenchmen in 1616 and had been publicly pardoned seven years later. A Frenchman, Pierre Magnan, who had fled to

Canada after beating a man to death with a club in his home town in Normandy, joined the party for the fun of it.

When the ambassadors reached the first Iroquois village, they were invited into the long house. The hosts set a kettle of water on the fire. "Are you not hungry?" they asked with an air of exaggerated courtesy.

"Why yes," said the Montagnais envoy. "We have traveled a long distance today without eating."

The hosts made sounds of commiseration. "It is only reasonable that we should treat you to a feast for the pains you have taken." One of the Iroquois drew a knife and slashed a piece of flesh from his guest's arm. He thrust the dripping gobbet in the kettle to boil. "Sing!" he commanded his visitor. The envoy, knowing well the protocol, and the end of it, sang loud and heartily. The Iroquois then gave him his own boiled flesh to eat.

"Are you still hungry? Do you want more?"

"Yes indeed! It is very good."

The Iroquois cut pieces from his thighs and put them in the pot. And so the straight-faced comedy continued until the envoy said that he had had enough. The Frenchman, Magnan, was then burned with lighted brands and birch bark until he died.

"Thus," comments Champlain, "does God sometimes punish men who, thinking to escape His justice by avoiding one path, are overtaken by it in another."

So, despite all Champlain's pleading and commands, the short-lived peace was at an end, the old war reigned along the great river and in the solitary woods.

With the summer came the annual ships from France, bringing old Pontgravé, good old Pontgravé, now in his mid-seventies and suffering terribly from the gout. Nothing could keep him from Canada. Everyone, says Champlain, was astonished.

The Jesuits were much disturbed because a promised ship with supplies and recruits did not arrive. Lacking provisions, Father Lalemant was obliged to embark nearly all his staff for France; to guard Notre-Dame des Anges were left Fathers Ennemond Massé and Anne de Noüe and six others. Father Brébeuf was far away in Huronia. The Jesuits were able to buy only ten casks of biscuit from the Company's storehouse, and that at the same high price charged the Indians: to wit, seven beaver skins per cask.

Fifty-five persons—men, women, and children, laymen, Recollects, and Jesuits—composed the settlement. Only eighteen of this number were workmen under Champlain's orders; half of these were required to tend the cattle and cut the hay at Cap Tourmente. Champlain seems to have been on bad terms with the Company's agents; he apparently lived in the fort and treated diplomatically with the Company's men in the Habitation. He was much disturbed by the shortness of supplies, and more by forebodings about the safety of his colony. He had learned during the summer that France and England were more than half at war and were seizing each other's vessels in the English Channel. Would the English overlook the rich prize of the Canada fur trade?

There was more misfortune. In October the Indians murdered two of the cowherds at Cap Tourmente while they slept. The pretext was merely that one of the French had refused an Indian a piece of bread. Again the problem arose of the policy to be adopted. It would be difficult, if not impossible, to find the actual murderers. Punishment of the tribe, then? "As to taking vengeance upon a number who were not guilty, there would be no sense in that. It would be to declare open war and to ruin the country for a time, until the whole race was exterminated, and at the same time to destroy our trade, or at least impair it greatly. We were besides in a miserable condition ourselves through lack of munitions of war."

Champlain therefore assembled the chiefs, displayed to them the maltreated bodies of the dead, with their heads crushed by tomahawks. He demanded that the murderers be surrendered. The chiefs protested that they had no idea who had committed the horrid deed. Champlain then seized a suspect, a notorious enemy of the French, and three boys, to hold as hostages until further information should be forthcoming.

The winter was hard and cold, but open. The lack of snow, preventing the hunt of the floundering moose, brought starvation to the Indians. A party of thirty Montagnais crossed the St. Lawrence on the heaving ice cakes to beg for food. Despite the shortness of supplies, despite the distrust aroused by the murder, kindly Champlain granted their request and served out to them the dried peas and beans kept for trade. The Indians felt bound to offer presents in return. But they had nothing to give, only their own bodies. They presented to Champlain three girls, eleven, twelve, and fifteen years old. Braving the lewd innuendoes, and certain dangers, on the part of the single men in barracks, Champlain accepted the gift. His reputation must protect him and his charges. "He was never suspected of any impropriety during all the years that he lived among these barbarous peoples," says Sagard, "and so these girls honored him as their father, and he took care of them as his own daughters."

He named them Faith, Hope, and Charity. He instructed them in Christian doctrine and in the occupations proper to gentle young women. He himself traced designs for them to embroider with wool, and he himself corrected their errors. And since there was very little wool, he would undo each task when it was completed and set them to another design. He loved them dearly, for these three Indian girls were his only children.

The spring of 1628 came and went. Champlain anxiously surveyed his supplies. By mid-June he had only four or five barrels of very poor biscuit and some dried peas and beans. The settlers found themselves forever staring downriver, watching for the little sails that would bring them relief. The rumors of the previous year of war with England grew in their minds. What if the succoring ships were taken at sea?

Champlain considered his predicament. If he had a pinnace he might embark his settlers and carry them down to Gaspé, where they would probably find some French fishermen. But he had no pinnace, and, in fact, no sailors. He must build a pinnace.

Couillard, Hébert's son-in-law, a wonderful handy man, did most of the work. Others collected gum and pitch from the spruce trees. An ox was killed for tallow, and also for food. Tow was made from scraps of old cordage. And so, with every sort of improvisation, the pinnace was built.

On July 9, two cowherds from Cap Tourmente appeared with an Indian who had paddled up from Tadoussac. The ships had

arrived! Six ships! The commander? Michel of Dieppe, known
as captain of a fishing vessel.

"This news cheered us up somewhat." But not for long. Why
six ships, persisted Champlain? Ordinarily the Company sent
out only two or three. And Michel in command? "He was not
the kind of person for so important a charge." There was
something funny about this.

Champlain summoned an interpreter, a Greek by race. (This
is his only appearance in the story; we should like to know how
the Greek came to Canada, and by what linguistic triumph he
learned both French and Montagnais.) Champlain ordered him
to disguise himself as an Indian, to slip down the river to
Tadoussac in a canoe, and to bring back a sure report. And
Champlain put his fort in order, his men on the alert, his women
in safety.

Shortly after, the Greek returned. In his canoe lay, wounded,
Foucher, who was in command at Cap Tourmente.

The English! The English with a band of French traitors!
What had happened?

"Why," said Foucher, "a pinnace anchored off Cap Tourmente an hour or two before daylight. The crew disembarked,
and I went to meet them. I was suspicious, and I challenged
them. One of them said, in French: 'We are your friends. Don't
you recognize us? We were here last year, and have come from
my Lord the Cardinal and Monsieur de Roquemont. We are
going to Quebec with dispatches, and in passing we thought we
would like to see you.' Indeed, I recognized several of them,
and so we were thrown off our guard. And while we were con-
versing, we found ourselves surrounded and threatened, and we
were forced to surrender. Then the English killed what cattle
they wanted, shut the rest in their stables, and burned them up.
And they burned our two houses and destroyed everything they
could, even the caps worn by the little girl. Then they took us
on their boat. But in the hurly-burly I escaped."

Champlain sounded the alarm, assigned men to their posts,
and put all hands to work on the trenches and barricades around
the fort. Anxiously he conned his munitions. He had just fifty
pounds of gunpowder, very little fuse or other equipment.

The next day, July 10, a small boat was seen nosing about the mouth of the St. Charles. Champlain recognized in it Nicolas Pivert and his wife and daughter, who had taken care of the cattle at Cap Tourmente. The boatmen were Basques.

Champlain summoned them ashore. One of the Basques explained that their ship had been captured by the English, and that he had been ordered to deliver a letter from the English general to Champlain.

Champlain read the letter aloud to his chief men. It announced that the writer had obtained a commission from the King of Great Britain to take possession of Canada and Acadia. He had seized the trading post in the Gulf at Miscou, and had captured all the craft on the coasts, including the ship bringing supplies to Quebec. "I had made preparations for going to see you myself, but I have thought it better only to send an advice-boat and two shallops to destroy and seize the cattle at Cap Tourmente; for I know that when you are distressed for want of food, I shall more easily obtain what I desire—which is, to take your settlement. And in order to prevent any ship arriving, I am determined to remain here until the season of navigation has closed, so that no ship may come to revictual you. Wherefore now consider what you wish to do: whether you are willing to surrender the settlement or not; for sooner or later, with God's help, I must have it, and I should desire for your sake that it might be rather with a good grace than on compulsion, so as to avoid the bloodshed which might occur on both sides. If you surrender the place with courtesy, you may rest assured of receiving good treatment in every respect, both as regards your persons and your goods, which latter, on my faith and on my hope of paradise, I shall preserve as carefully as if they were my own, without diminishing them by the smallest possible portion. . . . Awaiting your reply, and your decision to do as above expressed, I shall remain, Sirs, your affectionate servant, David Kirke."

David Kirke! Why, how small the world is! This must be David Kirke of Dieppe! Champlain, who had lived in Dieppe, certainly knew his father, Gervase Kirke, a man of Champlain's own age. He was a prosperous merchant with important London connections, an English Protestant who had married a French

woman. David was the eldest of his five sons, who were half
French by race, education, and language, but English still in
their loyalty. (Or were they merely seeking profit, under whatever flag?)

David Kirke's letter was a reasonable and courtly one, inviting to surrender without loss of honor. It indicated that the
English general was a competent commander; his intelligence
service was excellent; he had adopted the oldest, cheapest, and
most effective means of reducing an enemy, that of blockade
and starvation.

There were surely some of the hearers, prudent or craven,
who urged acceptance of the Englishman's honorable terms.
All must have thought with foreboding of the empty storehouse,
of the pitiable supply of weapons and ammunition. They were
in no case to withstand a siege, and in worse case to endure a
winter of starvation. But if there were palterers, they could not
prevail upon the indomitable spirit of Champlain.

He sat down to write a reply to the English summons. He
couched it in the same courtly style.

"Sir," he wrote, "we entertain no doubt as to the commis-
sions which you have obtained from the King of Great Britain.
Great Princes always choose men of brave and generous disposition, amongst the number of whom he has selected you to fulfill
the duty he has assigned to you. . . .

"It is true that the better a fortified place is provisioned, the
better it holds out against the storms of time; nevertheless the
place can make good its defense when good order is maintained
in it. That is the reason why, having still grain, Indian corn,
peas, and beans, not to mention what this country produces, a
diet that the soldiers of this place can content themselves with
as well as they could with the finest kinds of flour in the world;
and knowing well that, were we to surrender a fort and a settlement conditioned as we now are, we should not be worthy of
the name of men in the presence of our King, but rather be
reprehensible and merit chastisement in the sight of God and
men, honor demands that we fight to the death. For these
reasons I know that you will think more highly of our courage
if we firmly await the arrival of yourself and your forces than
if, in a cowardly fashion, we should abandon something that is

so dear to us without first making proof of your cannon, your approaches, entrenchments, and battery against a place which I am confident you will judge, when you see and reconnoiter it, not to be so easy of access as perhaps you have been led to believe, nor its defenders destitute of courage to defend it, seeing they are men who have tried the hazards of fortune in many different places. Then if the issue is favorable to you, you will have more cause, having vanquished us, to bestow your offers of kind treatment, than if without a struggle we should place you in possession of a place the preservation of which is enjoined upon us by the strongest considerations of duty that can be imagined. . . .

"We are now waiting from hour to hour to receive you and resist, if we can, the claims you are making to these places, which being excepted I shall remain, Sir, your affectionate servant, Champlain." [3]

The envoy, bearing this elegant reply, went down to his general in Tadoussac. The English were impressed by Champlain's bold front. What they wanted was furs and loot, not a glorious death storming a stronghold. Quebec, they decided, would starve itself out. General Kirke and his fleet left Tadoussac to look for French ships along the coast, "in order to pay for the cost of their expedition."

A few days later a small boat manned by eleven French sailors slipped into Quebec. This was their story: a new company, the Company of New France, had taken over the control of Canada. It promised a new and active policy of colonization. It had loaded four ships, under the command of Claude de Roquemont. There were two hundred settlers on board, and ample supplies. They had reached Gaspé safely, but on hearing of the English fleet at Tadoussac, Roquemont had halted and had sent the small boat to Quebec. The messengers had made their way upriver with the utmost caution, and had succeeded in dodging the Englishmen.

Champlain sighed. He had little hope that Roquemont's

[3] The most famous message of defiance in our times was that of General McAuliffe in Bastogne. His reply to the German summons, you remember, was merely "Nuts," which puzzled the Germans mightily. Here is a text for meditation on the military manners and prose style of two epochs.

merchantmen would escape or defeat the English fleet. In his uncertainty he could not send the sailors back. He would have eleven more mouths to feed during the winter. He must revise his calculations.

He questioned the sailors narrowly concerning the new company. And this is what he learned (though indeed I am piecing out their presumable knowledge with official records):

France was under the control of a great man, an irresistible dominating spirit, the Cardinal de Richelieu. Whatever he did, he did grandly, flooding away the past like a storm, designing great new symmetrical constructions for the future. His chief aide and confidante was the extraordinary Père Joseph, the Gray Eminence, Capuchin friar, mystic, and diabolic politician. Père Joseph was appointed Apostolic Commissary of Missions in 1625. In the following year he wrote a sensational memorandum on colonization, sea power, and the conversion of the heathen. It was doubtless Père Joseph who drew Richelieu's attention to the sorry record of the various fur-trading companies in Canada, and to the necessity of a thorough reform.

Richelieu's action was typical of him. He pointed out that in eleven years the monopolists, despite all their engagements, had taken out just eighteen colonists, and some of these had returned to France. There was only one family of genuine agricultural settlers in Quebec, the Hébert-Couillard family, and its members were forever oppressed and hindered by the Company agents. The de Caen monopoly, said Richelieu, had forfeited all its rights. He swept it out of existence and annulled all its claims.

The Cardinal drew up a formulary of a new company, grandiose and geometrical as the town of Richelieu he established in Touraine. It was composed of a hundred associates, each of whom would pay in 900 livres. Its members were in part merchants, in part the gentleman-bureaucrats so influential in France under the old regime. A tempting provision was the item that the Company would award twelve titles of nobility to its members. Richelieu was eager to break down the barrier between merchant and noble; an edict of 1629 proclaimed that sea commerce would not derogate from nobility.

In the roll of the Hundred Associates we find the name of Samuel Champlain, Esquire. He has officially acquired the honorable title of esquire, but he seems to have lost the *de*, the *particule nobiliaire*.

The Company was given control forever of the fur trade, and for fifteen years of all other Canadian commerce except the fisheries. It was bound to take out at least two hundred genuine settlers yearly, a total of four thousand within fifteen years. These would be supplied with all their needs for three years. Protestants and foreigners were forbidden entry to Canada. Three priests would be maintained in each settlement. Converted savages would have the rights of French citizens.

Now on paper this was a most imposing plan. It had, however, one serious fault: assuming that the profits from trade would support the enterprise through its difficult beginnings, it made no provision for government aid and subsidy.

Richelieu carried through the organization with his customary vigor. He appointed the Sieur de Roquemont his lieutenant, by some means gathered two hundred settlers and their equipment, and sped them off to Canada. One of the four ships, in charge of the Jesuit Father Noirot, contained ample supplies for the Jesuit mission.

But all this gallant enterprise came to nothing. General Kirke found the French ships off Gaspé. In a fourteen-hour naval battle he worsted the French and captured their ships, all save that of Father Noirot, which escaped and fled back to France.

Champlain in Quebec took anxious thought of his situation. He now had seventy-five French men, women, and children in his charge, plus an Indian prisoner suspected of being the murderer of two Frenchmen. (The other hostages were released.) He had also his two darling Indian girls Hope and Charity, for Faith, belying her name, had returned to her own people. To feed this assemblage through a Quebec winter he had a few barrels of dried peas in the warehouse, and nothing more.

He bought from the Indians 1,200 dried eels. As even trade goods were short, he had to pay the Indians with their own beaver skins, at the rate of one beaver for ten eels. He looked eagerly to Couillard's little farm; but all its surplus yield worked out to nine and a half ounces a week of barley, peas, and corn.

This, says Champlain with superb understatement, was a very small quantity among so many persons.

For the rest his charges must live off the country. They fished and hunted; but game had fled from the neighborhood, and powder was too short to be used on anything but a sure target. One party of hungry hunters killed a moose, but "devoured it like ravenous wolves, without giving us any share beyond about twenty pounds." Men bargained with the Indians for fish, giving even their coats for pay.

Day by day Champlain portioned out the supplies with a jealous hand: seven ounces of pease meal per head per day. Roots recommended by the Indians, expecially Solomon's-seal, were gathered in the woods. (Brother Sagard found Solomon's-seal a sovereign remedy for hemorrhoids, if sliced thin and worn in an amulet about the neck. The recipe had been guaranteed by a fine lady of Paris.) Peas, roots, and acorns twice boiled were combined in a loathly unsalted gruel with bran, straw, and an occasional fish. Many fell sick. But hungry stomachs seem to adapt themselves to hunger; no one, apparently, died. Old Pontgravé's gout even was relieved by this regime.

If the men could have passed the winter in drowsy ease they might have borne hunger better. But the strongest must be sent hunting; the others had to cut and carry wood. In twenty years the French had felled all the trees within two thousand yards of the Habitation, in the thoroughgoing way of the Canadian today. To cut wood and to drag it so far was a desperate task for starving men.

But somehow the winter passed, and somehow the spring found the Frenchmen still toiling up and down the Rock, still peering abroad with sunken eyes.

In May, one of the towers of the fort collapsed. Some took this to be a divine omen that their defenses would not be needed, though Brother Sagard blamed the blasphemies of the workmen during its construction.

The last of the vegetables were consumed. The daily soup was brewed with acorns, with rank and evil-smelling roots from the woods, with whatever fish the desperate anglers could take. The Jesuit Father Anne de Noué, once a page at court, became a fisherman of almost apostolic skill.

Champlain made incessant plans. If the war should end, or if the French should defeat the English on the coast, relief might come at any time. If he should receive no word by July, he would fill his wretched seven-ton pinnace with men and furs and send it downriver. The crew would look for French fishermen at Miscou or Gaspé, pay for their passage home with furs, and send the pinnace back to carry down a second load of refugees. Those left in Quebec might survive on the products of the Jesuits' and Recollects' gardens, and on the yield of Couillard's little farm. "The only difficulty I saw in this business was how to live until the month of August, to gather in the grain; for we must either have something to subsist on for three or four months, or perish."

If, as he feared, he should fail to make his pinnace watertight, he had a wild and noble plan. He would take his hardiest men, enlist the aid of the Indians, and march to Iroquoia. "We would then carry one of their villages by storm to get grain, or else die in the attempt. There we would fortify ourselves, and pass the rest of the summer, autumn, and winter, rather than die of hunger at the Habitation; and we would await news in the spring, through the savages, from those remaining at Quebec. The savages promised me that, if God gave us the good fortune of victory, the result would be the making of a general peace and keeping the country and its rivers free."

If he had put this bold plan into practice, history would have another fine adventure tale to tell.

Casting about for other issues, Champlain sent a Frenchman overland to the Abenakis of southern Maine to propose that they should receive the French during the following winter. Two others were dispatched in a canoe to Tadoussac, with instructions to look for French contrabanders and to propose to them peace and great gains if only they would rescue the settlers. Seven others were sent down in the small boat to make their way, if possible, to Gaspé and return with succor. The remaining settlers labored to make the pinnace seaworthy. "Thus we omitted nothing that we could think of that might help us out of our difficulties, dreading, as we did, a ruder shock than that of the year before, if our ships should not come."

So the month of May wore on, and June. Hunger and fear

dominated every mind, determined the action of every craving body. "The most deplorable and painful thing in this time of want was to see some poor families burdened with children that were crying with hunger to their fathers and mothers, who were unable to get roots for them; for it was with difficulty that anyone could find enough in the depths of the woods, even by going four or five leagues from the settlement, to half satisfy their hunger, pestered as they were with mosquitoes, and sometimes harassed and impeded by bad weather."

There was one unnecessary mouth to feed: that of the Indian prisoner held on suspicion of murder. To release him would mean a loss of prestige; to kill him would be unjust. Champlain's heart inclined ever toward mercy. After long conferences, high-flown speeches, and much tergiversation, Champlain turned him back to his own people. He had to be carried away in a blanket, for he had suffered terribly from confinement. Indeed, he declared that he would much prefer death to imprisonment.

On June 15 the small boat dispatched to Gaspé returned with its full crew to report that eight English vessels were scouring the coast. Thus there was little hope of French aid. It was necessary to put the emergency measures into effect. Champlain embarked thirty men on the leaky pinnace, under the command of Boullé, with orders to look for a French fisherman at Gaspé, Newfoundland, or Cape Breton, and if they should find none, to head boldly across the Atlantic to France. The ship's stores consisted solely of the harsh, queasy roots of wild plants. They took the best of the fishing tackle, to feed themselves out of the sea. Champlain did his best to persuade Pontgravé to take his place in the pinnace, but Pontgravé refused to leave Quebec. His obstinacy, magnificent in its way, was troublesome to Champlain, for it took four men to care for the helpless, exigent old man.

The pinnace set sail on June 26. Champlain and his settlers returned to their weary gathering of roots, a task that took them daily farther afield, even to a distance of twenty miles. The fishing went on, though hampered by the scarcity of nets, lines, and hooks. The stock of powder was down to thirty or forty pounds, and even that was of poor quality.

On July 17, twenty men arrived, including Father Brébeuf,

from Huronia. What food had they brought? Why, only six or seven bags of corn meal, weighing about fifty pounds; they had expected to banquet at the Habitation. The Indians were infuriated to find no trade goods in the warehouse. They prepared to carry their beaver skins all the thousand miles back to Huronia.

Two days later an Indian came running to the fort with word that three great ships, evidently Englishmen, were just below Quebec. "When this news came I was alone at the fort, some of my companions having gone to fish, and others to look for roots; my servant and the two little native girls had gone with them. About ten o'clock in the morning some of them came to the fort and to the settlement; and my servant arriving with four small bags of roots told me that he had seen the English vessels a league distant from our settlement, behind Point Lévis. I took care to put in order the little we had for defense, in order to prevent surprise alike at the Fort and the Habitation. The Jesuit and Recollect Fathers came in as fast as they could, on hearing the news, to see what could be done. I summoned those whom I thought proper in order to advise as to what was best to do in this extremity. It was decided that, considering our helpless situation in being without provisions, powder, or match, and destitute of help, it was impossible to hold out, and that we must therefore seek the most advantageous terms of capitulation possible, meantime awaiting what the Englishman might have to say. We were resolved, however, that in case they would not grant us terms, we would show them that they would lose some of their men by forcing a landing."

The white sails of three ships showed in the main stream off the Ile d'Orléans. There was a flyboat of nearly a hundred tons with ten cannon, and two cutters of forty tons and six cannon each. These, unless our records are at fault, were the largest vessels that had mounted the stream to Quebec since Cartier's time. They were piloted up the treacherous river by French renegades.

The ships stood prudently beyond cannon range. A small boat bearing a white flag was put overside. As it headed toward Quebec, Champlain hoisted a white flag above Fort St. Louis. The boat pulled in to the landing stage. An English officer stepped ashore and climbed the steep path to the fort. Here Champlain civilly received him, and the two doffed their ponderous beavers and bowed, under the gaunt and wondering gaze of the red men and white. The officer handed to Champlain a letter from his commanders. It was thus conceived:

"Sir: In pursuance of what my brother wrote to you last year, that sooner or later he would take possession of Quebec, unless it was reinforced, he has instructed us to assure you of his friendship, as we assure you of ours, and knowing well the state of extreme destitution in which you are with respect to everything, he calls upon you to place the fort and habitation in our hands, assuring you of the best treatment for yourself and your people, and also of as honorable and reasonable a settlement as you could desire. Awaiting your reply we remain, Sir, Your very affectionate servants, Louis and Thomas Kirke."

Champlain attempted to interrogate the Englishman. But as the officer had no French, Champlain summoned Father de la Roche d'Aillon and conducted the colloquy in Latin. He then withdrew with his principal men and read the letter aloud. After consultation he indited the following reply:

"Gentlemen: The truth is that negligence, or the hindrances caused by bad weather or the perils of the sea, have prevented the arrival of the relief that we were expecting in our suffering, and have put it out of our power to resist the carrying out of your design, as we did last year, without giving you an opportunity of making good your claims, which, if it please you, will only be realized now on condition of your carrying into effect the offers you made us of a composition, the terms of which we shall communicate to you very shortly, after we have decided on them; awaiting which, you will be good enough not to allow your vessels to come within cannon shot, nor attempt to set foot on land until everything shall have been settled between us, which will be for tomorrow. Meanwhile I shall remain, Gentlemen, your affectionate servant, Champlain. This nineteenth of July, 1629."

The English envoy bowed in courtly style, and Champlain's beaver hat described the correct arc. The Englishman retired; Champlain and his chief men drew up their articles of capitulation. These called, in brief, for their safe repatriation with all their property in a vessel to be placed at their disposal. They would pay for their supplies with their furs. Special mention was made of Hope and Charity, who should be permitted to accompany the repatriates.

Louis and Thomas Kirke, commanders, replied that while they could not supply a vessel to the French, they would guarantee safe passage to England and thence to France. They would permit the officials to carry out such arms, clothes, and furs as they might personally own, the soldiers and other employees to retain one beaver skin each, and the Fathers to hold only their cassocks and books. As to the two native girls, no, they could not go.

The clerks protested loudly at being stripped of their private gains. They vowed they would fight, not for France, not for Canada, but for their personal profit. But Champlain knew the hopelessness of resistance. He accepted the English terms.

The Kirke brothers formally occupied Quebec for England on July 20, 1629. They did their work with courtesy, nay with deference toward courageous Champlain and toward old bedridden Pontgravé, a famous personage to young men who had grown up on the Dieppe waterfront.

Louis Kirke, the new commander, tore down the French coat of arms from the stockade and nailed up his country's emblem. Above a bastion of the fort he hoisted for the first time the English flag. He paraded his men to the rattle of English drums, and fired a salute with the castle guns, which was echoed by a salvo from the anchored ships.

Louis Kirke was a kindly, courteous young man, French in disposition. "He found intercourse and conversation with the French more agreeable than with the English, to whom his nature seemed to be adverse." He was respectful to the French missionaries and granted every reasonable request of theirs.

To the widow Hébert and her son-in-law, who expected only the seizure of their little farm, he offered every inducement to remain, on terms far better than those granted by the French company. But of course they would have to do without the consolations of their religion. Mme Hébert and Couillard, shaken in their purpose to return to France, consulted Champlain. Recognizing their reluctance to abandon the fruits of twelve

toilsome years, only to arrive destitute in Paris, he said: "Were
I in your place, for this year I should reap my grain and trade
off as much of it as possible with the savages and with the French
vessels which will come, I hope, to resume possession. I should
sell my furs to the English and draw the money they have
promised for them, and then abandon my lands to them and return to France in their vessels. Because we must take more care
of our souls than of our bodies. And then, having some money in
France, you would be able to avoid want." This advice they
adopted.

At four shifty figures among the occupiers Champlain looked
askance. These were Étienne Brûlé and Nicolas Marsolet and
two other French renegades. Brûlé and Marsolet! The boys he
had brought out in 1608, who had survived the first terrible
winter in Quebec, who had become the colony's best interpreters, who had adventured so far and had suffered so much for
France! So they had sold their honor, and the respect of their
fellows, for some mean advantage with the English!

The waiting days seemed to Champlain like months. It was
bad enough to see the English patrolling the beloved settlement where he had ruled for twenty-one years; it was worse
to feel the dying of his dreams. And such a pitiable handful of
marauders had done the work! If only the French authorities had
had the wits to supply the fort with victuals and arms, he could
have defied any attacker, and have held all Canada for years,
till fortune should turn!

No more could he see in vision his shining city of Ludovica,
with its busy streets and noble towers and, over all, the spires
of the Church of the Redeemer. If the dream visited him it was
soon dispelled by English voices, uttering their whining vowels
and spitting consonants.

In the troubled, weary hours he made a solemn vow. If God
in His mercy would return Quebec to the French, he would
build a votive church, and he would dedicate it to Notre-Dame
de la Recouvrance, Our Lady of Recovery.

He begged Louis Kirke to let him leave this scene of torture,
to go down to Tadoussac and there await transportation to
England. He asked again permission to take with him his two
dear Indian girls, Hope and Charity. And Kirke, recognizing

the troubled spirit and the innocent affection of the kindly old man, granted both requests. On July 24 the three left Quebec in Thomas Kirke's flyboat.

Off Murray Bay, ninety miles downstream, a strange French ship was sighted. Battle was joined; the Englishman rammed the Frenchman and forced his surrender. The French captain was Emery de Caen; he was on his way to relieve Quebec, but obviously with insufficient strength. He reported that he believed that peace had been made between France and England. He had, however, no compelling proof.

The English brought their prize into Tadoussac. Here Champlain was courteously received by the English commander, David Kirke, the eldest of the five brothers. He had a fleet of five large vessels of 300 to 400 tons, well equipped with cannon and fire throwers. His rear admiral was a French renegade, Jacques Michel, who was treated by his superiors and inferiors with barely concealed contempt.

In Tadoussac, Champlain found faithful Eustache Boullé, who had been captured in his crazy pinnace after some wild adventures up and down the river.

Here too were faithless Brûlé and Marsolet, down from Quebec. Champlain treated them with lively scorn. "God will punish you if you do not mend your ways," he said. "If you knew that what you are doing is displeasing to God and to mankind, you would have a horror of yourselves. To think of you, brought up from boyhood in these parts, turning round now and selling those who put bread in your mouths! Do you think you will be esteemed by this nation? Be assured you will not, for they only make use of you out of necessity, watching your actions closely all the time, because they know that if someone else should offer you more money than they are paying you, you would sell them even more readily than you did your own nation; and when they have become acquainted with the country, they will drive you away, because people only make use of traitors for a time. You are losing your honor; you will be pointed at with scorn on all sides, wherever you may be. 'These are the men,' people will say, 'who betrayed their King and sold their country.' Better would it be for you to die than to live in the world under

such conditions, for whatever happens, you will always have a
worm gnawing at your conscience."

The pair were surly and defiant. "Well we know," they said,
"that if they had us in France they would hang us. We are
sorry for that, but the thing is done. We must drink the cup,
since we have begun, and make up our minds never to return to
France. We shall manage to live, just the same."

"Oh, what poor excuses!" said Champlain, and turned away
in contempt and bitterness.

The renegades suffered the usual lot of the faithless, being
scorned by their new masters as by the old. Hungry for favor,
they abjured even their religion; they ostentatiously ate meat on
Fridays, "thinking thus to curry favor with the English, who,
on the contrary, blamed them for it."

Shortly after, Brûlé left for Huronia, whence he was never to
return.

Marsolet took an opportunity for a private vengeance. Knowing how dearly Champlain cherished his two Indian girls, he
attempted to seduce one of them, but was repelled by her violence, greater than his own. He then wrote a letter to General
David Kirke, alleging that the Quebec chiefs demanded the
return of their girls. Champlain branded the letter a downright
lie, prompted by Marsolet's malice and his lewd purposes. He
persisted that the girls should accompany him to France, for
their safety in this world and their salvation in the next. But
the general was unwilling to discredit his own creature on the
word of his prisoner. The girls, on learning of the general's
obstinacy, "were so sad and distressed that they could neither
eat nor drink, but wept bitterly, so that I felt great compassion
for them. 'Is it possible,' they said to me, 'that this bad Captain
wants to prevent us from going to France with you whom we
consider as our father, and from whom we have received so
many benefits, even to taking the food you needed for your own
life to give to us during the hard times, and keeping us clothed?
We have such sorrow in our hearts that we cannot tell you.
Would there be no way of hiding us in the vessel? Or if we
could follow you in a canoe, we would do so. We beg that you
will ask this wicked man once more to let us go with you; if not,

we shall die of grief rather than go back with our savages.'
Thus did they express to me the sentiments of their little
hearts."

Champlain made another offer to keep them. He proposed
that the value of his beaver skins, amounting to a thousand
livres, be given to their tribesmen, to reconcile them to the loss
of the girls. He would arrive destitute in France, but with two
immortal souls. But no, even this offer did not sway the general.
He had spoken; he had chosen his course; nothing would make
him change. The girls must go back.

"Those poor girls, seeing that there was no remedy left
them, began to grieve and to weep bitterly, so much so that
one fell into a fever, and went for a long time without eating,
calling Marsolet a dog and a traitor, and saying: 'Since he saw
that we wouldn't yield to his desires, he has caused us such
distress that I can conceive of nothing like it short of death.'

"One evening, as the General was giving a supper to the
captains of his vessels, Marsolet being in the room, one of the
two girls named Hope came in. Her heart was very sad and
she was sighing. Noticing this, I asked her what was the matter,
whereupon she called her companion, Charity, saying: 'My
sorrow is so great that I shall have no rest until I unburden my
heart against Marsolet.' She then approached him, and looking
him straight in the face, she said: 'I can have no peace of mind
until I speak to you."

" 'What do you mean?' he asked.

" 'It is not in secret,' she replied, 'that I wish to speak to you.
All who understand our language will understand my meaning
well enough. All the savages know that you are a perfect liar,
who never say what has been said to you, but you make up lies
to get people to believe you. Remember that for a long time
now the savages have owed you a grudge. You report to your
captain things that were never said by the savages; but, villain,
you were careful not to mention what moved you to invent such
stories; it was that I wouldn't yield to your dirty pleasures when
you asked me to go with you, and you said I wouldn't lack for
anything, that you would open your chests and I could take out
whatever I liked—but I refused. You tried to make some im-
proper caresses, and I thrust you off, telling you that if you an-

noyed me further, I would make a complaint. After that you left me in peace, saying I was an obstinate creature. I assure you that I was not afraid of you. I want to go to France with Monsieur de Champlain, who has fed me and provided me with necessaries up to the present time, teaching me to pray to God, and many other virtuous things. I didn't want to destroy myself by staying here. The whole country had agreed to it, and my purpose was to go and live and die in France, and there learn to serve God. But, miserable creature that you are, instead of taking pity on two poor girls, you show yourself worse than a dog toward them. Remember that, though I am only a girl, I will procure your death if I can, and will do my best to that end, and I assure you that if you come near me again, I will plunge a knife into your heart, though I should die for it the moment after. Ah, traitor! You are the cause of my ruin; how can I look at you without weeping, seeing him who has caused my misfortune? A dog has a better nature than you; he follows the one who gives him his living, but as to you, you destroy those who have given you yours, without any proper gratitude toward your brothers, whom you have sold to the English. Do you think it was well done thus to sell your nation for money? But not content with that, you ruin us too by preventing us from learning to worship the God whom you disown, and who will visit you with death if there is any judgment in store for the wicked!'

"Thereupon she began to weep and could hardly utter another word.

"Marsolet said to her: 'You have learned that lesson pretty well.'

" 'O villain!' she said, 'you have given me plenty of cause to say more to you, if my heart could express it!'

"Marsolet then turning to the other little girl called Charity, said to her: 'Won't you say something to me?'

" 'All that I could say to you,' she replied, 'my companion has already said. I will only say this in addition, that if I had your heart in my grasp, I would eat it more readily and with better courage than the meats that are on this table.'

"Everyone thought highly of the courage and language of this child, who spoke not at all like a savage. That fellow

Marsolet was greatly taken aback by the truth of these words coming from a child of twelve; but nothing could move or soften the heart of General Kirke."

No further argument of Champlain could avail. He had his own cloak and dressing gown cut up to make clothing for his charges. He told them to take courage, always to be good girls, always to say their prayers. He gave one a rosary, as Boullé did to her sister, "for we could never give anything to one without the other having the same, on account of the jealousy existing between them." He arranged with Couillard that they should live on his farm, under the eye of Mme Hébert. Couillard promised to care for them as if they were his own children. The girls curtsied to Couillard, and said: "We will not leave you any more than we would our own father, in the absence of Monsieur de Champlain. What will console us and help us to be patient is that we are hoping for the return of the French; and if we had had to return to the savages, we should have died of grief."

So, with many embraces and tears, Champlain parted from Hope and Charity.

A few days later the ignoble Jacques Michel, rear admiral, died, in great remorse of conscience for his treachery to France. His death was obviously God's punishment for his incessant blasphemies and for a heinous attempt to strike the Jesuit Fathers. The English gave him a proper funeral, but there was more rejoicing than regret among them.

And now it was summer's end, and time to set sail for England. The ships embarked most of the French colony from Quebec, including all the clergy, including poor old Pontgravé, groaning and cursing. Five families remained: those of Couillard, Martin, Pivert, Hubout, and Desportes; also the surgeon Duchesne and certain interpreters and clerks.

On October 20 the English ships reached Plymouth. And there General Kirke learned that peace between France and England had been proclaimed on April 29. So his conquest of Canada was illegal! There would soon be great work for diplomats and lawyers, restitutions, claims, and counterclaims! Kirke was greatly angered, notes Champlain with satisfaction.

The French were landed at Dover, to be repatriated to

France. But Champlain went on to Gravesend and thence to London to see the French ambassador, to deposit his reports, pleas, and protests against the English actions in Canada. The ambassador had an audience with King Charles and emerged with an air of confidence.

Champlain remained for five weeks in London, and returned to France early in December.

He had been absent for three long and terrible years. He was over sixty; after a lifetime of effort he came home empty-handed. The empire he had built lay in the hands of his enemies. Well, the course before him was clear. He must make the Cardinal de Richelieu demand, and obtain, the return of Canada to France. Hope was still lively in his heart.

CHAPTER XX

The Last Voyage

CHAMPLAIN HURRIED to Paris to his wife Hélène. She was now a childless, unfulfilled woman in her early thirties, whose wifehood had been mostly separation from a husband distraught when he was not absent. Did she still keep a simulacrum of a home in the rue de la Marche? Or had she returned to her family? Or was she already consoling herself for her unsatisfactory spouse by lodging in the Ursuline convent? (Much as one may dislike the question-mark style of writing history, it is hard to dodge if one does not know the answers.)

At any rate, the husband did not long divert Hélène from her devotions. She recognized once more (with grief and anger?) that he loved a savage wilderness better than his own proper wife. The restoration of Canada, that ravished bride, was all his concern.

In this year of 1630 war was the habit and assumption of European life. The Western world was in the very middle of that long, dreary, bloody succession of tangled conflicts which history later decided to call the Thirty Years' War. Alliance, counter-alliance, strategic peace, strategic treachery, determined the destinies of great races and of little men. In all this moil and meddlement Champlain strove for one end: to save Canada for France.

He wrote letters to the King, setting forth once more the potential riches of his lost country, its fertility, its mineral wealth, its wild life. (He mentions, incidentally, a bird of prey the size of a chicken, gray-backed and white-bellied, one of whose feet is a talon to seize prey, the other a webbed paddle for swimming and diving. The bird is rare, he admits.) He held up again the hope of finding a passage to China. He concludes with the request that his pension, in effect for twenty-five years, be continued.

He importuned all those who might have to do with the settlement of Canada's status. He saw the King, the Cardinal, the influential Company members. "I made them listen, and hear all about my voyages, about what they should do in respect to the well-being of New France." England indeed admitted of necessity that Quebec had been seized after the proclamation of peace with France. But England had her grievances, and there were mountainous claims for indemnities by Kirke and others to weigh against the mountainous French claims. The negotiations dragged on and on, protracted by the restlessness of Louis XIII, who wandered forever up and down France, pursued by the infuriated commissioners, carrying a groaning weight of documents in mud-spattered saddlebags.

The dispute might well have continued forever had not King Charles of England raised the question of the sums still due him on the dowry of his wife, Henrietta of France. He was badly in need of money, for his hostile Parliament had refused to vote him subsidies since 1628. He therefore agreed that, in return for the payment of 400,000 crowns, the handsome arrears on the Queen's dowry, he would return Canada to France and, after a proper review, honor the excess of the French claims over the English.

Meanwhile the French merchants sorrowed for their lost business, the devout for their lost souls. The Jesuits said a daily Mass with the intention of Canada's restoration, and Ursuline and Carmelite nuns knelt in perpetual prayer to the same end. Prayer and business, faith and works, gained their common purpose. The treaty restoring Canada to France was signed at St.-Germain-en-Laye, on March 29, 1632.

Thus the English remained in control of the St. Lawrence

for three seasons. According to Champlain they did very well, taking out 300,000 livres worth of furs. But they paid for their profits with suffering. During the first winter they lost fourteen men from hunger and scurvy.

In 1631 Emery de Caen, who had many claims on behalf of his own old company, appeared at Quebec and demanded the right to trade. The English sent him back, empty-handed and raging.

In the following year, the new company of the Hundred Associates planned to send out Champlain to take charge of operations. As the company could find neither money nor ships, Richelieu granted to de Caen, in some compensation for his losses, the right to trade on the St. Lawrence for the year 1632 only. De Caen had evidently made his peace with the Cardinal by becoming a Catholic. He even carried in his baggage a morsel of the True Cross, which he used in the baptism of an Indian.

In this year of 1632 the Cardinal made a decision momentous for Canada's future. He annulled the rights of the Recollects in Canada and gave the Jesuits the exclusive rights to missionary labor. The decision was perfectly justifiable. The rivalry of the two orders was unedifying and wasteful; it was reasonable that the weaker should yield to the stronger. But the Recollects and their partisans were bitterly disappointed. Poor Father Joseph le Caron "groaned and sighed to the end of his days." His days were in fact few.

To the task of converting a continent the Jesuits assigned Father Paul Le Jeune, one of the noblest of a heroic band; Father Anne de Noüe, who had already suffered in Canada; and Brother Gilbert Buret. They embarked on the ship of Emery de Caen and set sail from Honfleur on April 18, 1632. Champlain was not of the party; he had no concern with de Caen's enterprise.

After the usual adventures and perils the expedition arrived at Quebec. De Caen showed to Captain Thomas Kirke the orders he carried, and Kirke perforce yielded up the fort. The Habitation had been burned, and briers and creepers had quickly hidden its shame. The little chapel was gone. The Jesuits'

home by the St. Charles, robbed of its windows, was inwardly
rotting.

There was an ugly bit of news. The English had freely exchanged brandy for beaver, and the Indians had become dangerous drunkards, killing and wounding in their cups. Some
wicked Frenchmen during the summer continued to satisfy the
wild men's craving. "Since I have been here," says Father Le
Jeune, "I have seen only drunken savages. They are heard
shouting and raving day and night, they fight and wound each
other, they kill the cattle of Madame Hébert, and, when they
return to their senses, they say to you: 'It is not we who did
that, but thou who gavest us the drink.' When they have slept
off their drunkenness, they are as good friends with each other
as ever, saying to each other: 'Thou art my brother, I love thee;
it is not I who wounded thee, but the drink which used my arm.'
I have seen some of them with very badly battered faces; even
the women get drunk, and shriek like furies. I expect that they
will kill some of us French people one of these days, as they have
already thought of doing; and after eight o'clock in the morning
it is not safe to go to see them without arms, if they have any
wine. Some of our men going to see them after dinner, a savage
tried to kill them with his hatchet, but other savages who were
not drunk came to their assistance. When one of them is very
drunk, the others tie him by his feet and arms, if they can catch
him."

The Jesuits found a strange inhabitant in Quebec: a little
Negro boy from Madagascar, who had somehow been transported to Canada by the English, and who now took refuge with
the hospitable Héberts. The priests put him with some Indian
boys to learn his letters and catechism. What became of him we
do not know. There was another exotic *Québecois*, a young
Bengalese, who had been converted to Christianity in France,
and who apparently shipped with de Caen. The spirit of adventure knows no restriction of time, race, or country.

Meanwhile Champlain, in Paris, was busy putting the finish-
ing touches to his fourth published book, the *Voyages* of 1632.
In his mind it was to crown his life's work, to be a necessary
handbook for historian and traveler, and to be a solemn lesson to

France of her glorious opportunities in the New World, of her necessary course of action, of the dangers she must avert. His purpose is proclaimed on the title page, which indicates France's right to America by discovery and settlement.

His book begins with a rosy description of New France and of its limitless bounty. The author then tells the long story of French enterprise in North America, from the first visits to Newfoundland in 1504. Snipping and cutting from his previous volumes, he recounts his own adventures, on the Atlantic coast, on the St. Lawrence, in Huronia. He brings the story through the capture of Canada by the English, with an appendix on the events of 1631. He adds a treatise on seamanship, with full instruction on the use of charts and instruments. He appends some examples of the native languages, contributed by Fathers Brébeuf and Massé. Included in the book is the largest and most up-to-date map of New France yet produced.

Bibliographers, comparing the text of this volume with that of 1619, make a curious observation. The whole story of the Recollects' first coming to Canada is omitted; everything in their favor is removed, and praise of the Jesuits substituted. The Abbé Laverdière, the great Canadian editor of Champlain, concludes roundly that the Jesuits tampered with Champlain's manuscript. Such a supposition rouses plenty of problems; authors so treated by their publishers make frightful outcries. The natural explanation is that Champlain made the alterations himself. He welcomed the rich and zealous Jesuits to Canada. Since the Recollect-Jesuit dispute was settled, for Canada's good, there was no point in encouraging recriminations.

Champlain's "Treatise on Seamanship and the Duty of a Good Navigator" has a special interest. It is his only effort to rise above the day-by-day journal, to create a work of conscious literary art. It was written, he says, for his own satisfaction. And it is a self-revelation, for his "good navigator" is clearly himself, or the man he aspired to be.

"The good navigator should above all be an upright, God-fearing man, not allowing God's holy name to be blasphemed on his ship, for fear, since he often finds himself in danger, lest His divine Majesty should punish him. He should be careful

night and morning to have prayers offered up . . . He should
not be dainty about his eating, nor about his drink, adapting
himself to the localities in which he finds himself. . . . He
should be robust and alert, with good sea-legs, inured to hardships and toil, so that whatever happen he may be able to remain
on deck and in a strong voice give everybody orders what to do.
Sometimes he must not be above lending a hand to the work
himself, in order to make the sailors more prompt in their attention and to prevent confusion. . . . He should be pleasant
and affable in conversation, authoritative in his orders, not too
ready to talk with his fellows, except with those who share the
command; otherwise in course of time a feeling of contempt for
him might arise. He should also punish evil-doers severely,
and make much of the good men, being kind to them, and at
times gratifying them with some friendly demonstration, praising them, but not neglecting the others, so as not to give an
occasion for envy. . . . He should be liberal according to his
opportunities, and courteous to defeated enemies, granting them
all the rights of belligerents, and above all keeping faith if he
has made any terms of surrender; for anyone who does not keep
his word is looked upon as a coward, and forfeits his honorable
reputation, however good a fighter he may be, and no trust is
ever reposed in him. Moreover he should not practise cruelties
nor be revengeful. . . . He should not allow himself to be
overcome by wine; for when a captain or a seaman is a drunkard
it is not very safe to entrust him with command or control,
on account of the mischances that may result while he is sleeping like a pig, or has lost all sense and discretion and by reason
of his drunkenness persists in insolence just when it is a matter
of necessity to find some escape from danger. . . .

"The wise and cautious mariner ought not to trust too fully
to his own judgment, when the pressing need is to take some
important step or to adopt some dangerous course. Let him
take counsel with those whom he recognizes as the most sagacious, and particularly with old navigators who have had most
experience of disasters at sea and have escaped from dangers
and perils. . . . He should be wary and hold back rather than
run too many risks, as in approaching land, particularly in foggy

weather, when he will bring the vessel to or stand off and on according to the position of the ship, inasmuch as in fog or in the dark no one is a pilot. . . .

"He should make the day his night and be awake the greater part of the night, always sleep in his clothes, so as to be on hand promptly for accidents that may happen, have his own private compass, often refer to it to know if the course is being properly kept, and see that every member of the watch is doing his duty. . . .

"He should take good care to have wholesome food and drink for his voyage and such as will keep well, to have good dry bins in which to keep the bread or biscuit . . . He must be a good manager in serving out rations, giving each man what he reasonably needs. . . . He should entrust the serving out of rations to a good trustworthy steward, no drunkard, but a provident fellow. . . .

"He should be particularly careful to see that everything is in good order on his ship, both to make it strong enough to support the weight of the guns it may mount, and to improve its appearance, so that he may take pleasure in it when he comes aboard and when he leaves, and may please those who see him on his craft, just as an architect is pleased when he has adorned a splendid building of his own designing. Everything on the ship should be very neat and clean, after the fashion of the Dutch, who commonly take first place in this respect. . . . He should often have the 'tween-decks cleansed of the filth that accumulates there, for it frequently causes a stench and gives rise to disease.

"Before embarking he must have everything requisite for giving necessary aid to the men, together with one or two good surgeons who are not ignoramuses, like most of those who go to sea. . . .

"He must be watchful of finding himself in ordinary dangers, be it by accident or through ignorance or rashness, as when you run inshore before a wind, or doggedly try to double a cape, or follow a dangerous course by night among sandbanks, shoals, reefs, islands, rocks, or ice. But when ill fortune brings you to such a pass, there you must display manly courage, make light of death though it confronts you, and in a steady voice and

with cheery resolution urge all to take courage and do what
can be done to escape danger, and thus dispel fear from the
most cowardly bosoms. For when they find themselves in a
hazardous situation, all look to the man who is thought to
have experience. If he is seen to blanch and give his orders in a
trembling and uncertain voice, all the others lose courage, and
it is often seen that ships are lost in situations from which
they might have got clear away if the men had seen their captain
undaunted and determined, giving his orders boldly and with
authority. . . ."

There is plenty of other advice, still sound for the master
of a little ship or a big. This "Character of a Good Captain"
might well be conned by the young gentlemen of our naval
academies.

The compendious volume of 1632 is Champlain's literary
testament. He assembles therein the facts, thoughts, and memories he wishes to bequeath to the world. He was tidying up his
life in preparation for a long journey, the longest of his journeys.

He made an act of mutual donation with his wife, a will, in
effect. He named among his heirs a cousin, Marie Camaret,
wife of Jacques Hersaut, a small official of La Rochelle. In this
document Champlain is represented as *"gentilhomme de la
chambre du roi."* The distinction was probably formal and unprofitable, but pleasing to an elderly gentleman's vanity.

In the autumn the ships from Canada returned, though
Emery de Caen himself remained to winter in Quebec. Champlain listened eagerly to the news. It was evident that Canada
needed him, as he needed Canada.

In November, Champlain was shocked to hear of the de-
capitation, by a primitive guillotine, of his old master and friend,
the Duc de Montmorency. The Duke had joined a rebellion set
on foot by the King's brother Gaston d'Orléans. The King's
brother was pardoned.

Winter was the time for plans and preparations. The Company of the Hundred Associates, which had suffered appalling
losses during the English war, was provoked to new enterprise
by the driving force of Cardinal de Richelieu, and encouraged
by the report of de Caen's profitable trip. Three ships were
fitted out.

Champlain was for the first time placed in absolute and undivided command of the St. Lawrence. He was the governor not only for the King, but for the trading company of which he was a member. No longer need he dispute with highhanded factors over the limits of authority, the apportionment of supplies, the assignment of men to necessary labors.

As commander he had the selection of the personnel for his journey. He admitted no bumptious Protestants to his ships, and certainly no more criminals fleeing French justice. There were two hundred men on board, some of them genuine colonists, but only one woman and two girls. He carried two famous Jesuits: Ennemond Massé, who had first gone out to Acadia in 1611, and great, burly Brébeuf, veteran of the Huronian mission, and destined for martyrdom and sainthood.

Faithful Eustache Boullé elected to remain in France; he felt the stirrings of a religious vocation. And Pontgravé? We hear no more of him. Probably the gout had shot its last shaft.

The expedition set sail from Dieppe on March 23, 1633, and made a good crossing. Champlain found three English ships trading in the river as far up as Tadoussac. As their strength was about equal to his own, he dared not risk his precious cargo in battle, but contented himself with sharp summonses and threats of legal action, which deterred the English not at all.

He arrived at Quebec on May 22. He disembarked a squad of soldiers armed with pikes and muskets. To the beat of drums they marched, panting, up the path to the clifftop. Their commander summoned Emery de Caen to surrender the fort. De Caen, after reading the orders of the Cardinal de Richelieu, resignedly obeyed.

The settlement was in woeful state. Of the Habitation, only the cellar and some sheds remained. Champlain could not even find a dry place to store his provision of flour. Well, he had rebuilt before; he would simply rebuild again.

He visited the Jesuits, in relative ease in their home across the St. Charles. He was cordially entertained at a dinner of bear's meat. Father Le Jeune returned the call on board Champlain's pinnace, bringing with him a choir of small Indian boys, who sang the paternoster in their native tongue.

The Jesuits gave him a good report of the behavior of the French in the previous winter. "I confess I had some fear that libertinism might cross the sea with us," said Father Le Jeune. "But the good example of the commanders, the distance from all debauchery, our small labors in preaching and in the administration of the sacraments, have held all strictly in the line of duty."

The relations with the Indians were on the whole good. When Father Le Jeune rang his bell for school some twenty boys responded. They were learning—though with what quaint misconceptions!—the elements of Christian faith, and they were docile and grateful scholars. But the Father was much perturbed by the taste for drink their elders had learned from the English, and which occasional Frenchmen were base enough to gratify. Champlain thereupon issued an order stringently prohibiting the sale or gift of liquor to Indians—an order that has never been rescinded.

When official business was dispatched, Champlain inquired for his two dear adopted children, Hope and Charity. Ah, they had gone back to their people, to the life of the camp and woods, and their souls were lost, as they had well foreseen. We never hear of them again.

Now the busy times began. Perhaps first of Champlain's tasks was to fulfill the vow he had made four years before: to raise a church to Our Lady of Recovery, if She would restore Canada to Her devotees. He built the chapel on the high land near the fort. It was ready by autumn, and the Jesuits there sang high Mass every Sunday. Its site is sanctified indeed; upon its ruins rises the high altar of the Cathedral of Quebec.

All available men were put to work clearing the site of the Habitation and building a new warehouse, with a platform for cannon. Everyone labored through the long summer days, driven by the will of Champlain.

He turned actively to the promotion of the fur trade. A party of English, with shifty Marsolet for interpreter, were encamped forty miles below Quebec, offering competition in prices, offering drink. Champlain countered their move, not by fruitless battle, but by establishing his trading post thirty-five miles above the city, on an islet off Pointe Platon which effectively commands the stream. He forbade the Indians to descend below this point. Few, it seems, dared disobey.

He held a parley with a deputation of Indians from upstream who came to complain of the growing boldness of Iroquois raiders. He promised them that he would build a fort at Trois Rivières, to protect them, and incidentally to secure the fur-trade route. This was an old project, which he had conceived on his first visit to the river in 1603.

The fear of the Iroquois which possessed the riverain Indians soon proved to be all too well founded. A party of French sailors hauling a shallop around a point were suddenly attacked by thirty or forty Iroquois. Two Frenchmen were killed and scalped; four were wounded, and one of these died. So the Iroquois were repaying, at the very headquarters of the French, the visits that Champlain had made them twenty years before.

Further reports of the Iroquois menace were brought by trading parties from the interior, Algonquins from Allumette Island on the Ottawa, Nipissings from their inland lake. "We shall put an end to this terror," said Champlain confidently. "Our King will send us men and arms. I promise you that within four years we shall attack the Iroquois in their homeland and render them helpless."

The anonymous author of an account published in the *Mercure François* for 1633 says: "I have often heard the Sieur de Champlain say that to conquer these Iroquois, we would need only a hundred picked men, courageous, calm, obedient, toughened to fatigue, who could get along with the Indians and eat their food. With this corps of rangers, who would be accompanied by three or four thousand savages, we would go to the Iroquois, and in twelve days we would make a surprise attack on one of their towns with the aid of grenades, mines, bombs, and cavaliers which we would construct to dislodge them from their parapets; and when they saw this they would make no resistance, but would assuredly abandon the stronghold. We would make short work of the others, for they have only five villages of any consequence. Then we would impose our law on all these peoples, subjecting them to our will, giving them what laws and customs we should desire, and so we would be feared by our enemies, and respected and loved by our friends, who would know the valor of the French when they are offended; and they would perforce learn that we know how to do something else than bargain for beaver skins. Such a war would be a master-stroke of strategy in this country, and it wouldn't cost much."

Champlain outlined his plan at a great council of the Indians. He promised that he would write to the King and Cardinal to insist upon prompt military aid.

In his letter, still in the French archives, he complains that the Iroquois hold over four hundred places in subjection, and that they menace all the water communications. He proposes that a general peace be made among all the victims and enemies of the Iroquois. "If this peace is made we shall enjoy every advantage. Possessing the interior, we shall drive out our enemies, both English and Dutch, and force them to retire to their coasts. By taking from them the commerce with the Iroquois, we shall constrain them to abandon everything. We need only 120 men, lightly armored to repel arrows. With two or three thousand savage allies, we shall render ourselves absolute masters of these peoples in a year or two, and that will spread the practice of religion and incredibly increase trade. The country is rich in mines of copper, iron, steel, brass, silver, and other minerals. Monseigneur, the cost of 120 men is little to His Majesty, and the enterprise as honorable as can be imagined, and all is for the glory of God, to whom I pray to give you increase in the prosperity of your days, etc."

In a second letter he proposes to lead the punitive expedition in person. "I know the forces of the enemy savages and their ways of making war, which gives me such an advantage that with God's grace I would reduce them easily to a dutiful state. The experience I have acquired in the many years that I have dwelt in this country ensures that with such help I would promise myself an assured victory."

These are certainly not very convincing sales letters, despite their naïve appeal to high policy, piety, and cupidity. The Cardinal, with perhaps a smile for the valiant old warrior, consigned the letters to the files.

But Champlain's confidential statement to his master may well interest us. Here he could outline his policy as he could not properly do in books that would soon find their way to England and Holland. The policy was one that he had followed, more or less, for thirty years: to reduce, first, the Iroquois power; then to impose a general peace, a *pax Gallicana*, among all the Indians, and under its sanction to bring the Iroquois into the French sphere of commercial influence; and then to starve out the English and Dutch traders, to force them back to the coast and out of America. The true rivals, the eventual enemies of France, were not the Iroquois but the Europeans in America.

One may amuse oneself by speculating on what would have happened if the Cardinal had sent a hundred and twenty commando troops to subdue the Iroquois. Even if the French had decisively won the war (a considerable supposition), they could hardly have imposed a secure peace upon the proud and vengeful enemy. Nor could they have altered primitive American geopolitics and diverted Iroquois trade from Fort Orange to Quebec. Nor, finally, could they have starved out the English and Dutch, who had by this time taken firm root in the soil, and who had learned, unlike the French, to be self-sufficient on their American farms.

But now let us return to the summer of 1633.

A great swarm of Hurons, a hundred and forty canoeloads, ran the Iroquois gantlet and arrived at Quebec. (The English traders had left in disgust, and Champlain had lifted his blockade.) The Hurons brought rich treasures in furs. But they had a secret, which was soon whispered in French ears. Brûlé, scapegrace Brûlé, had wintered among them, and in some quarrel, probably over a woman, he had been killed and formally eaten. His epitaph is thus written by the Recollect du Creux: "Long a transgressor of the laws of God and man, he spent the rest of his wretched life in vile intemperance, such as no Christian should exhibit among heathen. He died by treachery, perhaps only that he might perish in his sins. He was hurried to the Judgment Seat to answer for all his other crimes and especially for that depravity which was a stumbling block to the Hurons." [1] Let any who wish rehabilitate the memory of this extraordinary discoverer.

The Hurons feared that the incomprehensible French might

[1] Percy J. Robinson: *Toronto under the French Régime*, 9.

demand satisfaction for the death of a Frenchman. But no, Champlain told them that Brûlé, by cleaving to the English, had lost his nationality. The French had no concern for his life or death. Let not this incident disturb the harmony of the trading fair.

But there was another and more difficult case.

A Frenchman washing his clothes by a brook near the fort of Quebec was wantonly clubbed to death by an Indian. The murderer was captured; he was an Algonquin of Allumette Island, down for the trading. His only excuse was this: he was supposed to kill another savage in a blood feud. As he found his proper victim always on his guard, he simply slew a Frenchman instead. For honor's sake he had to kill someone.

Now this was too much. This was the fifth Frenchman to be treacherously and capriciously murdered in Quebec. In the other cases no one had been punished. But now, to save the face of the French, there must be an end of appeasement.

All the Indians came trooping to interview Champlain. Said their spokesman: "We know well that we have cut off a bit of your heart, and a bit of ours. This must be repaired. We cannot do so by gifts and presents, but only by a share of our own flesh." So saying, they presented two small children to Champlain. "We give them to you; do with them as you will. It is to replace the morsel which has been cut from your heart. And deliver to us the prisoner, so that we may all rejoice together."

Champlain made a long answer, patiently comparing the principles of savage justice with those of the French. He made clear that the French must punish the malefactor himself and no substitute. The Indians professed themselves convinced, but they were obviously sulky. Champlain put the prisoner in irons in the fort, postponing judgment until the fellow tribesmen should depart for their homes. The mood of the Indians grew uglier. The Huron chiefs retracted their promise to take three Jesuits to Huronia, on the ground that they could not restrain their young men from taking vengeance. Father Le Jeune asked Champlain to pardon the prisoner. "No," said Champlain; "it is a matter of life and death. I am responsible to the King for the punishment of a Frenchmen's assassin." Father Le Jeune then asked that the death sentence be deferred until it could be confirmed in France. Champlain agreed, although this meant a year's delay, the presence of a troublesome prisoner in the Fort, and a living grievance among the Indians.

Not long after, the prisoner escaped. He succeeded in loosening the pin that linked his irons to their chain, and fled while his guard was eating dinner.

In this episode Champlain reveals again, I think, his flaw as a commander. He did not adopt a firm policy and cleave to it. He understood perfectly the Indian logic of revenge, which might be exercised on any representative of the hostile side, and how incompatible was their logic with the French legal conception of crime and punishment. He understood also that a judicial sentence and execution of the culprit might become a *casus belli*, might alienate all the Algonquins who commanded the Ottawa River, the great trade route to the west. And he shrank from the grisly business of shooting or hanging. Quick, sharp justice, trial and punishment, might have worked. But no, Champlain delayed, argued, paltered, explained, until finally the situation became intolerable to all. And the prisoner escaped. Who gave him the means to file the pin of his shackles? I have my suspicion.

Now let us look at a more pleasing contrast of the savage and civilized codes, of the clash of two incomprehensions. Father Le Jeune tells the story. "A Nipissing Indian was looking very attentively at a little French boy who was beating a drum; and going near to him so as to see him better, the little boy struck him a blow with one of his drumsticks and made his head bleed badly. Immediately all the people of his tribe who were looking at the drummer, seeing this blow given, took offense at it. They went and found the French interpreter, and said to him: 'Behold, one of thy people has wounded one of ours. Thou knowest our custom well; give us presents for this wound.' As there is no government among the Savages, if one among them kills or wounds another, he is, providing he can escape, released from all punishment by making a few presents to the friends of the deceased or the wounded one. Our interpreter said: 'Thou knowest our custom; when any of our number does wrong we punish him. This child has wounded one of your people; he shall be whipped at once in your presence.' The little boy was brought in; and when they saw that we were really in earnest, that we were stripping this little pounder of Savages and drums, and that the switches were all ready, they immediately began to pray for his pardon, alleging that he was only a child, that he had no mind, that he did not know what he was doing. But as our people were going to punish him nevertheless, one of the Savages stripped himself entirely, threw his blanket over the child, and cried out to him who was going to do the whipping: 'Strike me, if thou wilt, but thou shalt not strike him!' And thus the little one escaped."

The Indians were mollified; the pledges of friendship were made anew. One night, according to their custom, their entire body disappeared. "They flew away like birds," says the Jesuit Father. A few days later, in mid-August, the French vessels sailed, loaded down with furs. And the long silence settled down on Quebec.

Now began the happiest period of Champlain's life. He was in sole command of Quebec and of all the great country to the west. He had the respect, the love, of all his colony. His work was recognized in France, his purposes endorsed by his master the Cardinal. Supplies were received in comforting quantity from home: flour, wine, pork, butter, even codfish. Honest, pious families were beginning to arrive, ready to make new homes in New France. No longer need he dispute forever with shabby fur-merchants, whose only aim and measurement was profit. Adventure was over; peace had come. "The advice I give to all adventurers," he had written in his last book, "is to seek a place where they may sleep in safety."

I like to fancy that he occupied the tranquil winter days by taking up again his water-color brushes, limning the majesty of Quebec. I like to think that some day I may see those loving sketches.

Within the fort, life was ordered, says Father Le Jeune, as in a well-conducted school. "Monsieur de Champlain has someone read at his table, in the morning from some good historian, and in the evening from the Lives of the Saints. Then each one makes an examination of his conscience in his own chamber, and prayers follow, which are repeated kneeling. He has the Angelus sounded at the beginning, in the middle, and at the end of the day, according to the custom of the Church. In a word, we have reason to console ourselves when we see a chief so zealous for the glory of Our Lord and for the welfare of these Gentlemen."

A school, perhaps, but a military school. The day began with the *diane*, the drums at dawn. Sentries paced their rounds, and all the garrison turned out for drill. Rations were served out at the rate of two great loaves of bread per man per week, and two pounds of bacon, a pound of codfish, two ounces of butter, and oil and vinegar. The rest of the subsistence was made up by hunting and fishing. The healthy weariness that resulted helped to quell the quarrels and grievances of lusty men in barracks. Life was on the whole cheery. There was music and song in plenty; one young Frenchman had a sort of zither or hurdy-gurdy, which the Indians adored.

True, the innate depravity of human nature sometimes asserted itself, especially when the French ships came to port in the summer. Then there were some drunkenness and thievery, to the wonderment, ironic or scandalized, of the Indians, and to the grief of the Jesuit Fathers. But the authorities in France were now very careful in their selection of workmen, soldiers, and sailors. Only the godly and honest might embark. Their conduct in Canada was on the whole exemplary.

A good-sized party of genuine colonists, headed by Robert Giffard, came out in 1634 and established themselves at Beauport, just below Quebec. A settlement was made at Trois Rivières, with a pair of priests to serve it and the Indians round about. Building went on steadily at the fort of Quebec, and at Notre-Dame des Anges. A census of cattle showed ten cows, two heifers, and a small bull. And the heart of Champlain was gladdened as he looked upon the fatness of his land.

He loved and respected the Jesuits, especially gentle, virtuous Father Lalemant. "The Governor never omits any occasion to show us his good will," says Father Le Jeune. He stood godfather to converted Indians, and when one such died he turned out all his men to attend the funeral. (The baptisms, to be sure, were nearly all of small children at the point of death. The inconstancy and incomprehension of the adults were a perpetual sorrow to the missionaries. One likely prospect could not get it out of his head that the priests' "water of importance" must be brandy.)

To the Indians, Champlain was kindly and politic, an under-standing father. He knew how to deal with them; he had learned savage tact as well as civilized tact. "One must always give reason for every decision," he explained to the Jesuits. But the decision must be strictly enforced, as in the prohibition of strong drink. It is true that Champlain never mastered the native languages. On every public occasion he used an interpreter. Sagard tells us that the Montagnais were hurt because in all his years among them Champlain had never learned their tongue; they were always suspicious of the interpreters' knowl-edge and private interests. To be sure, he must have had some smattering of the language. He used the common "baragouin" of the settlement, a medley of French and Montagnais, "which is neither French nor savage, but when the French use it they think they are talking savage, and the savages, speaking it, think they are talking good French."

With his great children, Champlain's manner was genial, playful. "You always say something jolly to cheer us up," said a chief to him. One day when Champlain and the ship captains were assembled in the Jesuits' chapel, the inquisitive Indians peered in at the window. "The Sieur de Champlain, enjoying their wonder, gave a piece of lemon peel to one of them, who, on tasting it, cried out: 'Oh, how good that is!' He divided it with those who were with him, who were all seized with the same admiration. They asked what it was; the Sieur de Champlain said to them, laughing, that it was the rind of a French pump-kin. This astonished them very much, and they said to each other that our pumpkins were wonderful. Thereupon those who had not tasted appeared at the window and asked the Sieur de Champlain if all the pumpkins were eaten, saying that they would like to taste them, so as to tell about them in their coun-try. You can judge for yourself how all in the room began to laugh."

A poor enough joke, heaven knows, but you observe Cham-plain's kindly manner, you feel his warm heart.

He still urged peace with the Iroquois, but without much hope or conviction. Chiefly he sought to bind the natives to the French with every bond of sentiment and interest. Twice, in his speeches at the annual fur-trade banquet (when his hearers were distended with peas, powdered sea biscuit, and prunes, boiled, saltless, in a beer vat) he proposed the inter-marriage of French and Indians. "Our young men shall marry your daughters, and we shall be one people. . . . The French will marry your daughters when they become Christians." But his dream of the amalgamation of the races was disavowed by his successors. The Jesuits steadily refused to marry colonists to Indians, suspecting that the desire of these Frenchmen was to descend to the barbarian level.

Another dream, the old dream of the Northwest Passage, haunted Champlain to his death. Many years before, he had seen the South Sea at Panama; the memory of those golden waters was ever bright in his mind. His agents among the Indians had standing orders to gain information about the west, and to explore, if occasion should arise.

One of the best of his interpreters was Jean Nicolet. He spent ten years with the Island Algonquins and with the Nipissings, suffering much; in one winter he was seven weeks with only bark for food. In 1634 he was sent to make a peace between the Hurons and some tribes of the Great Lakes.[2] Provi-dently, he took in his baggage a robe of China damask, with flowers and birds of many colors, to wear if by chance he should reach the court of some Oriental potentate. In fact he got no nearer China than Green Bay, Wisconsin.

The dream of China lingered on, to recur occasionally in the *Jesuit Relations*. The memory of that phantom is still preserved at Montreal in the very name of the Lachine Rapids.

But there was another dream more and more in Champlain's thoughts: the dream of a country fairer even than Canada. He was sixty-eight years old, and tired after a lifetime filled with suffering and privation. Now that his colony seemed to be set-ting fair toward success, he felt that his work on this earth was done.

In October 1635 he was smitten by a paralytic stroke. He was put to bed in the governor's chamber of the fort. Surely his window looked down on the noble river, and across to the heights of Lévis. He could watch the leaves falling, the first

[2] Though it may have been 1638. Brebner: *Explorers of North America*, 188. See his references.

ominous snows whitening the evergreens, and he could live again in memory many another Canadian winter.

He dictated his final will. "I nominate the Virgin Mary my heir," he said. He left his furniture and his funds in the Hundred Associates to his little Quebec church, Notre-Dame de la Recouvrance.

His friends would gather by his bedside, and to them he would give painfully admonitions for the good of the colony. "He crowned his virtues with sentiments of piety so lofty that he astonished us all," says Father Le Jeune. "What tears he shed! How ardent became his zeal for the service of God! How great was his love for the families here! He said that they must be vigorously assisted for the good of the country, and made comfortable in every possible way in these early stages, and that he would do it if God gave him health."

On Christmas Eve midnight Mass was celebrated in Notre-Dame de la Recouvrance. At the *Te Deum*, the cannon of the fort boomed three times. And Champlain, hearing the familiar sound, knew that this time the cannon celebrated victory.

On Christmas Day he died.

Amid the common grief of French and Indians he was buried with all the pomp the colony could command. Shortly after, a chapel, *la chapelle de M. de Champlain*, was erected to contain his tomb.

"The advice I give to all adventurers is to seek a place where they may sleep in safety."

The chapel stood, probably, within the courtyard of the present post office. But concerning the site, and concerning the present location of Champlain's remains, a long and unprofitable dispute has raged.

It was, perhaps, by God's mercy that Champlain died on this high holy day of 1635. For in Paris the Hundred Associates, under the guidance of Cardinal de Richelieu, were meeting to choose a new governor. The reason is not clear—whether Champlain was regarded merely as too old, whether his policy had crossed that of the Cardinal, or whether some intrigue was at work. There was indeed a plan afoot to turn Canada over to the Knights of Malta; but for all we know, Champlain may have approved the project in advance. The Governor chosen, Charles Huault de Montmagny, was a worthy and capable officer, who ruled Canada well for a dozen years. When he reached Quebec in the summer of 1636, he was at least spared the painful duty of serving Champlain with the order for his dismissal and return to France.

Father Lalemant went back to France that summer and informed Hélène de Champlain of the death of her husband. She took the news with Christian fortitude and immediately entered an Ursuline convent in Paris as a novice. In 1648 she gave 20,000 livres to found a convent of the order at Meaux, and there took her final vows. As a foundress she was allowed fire in her room and a lay sister to wait upon her, and she was dispensed from rising at four in the morning. There she died in 1654, in the odor of virtue.

Her brother Eustache spent ten years in Italy and then became a Minimite monk.

There was a troublesome business about Champlain's will. His widow, respecting his pious dispositions, and obviously well provided for, did not contest his gifts to Notre-Dame de la Recouvrance. But his cousin Marie Hersaut, née Camaret, protested that the will was invalid, improperly executed, and in violation of the terms of the marriage contract. The court ruled in her favor and awarded her the value of Champlain's share in the Hundred Associates. Notre-Dame received only 900 livres, the product of the sale of Champlain's personalty. It is evident that he had not enriched himself. He had disdained every opportunity his position afforded for shady profits.

In France, Champlain was soon forgotten. The French, busy with their wars, the intrigues of nobles, the disputes of religion and class, were extraordinarily oblivious to the fate of New France beyond the seas. The drama of forest and sea, of white man, red man, and black, was too unclassical for French taste; it did not observe the tidy unities.[3]

But in Canada, Champlain's memory lingered and grew. He is referred to in the chronicles as *"Monsieur de Champlain d'heureuse mémoire."* When Father Le Mercier, in faraway Huronia, received the news of his death he and his companions

[3] See Appendix H, "The Awareness of Canada in Seventeenth-Century France."

redoubled their vows, "for we could not do too much for a person of his merit, who had done and suffered so much for New France, for the welfare of which he seemed to have sacrificed all his means, yea, even his own life. Therefore God rewarded him after this life by a death accompanied by so many sentiments of devotion and piety that his memory will be forever honorable." The Hurons venerated him; when they came down to Quebec in the summer they brought special presents to help the French to dry their tears and swallow their sorrow. Several years later they were still marveling at his virtues, especially his chastity. And the good missionary among them wrote: "Would to God that all the French who first came to this country had been like him; we should not so often have to blush for them before our savages."

He was a good man. He had the qualities necessary for the adventurer: toughness, tenacity, foresight, courage. But it was the natural virtue of his spirit that little by little impressed itself on the hard fur-traders and on the perfidious Indians. Not many of the great conquerors of our continent have been eminently good men. There was Cabeza de Vaca, and Las Casas, and perhaps some of New England's saints, though their godliness may seem today less virtue than an assumption of virtue. The reader of Champlain's works, the student of his life, must feel himself constantly in touch with a man to whom good was a reality, one who believed in the goodness of God's purpose, and who sought to realize it in the welfare of his fellow men, both white-skinned and red-skinned.

In other words he was an idealist. He was still young when he found his ideal. It appeared to him faintly in Mexico when he saw a colonial system devised only for the advantage of the ruler. It appeared to him clearly when he first came to Canada. Thenceforth all his life, all his thought, was devoted to one end: to the foundation in America of a great kingdom, to be ruled with justice and mercy, by France, but for God.

He had the faults of the idealist. He stood a little apart from men. He was not sly enough to overreach the sly. They often befooled him, laughing in their sleeves. He dreamed too far ahead; he could see the Pacific, China; he could walk in vision in a shining city, where the eye of flesh saw only a log warehouse and a tumbledown fort. He aroused mistrust in the fur merchants, practical men, on whose good will he depended for so long. He was too understanding of others, of their purposes and justifications. At the high moment of decision he would be visited by a paralysis of action, and suddenly he would forget even the interests of his own ideal and surrender to the specious loquacity of mean-minded men.

But in his high policies he was right. He saw the future with just eyes; he prepared for that future; he helped to make it. The principles he laid down for his colony enabled Canada to live, a strong, self-sufficient, permanent community. His Indian policy brought the French to the Rocky Mountains at a time when the English were still cautiously pushing forward to the Alleghenies.

Suppose he had never lived, or suppose he had been turned from his task by one of fate's perversities. For years Quebec would have been a mere summer trading post. The enterprising Dutch, with their Iroquois allies, might well have forced the northern fur trade into their sphere of influence. The English, planting colonies in Newfoundland and Nova Scotia from 1622 on, would have found no serious bar to an advance up the St. Lawrence and the capture of all Canada.

But Champlain, indomitable Champlain, with a few dozen men, held the country for France. Well is he termed today the Father of Canada. Canada was his child, the only love of this lonely, visionary, good man.

APPENDIX A

The Date of Champlain's Birth

THE *Biographie Saintongeoise* of 1852 gives Champlain's birth date as 1567, but we have no means of knowing whether the editor had access to material since lost or whether he was guessing. In attestation of the date of 1567, the legend beneath the familiar portrait has frequently been invoked. However, the portrait was painted by the gifted toes of Ducornet, in 1854 or shortly before, and the legend has no value. We must fall back on circumstantial evidence.

Champlain was serving as *maréchal des logis*, billeting officer, in 1593 or thereabouts. To hold this responsible position, which requires an air of mature authority, he could hardly have been under twenty. We have therefore 1573 as the latest probable birth date.

In 1619 Champlain writes of his friend Pontgravé: "His years would lead me to respect him as I would my father." (*Works*, IV, 363.) Sagard says Pontgravé was over seventy in 1629. (*Histoire du Canada*, Paris, 1866, IV, 891.) Thus in 1619 Pontgravé would have been over sixty; he was born about 1557 or earlier. One does not ordinarily respect another as one's father unless there is a difference of ten years or so in age. According to that, Champlain would have been born in the neighborhood of 1567.

In 1634 Champlain proposed to Cardinal de Richelieu that he should lead a punitive expedition against the Iroquois. Make every allowance for a valiant old gentleman's sense of well-being; he could still not be over seventy. That gives us 1564 as the earliest possible date.

On the whole, 1567 seems about right.

APPENDIX B

The Chronology of the Journey to the West Indies

CHAMPLAIN'S CHRONOLOGY of his journey is very confused, and often palpably in error. L. Cabrera de Córdoba, in his contemporary *Relaciones de las cosas sucedidas en la Corte de España* (Madrid, 1857), says (p. 9): *"Don Francisco* [Coloma] *partió con 12 galeones de San Lúcar, a los 3 de este mes* [February, 1599]." Champlain says: *"à commencement du mois de januier de l'an 1599."* From then on he never gives a date, but refers occasionally to the passage of eight days, a month, etc. The total of his statements of elapsed time, plus reasonable surmises for intervals and journeys of unspecified length, is about sixteen or seventeen months, which would land him in Spain about June or July 1600. (His admiral, Don Francisco Coloma, was back in Spain by February, 1600. See *Archivo Histórico Español: Col. de documentos inéditos para la historia de España y de sus Indias*, Madrid, 1930, III, 4.) But Champlain says that he returned to Spain two years and two months after his departure, which gives us March 1601, if we accept his own date for setting sail, or April 1601, if we accept Cabrera de Córdoba.

Cabrera de Córdoba reports incoming convoys on August 11, 1600, January 4, 1601, and September 26, 1601. It is evident that either Cabrera de Córdoba failed to report the arrival of a fleet in March or April 1601 or Champlain's chronology is all wrong. Now Cabrera de Córdoba regarded the appearance of the Indies fleet as most important news, for it brought the precious metals that sustained the government. Further, it would be very unusual for more than two Indies fleets to arrive in one year. I conclude that Champlain's reckoning of his date of return is wrong.

Did Champlain arrive in Spain, then, on August 11, 1600, on January 4, 1601, or on September 26, 1601? Nearest to Champlain's own date is January 4, 1601. However, this convoy underwent a hurricane in the Bahama Channel and other bad storms in the eastern Atlantic. One of the vessels found its way up the African coast to Gibraltar and came to port in Málaga; one ran aground and was lost off Cape St. Vincent; the flagship arrived, leaking badly, in Cadiz. Champlain says nothing of these misadventures, but reports a normal arrival at Seville. This date is, then, hardly possible. We are left with August 1600 and September 1601. But September 1601 is out, for we know that Champlain appeared in person before a Cadiz notary on July 2, 1601 (A.-L. Leymarie, in *Nova Francia*, I, 80, October 1925). August 1600 is more likely anyway, as it fits with a rough reckoning of the elapsed time of the journey, and as there is no evident reason why the *St. Julien*, chartered by the month, should have been left in the Indies while its companions returned. There was a chronic shortage of ships for the Spanish transatlantic service.

To be sure, this reasoning raises another problem. If Champlain returned in August 1600, how does it happen that he was in Cadiz a year later? Perhaps his ship was commissioned for further Spanish service, which he preferred not to dwell upon. Perhaps, perhaps. We just don't know. At any rate, we don't know of his being anywhere else.

A search made at my request in the Archivo de Indias has failed to reveal Champlain's name on the manifests of Don Francisco Coloma's convoy of 1599, or any mention of him in accessory documents. Sr. C. Bermúdez Plata, Director of the Archives, writes: "*Se han consultado muy detenidamente los legajos Contratación, 1133 ('Registro de ida del año 1599, de los que fueron a Santo Domingo, con los galeones y armadas del General Don Francisco Coloma'); el legajo Contratación, 2965, referente a la armada de Don Francisco Coloma) Contratación 2966, referente al mismo General Coloma, y a su salida en 1593 y 1599) el legajo Contratación, 2957, sobre el repetido General Coloma, y por último el legajo Contratación, 2958, que trata de los papeles de la armada de Coloma. En ninguno de los citados legajos se ha encontrado nada sobre el indicado Samuel Champlain.*"

Maybe he was using a false name.

APPENDIX C

The Marquis de la Roche and Sable Island

AFTER THE FAILURE of the expedition of the Marquis de la Roche in 1584, he kept his rights to colonize Newfoundland and the surrounding region. For five years he was apparently unable to raise money for a new effort. He was then seized by the Duc de Mercoeur, the leader of the opposition to Henry IV, and was imprisoned for seven years. He was released for a thumping ransom and immediately organized a raid on the island of Ushant, which was held by his own side. He was an unreliable person, to say the least.

The civil wars ended, and La Roche bethought him of his post as lieutenant-general and viceroy of the King in Newfoundland. In 1597 he chartered a Newfoundland fishing ship, Thomas Chefdostel, master, to land a company of soldiers on Sable Island, thence to control the fish and fur trade. Sable Island is a dismal, fog-bound strip of sand, twenty miles long by a mile in breadth, off the coast of Nova Scotia. Ringed with wrecks, the graveyard of the Atlantic, it is the enemy of all life. As no soldiers or colonists could be tempted to settle this ominous waste, La Roche obtained two hundred sturdy beggars, male and female, from the Rouen jail. He apparently released 140 of them for pay. In the spring of 1598 he deposited sixty penniless unfortunates on the island. Were some women among them? I hope so, for drama's sake. But certainly no women survived.

The sturdy beggars, *mendiants vigoureux*, trained only in the villainies of a crowded city, surveyed their republic. It is a treeless, shelterless waste of sand, rising at the summit eighty feet above the water. It is frequently wrapped in dense fog, and is assailed by terrific storms, when the great breakers shake the narrow land, and the wind carries to sea anything it can pluck loose. Three sea currents meet here; bodies from wrecks circle round and round the island, forlornly seeking a dry grave. The phosphorescence is legendary; the whole ocean seems ablaze; the sea breaks in a wall of fire fifteen or twenty feet high. The shore is studded with wrecks, with stumps of masts bedded in sand.

In the center of the island is a fresh-water lake. Wild peas, strawberries, blueberries are abundant. There are plenty of ducks and other wild fowl, and though we may presume that the settlers soon wasted their ammunition, if indeed they were entrusted with muskets, they could at least subsist on gulls' eggs. Shellfish abounded, and the silly seal offered himself for massacre. What is more, the Portuguese had put ashore some cattle and swine to breed about 1567, and these throve in the feral state. At some time, though probably later, some horses were left here or survived a wreck. About fifty years ago there were still some two hundred of them, living in hostile gangs, each led by an old male. According to a Toronto paper of July 1947 (which I seem to have lost), they are still there. Their habits should be an entrancing study for the zoologist.[1]

[1] "The gang consists of mares, colts, and young horses. When the latter attain their full growth, the leader generally turns them out. These then wander about the island, until they manage to steal a few mares away from some of the others and form new gangs for themselves. On these occasions severe fighting ensues between the leader and the intruder, the conflict not infrequently lasting for hours, each biting and tearing the other until one is overpowered. If the intruder beats the leader of the gang, he takes his place and appropriates to himself the mares, or as many as he wants. It sometimes happens, when a young stud horse wants to form a gang, that he proceeds surreptitiously at night and inveigles away a mare to some other part of the island. When her master finds her missing, he searches for her, and if he finds her a furious battle with her captor ensues. If victorious, he marches her off with him back to the gang. If defeated, the conqueror will in all probability despoil him of other females, and thus break up the gang. The mares accept the situation when the fighting is over, give in their allegiance to the conqueror, and live peaceably with him till some new domestic trouble arises." Dr. E. Gilpin, about 1864, quoted by the Rev. George Patterson, in *Proceedings and Transactions of the Royal Society of Canada*, XII, part 2 (1894).

The same article gives a very curious picture of the balance of nature, as it has operated in this isolated environment in our own times. "English rabbits were introduced and multiplied, and formed an agreeable change in the food of the employees. But the rats landing from wrecked vessels multiplied to such an extent as to become a plague, comsuming the stores so as to threaten famine, and then by killing the young rabbits nearly annihilated the stock altogether. Then the

A supply ship arrived annually from France. (This item, with a number of others, appears in a precious *mise au point* by Gustave Lanctot, in the *Annual Report of the Canadian Historical Association* for 1933. The article is based on a newly discovered document, which goes far to absolve La Roche from blame.)

The colonists on their Devil's Island responded to their master's promptings. They assassinated their captain in his sleep, and then the lieutenant. Other murders followed. When news of the uprising reached France, no doubt by means of a fishing vessel, la Roche decided to send no more supplies, and let them die. But they lived somehow, even domesticating the wild cattle and milking their tiny udders. They reverted, like the cattle, to the feral state.

Eventually the Parlement of Rouen got wind of their straits, and the pilot Chefdostel was ordered to bring them back on his next trip. "This he did and found twelve alive [Lanctot says eleven], to whom he did not reveal the King's command, wishing to get possession of a large store of hides and sealskins, which they had got together during these five years. In short, on their return to France, they appeared before His Majesty clad in these sealskins. The King ordered a sum of money to be given them, and they withdrew. But a suit arose between them and the pilot about the hides and furs which he had wrung from them, though they afterwards came to a friendly settlement." [2] Lanctot says la Roche was indignant because the survivors were rewarded instead of being executed.

Thus the waifs of Sable Island disappear. A visitor to the island in 1894 writes: "There were till recently, and probably are yet, grounds enclosed by an embankment of sods, known as the French gardens, said to be the work of la Roche's convicts. The work is older than the present establishment, and the tradition may be well founded." [3]

What a scenario for the historical romancer! What notes for a drama of courage, despair, lust, and greed! May not this story set some imagination afire?

---

government sent cats, who first killed the rats and then finished the rabbits. Next the cats became so numerous and wild as to become a trouble, when dogs were imported, and by means of them and shotguns the cats were exterminated. The island was then stocked with rabbits, which multiplied freely, when a snowy owl, having visited the island, seemed delighted with the prospects. But without staying to regale himself on the abundance before him, he started off seemingly to invite old friends to the feast. At all events a number of them immediately joined him on an expedition to the island, where they extinguished the rabbits, so that only a few tame ones are now to be seen. The rats still remain, and burrow as the rabbits."

[2] Lescarbot, II, 195.

[3] Patterson, *Trans. Roy. Soc. Can.* XII, part 2, 8*n*.

APPENDIX D

The Iroquois Wars

THE THEORY that the Iroquois wars were actuated by rivalry for the control of the fur trade was first stated, to my knowledge, by Léon Gérin in *Nouvelle-France*, Quebec, 1903, II, 273. He propounds further that the war was a social necessity, from the need of the Iroquois to recruit women prisoners to carry on their agriculture.

George T. Hunt (*The Wars of the Iroquois*, Madison, 1940) has argued, with great plausibility, that the wars were inspired solely by commercial needs. The supply of beaver in the Iroquois' hunting grounds was soon exhausted; to meet the insistence of the Dutch traders, the Iroquois were forced to attack the trading nations of the north, particularly the Hurons. Until 1640, he insists, the Iroquois were a pacific, agricultural people, whose political organization had not yet developed, who had no particular advantage in armament. Parkman's statement that the Iroquois were murderous by nature he regards as simply absurd, not the sort of thing a historian should say.

Professor Hunt's brilliant book demolishes many legends, and establishes the whole question on a tempting socioeconomic basis. There is, however, one large difficulty: the Iroquois and the St. Lawrence Indians were constantly at war for a century before the commercial rivalry could have existed.

The Indians Cartier found at Hochelaga (Montreal) in 1535 were almost certainly Huron-Iroquois. These had disappeared when Champlain arrived in 1603, but whether they had been expelled by the southern Iroquois or by the Algonquins, or whether they migrated under no compulsion is hard to establish. (See W. J. Winterberg, in *American Anthropologist*, XXIX, 251.) The Indians whom Cartier met at Stadacona (Quebec) were certainly of Iroquois stock, though one may dispute whether they were Hurons, or an offshoot of the southern Iroquois, or a mysterious separate tribe (A. J. Bailey, in *Trans. Roy. Soc. Can.*, XXVII, 97–108; Frank G. Speck: *The Iroquois*, Cranbrook Inst. of Science, 1945; W. N. Fenton, in *Smithsonian Miscellaneous Collections*, Vol. C, Washington, 1940, p. 173–239). At any rate, their King told Cartier of the Toudamans, who carried on continual war with them, and these Toudamans are readily identified with the Tsonondowanen, the Senecas, or the Senecas and Onondagas together. (But W. N. Fenton thinks the Toudamans were eastern Algonquins, perhaps Etchemins.) A tribal war with the southern Iroquois, resulting in the expulsion of Cartier's friends from the St. Lawrence valley, and its occupation by Algonquins, seems pretty clear.

In any case, by 1603 the Iroquois menace had become so acute that the far-flung Algonquin alliance was formed. As the Algonquins told Champlain that their total numbers were less than those of the Iroquois, there is a strong suggestion that the alliance was defensive rather than offensive.

As for the responsibility of the Dutch in encouraging a trade war, the Dutch did not come to New York until 1609; they established Fort Nassau at our Albany in 1614, abandoned it in 1617, re-established it as Fort Orange in 1624. Champlain makes clear that the wars were waged violently before this time. Therefore Hunt's theory that the wars were commercial in origin seeems to me untenable.

It may still be argued that the war was based on economics, that in the second half of the sixteenth century the mysterious, unrecorded fur trade in the Gulf of St. Lawrence had grown so greatly that its effects were felt in Iroquoia, and the Iroquois were clearing the way to the source of supply of knives and kettles. But this is only an hypothesis, without evidence. There is no indication that the Iroquois had ever made direct contact with the merchants. In 1609, says Champlain, they still used stone hatchets, and "poor axes they sometimes win in war." His arquebus was a total surprise to them. Evidently they went to the St. Lawrence only for manhunts.

Is Parkman's theory of the "homicidal frenzy" of the Iroquois so absurd? They had established themselves in the happy, fertile country of central New York, by valor, by aggression and domination, by expelling or submerging the local inhabitants. They remembered ancient grievances against the St. Lawrence Algonquins, who had perhaps expelled them from their previous homes. Their memories were long. Hunt himself argues that in 1691 they remembered the coming of Cartier in 1535 (*The Wars of the Iroquois*, 25–8). A traditional war of revenge on the Algonquins seems consonant with Iroquois character, with human character. Aggression and domination had given their race a home. That tradition, prized and encouraged, became for each new generation a requirement that manhood should be demonstrated by symbolic raids and the torture and death of Algonquin captives. This tradition may well be called "homicidal frenzy." The commercial war came afterward, with its sanction in the holy traditions of the race. After all, we have seen the same transfer of values in the greater world.

APPENDIX E

The Site of the Battle of 1609

THE DETERMINATION of the site of the first Battle of Lake Champlain has provoked the flow of a good deal of ink and bad blood. Of the various arguments alleged, not much can be proved from Champlain's dates, of which he was notoriously careless. He says (*Works*, II, 73) that he left Quebec on June 28, arrived fifteen leagues upstream on June 1, and at Trois Rivières on June 3. He means, of course, July. He then says that he left Chambly Rapids on July 2. This being impossible, the Champlain Society editors propose July 12, which is reasonable. We may still wonder why a war party should take two weeks to proceed a hundred miles along Lake Champlain. My own guess is that it did not. Champlain's habit was to put down exact dates, as in a ship's log, but when, as in this case, he could not keep a log, he attempted, some time later, to follow the ship's log style. He put down exact dates—but wrong ones.

Not much more can be proved from Champlain's statements of latitudes. They seldom agree with modern determinations; they are likely to run half a degree to the south. Either he was careless or he could not take fine observations with his clumsy astrolabe. I doubt if he took his astrolabe to Lake Champlain anyway; he says he traveled light, carrying only weapons and ammunition. More likely his latitudes are estimations after the fact.

There are two significant passages in his account. One is *"nous fismes recontre des Yroquois sur les dix heures du soir au bout d'vn cap qui aduance dans le lac du costé de l'occident."* The most striking cape on the west shore is Crown Point.

The other passage is in his description of the reported passage to Lake George and the Iroquois country. The Indians told him *"qu'il falloit passer par vn saut d'eau que ie vis depuis."* This is the outlet of Lake George. He says also that three hours after the battle his party set out on the return journey. As he was never again to visit Lake Champlain, the only time he could have seen the Lake George outlet was in the three hours after the battle. But Crown Point is sixteen miles north, and is hence ruled out. The only site that fits is the small promontory just to the north of the outlet, at Ticonderoga. There, in fact, a marker now stands.

For arguments on both sides see Guy Omeron Coolidge, in *Proceedings of the Vermont Historical Society*, VI, 148 (September 1938), and S. H. P. Pell, in *Bulletin of the Fort Ticonderoga Museum*, V, 5 (January 1939).

APPENDIX F

The Location of the Onondaga Fort

THE DETERMINATION of the site of the fort attacked by Champlain and his Hurons in 1615 is a pretty exercise in the use of evidence.

Parkman, Lavardière, and others located the fort on Canandaigua Lake. Their arguments were unsound and need not be here detailed. Parkman, in later editions of his *Pioneers of France*, abandoned the Canandaigua Lake location in favor of Nichols Pond.

An examination of the lakes and ponds of central New York reveals only two sites that fit the specifications at all nearly. These are Onondaga Lake, on which stands the city of Syracuse; and Nichols Pond, three miles from Perryville, in the township of Fenner, Madison County.

The Nichols Pond site has gained general acceptance in recent books and studies. Markers, bearing the authority of the State Education Department, point the tourist thither.

For the study of the question, we have three pieces of documentary evidence:

1. Champlain's text, as printed in 1619 and reprinted without material change in 1632.

Is this text to be taken as an accurate record? Not necessarily. It was Champlain's habit to carry "*tablettes*," for making maps, sketches, and notes, and for sending messages. He refers to them in his account of the 1613 journey. But after the battle of 1615 he was carried on an Indian's back from the fort to the boats, a distance of sixty miles. Would the Indians have transported his paper and inkhorn? Possibly

355

not. Did Champlain have a chance to write up his notes during the long winter retreat across Ontario? Possibly not.

In any case his reckonings of time and distance are highly suspect, to say the least. In his record of the 1615 expedition he gives seven reckonings of distance that can be checked on modern maps. By reducing his leagues to miles, we find that his estimate of a league ran anywhere from 1½ to 3 miles; the average is about 2 miles. The normal French league of his time was almost exactly 2½ miles. However specific his reckonings may be, they are to be treated warily.

What we can accept without question are those facts which would have impressed themselves indelibly on his memory, and would reappear when he came to re-create the story: the layout and structure of the fort, the incidents of the battle, the high wind, the snow flurries. The rest can be brought in as supporting evidence, not as irrefragable proof.

2. The illustration accompanying the text. This has a high probative value. Champlain refers to it in his text as to a satisfactory representation of the fort and the battle. There can hardly be any question as to the origin of the illustration. Champlain made one of his watercolor sketches, like those now preserved in the John Carter Brown Library; he gave his sketch to the engraver, who "improved" some of the details, representing the cavalier, for instance, as a structure of neatly squared timbers; Champlain, little concerned by such details, passed it for publication.

3. The map that appeared in the edition of 1632. The segment showing the area of our concern is very puzzling. It agrees ill with Champlain's text and with the geographical facts. Some students (Lavardière, Harrisse, Margry, Marshall) conclude that the map is by some publisher's hireling. This seems most improbable. Champlain was in Paris when the book was published; cartography was his first trade; he would not conceivably have turned over the making of his map to some hack. Still, the section of his map dealing with the area under discussion is too unreliable to be alleged as final proof. It can, however, be adduced in support and corroboration.

Now we are ready for the problem.

Who were these Indians whom Champlain was attacking?

He calls them "Entouhonorons." He was approximating, evidently, the Huron word for "Onondagas," which was "Onontaerrhonons." It was understood from the beginning that the expedition's purpose was to wipe out the Entouhonoron stronghold. Hence we should look for a fort in the Onondaga country. Yes, but Champlain seems to divide all the Five Nations into two: the Mohawks, whom he calls the

Iroquois, and the four other nations, whom he seems to regard as Entouhonorons. Hence a fort in Oneida or Cayuga country should not be excluded. But the Onondaga hypothesis is the likely one. Champlain misunderstood the application of the word "Entouhonoron." The Hurons, shouting "Kill the Entouhonorons!" were referring only to Onondagas.

According to the text, the last fixed point is the outlet of Oneida Lake, at Brewerton. On this everyone agrees.

"On the ninth of October, our savages, when out scouting, met with eleven savages whom they took prisoners, to wit, four women, three boys, one girl and three men, who were going to catch fish some four leagues from the enemy's fort."

The south end of Onondaga Lake is eleven miles from Brewerton, almost exactly four leagues. This fits.

Nichols Pond is twenty-five miles by airline from Brewerton. Wide Cicero Swamp bars the way thither. It would be at least thirty miles by trail. It seems unlikely that a fishing party from Nichols Pond, including four children, would come so far. The Nichols Pond advocates suppose, therefore, that the Hurons turned east, following the southern shore of Oneida Lake, and found the fishing party at the mouth of Chittenango Creek, eighteen miles by air line from Nichols Pond. That is still a long round trip for children, even Indian children. The Onondaga Lake hypothesis is much better.

"On the following day, about three o'clock in the afternoon, we arrived before the enemy's fort." Either location would fit this.

The fort itself, according to the text, was strongly palisaded. "They were near a pond where there was no lack of water."

What does Champlain mean by a pond, *"un estang"*? The *Dictionnaire de l'Académie* of 1684 defines the word thus: *"Grand amas d'eau soustenu par une chaussée, et dans lequel on nourrit du poisson."* Champlain uses the word for the lagoons on the east shore of Lake Ontario, including North Pond, 3½ by 2 miles in area. In Canada he calls Coldingham Lake, two miles long, an *"estang,"* and calls Olmsted Lake, 4 miles long, *"un estang qui pouvoit contenir une lieue de long."*

Onondaga Lake is four miles long and one mile broad. It would fit his definition of an *estang*. Nichols Pond is hardly more than an alder swamp, an acre in extent, with standing water a foot or two deep, occupied by a rank growth. It often dries up entirely. It is not now an *estang*. But of course, it may have been larger in 1615; vegetation may have since encroached upon it.

Let us look at the illustration for corroboration. This depicts a large village with an open body of water beyond. It looks much more like Onondaga than Nichols Pond. It shows, further, two streams moating the fort and flowing into the open water. A sluggish rivulet a yard across flows into the marsh surrounding Nichols Pond; another sluggish brook at the opposite side is its outlet. At Onondaga Lake, Onondaga Creek, a considerable stream, empties into the lake after passing through a mile of flat land. Mud Creek flows from the east through marshy lowlands, reaching the lake near the outlet of Onondaga Creek. This fits much better than the Nichols Pond layout.

The topography has changed in the Onondaga Lake region. Mr. Mansfield J. French, historian and antiquarian of Syracuse, writes me: "Onondaga Creek and Mud Creek united, in the early days, at the original shore line of the lake. There was a marshy area along the shore when salt operations were first undertaken, and when the State Ditch was dug to give direct drainage into the Seneca River, a row of 'Reclaimed Lots,' entirely surrounding the lake, reduced the lake to its present bounds. The earliest salt operations were undoubtedly begun near the confluence of the two creeks, as Reclaimed Lot No. 1 is at this point. The land slopes quite abruptly to what was the early business center of the village of Salina."

This fits even better with the indications of Champlain's illustration.

Now let us see if we get any help from Champlain's map. It is really pretty bad. A dotted line shows the presumed course of the expedition. According to the map, it crossed the east end of Lake Ontario along a string of islands ranging from northeast to southwest. In fact these islands range from west directly east. I conclude that Champlain remembers the islands, but he has lost his notes and observations, and has forgotten the compass directions. We recognize the lagoons along the east shore (which he makes the southeast shore) of Lake Ontario. He turns inland, past a chain of lakes, and crosses the outlet of one of them. But there is only one lake, Oneida Lake, in this region. I suppose that where his dotted line crosses the outlet of the southeastern lake, he is at the outlet of Oneida Lake, though he has the orientation all wrong. He has forgotten; he has lost his notes. And the other lakes? Perhaps—this is the merest supposition—he half understood his Hurons talking of the chain of Finger Lakes. He had lost his Huron interpreter Brûlé; he was bewildered. He could not remember, later, exactly whether he saw those lakes or not; he had passed so many lakes!

Beyond the outlet of Oneida Lake the dotted line turns southwest (but we can't take the directions too seriously) to a palisaded village beside a lake. The proportions are of course all wrong. But the lake is represented as of the general size of Oneida Lake; it is not a mere puddle. Its outlet flows west and north into Lake Ontario. This could be Onondaga Lake; it could not be Nichols Pond.

What would be likely to remain in his mind? The relation, and the proportion, of the fort to the water. Also, I think, the general orientation. For remember that a high wind blew for two days, followed by snow flurries. This can only be our northwest wind. Champlain, in his anxiety to burn the village, would naturally keep the general layout in mind, and he would call upon his memory for all recoverable details when he came to make his map. His layout fits Onondaga exactly; it fits Nichols Pond not at all.

How about Indian remains? Onondaga Lake was by way of being holy ground, where Hiawatha himself had founded his League of Nations. But at the crucial point, the southeast end of the lake, between the two streams, there is no record or memory of a palisaded fort, only of a fishing village. However, the absence of remains proves nothing. Iroquois villages were migratory; in a dozen or fifteen years the surrounding cultivated land would be exhausted, and the villages become so foul that the inhabitants would gladly move. If there was a fortified town at this site in 1615, it would naturally have left no relics. Mr. French writes me: "The early salt boilers probably used all of the timbers from the fort to build the block-house and then used the timbers for fuel, when the block-house was not needed."

At Nichols Pond there was certainly an important Indian village, of which many relics have been discovered. Its date cannot be determined. But it was an Oneida village, not an Onondaga. While Champlain might have lumped the Oneidas with the Onondagas, it is more likely that he did not.

In short, it seems to me that the weight of evidence tips the balance definitely in favor of the southeast rim of Onondaga Lake, where, in past, Onondaga Creek and Mud Creek met at the lake shore.

It is difficult, if not impossible, to reconstruct the courses of these creeks through the lowlands in 1615. Mr. French's patient efforts do not enable him to point to a site for Champlain's fort with absolute exactness. However, his evidence would show that it stood near the junction of North Salina Street and Hiawatha Boulevard.

I fear that this conclusion may evoke angry rejoinders and accusations of corruption from the Madison County Historical Society. I can only suggest that the Madison County Historical Society fight it out with the Onondaga Historical Society; perhaps with bows and arrows.

APPENDIX G

Did Champlain Oppose a Huron-Iroquois Peace?

GEORGE T. HUNT (*The Wars of the Iroquois*, Madison, 1940, pp. 35, 70) says that the Iroquois effort to make peace was "foiled by Champlain's tactic," and that he sent Father le Caron and Brother Sagard to Huronia in 1623 "with instructions to break up any such negotiations." The allegations are based only on the two passages from Sagard and Charlevoix quoted on page 286.

But the quotation from Sagard makes no mention of Champlain, only of some *"Messieurs de la Société,"* who, whether in France or on the St. Lawrence, were ill-informed of the actual state of affairs. Sagard quotes them as if to show how ignorant and mean-spirited they were. And Charlevoix, writing a hundred years later (his book was published in 1744), is only a secondary authority.

Champlain insists that he did everything to promote a general peace among the Indians. Every argument from common sense supports his veracity. His colony at Quebec was in constant danger from the Iroquois. Never, in his lifetime, did he have more than a dozen proper soldiers to protect his settlement.

The interests of the fur trade were better served by peace than by war. True, the French merchants feared the competition of the Dutch in Fort Orange. But the trade route to Fort Orange offered no advantages to the Hurons. It added distance and two very long and hard portages to their journey. The Hurons were middlemen, not producers

3 6 0

of furs. The beaver was soon extinct in their own country (*Jesuit Relations*, VIII, 57). They collected their furs from the hunting tribes, on the northern shore of Lake Huron, around Lake Nipissing, and even farther north and west. From these areas their shortest route to market was down the Ottawa to the St. Lawrence.

The Iroquois also were middlemen. They would not have permitted the Huron traders direct access to the Dutch. Their middlemen's charges would have made trading with the Dutch disadvantageous to the Hurons.

The fact that thirty-five canoes of Iroquois came to the trading fair on the St. Lawrence in 1624 proves that the French traders could offer serious competition to the Dutch. In 1634 a party of Canadian traders established themselves among the Oneidas, in the heart of Iroquoia, and sold the Indians better goods at lower prices than did the Dutch (*Narratives of New Netherlands*, 139–50). Such facts are ample vindication of Champlain's peace policy.

It seems that the Dutch were not yet making a serious effort to use the Iroquois as agents to capture the northern fur trade. In 1626 a party of Fort Orange Dutch joined the Algonquin Mohicans in a war against the Mohawks, contrary to the official policy of neutrality, to be sure. Incidentally the Dutch musketeers were defeated by the Indians' arrows, as Champlain had been defeated in 1615.

Thus the Dutch competition was not yet, in fact, a serious matter, while the menace of Iroquois raids on the Huron fur flotillas was very serious. Peace was to the advantage of the French, not war.

Champlain's peace policy was justified by the event. Peace, though an insecure peace, was made. And we hear nothing of any diversion of trade to the Dutch.

For a judicious and well-informed treatment of the question, see Leo-Paul Desrosiers: *Iroquoisie*, Montreal, 1947, 74–109.

The Awareness of Canada
in Seventeenth-Century France

PIERRE CORNEILLE was born in Rouen in 1606. He grew up there, and became *avocat du roi au siège de l'amirauté*. In the course of his duties, he must have been frequently on board ships back from the western ocean and from Canada. Yet he never mentions America in his extant correspondence, nor did it ever occur to him, when he was seeking a subject for drama, to use any of the stories of venture and heroism he must have heard on board.

This obliviousness is characteristic of seventeenth-century France. The works of Champlain, Lescarbot, and other adventurers, the Recollects' reports, and especially the great series of *Jesuit Relations* must have had a circulation among the curious and the pious. Canada had its meaning to the business world, to the inquiring in various fields. Canadian products were being acclimatized in France by enthusiastic amateurs. The statesman Peiresc writes in 1626 that he has eaten Canadian strawberries and melons and found them delicious (*Lettres*, VI, 530, 576).

But the literary men, searching for themes, hunted forever through the authors of Greece, Rome, and Spain, and never once thought of looking to the west. In the world of letters "Canada" was used only as a joke, a synonym for frightful exile. A comic poet, Neufgermain, asserted that he was trying to send his wife there. Saint-Amant wrote in 1631 that the tarts and madams of Paris would be sent to populate Canada:

Adieu, maquerelles et garces . . .
Dans peu vous et vos protecteurs
Serez hors de France bannies
Pour aller planter colonies
En quelque Canada lointain.

His inference that women of evil life were being shipped to Canada, though supported by a silly tale of Tallemant des Réaux, is totally false.

The exotic names of the Hurons and Iroquois became a byword signifying barbarity. They so appear in La Bruyère's *Caractères* in 1685.

Scarron is said to have had three thousand francs in the Company of New France, and to have contemplated moving to America. But after his marriage to the future Mme de Maintenon, he changed his mind, and incidentally lost his money. I find no mention of Canada in his works.

Only such meager gleanings turn up in French literature of the century. Yet certainly the *Jesuit Relations*, at least, were widely read. Chinard (*L'Amérique et le rêve*, 125–48) ascribes to them much importance in the development of the idea of the noble savage and of the virtue of the primitive, ideas that Rousseau was to make popular. An excellent task for some young scholar would be the study of the diffusion of the *Relations*, and of their effect on popular thought.

ACKNOWLEDGMENTS

THIS BOOK is based mostly on the accounts of Champlain and his contemporaries. If the scholar is alarmed at the sight of conversations, he may be appeased on learning that they are either directly transcribed from the originals or are reconstructed from clear indications. On only a few occasions have I given imagination some play, and in those cases I have warned the conscientious reader.

Since most of my material is taken from a few books, with which the specialist is well acquainted, I have thought it unnecessary to encumber the pages with constant footnotes. I have appended notes only to stay a controversial opinion, or when I could point to a little known or hitherto unreported reference.

The mainstay of this book is the monumental series of publications of the Champlain Society of Toronto, especially *Samuel de Champlain's Works*, in seven volumes, 1922–36, edited by H. P. Biggar, H. H. Langton, W. F. Ganong, J. Home Cameron, John Squair, and W. D. LeSueur; Marc Lescarbot's *History of New France*, edited by W. L. Grant; and Sagard's *Long Journey to the Country of the Hurons*, edited by George M. Wrong and H. H. Langton. I am naturally under constant indebtedness to the *Jesuit Relations*, to the classic historians, Parkman, Slafter, Laverdière, Sulte, Dionne, and to the moderns, Leo-Paul Desrosiers, Gustave Lanctot, H. A. Innis, J. Bartlet Brebner, and many others. As Pascal said: "Some authors, speaking of their works, say: 'My book, my commentary, my history, etc.' They would do better to say: 'Our book, our commentary, our history.'"

My gratitude to the Cornell University Library cannot be measured or expressed. I am thankful also for important aid from the John Carter Brown Library, the Archivo de Indias of Sevilla, the Quebec Provincial Archives, the Laval University Library, and the Public Archives of Canada, and also for the precious system of Inter-Library Loans.

Many individuals have given me valuable suggestions and have aided in the settlement of special problems. I am in particular debt to Messrs. Percy J. Robinson, Aurora, Ontario; José M. Gallardo, Crawfordsville, Indiana; Lawrence C. Wroth, Providence, Rhode Island; R. W. G. Vail of the New York Historical Society; Mansfield J. French, Syracuse, New York; Arthur C. Parker, Naples, New York; Alexander M. Stewart, Rochester, New York; Loren C. Petry, Ithaca, New York; Dr. Erl A. Bates, Ithaca, New York; and S. H. P. Pell, Ticonderoga, New York.

INDEX

i

Index

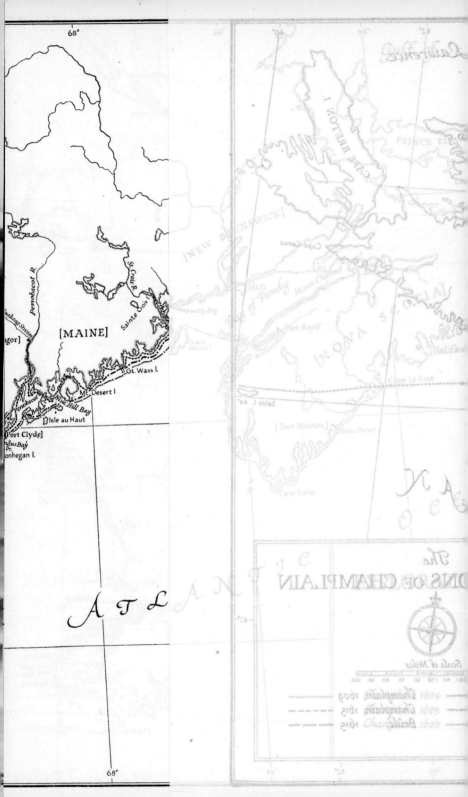

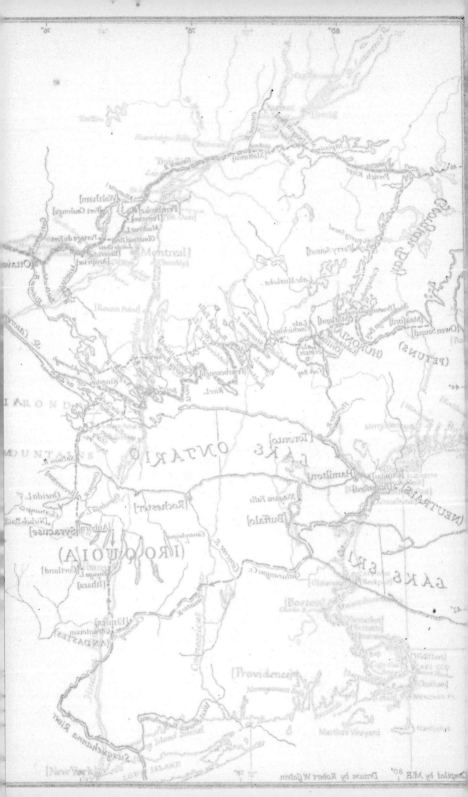

A NOTE ON THE TYPE
IN WHICH THIS BOOK IS SET

This book is set in Monotype Bell, a copy of the English Monotype face of the same name. The Englishman John Bell (1745–
1831) was responsible for the original cutting of this design. The
vocations of Bell were many—among a few might be mentioned
bookseller, printer, publisher, type-founder, and journalist. His
types were considerably influenced by the delicacy and beauty of
the French copper-plate engravers. Monotype Bell might also be
classified as a delicate and refined rendering of Scotch Roman.

Composed, printed, and bound by Kingsport Press, Inc.,
Kingsport, Tenn.